An Especially Good View

Watching History
Happen

Peter L.W. Osnos

PLATFORM

NEW YORK

Platform Books are available for bulk purchases at a discount in the United States. For more information, please contact Platform Books, info@platformbooksllc.net.

Platform Books authors are available for speaking events. For more information, please contact Platform Books, info@platformbooksllc.net.

The publisher is not responsible for websites (or their content) that are not owned by the publisher.

Peter Osnos and Susan Sherer Osnos, Publishers
Platform Books
900 West End Avenue, Suite 16A
New York, NY 10025
Christine E. Marra, Managing Editor

Book design by Maryellen Tseng
Set in 11.5-point Adobe Caslon

Editorial production by *Marra*thon Production Services, www.marrathoneditorial.net

Library of Congress Control Number: 2021933367

ISBN 978-1-7359968-0-6 (HC); ISBN 978-1-7359968-2-0 (eBook)

Printed in the United States of America
First Edition: June 2021

10 9 8 7 6 5 4 3 2 1

To

Families:

Past,

Present,

Future

Contents

~

*As a preteen, my son Evan joined the Hilltop Texaco base-
ball team in the Bambino (Babe Ruth) League of Greenwich,
Connecticut, where we lived in an old frame colonial near
the estates for which the town was famous. He was a reserve
outfielder.*

*The team was the runner-up for the town championship,
and the awards evening was on a Friday in October at the
Old Greenwich Civic Association building. I arrived from
the city in a tweed jacket and suede vest—natty, I thought.
Evan looked at me and said, "Dad, the vest has got to go."
It did.*

*The sports teams in Greenwich were mainly sponsored by
the town's shop owners and by the police and firefighters.
They tended to be Italian- or Portuguese-Americans. And
the dinner reflected that ethnic heritage, with tinfoil plat-
ters of lasagna, ziti, and many varieties of sweets. There
were speeches, including an appearance by Tim Teufel, a
graduate of Greenwich High School and then a player for
the New York Mets. All in all, it was a great evening.*

*For the next two weeks or so, everyone who came into our
house heard me describe this—to me, at least—exotic event
in detail: tinfoil, Teufel, and all. One night after hearing
this routine, Evan looked up and said, "Dad, you remind
me of Jane Goodall"—the renowned chimpanzee specialist.
"You go to the dinner with your notebook and your tape
recorder and you say, 'Isn't it amazing, how they show affection for their young …'"*

Nailed.

*Just get it down on paper and then
we'll see what to do with it.*

—MAXWELL PERKINS

*Write a book. . . .
It is better than a building.
It can't be torn down.*

—P.L.W.O.

Who, What, When, Where, Why

FOR A MIDDLE SCHOOL PROJECT a few years ago, my grandson Ben asked me to tell him about "my" family in World War II. "Ben," I said, "it's *our* family." In a way, that is the origin of the book you have in front of you. This is an answer to a grandson's question and, as it happens, a great deal more about what I saw, learned, and felt in my own life, at the time and in retrospect.

As an editor and publisher, I have encountered memoirs of all kinds—bracing, tragic, illuminating, mean, kind, boring, revelatory. I have published the memoirs of some of the most famous people in the world: presidents of the United States and Russia, first ladies, those responsible for waging war and peace, billionaire philanthropists, advisers to the high and mighty, political prisoners, celebrated athletes, and journalists of every sort. I have encountered authors who were too self-deprecating and others who were comically self-aggrandizing.

I know from memoirs.

Maybe that is why I approached my own memoir with trepidation. What would I find as I explored my life? I knew what I remembered, but how good, really, was my recall? Suppose the person I uncovered was unappealing to me? Perhaps I too was self-important, vain, too eager to please, greedy and grumpy—all the things I did not like about other people of the great many I have encountered. There was a basic tale to start with: I was raised in a good home, properly schooled, had a family, and embarked on the career that is so much a part of this saga. As I write, I am in the latter half of my eighth decade and it is now or never to put down this story. In this book, I am a self-proclaimed observer as much as a participant. In Yogi Berra's (actual) insight, "You can observe a lot, by watching."

When I started writing this book, I was surprised to discover how little I knew about my family background, aside from the outlines and selected legends. My parents were upper-middle-class Poles and Jewish. They and my eight-year-old brother escaped Poland after the start of World War II in 1939. With astonishing courage, resourcefulness, and luck, they made it to India and then to the United States. I arrived with them on February 6, 1944, in San Pedro, California, four months old, in a basket.

By the time I was in early grade school, Józef and Marta (they became known to work colleagues as Joe and—in her laboratory, and unexpectedly—Ossie) were building their first weekend home on a lake in Morris County, New Jersey. My mother was a biochemist at Columbia's medical school, Physicians and Surgeons, a leading research institution. My father, an engineer, started a business that rode the crest of air-conditioning, which was becoming a requirement in homes, offices, and institutions. My mother loved theater and the arts. My father was a master at bridge. I leaned in mother's direction when it came to entertainment and card games. My brother, Robert, age twelve as they made it to New York, having endured unimaginable childhood traumas he never talked about, got his bachelor's, master's, and medical degrees at Columbia. He then had a fifty-year career in psychiatry, admirable for the breadth of his patients and practice, from the neediest to the best off. He died at age eighty-eight, at home in the midst of the 2020 pandemic, with his wife Naomi by his side, on his own terms.

Our parents made it to their eighties and nineties also, passing peacefully after very full lives. On her last afternoon, Marta had a visit from a colleague in one of her former laboratories. After the colleague left, her comment was, "Such an intelligent woman and such ugly jewelry!" In my father's final hours at Roosevelt Hospital—he was only admitted that day—I hummed an off-key "Moscow Nights," a classic Russian song, in his ear. My brother listened to Schubert's *Fantasie in F Minor* as he faded. His daughter Jean, with his other daughter Gwyn nearby, asked whether the music was "annoying or pleasant." "Both," he replied. Irony was essential to the family lexicon.

My immediate family was very small. They were, after all, refugees from the Holocaust. We had only a handful of relatives in the United States, who, as I reflect on them now, were a fascinating if small band of professionals and thinkers. None of them ever shared with me a sense of regret at all that had been lost. I know they were grateful—to use an inadequate term—for what they had made of their American lives.

Too often in memoirs, the protagonist takes pride in being "an outsider." I really was. I came of age in a world completely different from that of the first half of my parents' lives. They spoke Polish to each other. My language was English. In many ways, I was an only child: my brother was twelve years older than I and went to college at sixteen. (Only late in life did I realize, looking at photographs of us together, that I was his much-loved baby brother.) I went to public schools in Manhattan with other children from comfortable homes and did well until my teens, when I favored social activities over studies. So, I was sent off to boarding school in Connecticut, where I identified as so many teenage boys did in those years with Holden Caulfield in J. D. Salinger's *The Catcher in the Rye*. I went to Brandeis University, got a master's in journalism at Columbia, and embarked at twenty-two on my life's work.

In 1970, in Saigon, South Vietnam (where I was a reporter for the *Washington Post*), I met Susan Sherer, who at twenty-three was in a war zone working for a group of lawyers who provided free legal assistance to GIs in trouble. Her office was next to mine. A year later we were a couple and have been so since, with children, grandchildren, and an extended family on Susan's side—known collectively as the Russells—that is a community bound by devotion, mutual respect, and a compound on the shores of Lake Michigan. The Russells number more than eighty people now in five generations, all of whom would tell you that Lakeside, where they convene in August, is much more than a place.

This is a reported memoir. I have done what I could to take each event and experience described herein as a test of my skills as a researcher. That has involved many trips to places where I, and later we, lived and worked—Poland, Bombay, Indochina, London—and conversations at length with people I encountered. What did they remember? Why did matters unfold the way they did? And, awkwardly, what did they think of me? I especially want to recognize the three persons who were my mentors in career and style: I. F. Stone, Ben Bradlee, and Robert Bernstein. Readers will get to know them a bit along with luminaries who were, on the whole, a privilege to work with, plus a few I disliked.

Fortunately, when it came to the lengthy list of major personalities I covered and worked with, my recall was extensive and, on the whole, reliable. I have the resulting articles and books to enhance memories. With the assistance of search engines, the *Washington Post* library, my home shelves, and more memorabilia and notes than I realized there was, I have been able to add texture and details to my recollections.

Imagine my delight, for example, at the discovery of a telegram sent to my parents in April 1943, signed by Princess George of Greece, announcing that they could collect their US visas, which were exceptionally hard to get at the height of the war. That story can now be told in full. I do not display diplomas on my wall, but I do have a "top secret" Soviet Politburo memo about how best to deal with a nuisance—me, "correspondent" Osnos—and a CIA memo to see whether I really did have intelligence connections, as the KGB was insisting. (I am relieved to say, I did not.) Also on my wall is a photograph of Susan, our daughter Katherine, our son Evan, and a team of Sherpas at the end of a ten-day trek in the Himalayas to mark our twenty-fifth wedding anniversary. I found my first byline in a piece for the *Brandeis Justice* about a 1962 student trip to Mississippi, more important than any course I took that year. My last byline as a full-time reporter for the *Post* was a story in April 1984 about President Ronald Reagan's ancestral home in Ballyporeen, Ireland, "land of the small potatoes," that was awaiting his first-ever visit. I have continued writing regularly since and some of that is excerpted in these pages.

All this material and a good deal more, which is the equivalent of a foray into a well-kept attic, is on a website—an especiallygoodview .com—which is a supplement to the narrative and also includes video and audio links.

$\sim$

WHEN I SENT A DRAFT of this book to Lisa Kaufman, who was my young assistant at Random House in 1985 and later a wonderful colleague at PublicAffairs, as well as an editor of remarkable insight for the thoughts beyond the words, she said, in effect, this book is enjoyable but a mite cautious. In this version I have done what I can to unlock emotions and judgments.

Next I sent the manuscript to Paul Golob, another former colleague of extraordinary editorial finesse, who gave the material a thorough going-over, urging more of some things and less of others. It helped that Paul and I laughed at the same things, with and at each other. After considering the counsel from Lisa and Paul, I wrote the book that is now before you.

Some caveats I have learned as an editor: Not all revelations need to be shared. A very close boyhood friend was a closeted gay man. His family only learned about his struggles after he died. He will not be named, although otherwise described. A work colleague told a gossip columnist for *The New York Observer* that I had fiddled with the acknowledgments in Nancy Reagan's book to make myself seem more important. That was not true, and I had to beg the *Observer* not to use the item. Revenge is not the purpose of this book. Not all scores need to be settled.

I have also learned that describing people by their physical characteristics or personal tics is very tricky. Suffice to say, I have done what I can to bring you portraits of people close to me and some of those more distant without saying things about them that they did not already know.

Lisa also told me that I needed to tell readers of this book—aside from friends and family—why they should bother. My parents were, in their way, extraordinary, as were so many of the European Jews in World War II who defied the Nazis in one way or another. Their tales, as the last of them die, should be preserved. My years reporting many of the world's biggest stories in the Cold War era offer a perspective that is different, especially when as an editor and publisher I had unusual access to the characters and events. I felt I was a partner in examining their distinction and not an employee. As a journalist, I never intended to be a businessman, but I became one when I started and ran PublicAffairs. There are lessons about that process to be offered. If money is your objective, a lifetime in news and books is not the best means to that goal. In publishing, especially when I became an entrepreneur, I was as much an instigator as an observer, learning how to conjure books, handle authors, and manage the enterprise. I called us a seeking-profit company. Our focus was more the quality of the books than the financial return on them. We did, however, have to pay our bills.

The chapters in Passages about growing up describe experiences before I was immersed in the greater world, which is most of this story. I decided that to understand who I became, I should describe how I got this way.

An explanation about structure. Much of this book is chronological: the origins, schooling, the early career. Some sections, especially those about Vietnam and the Soviet Union, presidents and other major personalities, bounce back and forth a bit in time to collect themes in the experiences. What it was like to be a reporter in Moscow and Saigon in the 1970s will be described quite differently from accounts of being the editor and publisher of books by the people who defined the character and history of those years in those places.

There are also occasions where I mention more names than a reader might think necessary in storytelling. As an editor, I learned that people tend to notice when they are omitted with more attention than when they are mentioned, and are usually resentful. "Don't I matter?" is the natural reaction. So, if the names bother you, skip over them. Just know that someone is likely to be glad they are there.

Late in the reporting process for this book I was allowed to read a personnel file from my years at *The Washington Post*. What I discovered was that my standing at the paper was substantially different from what I had always thought.

The book concludes with stories and reflections from later in my life, recollections of a more personal nature and times when I found myself confronting upsetting or previously hidden truths. This would not be a real accounting if I left them out.

In the process of writing this book, it has only been read by people who might be interested in what it says. Now the book will be available to readers of other generations, including millennials. So let's calculate: my first memories and stories are from the 1940s, about eighty years ago. Eighty years before that was 1860. So if reading about these events and personalities seems remote to you, it is. This is, in a way, a book of history; not always historically significant, but certainly some of it was.

I close this opening with these thoughts about the book: Is it accurate? I have tried to make it so. Is its spirit fair? Again, I hope so. Is it interesting? That is up to you.

PART ONE

~

Passages

Chapter 1

Caste: Polish

MY BIRTHDAY HAS ALWAYS BEEN October 13. But the report from Dr. J. Hagemann, MD, DGO, in the Cambata Building, Eros Cinema, Churchgate Reclamation, Bombay, says, "Peter Osnos has been delivered by me on 12th October 1943. He has perfect health and has been vaccinated on 17th Dec. 43 against smallpox. The vaccination took alright."

A bill from St. Elizabeth's Nursing Home, Harkness Road, Malabar Hill, Bombay 6, says, "Warding charges at 15 Rs [rupees] per day for 14/10/43 to 23/10/43 150 Rs. Extras: Confinement 25 Rs. Circumcision 5 Rs."

The Certificate of Birth Registry from the Public Health Department on November 11, 1943, lists the address as Maskati Court, Queens Road, Esplanade, the name as Peter Lionel (my grandfather) Winston (for Churchill) and Caste: Polish. It is signed by the executive health officer.

October 13? October 12? We'll never really know for sure. A memoir is a record of memories. To me the word *autobiography* suggests factual precision about the life in question, whereas a memoir is more likely to have the strengths and shortcomings of the passage of time in determining what happened and how the writer felt about it. These are flashes inspired by family lore—some myths perhaps—and, over the decades, events of particular note. I met with as many of the main characters in this saga as I could reach. For the earlier parts of the story—before I was born, when my parents were already in their late thirties—I supplemented my interviews with books about our family.

In the Garden of Memory: A Family Memoir by Joanna Olczak-Roniker, published in Polish in 2002 and in English in 2004, is an incalculable gift. A brilliant writer and storyteller, Joasia, as we called her, pulled together strands of a remarkably colorful epic that features virtually all aspects of our background over more than a century and a half. That book was the recipient of Poland's top literary prize. *Isaac's Army: A Story of Courage and Survival in Nazi-Occupied Poland* by Matthew Brzezinski and published by Random House in 2012 used the story of my parents' escape from the Nazis in 1939 as an account of how one family outsmarted what would have been certain death. My father, Józef, would be immensely flattered to know that Brzezinski described him as having a passing resemblance to the actor Errol Flynn. My mother and brother wrote a short book of their memories of the years from the 1930s until they arrived in New York in 1944. My only regret is that I did not ask them for more—much more.

In recent years Susan and I traveled to Poland to connect with relatives and to be reminded of the horrors of the Holocaust. We visited Auschwitz and Birkenau; Cambodia, two generations removed from the massacre of millions by their own countrymen; and Bombay, to re-create the life my parents and brother had there from 1940 until the end of 1943. These trips and others added depth and texture to what I had known or experienced.

I also learned a great deal about the Osnos family from books by and about my cousin Marie Syrkin, whose mother was an Osnos and whose stepmother was also an Osnos. Marie's father, Nachman Syrkin, was one of the major figures in the origins of Labor Zionism, one of the leading political groups whose work culminated with the establishment of Israel in 1948. I never met Nachman, but Marie became a significant mentor to me as a professor, activist, writer, and source of pride. When Sam Norich, the president of *The Forward*, a major Jewish newspaper in New York, learned I was related to the Syrkins, he said, "They were as close to aristocracy as there is among Jews." He certainly didn't mean it in the royal sense, but I liked the suggestion.

I benefited as well from the diligent research of my grandnephew Eli Osnos White, who located and digitized documents that miraculously were kept through the very long passage of time.

~

I THINK MY FIRST MEMORY is of the day Mahatma Gandhi was assassinated in 1948. I was sitting in the kitchen of my parents' apartment, #806, in the Belnord at 225 West 86th Street in Manhattan. My family, I was told, had three heroes: Churchill and Franklin Roosevelt for their wartime leadership, and Gandhi for his role in the liberation of India, where after all my parents had found safety from the war. Their apartment rented for $150 a month. I went to see it as the building became a co-op in 2019 and was told that it was in contract for $7 million and would be combined with the apartment across the floor, which had sold for $6 million. We had an icebox, a gas-lit covered stove, and old-fashioned DC current suitable for radios and fans. Bits of furniture acquired from the Salvation Army in their early days probably was still around when my parents moved to the Beresford on Central Park West in 1962.

So, from the beginning, I was a spectator to their lives as they adjusted to New York and the United States. My life was to unfold in a place and a culture that was completely different from the one that had shaped my parents and my brother. In that sense, I was destined to be a reporter from the outset.

Marta Judith Bychowski, my mother, came from what was clearly an upper-crust Jewish family in Warsaw. *Acculturated* was the term for the Jews in their social circle, meaning that their first language was Polish and then the European languages. Yiddish was not their language, as it was for so many of what were known as shtetl Jews. Marta's mother, Gizela Horowitz (or Horwitz), was descended from one of the most prominent rabbis in the Austro-Hungarian Empire. It was said that he was responsible for the revision of the Jewish practice of having a mohel bite off the tip of an infant's penis at the time of circumcision. The rabbi's son was a scholar of the Dutch-Jewish philosopher Baruch Spinoza and was married by arrangement to the daughter of a wealthy salt merchant based in Warsaw. Gizela was one of their nine children. One sister married into the Citroën family, founders of the auto company. A brother, a member of the Communist Comintern, was executed in 1937 in a Stalinist purge. He and another sister spent time in Zurich before the Bolshevik revolution, where they were part of a group of radicals that included Vladimir Lenin. There is a family legend—impossible to verify but unquestionably tantalizing—that this sister's son, Janek Kancewicz, 103 years old when he died in 2020, was in fact the son of Lenin and not of a passing Ukrainian soldier, as he'd been told. Some stories are too good to check.

Marta's father, Zygmunt Bychowski, was a well-known physician, a senior medical officer in the Russian and later Polish army (Poland was embedded in the Russian Empire until World War I), a city councilor representing the Jewish community, and a follower of Theodor Herzl, the founder of modern Zionism. He was a contemporary of Sigmund Freud and a neurologist, a precursor to modern psychiatry and psychoanalysis. Marta had two brothers. The one who survived to maturity was Gustav, a Freudian psychoanalyst who made it to the United States from Poland through Switzerland early in World War II. Gustav's son from his first marriage, Ryszard, was a navigator in a Free Polish squadron of the Royal Air Force and was killed when his plane crashed in May 1944. He was twenty-two. Gustav's second wife, Maryla, and their daughter Monica were major figures in our New York life.

A brief digression: Marta had a cousin with the same name as her nephew Ryszard, described above. She didn't think much of that fellow—"a shoe salesman" is how she described him to me. In Vienna in the 1930s, this Ryszard met and married Magda Gabor, the eldest of the Gabor sisters—Zsa Zsa and Eva were the other two, married eight and six times respectively. Magda also married six times. She renamed this particular spouse Count (sometimes Prince) Jan Ryszard de Bychowski, allegedly from a Polish noble family with a castle in

Warsaw. (Nonsense.) The couple made it to England when the war started. Magda told later biographers that her husband was a pilot and was killed in 1944, effectively giving him the identity of cousin Ryszard. How do I know? I checked the record and also because the "count" wrote my mother from Paris in 1960 saying how pleased he was to have an apartment with an en suite bathroom. I read about his heroic nondeath in a celebrity biography of the Gabors, who, lest you don't recognize the name, have a contemporary parallel, more or less: the Kardashians.

Józef Osnos came from a well-to-do merchant family, one of eight children of Leib (Lionel) and Olga Osnos. The family spoke both Russian and Polish, tending toward Russian at home. Józef was a man of striking good looks: tall, with olive skin, a barrel chest, jet-black hair, and blue eyes. Osnos is an unusual name, not typically Polish, Russian, or Jewish, and I always wondered whether my father's family origins were further south or west in Europe. My DNA test says that I am 100 percent Ashkenazi Jewish, which would indicate a notable clarity of heritage.

One unsolved question is the presence of the Osnos name in nineteenth-century Norway and baptismal certificates there. I found the church listing but couldn't figure out whether or how it was related to the family I come from. Family lore was that Osnos was a unique name but over the years I learned about the family of Max Osnos, a prominent department store owner in midcentury Detroit with a large family. Marta always looked in phone books when she arrived in a city to see if there were any Osnos names. I don't remember any. We did know that an Osnos was a Russian chess grandmaster and a coach to Viktor Korchnoi, a world champion in the 1970s. Another Osnos was a celebrated inventor based in Berlin in the Edison era. How all these people were related and where the name came from remains something of a mystery. I did a search for the origin of the Osnos name, and with the help of a French cousin, Elie Vannier, I traced the name as far back as a man named Mendel Osnos in 1740. It was about this time that the Jews in eastern Europe were either mandated or permitted to choose family names in addition to the first name and patronymic that was standard. Apparently, Osnos was an Old Testament derivative of the "feminine biblical personal name Asenath (in Hebrew, Asnat/Osnat mentioned in Genesis 41.45) . . . other related family names are Osnas and Osnos," according to the Researchers of the Museum of the Jewish People at Beit Hatfusot. My guess is that Asenath, a biblical name, was a choice made by more than a single family.

At Auschwitz there are scrolls listing every Jew who died (one way or another) during World War II. I found eight Bychowski names and nineteen Osnos names, including at least three who were siblings of my father. His parents had died before the war. The only sibling of my father we were aware of was a Soviet army officer exiled to Krasnoyarsk in the late 1940s. When I was living in Moscow in the 1970s as *The Washington Post*'s bureau chief, I once received a phone call from someone who said he was my cousin from Siberia. At the time I was under close KGB surveillance, and so I treated this as a probable provocation and ignored his offer to meet. I'll never know.

As I wrote above, two of Józef's aunts, Bassya Osnos and her younger sister Machete, were (in succession) married to Nachman Syrkin, a sufficiently notable figure in Zionism for Israel to deploy a naval vessel in his name.

My father did have one nephew in New York, Zarka Auer. Long after he died, Susan and I saw a taped interview with Zarka on how he and his father survived the war when all else was lost. Zarka said it was because as a student engineer he had become fluent in German, and didn't look especially Jewish. What I have come to understand is that every Jew who made it to safety in the midst of the Holocaust had a survival story about defying the odds. I also came to realize that my family's saga was one of thousands of comparable accounts, all by the people who used courage, ingenuity, connections, and money to avoid the gas chambers. What can never be told are the stories of the millions who were executed. What went through their minds as they were marched to oblivion?

Marta studied biochemistry in Warsaw but never received a doctorate because, presumably, she was a woman and Jewish. Józef finished his engineering studies in Prague. Early photos of my parents show them at the beach, Józef a glamorous young man with a tidy mustache he wore his whole life. Marta had an animated, handsome face but was not what would be thought of as conventionally pretty. Their 1930 wedding was a big local occasion given Zygmunt Bychowski's prominence and Gizela Horowitz's family heritage. Shortly after the wedding the newlyweds moved to Paris, where Józef had what was described as a very good job. He would travel back and forth to Brussels as a merchant of diamonds and gold, a trip he especially enjoyed because on the train he could indulge his life-long fascination with bridge. One family explanation of their move to France was that Marta and Józef also thought it was time to get out of the domineering Bychowski orbit. Zygmunt, in particular, was said to be a snob who thought that Józef's family was less important than his.

There is no way to be sure, but I think there was subtle class tension between my parents' families long after the families arrived in New York. The Polish intelligentsia and professionals thought themselves superior to Russian engineers and merchants. My parents' circles in New York tended toward elegantly coiffed Polish ladies and their eminently successful spouses, all of whom, of course, had survived the Nazi terror. The Poles had faced west and spoke the languages of Western Europe, French and German. Russia has always had a different vibe, more eastern Orthodox Christianity rather than popes or Protestants. Wherever they were, Jews were considered—and considered themselves—a group apart. Being Jewish was a defining fact that obscured the reality that Judaism comprised a very broad spectrum of peoples, from the wealthiest to the poorest, the most religious to the most secular.

Some months after my parents arrived in Paris, my brother, John Robert, was born. He was always known as Robert, and he would later add Bychowski as a second middle name, probably because there were no other male descendants with that surname. In 1935, Marta and Józef returned to Warsaw, perhaps because her father died or for business reasons. Józef established an appliance factory that he maintained until the war. Marta worked for a pharmaceutical firm.

Now in their early thirties, they settled into what seems to have been a comfortable life. Decades later, a film called *Image Before My Eyes* was made about the Jews in Poland before World War II. Watching it on assignment from *The Washington Post* to write a review, I was startled to see a frame of two fashionable couples in a convertible in the late 1930s. One of those couples turned out, incredibly, to be my parents—an eerie glimpse of their lives. I asked my mother about it, and she recalled that it was an afternoon trip for a small-plane excursion around Warsaw. She also remembered regularly meeting friends in the café of the Hotel Europa (where she and my father would stay again on visits to Poland in the 1970s). Central European cafés were the center of a certain kind of lively socializing for Jews of the young Osnos family set. They lived in an apartment block in central Warsaw and had very active lives, which was always the case wherever they were.

On September 1, 1939, Nazi Germany invaded Poland. That began a five-year journey of extraordinary peril, daring, luck, and, still in many respects, mystery. There is a fixed narrative of that time as described in the family books and memoirs, but how much of it is left out or shaped by preferred memory is hard to know. The story is that as the war started, an order was given for all military-age men to travel east from Warsaw and join regiments there. Private cars in Poland were still unusual and a couple asked Józef, who had an international license, to drive them to the assembly point in their car. The expectation was that the war would not last long, and so it was agreed that Marta and Robert would stay in Warsaw.

The succeeding months were harrowing. Marta fell ill with scarlet fever. Her nephew Ryszard was by her side and Robert's during her illness. It was only after she recovered and his family had made it to safety in the United States that Ryszard joined the Polish wing of the

Royal Air Force, ultimately losing his life in the war. Our son Evan carries Richard as one of his middle names.

Marta and Robert moved from their apartment to live with one of Józef's brothers. Bombs were dropping, and she had an especially close encounter with the SS, who insisted on going to her apartment. Somehow Marta kept her wits. Robert's recollection of that time was largely of reading Jules Verne books and playing with toy planes while huddled here and there with his mother. Was he terrified? That is one of the mysteries. He was scared several times, but his very firm view is that he was not a war "victim." After all, he made it through and once the family arrived in India, they were safe and sound. I always wondered how that attitude had impacted Robert's life. Incredibly, in retrospect, neither he nor my parents dwelled on or would allow others to dwell on their wartime experiences. Decades later his wife, Naomi, told me that when Robert underwent psychoanalysis as part of his psychiatric training, the analyst said his deepest emotions were inaccessible. Did he repress them or was it possible that as a child he felt protected by his courageous mother and his intrepid and resourceful father? Robert's explanation always was that he was too fortunate in the war to have to wallow in past dangers. When he was in his late eighties, I was told that Robert's recollection was that the last time he had cried was in 1937, when he was six.

When Józef arrived at the assembly point east of Warsaw, the Polish army was already in disarray. With a car and hard-to-get gas, he chose to head for the Romanian border rather than run interference through the rapidly expanding enemy lines. Of all that happened in those chaotic early weeks of the war, his decision then was the most impressive by some measures and problematic by others. I never heard either Józef or Marta discuss their separation, which lasted nine months. She managed brilliantly to stay alive and navigate what very few other people could do: get out of Poland under siege. And Józef, almost miraculously, made it possible for them to cross into Romania and led them to eventual safety in India. To do that, Józef used ingenuity and guile. For instance, he knew enough to trade some gas for a ten-zloty gold coin with which he bought clean clothes after days on the road, and stopped looking like what he was, a bedraggled refugee. (The unlikely theme of nice clothes, preferably with creases in the right places, will recur. This would indicate that certain traits are handed down in generations—in this instance, father to son.)

It was months before Marta received word that Józef had made it to Bucharest, the Romanian capital. Once there, Józef found work, including selling used cars. There were many Polish refugees in the city, as Romania was technically still neutral in the war. With his earnings, Józef went to a tailor and had a suit of clothes made and purchased a homburg hat, which only the European elites would wear. Well dressed and speaking fluent French, he showed up at the Romanian foreign ministry, where he ended up in the office of the foreign minister. Impressed by his well-dressed and eloquent visitor, the foreign minister told his secretary to take Monsieur Osnos to the consular officer, who by coincidence had the same surname as the minister. Having been sent by the foreign minister himself, Józef was given a *promisa*, which was a voucher for a Romanian entry visa to be obtained by Marta in Berlin. That process required among other things for Marta and Robert to obtain papers saying that they had been baptized, so they could board a train into Germany—the opposite direction from everyone else trying to escape. Her new name was Irene. In Berlin, a cousin of Marta's agreed to give her money to continue the trip, but only after Marta stood on the balcony with Robert in her arms, saying she would jump. The cousin expected to be repaid but ended up soon thereafter in a concentration camp with his younger wife. A descendant with whom I connected years later was aghast at the story of the "loan." She said that the wife was determined not to lose her household possessions, including a collection of Persian rugs, which is why they stayed in Berlin.

When Marta and Robert arrived at the Bucharest train station, Józef was there to greet them with roses. It is undeniable, as Robert always insisted, that he and my parents were not victims. After all, they made it out.

When I read Roger Moorhouse's book *Poland 1939*, published in 2020, the full scale of what was happening in Warsaw became even clearer. By any measure, it was horrible. The streets were littered with decomposing corpses. Food was increasingly scarce. Nazi butchering of Jews was routine. A doctor who compiled a report on hunger disease, which my mother translated as a book, told an interviewer in 1984 that he first met Marta in an "underground medical course in the ghetto." This was probably before the ghetto walls were erected, so the precise meaning is unclear. Starting in 1940, there was an underground Aryan medical school and a Jewish one. It was thought that when the war ended in a few months, they would merge. That never happened. Learning that my mother was connected in some way to an underground medical course in the ghetto, which I never knew, emphasizes the realities of their experience and the valor they displayed.

In Bucharest, one predawn, there was a major earthquake, which Robert said was the most frightening thing he had ever been through. But once the family had exited their apartment building, Józef found himself by chance standing next to the Turkish consul, both in their pajamas. Not long after, the consul gave them a transit visa to Turkey, which enabled them to reach Baghdad. There they encountered John Mis, a Christian Pole and a fluent English speaker who was in Iraq as a teacher and translator. I have always suspected that he had some other role, perhaps MI6. He helped the family arrange a transit visa to Bombay, where it was understood they would be able to stay. They arrived in British India in the early fall of 1940.

Józef and Marta soon found their footing, thanks in part to the Hebrew Immigrant Aid Society (HIAS), a global organization to assist displaced Jews (and, in recent years, others) to get early traction in their new countries. They must have been helpful. In his will, Józef left a donation.

In time, Józef became the respected (and I gather well-paid) manager of a firm that made rafts for the British navy in a building converted from a furniture factory. A man in the Polish consulate (probably in exile) told my father that he would have to acquire a tuxedo to be accepted in high society. He said that my mother would be looking after the cook. Marta bristled. She found a job in a pharmaceutical firm and later became a censor of mail from occupied France and Poland. Marta came to regard John Mis, the person in Baghdad who had helped with their visas to India, as their "angel." He later turned up in Bombay as a senior official of the police's Criminal Investigation Division, having apparently dropped the pretense of being a teacher. After the war, he moved to New York where he became a language specialist at the New York Public Library because he was expert in twenty-seven languages. I knew Mis as a bespectacled scholarly sort, but I never understood his full significance to my parents.

In their early months in Bombay, money was short, but before long they had five servants. There was an eclectic refugee community in Bombay, alongside the British colonialists and prosperous "Baghdadi" Jews who had arrived there long before. A number of those friends from India stayed in my parents' lives thereafter. Joseph Hitrec, a novelist, was also the translator of Nobel laureate Ivo Andric. Another Polish Jew they knew in Bombay became professor of Sanskrit at the Sorbonne.

Robert was sent to a boarding school in Panchgani, a hill town several hours from Bombay. When, only months before he died, I asked him why he thought they had sent him to a boarding school, he said with characteristic terseness and a smile, "They must have thought it was convenient." His main memory was that he was told not to admit he was Jewish in what was a Christian school. He went to catechism, took castor oil, and wrote plaintive letters home that I only read when he was well into his sixties. His teachers were largely English, and Robert developed a British accent. His accent came in handy years later when his Columbia medical school professors characterized him as of "British origin" rather than a Polish Jewish refugee. He learned that fact at his fiftieth medical school reunion.

Józef instinctively understood that the family would have to leave India eventually because once the war was over there was likely to be a sustained conflict over the country's colonial status. Again, his instincts were right. Plans were devised to arrange immigration to the United States, a major undertaking when visas for Jews were very hard to obtain. But on April 29, 1943, at 10:29 P.M., a telegram arrived at the Jewish Relief Committee in Bombay with this message: "Transit visa union Osnos Marthe and Family at last obtained. Please let her know go consulate. Princess George of Greece." Princess George was Marie Bonaparte, a great-grandniece of Napoleon and a psychoanalyst who used her connections and money to rescue or support Jews needing emigration to safety, including most famously Sigmund Freud. She was from all accounts an extraordinary character who, among other things, wrote books under a pseudonym about sex, especially female frigidity. Brancusi dedicated a sculpture to her which, according to a photograph, is a phallus. She was married to Prince George, of the same royal family that included Britain's Prince Philip. What seems to have happened is that Marta's brother Gustav, who made it to New York in 1940, was in Marie's psychoanalytic orbit. This is yet another example of rare good luck that I never heard discussed at home.

Although the visa telegram arrived in April, the family did not set out until December because Marta was already pregnant with me. They booked passage on an American ship that had been seized from the Italians, the USS *Hermitage*, which carried a small number of civilian passengers. The main purpose of the voyage was to transport Italian prisoners of war to Australia, and then pick up American GIs to be brought home. The trip across the Pacific took thirty-four days. I was the youngest passenger, dubbed "Prince Peter" because of my special status. Forty years later I happened to meet a Yale professor, an

Iranian who had also been on the boat as a teenager. He and Robert reunited and from memory shared dialogue from the few Hollywood movies that were shown on alternate nights, featuring stars like Cary Grant and Clark Gable, and which they faithfully attended. Forty years after the fact, the professor remembered my family and even the basket that was mine. There were nightly blackouts. Józef was encountered one evening in a women's bathroom mixing formula for me and was under suspicion until he was able to satisfactorily explain that he was on a baby-related errand in the darkness.

The exact number of Jews granted US visas in 1943–44 is unclear, but figures at the US Holocaust Memorial Museum in Washington appear to say that only 8 percent of a quota from Nazi-occupied Europe was filled.

When the ship docked in San Pedro, California, on February 6, 1944, Robert's first memory was of a man on the street observing him in short pants who snapped, "Here's a quarter, kid. Buy yourself the other half of your pants." The family traveled across the country by train to New York, where they took a room at the Hotel Wales on Madison Avenue. Marta would recall sitting with Józef on a bench near Central Park wondering how they would be able to start over. He was forty-one. She was thirty-eight.

Chapter 2

The Belnord

MARTA, JÓZEF, AND ROBERT embarked on their new lives with brio—not that they really had a choice. As for me, having been born after their escape from Europe, my path was (by any measure) smooth, and yet, it was shaped by what they had lived through. I was a first-generation American and a post-Holocaust Jew, but my experiences were different from what my parents and brother had overcome. We were in many ways strangers with the same DNA.

The Belnord is one of Manhattan's most formidable apartment buildings. It covers a full city block from 86th to 87th Streets and from Broadway to Amsterdam Avenue. It was built in the early twentieth century, in part (so it is said) as a response to the construction of the Apthorp, a slightly smaller building on 79th and Broadway. The Apthorp was "restricted," meaning no Jews could live there. The Belnord was bigger and grander in scale, with more cherubs embedded in the entry arch. A defining feature of both buildings was the center courtyard with a large fountain. There were separate "halls" around the circumference. Curious children in the Belnord, of which I was one, could explore the basements, including a circuit for horse carriages and a "penthouse" that may have been there for servants.

My parents couldn't afford an apartment at the Belnord on their own, so they joined with another Polish family of three and a cousin of my mother's, Edzia Markoe, and rented a spacious and airy apartment with eight rooms, including a kitchen and maid's room. After a year, the other Polish family left and moved further up 86th Street. Edzia, who never married, had a small greeting card company, and she stayed for what must have been a decade until she inherited an apartment in Greenwich Village. The notion of her sharing the space with us did not seem strange. It was, in its way, central European, where large apartments would have boarders. She was a lovable person, born seemingly in middle age, who had a closet where she kept a supply of small gifts.

Writing about this now I keep having to remind myself that this was only a few years after the end of the war, in which so many millions perished in ghastly ways. And yet there was no inkling at home—that I can reconstruct—of what had transpired nor its consequences for our family. I had my own good-sized room and used the windowsill as a stage for "plays" and the walls for bouncing a rubber ball in what I imagined was a tournament of some kind. I had my own bathroom and hid vitamin pills that I didn't want to take under the radiator, until I was busted.

Marta, Józef, and Robert embarked on their new lives with what seems, in retrospect, extraordinary speed and focus. Robert went to Stuyvesant High School, a highly selective public school where he graduated at sixteen before entering Columbia College in 1947. Marta worked full-time at Columbia's Physicians and Surgeons, mainly on cancer research, for a succession of laboratory leaders. The most significant of these was Alfred Gellhorn, the brother of the journalist Martha Gellhorn, one of the wives of Ernest Hemingway.

After three years or so, Józef and two engineers from Europe started a firm in midtown selling air-conditioning, still a new item of personal and business convenience, from window units to whole buildings. Józef's view was that in the aftermath of the Depression and war, Americans would want to reward themselves. The company was called Airvel and it still is in business, now in Long Island City. He had two partners: Stephen Fay (né Feigenbaum), a fellow as elegant as Józef but as the years progressed more of a dashing rogue than was probably excusable—Fay died in the arms of a paramour—and John Edwards (né Pincus), a man of unusual wit and charm who lived well past one hundred. I last saw him in an open casket at the Frank E. Campbell Funeral Home wearing a fedora.

After five years in the United States, they, Robert, and I received naturalization papers, ending our tenure as "resident aliens"—a designation that sounds more demeaning than I think it felt to my parents.

The household was so busy that as a toddler I had to be cared for elsewhere. I went to a preschool for two- and three-year-olds nearby, which was still sort of unusual. Józef kept with pride a report that said that I showed leadership skills. In the summer before my fourth birthday I was sent to a sleepaway camp in Hunter, New York, for eight weeks. I have no real memories of that experience other than a few photographs of a little boy dressed for a play and looking out of a bus window. Robert recalls that when our parents came to visit, I refused to talk to them.

After nursery school I was enrolled in PS 166 on West 89th Street. (Today it is called the Richard Rodgers School after the composer and proudly claims to have had J. D. Salinger as a student also.) I would walk there unaccompanied and came home for lunch. We had a housekeeper (we always said "maid") named Ressie Porter, who came before noon and stayed until Marta arrived home from work. She was a dignified presence whose husband was a part-time preacher and driver. They had a Cadillac and lived in a walk-up brownstone in Harlem, which I visited. On Fridays she made amazing southern fried chicken, a favorite food thereafter. Ressie stayed with the family for decades until she retired.

Most of the year I would join other children in the courtyard playing city games like ringalevio, tag, and handball. I learned to ride a bicycle. I remember many of my playmates, especially Bobby Dublin, who had polio and used crutches. He took me to the filming of several children's television shows like *Rootie Kazootie* and *Howdy Doody*, and I was always impressed that we were seated in the front row, an enviable perk for a disabled child.

My most famous playmate was Brandon De Wilde, one of the best-known child actors of the 1950s. He was a star of the classic Western *Shane* with Alan Ladd and of *The Member of the Wedding* on Broadway. He lived on the fourth floor, and we used to run up and down the stairs to each other's apartments. De Wilde continued acting until he was killed in a car accident in Colorado when he was in his twenties. Another local boy was Johnny Strasberg, who announced one afternoon that his sister, Susan, was going to be on television that night as Juliet in Shakespeare's play. She was becoming a major star, playing among other roles Anne Frank.

Their father, Lee Strasberg, was the head of the celebrated Actors Studio. One of his students was Marilyn Monroe. She moved into the building to be close to him. Trust me this happened, although I wouldn't swear to the time frame. One evening in the midfifties, Robert and I went out for ice cream and I saw a small blonde figure walking ahead of us toward Amsterdam Avenue, where she bought a newspaper and stood reading it under an all-night light of a dry cleaner. A police car pulled up and, apparently thinking she was a lady of the night, must have told her to move on. When he passed us, Robert flagged down the officer and said that woman was Marilyn Monroe. Presumably aghast, the policeman did a U-turn and apologized to the young blonde he had been so mistaken about. How I wish we'd had a photographic device of some kind to verify every last detail of that story.

PS 166 was a classic New York public school of the 1950s. Miss Finklestein was my kindergarten teacher. Miss Gross taught me in third and sixth grade. Mrs. Wolfe was especially memorable in the fifth. Most of the students were Jewish. I remember one or two "Negroes," an Asian, and several children called "Christians." Johnny Deutsch's father was a butcher at Macy's. He lived in a brownstone, not thought then to be fashionable. The majority lived in the prewar apartment buildings from Riverside Drive to Central Park West from 86th to 90th Streets. Again, the war was not a factor in the culture in any way I was aware of. I did know my mother was a bit older than others and worked. She and my father had accents. Once, in an effort to understand why they were different, I asked them, "Why don't you like Coca-Cola?" That was as close to an exploration of who we were as I was capable of at the time.

My fellow students and I wore military-style dog tags for identification and did civil defense drills—"duck and cover"—for the possibility of a nuclear attack, which meant hiding under our desks. Thinking about that now, it was less terrifying than the school shootings of today with the warnings of "shelter in place."

Our home routine was fixed. Józef read *The New York Times* in the morning while drinking tea in a glass with jam (a Russian custom). When he came home, he would read the *World-Telegram and Sun* for the final stock prices and usually the first edition of the *New York Herald Tribune* in the evening. I don't know when I started reading the newspapers also, starting with the comics, but it must have been early, and I have been doing so with enthusiasm ever since. Harry Truman, Adlai Stevenson, and later John F. Kennedy were Józef's political standard bearers. My most memorable father-son outing was a rally for Stevenson during the presidential campaign of either 1952 or 1956.

Before dinner Józef would put on a wool checked shirt he called his "native" and take a nap. I listened to radio serials, especially *The Lone Ranger*, which was preceded by fifteen minutes of news commentary from H. V. Kaltenborn, who for some reason I also enjoyed. We had family dinner most nights because Robert was a commuter to Columbia through his undergraduate years and medical school. One especially eventful occasion involved Robert declaring that he could eat five pounds of steak at one sitting. Józef said he could not. A bet was made, and steak was produced. With extraordinary difficulty Robert swallowed the last bit but did not eat steak again for a very long time.

There were a great many books in the house and records of Broadway musicals, which I loved, spending hours sitting in front of the big console, and classics which I did not listen to except for Tchaikovsky's *Peter and the Wolf.* I was given piano lessons by my cousin Zarka's fearsome mother-in-law, Frina, who lived past one hundred and said that she survived Stalin and Hitler, but the worst experience of her life, figuratively, was trying to teach me piano.

As a teenager, I remember discovering Alfred Kinsey's landmark book about sex habits and reading it with fascination. I also found Arnold Gesell's books about child development (really). These books were my birds-and-bees education. Discussion on these matters with my parents never happened.

When I was about twelve, Marta said she would give me five dollars if I would read Leon Uris's novel *Exodus* about refugees struggling to get to Palestine after the war. That was really the extent of Jewish input. There were many Poles, Jews, who were family friends. But none, that I recall, were religious. No synagogues and no Sabbath rituals. The two biggest family holidays were Thanksgiving (initially at Uncle Gustav's Fifth Avenue apartment) and Passover at the Belnord, where Marta would always invite some of her scientific colleagues, including, unforgettably, a Laotian prince and Stefan Zamenhof, whose father was the inventor of the international language Esperanto. Most of the time Marta and Józef spoke Polish at home but I always answered in English. Robert's command of Polish never grew beyond what he had learned in childhood.

Marta and Józef had an active social life and relatively early—too early—they began to leave me at home alone. I was scared enough to keep a kitchen knife under my pillow. For a time, I developed a routine of nightly vomiting, a likely sign about how I felt in an empty apartment. Thinking about it now, it was assuredly much less dangerous than being bombed by the Nazis at that age, although it must not have felt that way.

Television was a big issue for my parents. They were convinced that watching too much would make rubbish of my mind. (Think about today's struggles over "screen time.") Finally, because Marta wanted to watch the coronation of Queen Elizabeth in 1953, a small TV set was placed in a corner of the living room. Józef, with great solemnity, took me to a neighborhood notary public to sign a formal agreement that I would only watch a half hour a day Monday to Friday and one hour on weekends. Only years later did I realize that the "agreement" was only for a year and was never renewed. The Belnord's old-fashioned DC current meant that to make the television work, a converter was required. And when my parents went out on the weekends, I was led to believe that the converter would blow up after thirty minutes unless the fuse was removed to cool off. I dutifully removed the fuse on the half hour several times until I came to realize that the warning, like the restriction-on-watching-time agreement, was nonsense.

Every week I went to the Saint Agnes branch of the New York Public Library on 83rd Street and Amsterdam Avenue to take out a selection of books. The Landmark series of history books in hardcover for children by prominent authors was a favorite, and over time I probably read most of them. Decades later, when I arrived at Random House, I thought about reviving the series. The first book my assistant Lisa Kaufman and I examined was Robert Penn Warren on the Alamo. Lisa corresponded with Warren who, she said, was appalled at the datedness and racism of his book. (He had referred to Native Americans as "savages.") Warren made the necessary changes, but we never went ahead with the project, which was rude and a commercial mistake. I had learned history from Landmarks.

I did well in school. IQ tests were a very big deal and in the sixth grade, I managed to sneak a peek at my score, which was more than 130, a good number. That year I was elected president of the student council. My election slogan was "Student Council Four Years Straight Makes This Peter Really Great." There is a photograph of me at that age, a little chubby with a pompadour. I was active in school plays and was assigned a double bass in the school orchestra. In the afternoon in the lower grades I was picked up at school by a bus from "Schwartzie's Rangers," an afterschool program housed in a basement on West End Avenue and 89th Street. We doubtless went to the park on most days, but I especially remember watching black-and-white Mickey Mouse movies when the weather was bad.

Robert called me, affectionately, "Zuzu," but he was so much older that, as I said, in many respects I was an only child—born midway through my parents' lives and in a completely different culture from theirs. The astonishing thing is that Marta and Józef established themselves so well in their new roles that in the early 1950s they bought land at White Meadow Lake in Rockaway, New Jersey, an hour from New York, and built a comfortable weekend home with large picture windows on a lakefront overlooking a steep wooded hill.

They were two of the first people to build on that side of the five-mile lake, which made the property especially fun to explore. I had a raft tied up to a wooden dock and roamed up and down the shoreline with a paddle. Eventually they bought me a small boat with a 5 or 7½ horsepower motor, which was an especially exciting object and gave me a sense of (controlled) speed. There were many other children at the lake in the summer, but much of the year I would play alone on weekends or bring a friend from the city. For two years I was sent to a sleepaway camp in Vermont and spent one summer at Boy Scout camp where I earned eleven merit badges. (My scouting career came to an end in junior high school when I skipped an evening event to go to a party and was required to return my "most improved scout" trophy from the previous year.)

From twelve on I went to the White Meadow Lake day camp, eventually ascending at fifteen to the position of counselor-in-training in swimming for the younger children. For reasons I never understood, I wasn't interested in team sports like baseball. I would throw balls in the air by myself on our lawn and catch them with a well-broken in glove. But I would avoid any position except right field, the least likely to be confronted with an actual hit. I don't ever remember attending a sports event with Józef or Marta. I did go to see plays and musicals with Marta, particularly Gilbert and Sullivan on Saturday afternoons and at Christmas, *Amahl and the Night Visitors* by Gian Carlo Menotti.

I discovered a social life. There is a photograph of me with a group at Tavern on the Green celebrating something. I was in the sixth grade (maybe seventh) wearing a suit and tie. My "girlfriend" was a very pretty classmate name Paula "Poppy" Wool. We had dance parties at apartments in the neighborhood and boy-girl stuff was a significant part of our out-of-school activity.

In the 1950s, there was a belief that bright children should be moved through school with extra speed. In retrospect, I think that was almost certainly unnecessary and probably a mistake. It perhaps reflected a sense of urgency among aspirational Jews about getting ahead. (Today's equivalent is getting into the "right" schools.) In any case, I was selected for an SP (special progress) class at Joan of Arc Junior High School, a large building on West 93rd Street housing seventh, eighth, and ninth grades. SP students were in a separate class and the approach was to move fast enough to skip the eighth grade. It never occurred to my parents or to me to question this concept, so I went headlong into being a ninth grader. I don't remember what kind of student I was, but I was no longer spending so much time alone reading books and listening to musicals on the record player. I liked girls and it turned out there was one or another that liked me. There were boys—only boys—having bar mitzvahs. And in what I regard as a shameless exercise in wanting presents and joining the crowd, I persuaded Józef and Marta to join the Stephen Wise Free Synagogue (I thought "free" meant that they didn't pay for the privilege). I completed the training and my Torah portion was about the circumcision of Abraham, which was a little embarrassing. Instead of a party in a rented space there was a party at home. At some point I remember the lights were lowered and I canoodled in the living room with a girl named Judy Elliott, who was different because she wasn't Jewish and not in an SP class.

Once, on the way to a scouting event outside New York on Palisades Parkway, my friend Bennett Shapiro and I started squabbling in the back seat and Józef said he would leave us by the side of the road to proceed by bus. He did. We managed to get where we were going, but Bennett's parents were (not surprisingly) furious.

~

AS THE ISSUE OF high school choice approached, I decided to apply to the High School of Music and Art on 137th Street and Convent Avenue instead of taking the test for Stuyvesant, then a highly selective all-boys school, where Robert had gone. To be admitted to M&A, you went through an audition to test your potential. I chose voice and, inexplicably, sang the spiritual "Go Down Moses." One of the girls in my junior high school crowd was the daughter of a senior administrator at the school. I don't know whether she was the reason I was admitted, because my musical background and skills were not particularly impressive. But I did have musical instincts (and still do). I was assigned to the timpani section of the intermediate orchestra, which in retrospect was a little like playing right field in Little League.

In the afternoons and on weekends, small groups of us would gather in front of a candy store on Broadway, a coffee shop called Esquire on 86th and Broadway, or a fancier place called the Croyden on Madison and 86th. I was accepted in all these places for some reason, although on the East Side the kids all went to private school. I have a photograph of me on Broadway with two other boys, Eddie Rosenfeld and Stephen Bochco, who went on to a very successful career in television (he created *Hill Street Blues*, among other successful shows). On the East Side, one of the boys, Nelson Peltz, became a billionaire investor known for being especially tough on CEOs. Andy Finklestein was the first among us to shave and became (as Andy Stein) president of the New York City Council. He was later celebrated in the tabloids for the quality of his toupee. I gather that all these little street corner groups, cliques, were considered "fast" by outsiders, whatever that meant at the time. I think that by being in three, I was not all that deeply embedded in any.

My tenth-grade tenure at M&A was brief. There was a transit strike that kept us from school but even when I was there my record was weak. I did poorly in Spanish and missed the minimum grade in music theory, although I did better as a timpanist and was elected home room class representative to the student council. Marta and Józef were, as they should have been, baffled by this person evolving in their midst. Our cultural differences were significant, except for Józef's and my interest in the political world. Most children in the 1950s, I suspect, did not read *The New York Times* daily or listen to the news on radio and television. I didn't really know what journalists did, but somewhere I wrote that I wanted to be one.

Either my parents or I raised the issue of sending me to a boarding school. It was now mid schoolyear. Private school in New York was for some reason not an option. They wanted me out of town. With a consultant's advice, I took a test and applied to three schools. I was told that I could attend Exeter the following fall if I agreed to repeat the tenth grade. Westminster accepted me but also for the fall. Cheshire Academy in Cheshire, Connecticut, said I could be enrolled as soon as the check cleared. So right after the New Year, I left the Belnord for Cheshire. I was driven to the school in my father's Chrysler by Marvin Fink, the service manager of Airvel. I don't know why Marta and Józef couldn't come. I never lived at home again except for summers. I was fourteen.

There is a debate these days about "helicopter" parenting, especially in the upper-middle classes: an overinvolvement in children's lives. Making sure that they are on teams and the right clubs, get extra help for school with a goal of getting into top colleges, and so on. In many cases, parents see their offspring's success as a reflection of their own. If you have the material needs taken care of, a splendid career and a weekend home, basking in the glory of an excellent child is very satisfying, another notch of prestige.

For most of my childhood, Józef and Marta were the opposite. They were loving but largely disengaged by temperament and background from my "American" choices. They never said "Play baseball" or "We'll go to the PTA meeting," or guided me carefully through the preparation for high school and college admissions. Every one of those decisions I either made or didn't make on my own. Their contributions were something I did not appreciate fully at the time: the courage and self-assurance they displayed to have outsmarted personal catastrophe from 1939 to 1944, and the unexpressed but unquestionable determination to make the best possible lives for their family in a new world.

That is quite something when you think about it.

Chapter 3

Founded in 1794

CHESHIRE ACADEMY was founded in 1794—proudly proclaiming 225 years of history (as of this writing), making it one of the oldest private schools in continuous operation in the country. It began as the Episcopal Academy of Connecticut. In 1917 it became the Roxbury School and was a feeder for Yale, especially postgraduate high school students who needed a year of preparation before joining the football team. In 1937 it became Cheshire Academy and was led by headmaster Arthur Sheriff, who was still there when I arrived in January 1958. I was given a second-floor single room in Horton Hall. One of the first things you heard from boys along the corridor was that Cheshire had boys who had been kicked out of the finest schools in America. From all accounts, the school, now coed, is doing well with students from many countries (paying full tuition) or whose parents are intent on giving their offspring better educations than they had.

I am proud to say I was once a commencement speaker and have donated enough books that I have published to establish an Osnos section in the school library.

The closest analogy to my sense of the place are the opening pages of *The Catcher in the Rye*, in which Holden Caulfield describes Pency Prep as a somewhat raffish institution on the prep school spectrum. We had a great many rules and rituals. Ties and jackets were required. There were Saturday morning classes. Boarders had higher self-regard than "day hoppers." We were prohibited from talking to town girls when we encountered them in the street. Classes were no larger than eight boys. A grade of 75 was considered good. Report cards were issued weekly. Like most boys in the school I complained about the restrictions but, on the whole, made it through, unscathed by disciplinary trouble.

The teachers were an eccentric and colorful bunch. "Doc" Brink, the geometry and algebra teacher, was said to have designed a camshaft for Cadillacs. He had a Santa Claus belly and would write on the blackboard with a piece of chalk on the end of a long stick. Larry Kelley had been a Yale football star, the second recipient of the Heisman Trophy in the 1930s. "Brother" Houghton was part of the distinguished Houghton publishing family. Morris Sweetkind, the English teacher, was widely published in the field. He introduced me to the works of F. Scott Fitzgerald, who I found especially appealing. Like Salinger, Fitzgerald must have appealed to my teenage sensibility about the social norms of the prep school life in which I had found myself.

The disciplinarian was Fred Linehan, another former Yale All-American with the face and bearing of a bulldog. Getting in trouble meant having what was described as a wall-to-wall conversation with Linehan. In recent years, it has turned out that at so many prep schools there were cases of teachers who preyed on the students, but I never had that experience—although thinking about it now, one of the school chaplains made me uneasy with his interest.

Hurley Hall was where the daily sit-down meals were. Students had to take turns as waiters. All requisite criticisms of the food were shared: saltpeter in the soup to diminish sexual urges; mystery meat with gooey brown gravy. In the considerable expanse of the dining room there was only one girl regularly in attendance. She was the daughter of an English teacher named Mitchell and was cruelly called "liver lips," as in, "When she starts to look good, it's time to go home for a weekend." There were occasional dances with girls from other schools or "a date" from home, but the overall goal was to put a firm lid on teenage libido.

Because I had skipped the eighth grade, the other boys in Horton Hall were at least a year older than I was. Our dorm master was a gangly fellow named Michael Smith, who later became a clerk to a Supreme Court justice. The boy next door to me was Jewish. There was a boy down the hall who, because of his mannerisms, was called "Lucy." The corner room at the end belonged to one of the three Buchmayer triplets, the sons of the owner of a major ski shop in Manchester, Vermont. The other boy in that room, Joe Heaslip, was also from Manchester. He was a square-jawed six-footer who was the quarterback on the Cheshire football team, the Cats. (From the class of 1958, two players made it to the NFL.)

The Manchester boys introduced me to anti-Semitism. Lest I missed the point, they told me what they thought of Jews. This was only thirteen years after the end of World War II, and the full meaning of the Holocaust was not yet understood, even by me. One day I returned from class to discover that all the furniture in my room had been upended. But curiously I don't remember being especially unnerved at the bullying. By senior year, Heaslip and I were best friends. I introduced him to a Jewish girl from Central Park West who he took to the senior prom. I called him "Jaws." Joe went to Boston University and served in the army. I lost track of him. In 1988, I asked the owners of a Manchester bookstore whether they knew Joe. Joe had come home, they said, joined the family oil business, and died in his midthirties, leaving a wife and daughter.

I needed to know more. Recently I located a death notice in the *Bennington Banner* that said that Joe had died unexpectedly. His wife and daughter were named. Putting the daughter's name in Facebook worked. The first post I saw was what she said was one of her favorite pictures of her dad. There, for the first time in fifty years, I saw my friend's face, very much the same guy. The daughter agreed to talk to me. Her mother, now living in Texas, wondered why after all these years I was interested in Joe, but she sent me a picture of his gravestone in a Manchester cemetery.

To my surprise, it turned out that after college and the military, Joe had gotten a master's degree in social work at Washington University in St. Louis and was on his way to a PhD. I would not have

guessed he would get a graduate degree and choose a career in a helping profession. His wife worked in an office and supported them. His
father, who apparently was tough and nasty, summoned him back to
run the family oil business and Joe went, despite his wife's misgivings.
But what struck me most was that this square-jawed Vermont foot-
baller had become my best high school friend. Much was going on in
Joe's mind and spirit that I might easily have influenced and yet never
recognized.

~

ANOTHER BOY WAS Bobby Goldfine from Newton, Massachusetts. His uncle, Bernard Goldfine, was the focus of a political
scandal in which President Eisenhower's chief of staff, Sherman
Adams, received a vicuña coat from Goldfine (who was under federal
investigation) and had to resign. Another student was the son of
Zeppo Marx, the straight man of the Marx brothers. His stepmother
later married Frank Sinatra. The closest thing I recall to a "person of
color" was Mengasha Adamsou, known among us as the "bastard son"
of Ethiopian emperor Haile Selassie. That was as much as we knew
about him and we never pursued the topic. He would march around
outside the dorm with a broomstick as he hoped to go to West Point.
James Spruance was Navy royalty. There was a class of ships named
for his forefather. My favorite prep school names were (phonetic)
Herksher Tweed and Barnum Beech Burrall. Peter Strongwater was
known as Peter Weakpiss. I was apparently known, according to my
senior roommate Jeff Cates, as Peter Prep because of the way I dressed.
I did like striped button-downs, which Józef got for me by the handful because Airvel had air-conditioned a Manhattan shirt company's
showroom.

In my junior year, I made the honors list with an over-75 average
and did especially well, for the one and only time, in math beyond
addition and subtraction, thanks to Doc Brink. I made the mistake as
a senior of taking mechanical drawing and calculus, which were not a
fit. History and English rescued me for graduation.

We spent weekends on campus, although you could take a few Saturday-Sunday breaks and very occasionally leave on Friday. I met a girl from Westport through another student and was, more than I ever had been, smitten. We exchanged letters that she would spray perfume on. When we were together at her home we would "make out." Among my high school romances, this was the most intense. She eventually broke it off and I was crestfallen. The reality is that teenage boys find it hard to submerge their adolescent urges. I once wrote an editorial for the school paper advocating for the chance to talk to town girls. Arthur Sheriff refused to publish it.

Whenever possible, I always seemed to have a girlfriend. In the summer when we were at White Meadow Lake I would have what Marta called "the substitute" for whoever was the primary crush in the school year.

I doubt we ever saw a newspaper and had no television (there was a record player for early rock and roll and ersatz folk like the Kingston Trio). I remained interested in politics nonetheless, I guess, because of Józef's example. For instance, I vividly recall watching the 1956 Democratic convention on television with him at White Meadow, which almost nominated John F. Kennedy for vice president. Like so many of my generation, Kennedy became my beau ideal of a public figure.

My extracurricular activities at Cheshire included the school paper (where I was the features editor), the yearbook, and the nondenominational but affirmatively Christian chapel committee because I found the Sunday services comforting. Also for some reason I was in the glee club, which was distinctively undermined by the fact that the school song had a line that went something like: "Cheshire fields are proud and hoary." And I played the snare drum in the school band, building on my brief experience as a timpanist. I think the closest I came to a team sport was as an occasional participant in track events. The school would have served me well by encouraging or requiring me to be on a team. Except for running groups years later, I never joined a sports team, which I regret. No one had ever told me that to be especially good at a sport, you had to work hard at it.

One night in the spring of 1960, my senior year, I "ran away," as we called it. I stuffed my bed with pillows and went by bus to New Haven. The only person I knew there was Andy Glass, the son of close friends of my parents, a Yale graduate who was then a reporter for the *New Haven Journal Register*. He bought me a meal and told me to go back to school, which I did. My absence had not been discovered. Jeff Cates, my roommate (now a retired Arizona judge), told me that he remembers that it was the day I was turned down at the University of Pennsylvania. I realize that I had never been turned down for anything before. You had to start somewhere to learn how it feels.

The college application process was another period in which, in retrospect, I didn't have any real guidance. I don't know what if anything Cheshire provided. I applied to Penn, Columbia, Syracuse, Colby, and Brandeis. I was accepted early enough to Syracuse to feel relieved, turned down at Penn (my first choice), never heard from Colby, and put on the waiting list at Columbia. Robert had three degrees from Columbia and Marta had a position at the medical school, so I expected to have some leeway. What I had always heard about that class of 1964 and thought was a myth turned out later to be true. Columbia's future provost Jonathan Cole was in that class and confirmed to me the story that for that one and only year, acceptance was based solely on grades and board scores—nothing else. As a result, the class came overwhelmingly from New York City's selective public schools (Stuyvesant and the Bronx High School of Science) and was nearly all Jewish. Too many of the boys (the college was all male) who had been accepted chose to attend, exceeding the dormitory capacity. The entire plan was considered a disaster, and the dean of admissions was fired.

I applied to Brandeis because I was encouraged to do so by my mother's very formidable cousin, Marie Syrkin. Marie was a professor of humanities there and recommended me to the admissions director, Philip Driscoll. Despite the fact that I was Jewish, along with the vast majority of the student body, admitting a New England prep school graduate was at Brandeis a tepid form of diversity.

Marie had gotten her position at Brandeis despite reluctance from several senior male academics who thought she was insufficiently scholarly. She had never completed her PhD and had been a high school teacher for a time. In addition to a biography of her close friend Golda Meir, Marie wrote a number of other books, including *Blessed Is the Match*, one of the first accounts of Jewish resistance in World War II. On the back cover of the paperback is a quote from I. F. Stone: "To call this book terrible and tragic is an understatement. To read it is an obligation." Many years later, Izzy and Marie both came to our family Seder. By that time they disagreed on Israeli policies toward Palestine. Even so, it was an honor to have them both.

Marie married three times. Her last husband, Charles Reznikoff, lived in New York, where they kept an apartment. Only when he died did we realize that he was a major figure in what was known as the "concrete" school of midcentury poetry. Many of his books are still available.

So, without knowing much about Brandeis—in 1960 the university was only twelve years old, founded in 1948—I decided to go there instead of to Syracuse, which was known as a party school. After the boys boarding life, the attractions of one of the Jewish fraternities there (that was still the segregated rule then) would have been a social activity to be savored and would have become a distraction to academic life. I am sure that the festivities of a frat house wouldn't have been a lasting plus compared to the political consciousness and values that were my main takeaway from Brandeis. There were no fraternities or hard-to-get-into clubs. The university had just dropped the football team. School "spirit" was not what cooler students wanted to display. In other words, Brandeis was the best school that would have me, not my strong choice.

Off I went in September 1960. For the first month, I was still sixteen years old.

Chapter 4

The Harvard of the Jews

BRANDEIS UNIVERSITY in Waltham, Massachusetts, was founded the same year as the establishment of Israel. In the aftermath of the horrors of World War II, which were still being absorbed, the creation of a secular Jewish university had many supporters in the United States. With quotas and restrictions of various kinds in place at many of the elite universities, the Brandeis aspiration was to be the "Harvard of the Jews." The list of professors was illustrious in part because so many Jewish intellectuals had fled to American safety from Europe. In the period of Senator Joseph McCarthy's portrayal of communists under every bed, there were also political pressures on scholars thought to be left-wing who were welcome at this new up-scale academic institution. The Brandeis faculty—Herbert Marcuse in political philosophy, Abraham Maslow in psychology, Philip Rahv in English, Frank Manuel in history, Eleanor Roosevelt in whatever she chose—immediately gave the university stature beyond its size.

The founding president was Abram Sachar, a historian who was so prodigious a fundraiser that the campus newspaper *The Justice* called him "the Prince of Schnorrers," Yiddish for someone who is always trying to get something for nothing. The progressive sense of transparency and openness to a range of ideas was said to reflect the legacy of Justice Louis Brandeis. But aside from the presence of three chapels on the campus—Jewish, Catholic, and Protestant—the over-riding culture was a mishmash of Jewish identities of the era, largely liberal in a mid-twentieth-century way. I never entered any of the chapels in my four years on campus, nor did I join in any activities

43

that were specifically Jewish in character. And yet the core of the university was a traditional Jewish respect for education and a tolerance of other people's backgrounds and views.

Most students were the children or grandchildren of immigrants. Achievement was a holy grail, and graduates tended toward the secure professions: law, medicine, academia, social work, and insurance. Corporate business careers apparently were less available to Jews in that era. Journalism and the arts were considered a bit offbeat, even daring. I don't remember banking, finance, or creative entrepreneurship to be considered "Jewish." Technology as we know it today was still "engineering" and was not, as I recall, especially popular.

There were very few American "Negroes" at Brandeis and I do not remember anyone who was introduced as a Muslim. If there were students in skull caps (yarmulkes) I didn't notice them. Identities, aside from being Jewish or a non-Jew, just didn't seem to matter. The lack of bias wasn't a political or social stance. This was pre-consciousness. In the early 1960s, the students seemed to be more homogeneous. The assumption was that the overwhelming majority were Jewish. I don't recall paying much if any attention to who was not Jewish, except perhaps to wonder why they had chosen Brandeis. So I was surprised to learn that in a 2016 study called "All Together Separate: Race, Ethnicity, and Gender at Brandeis," 40 percent of the students said they were "atheist, agnostic, or nothing in particular." Thirty-one percent said they were Jewish, the figure declining from 36 among seniors to 24 percent among first years. Another 3 to 10 percent said they were Jewish, aside from religion.

The detailed sixty-four-page examination showed that 51 percent of the students were white and 25 percent were East Asian (Chinese, Japanese, and South Korean, presumably), including many who were not classified as US citizens. Six percent were Black, two percent were Muslim, and 86 percent said they were heterosexual. Every nuance of difference was noted.

In my era, for all the anti-Semitism that had nearly wiped out European Jews not even a generation before, there was strikingly lit-

tle focus on that issue. Anti-Semites would not choose Brandeis anyway. It was recognized that the elite WASP-dominated institutions
limited Jews, but that was sort of an accepted fact, which is why there
was room for Brandeis to set out to be an equal of the Ivy League.

There were a few dozen foreign students under a program funded
by the New York philanthropist Lawrence Wien. They were called
"Wienies" and came from all over the world. They were considered
exotic. That program still exists, and its alumni ranks are impressive.

Among the more notable Brandeis graduates in its early years
were Marty Peretz, who later taught at Harvard, married rich, and
became the longtime owner of *The New Republic* as he moved to an
obstreperous crankiness in his views. (But he was a great admirer of
Marie Syrkin, for which I always liked him.) His wife funded a group
of civil liberties lawyers in Vietnam, where my wife-to-be, Susan,
worked. For that I am eternally grateful. Stephen Solarz became a
congressman from Brooklyn who was one of the visible and energetic
foreign policy whizzes of his generation. William Singer would
achieve a national profile when he challenged Mayor Daley and his
machine in Chicago as a reformist Democrat. My favorite statistic
about Brandeis in the late 1960s period of social turmoil is that, over
time, it had four people on the FBI's Most Wanted list: Angela Davis,
the civil rights activist and communist who was implicated in a murder and eventually became a civil rights icon; Abbie Hoffman, a ren-
egade with a drug record, who was founder of the "Yippies"; and two
female bank robbers who were part of a radical group. My guess is
that the wealthy donors in Palm Beach must have been appalled. This
was a Brandeis paradox—the rich tended to become more conservative and the policies of Israel a divisive matter—that would endure as
a fundamental problem for the university's self-image.

The student culture was somewhat bifurcated, as most student
cultures are. There were the "collegiate" types who were by most standards conventional. The boys enjoyed sports, although Brandeis was
far from a powerhouse on that score. The girls wore skirts and circle
pins. The "bohemians" wore jeans and listened to early folk stars like

Joan Baez and Bob Dylan (both amazingly still around nearly sixty years later). This was the time of poetry by Allen Ginsberg and anomie from Jack Kerouac. These students were the mellow progenitors, on the whole, of the more radicalized student disrupters of the late 1960s. Our time was the relatively optimistic "New Frontier" of the Kennedy years. There was no Vietnam war to speak of yet. The civil rights movement was mainly in the South. Everyone would agree that the tensest moment came in October 1962 when the Cuban missile crisis raised the prospect of nuclear war. I remember being in the smoking room of Goldfarb Library pondering our fate, but, curiously, I don't recall that I was exceptionally spooked. We did not, after all, have a television in our dorm that I ever watched.

While I certainly wanted to look "collegiate" and dressed neatly in crewneck sweaters, I didn't really fall clearly into any category. I had a full complement of friends who, as I think about it now, were a mix of types from various streams. My friends included a playwright, a journalist, and an artist. The girls we dated were pretty, a term no longer in vogue. What attracted people to each other was then, as it is now, a mystery: appearance, personality, background? The rise of online dating, in which the first thing you are likely to see is a picture, suggests that how a person looks is still influential.

I arrived at Brandeis in the fall of 1960 as the torch was being passed to a new generation. That meant the Peace Corps, the space race, the nobility and dignity of civil rights protestors, and the Russians as satisfying villains in the Cold War. It was also a time of a growing middle class, cars with fins, and pervasive new appliances—televisions, air-conditioners, and other suburban comforts. Having the Kennedys coming into the White House made the era seem glamorous, especially in contrast to the Eisenhower years. The country felt young and so were we. My parents had fled what was certain annihilation. My life was safe and secure. They were Europeans. I was American. What we shared was a sensibility that was not based on grievance of what was lost. The terrifying past seemed not to interfere with the successes of the present.

My freshman roommate came from Modesto, California, because I had asked for someone from another part of the country. We lived in Fruchtman Hall. Brandeis buildings carried the names of the donor base: five Shapiros and a Gryzmish, Kutz, and Olin-Sang (whom we said were Oriental Jews).

The most memorable moment of that year was the response I got on my first paper in humanities. The professor was Alan Grossman, who later became a prominent poet. The subject was *The Iliad*. The grade was a C+. The notation at the top was: "Not a stupid paper, Mr. Osnos, but an ignorant one," which was actually not the worst place to start a college career. I endured the required courses in math and science and did not do especially well. I didn't particularly care about what was happening in classrooms. I was biding my time until things would come along inside the classroom, or more importantly outside, to capture my interest.

Among that year's girlfriends was Charlotte Moses. I would put lush music on the record player in my room. I cringe now at how feckless I was in so many ways. By contrast Charlotte was exceptionally bright and witty. She later had a major legal career in New York. The biggest influence of the year came in the summer. Bob Greenberger, who was a sophomore, a basketball player from Neponsit, Queens, and I planned what turned out to be an eighty-day trek around Europe and the Soviet Union. We carried *Europe on Five Dollars a Day* and basically kept to it. We arrived in London on the day that Ernest Hemingway's suicide was in the news. We weren't used to shocks like that. We checked our big suitcases, quickly realizing we did not need as much as we had brought.

We set off with our Eurail passes through Amsterdam up to Scandinavia and on to an organized trip to Leningrad and Moscow. In 1961, going to the Soviet Union was still amazing and uncommon. Our trip, as nearly as we could tell, was unsupervised by the Soviet authorities. I remember selling a madras belt on the street for enough rubles to buy mementos. I must have had another belt. The main value of the Russia trip was that it gave me a baseline of comparison for when I returned as a newspaper correspondent thirteen years later.

After an overnight train trip to Hamburg, Bob and I arrived just as the loudspeaker bellowed *"Achtung!"* We looked at each other in disbelief, agreed that Germany was not for us two young Jews, and headed off to Switzerland. I didn't get back to Germany until the mid-1970s, by which time "Achtung" was not so disturbing.

(One of my favorite teenage memories was traveling to Europe with my parents the summer when I was fourteen. We were standing in line at the Doge's Palace in Venice when a German edged into line ahead of Marta. She blurted an epithet: *"Schweinhund* [pig], get back where you belong." I'm sure he did. She was small but tough.)

My parents had given me several hundred dollars spending money for the trip, and I was determined not to let it run out. Having left my suitcase behind, I had two drip-dry shirts, quick-dry underwear, and at most two pair of pants. Near the end of the trip Bob and I were to meet my parents at an elegant resort on the Costa Brava in Spain. When we got off the bus from Barcelona, Marta burst into tears. "You look like you just got out of Auschwitz," she cried. I guess I was haggard at 120 pounds or so in a white shirt gone gray. The resort was exceptionally luxurious (Bob and I stayed in staff quarters), and I ate so much at the sumptuous meals that I couldn't stand straight when I left the table. It was a great voyage; so much to discover. I was now nearly eighteen.

My second year at Brandeis was marked by three experiences that were, in their way, profound, moving me from adolescence to the next stage of awareness. None of these were in the classroom. And the truth is I don't remember my classes with the clarity with which I recall what was happening outside.

The first of these experiences was a trip of about ten days to Mississippi in February 1962. Our guide was a young lawyer named Bill Higgs, said to be one of the very few white lawyers in the state who would take civil rights cases. He was at Brandeis on a semester-long fellowship. He invited three of us—Fred Gordon, Dave Tierney, and me—to join him on the trip. I don't know why I was asked to join but was very lucky that I did.

By any measure it was extraordinary. We drove down from Waltham and went to Jackson, Greenville, and Oxford and met virtually everyone who in the years that followed would play a major role in the great civil rights period of the 1960s: Medgar Evers (murdered a year later); Fannie Lou Hamer, a founder of the Mississippi Freedom Democratic Party; James Meredith, later to be the first Black student enrolled at Ole Miss; James Silver, the white Ole Miss professor who wrote the classic book on the nature of the state's "closed society"; Governor Ross Barnett, who told us that God meant the races to be separate, "sure as he made little green apples"; members of the White Citizens Council, a more respectable version of the KKK; Hodding Carter, a principled newspaper editor; and William Faulkner, who entertained us at his home in Oxford, only six months before he died.

When we returned, I wrote my first articles for the Brandeis paper, *The Justice*, describing the scale of rural poverty we had seen and the impact of systemic segregation. Nothing in my life up to that point had made so deep an impression on me in ways that have lasted to this day. Years later Higgs was disbarred in Mississippi on the grounds that he was gay. I could not be more grateful to him. After he left Brandeis, I never saw him again.

The second experience involved a girl named Ann Marcus, a freshman. I don't know what the proper term was at the time, but I was besotted. Why I was so taken with her is a mystery of youth. She liked me, in the parlance of the day, but not in the way I was drawn to her. She had a boyfriend from her neighborhood who was in school in Philadelphia and I seemed to be in competition with this phantom. Within the limitations of college "parietal hours" we would convene in my dorm room (hers was off-limits), in ways that were by the standards of late teenage relationships of that time enticing.

The third experience was connected to the Ann infatuation. On the evening of May 3, 1962, in my dorm room, she broke up with me. After dropping her off at her dorm, I turned to the glass door in the dormitory and hit the horizontal metal handle hard enough to break through the glass, shattering it and my right wrist. I was bleeding badly and a couple in the parking lot drove me to the Waltham hospital emergency room. The next thing I remember was my mother when I awoke from surgery, clearly injured but stable. The rest of the term, my arm was wrapped in bandages and I had to take finals orally because my writing hand was incapacitated. The gesture was obviously dramatic and the source, I'm sure, of much campus buzzing.

It never occurred to me or to my parents to blame the Brandeis door for the mishap, but the report of the incident said, incorrectly, that I had been drinking. I was placed on disciplinary probation. Over the summer I was able to restore some movement, but surgery was scheduled for the following fall to reconnect a severed medial nerve in my wrist. The operation took place in October at Columbia Presbyterian Hospital.

I remember those days especially well for an unrelated reason. In Mississippi I had asked James Meredith to write me a letter about his plan to attend Ole Miss and his hopes for the state. He had sent it to me, and the week he enrolled in Oxford—which was a huge national story because of the racial confrontation—*The Justice* ran the letter as a "world exclusive." The letter even made it into *The New York Times* as a wire service item and I was named as the recipient. In my New York hospital bed, I was thrilled.

The net effect of the injury was that I never regained full feeling in two fingers of my right hand and have a dramatic scar on my right arm. When I was summoned to the draft board in 1966, the lack of an effective trigger finger got me a 1-Y classification (only eligible to be drafted in an acute crisis) and so I was able to go to Vietnam in 1970 on my terms and not the Pentagon's. In my judgment, the physical discomfort was well worth it, given what it did to introduce me to a degree of maturity and the chance to cover the war without serving in it.

Speaking with Ann decades later, I was surprised to learn that she had been more affected by my accident than I had realized. She went to Israel on a fellowship and almost didn't return to Brandeis. Ann and I had stayed in friendly contact for a while after college, without ever talking about what had happened. She went on to a major career as a dean at NYU. She showed me a note Marta had sent her when the appointment was announced in the *Times*, saying how warmly she was remembered.

The only thing that made a lasting impact in my junior year was a psychology course that involved weekly visits to Metropolitan State, a vast nearby mental hospital where I was assigned to spend time with a long-term patient on a closed ward named Eddie Galvin, who was in his thirties. Met State was probably considered a respectable asylum, but it was horrifying to walk through the wards of long-term "inmates." Galvin was lucid enough for me to get a sense of him. He was on a strong medication called Thorazine. Aside from the pills, the only major care he received was removal of his teeth. I was once permitted to take Galvin on a car ride out of the hospital. Asylums like Met State fell out of favor a few years later and virtually all the patients were sent back to the community.

I wrote about Met State for my final paper and how care of the mentally ill had evolved from physical constraints to medicated control. Whatever my grade was—not memorable—the course gave me vivid life lessons. College for me was more about experiences than grades.

The other big development of that year was a gift from Józef of a brand-new 1962 black Plymouth Valiant convertible with red upholstery, one of the snazziest cars on campus. What prompted so grand an offering I don't know. My first, beloved, car had been a 1954 black Pontiac convertible with wire wheels and a continental kit on the rear bumper. It cost $350. My close friend (to this day) David Epstein also had a Valiant convertible that year. At Brandeis that kind of showiness was unusual to the point of being memorable.

I accrued enough parking tickets on the Pontiac to again receive a disciplinary warning. The problem was that the parking spot I had been assigned was about a half mile from our dorm, which I clearly considered an obstacle. This was not my most mature reaction, it needs now to be said. I had a part-time job chauffeuring visiting VIPs to campus, which amused my friends because I was considered a somewhat unreliable driver.

In the summers I found internships working with inner-city so-cial welfare organizations: a settlement house on the East Side; Mo-bilization for Youth, on the Lower East Side. I was a counselor and took the boys to parks and on day trips. I enjoyed what seemed to be insights into the world of children—mainly Hispanic and Black—from backgrounds so different from my own. And once I had the Valiant, on summer nights with the top down listening to Motown, I felt very sophisticated. After junior year, a White Meadow Lake friend, Fred Yerman, and I drove cross-country. We managed to stay in the only motel in Las Vegas that had no air-conditioning and lis-tened to Martin Luther King's "I Have a Dream" speech on the radio as we overlooked the Grand Canyon.

The last year at Brandeis was the best. Six of us rented a house on Norumbega Road, in a park near campus on the Charles River de-scribed in a sign as "Duck Feeding and Parking Area." The house had been built close enough to the path of Route 128, which encircles Bos-ton, to earn the builder a substantial payout when the house had to be moved. This was clearly more a financial play than a devotion to archi-tecture. The house was sprawling, with rooms of odd sizes. Probably by lottery I got a corner bedroom and furnished it with stuff from our White Meadow Lake house. It was way better than any dorm room or most off-campus housing. The five other boys and I had been friends from our first year. Eli Segal had the room next to mine. Eli was then and throughout his life an extraordinary presence with immense nat-ural charm and leadership skills. He would go on to work on presiden-tial campaigns from Eugene McCarthy's in 1968 until Bill Clinton's successful runs in the 1990s. "E," as we called him, would be responsi-ble for the establishment of AmeriCorps, the national service pro-gram, and Welfare to Work, two of the Clinton administration's great achievements. In that year he spent a great deal of time writing an honors thesis on politics. It took him so long to finish that we would regularly look in on him and he would say "JAD"—just about done.

Eli said that I always told him not to be so worried about grades, assuring him that he and I would both make our way in the world.

His intention was to make a million dollars in business by the time he was forty so he could devote himself to public service. And he achieved that goal.

The others in the house were Lenny Oshinsky and Arnie Kanter, now lawyers; Mike Oberman, who went into business; and Stuart Paris, a Brandeis basketball star who in middle age became a rabbi. Oberman was a big fellow, known as Bear, and provided us with an irresistible opportunity for a prank. Every day for most of the year Lenny or Arnie would lift one item from Mike's room and put it in a trunk—a pencil, a light bulb, a pair of his underpants, even a few books. He never caught on and at the end of the spring term we presented him with his possessions. By the standards of raucous student activity, this was certainly tame. As for me, every day one or another of the group would hold down my legs while I did sit-ups off the end of the bed with a five-pound weight in my hands. No one involved forgot their pleasure in making fun of me.

Only a few years later students like us were in rebellion on and off campuses. By contrast, our years were mainly an idyllic pause.

My girlfriend of that period was Nina Felshin. She was a terrific ranked amateur tennis player and an extremely talented artist of what later was known as Pop Art. Her drawings, pictures, cartoons, and assorted geegaws always had a humorous edge. Of all my college relationships, the one with Nina was the most upbeat. Nina came from the Upper West Side of Manhattan and had attended M&A. Our geographic symmetry was part of our compatibility. She would later tell me (for the first time when we were in our seventies) that we had been in junior high school together; she was a year behind and had a crush on me. She thought, however, that I was in a "fast" crowd and didn't notice her. Ha!

Nina's parents had a business that imported artifacts from Mexico and supplied wardrobes for children's summer camps. They were very left-wing and read *The Guardian*, a weekly socialist newspaper. Her father, Seon, ran for Congress on the American Labor Party ticket, a left-wing political group that was still recovering from the harassment of the Joe McCarthy period of the 1950s.

Unquestionably the most vivid event of my senior year happened on November 22. Leaving a constitutional law class at about 1 P.M. on that Friday, I saw students, aghast, coming up the hill and saying that President Kennedy had been shot. In the context of the time, the notion that the president would be assassinated was simply not in our realm of imagination. (Years later, when I was working with Robert McNamara on his memoirs, he told me of receiving the first call at the Pentagon and thinking that the president had been "shot at," not killed. His death was inconceivable.)

That afternoon I walked around Norumbega Road with David Epstein, both of us reeling from the news. Much of the weekend was a blur, but I know that Nina and I went to downtown Waltham to see the film *Lawrence of Arabia*. One of the reasons the days were such a blur is that the Norumbega house did not have a television, an amazing fact for 1963, and *The New York Times* was not delivered to us. While we were transfixed by the news, we were less exposed to it than we would have been even a year or two later. All the students then went home early for Thanksgiving, and it was there I remember watching television. Józef was profoundly affected by the news and bought an advertisement in the *Times* advocating for prizes to be established in Kennedy's name for arts, culture, and peace. His proposal was included in news roundups of how Kennedy's legacy should be honored.

By now I was only taking courses that appealed to me: popular culture in the nineteenth and twentieth centuries, art history, twentieth-century American history, constitutional law, and most memorably, a twentieth-century literature course with the novelist Hortense Calisher, where I read Saul Bellow, Günter Grass, Albert Camus, Malcolm Lowry, and others. I was fascinated and inspired.

Calisher would come to Brandeis weekly for the seminar, and I would pick her up at the airport and drive her to visit her son, who was then a patient at McLean, the private mental hospital that was later immortalized in the book and film *Girl, Interrupted*. As distinct from Met State, McLean was on a leafy campus and associated with Harvard Medical School. Its reputation was as a respite for troubled youth rather than an asylum. Fifty years later that mistaken impression would come back, to my regret.

In another class I wrote a paper on the bombing of a church in Birmingham, Alabama, that killed four little Black girls; and for yet another class I wrote about the popular misconception that Soviet leader Nikita Khrushchev's declaration at the United Nations that "we will bury you" was actually more a metaphor than the chilling threat it was said to be. The thread that connected all these courses was a developing interest in the world outside campus.

At last, as the work was appealing to me, for the first time I elevated my grades to make the Dean's List. With graduation in the offing, I applied to two graduate journalism programs, at the University of California, Berkeley, and Columbia. Berkeley accepted me quickly. At Columbia, I took a writing test and was accepted. The issue of tuition and living costs never arose—even graduate education was affordable in those days—and I was very pleased and my parents very proud that I finally made it to my brother's alma mater and Marta's workplace.

Eli and I were co-heads of the Student Political Education and Action Committee (SPEAC), whose main role was to bring speakers to campus. I remember Malcolm X, the writer Mary McCarthy, and Mark Lane, who was the principal proponent of the theory that a conspiracy was behind the Kennedy assassination. We were sufficiently interested in Lane's ideas that we invited him to stay at Norumbega, and I turned over my room to him. The ABC News commentator and anchor Edward P. Morgan visited Brandeis as well. In retrospect, Nina remembered this as CBS's Edward R. Murrow and that I told her to get him a roast beef sandwich, which she (correctly) resented.

We organized a mock nominating convention for Lyndon Johnson. I began reading *I. F. Stone's Weekly* newsletter and was attracted to liberal politics. But ours was hardly a hipster lifestyle: no drugs, little if any alcohol. Lots of mocha chip ice cream from a nearby Howard Johnson's.

Our years at Brandeis were bookended, more or less, by the election of John F. Kennedy and his murder. These were, by the standards of

American life since, an innocent period. I don't think it is possible to overstate how different it was from the years of upheaval at home and the Vietnam War that followed. As Daniel Patrick Moynihan said after Kennedy's death, "We may laugh again, but we'll never be young again."

The Democratic convention was in Atlantic City that August and I got some kind of pass to volunteer. After the first day I was put off by the battle over the seating of an all-white Mississippi delegation instead of the integrated Mississippi Freedom Democratic Party led by Fannie Lou Hamer (whom I had met in 1962). I gave up being in the hall and joined a demonstration on the boardwalk. A clean-cut white boy in a suit and tie, no less, I was placed in the front row standing next to Stokely Carmichael, a charismatic leader of the Student Nonviolent Coordinating Committee (SNCC), later to be a pillar of the Black Power movement. Martin Luther King visited us on the boardwalk, a thrill. The MFDP finally gained modest representation in the delegation. I think that was the only time I directly participated in a political protest, because going to journalism school reinforced my instincts to be an observer of what was happening around me.

In the fifty-five years (and counting) since I left Brandeis, it has continued to be a first-class university in most respects. But over time its original sense of exemplary social and political engagement has diminished. At its founding, Brandeis, like Israel, was a response to the Holocaust, as well as to quotas and anti-Semitism in the Ivy League, private clubs, law firms, and Wall Street. Its leading professors were refugees from Europe and from American McCarthyism. There was a determined and admirable motivation to establish a top-quality institution of openness, tolerance, and social justice for the offspring, on the whole, of middle-class families that had navigated the hard years of the 1930s and '40s.

As the Jewish population of America prospered and traditional obstacles were lowered, Brandeis became, in my view, less distinctive. Abram Sachar's successors as president were of mixed quality. There were regular instances of clumsy moves by administrators tied, somehow, to fundraising. At one point it was summarily announced that the university would sell off its (donated) art collection to, in effect, pay the rent. In the 2000s Brandeis struggled, as so many universities did, with the illiberal contradictions of political correctness. On the one hand the university accepted the papers of Lenny Bruce, a crude, lewd, and very funny comedian of the 1960s, but it was unable to proceed with a play about Bruce, written by alumnus Michael Weller, because students objected.

I maintained a periodic connection to Brandeis. I was invited to be the speaker at the Phi Beta Kappa ceremony at my class's twenty-fifth anniversary. I like to say that Phi, Beta, and Kappa were all rolling in their graves at that irony, given my academic record. When the three-time Pulitzer Prize winner and Brandeis graduate Tom Friedman had to cancel a speech to the President's Council, a fundraising group, I was asked to replace him at the last minute. I was profiled in alumni publications. After Eli Segal's death in 2006, when his family established a citizen service and mentoring program in his name, Susan and I gave it the largest gift of any in our lifetime, which were the proceeds of our investment in Eli's son Jonathan's successful launch of a national publication on high school sports. I became, myself, a member of the President's Council, although I never again could make that kind of donation. All that honorific meant was an invitation to graduation and a pro forma birthday card.

I never felt especially close to my alma mater. I did benefit enormously from my years there, to be sure. Yet, as is the case with so many American Jews and our changing attitude toward Israel and its policies, and our complicated feelings about our attachment to a religion that was a proud heritage but that we did not practice, over time I found Brandeis to be less meaningful as a force for the universal values I believe in. Brandeis and Israel were both founded in 1948 and their trajectory is comparable: admirable as a Jewish contributor to the situation of Jews, generally, and less a source of personal admiration. Alumni tend to become prouder of their institutions over the years. That, alas, was not what happened to me. From time to time, Brandeis would solicit my opinion by email. When I wrote, I don't believe I ever got an answer.

Chapter 5

The J School

THE GRADUATE SCHOOL OF JOURNALISM at Columbia University, technically the Joseph Pulitzer School, was the only degree-granting journalism program in the Ivy League in 1964. Founded with Pulitzer money a half-century earlier and home to the annual Pulitzer prizes, the J School (as it was known) was always considered the most prestigious journalism school in the country. But at Columbia itself, it was considered more of a trade school than a place of scholarly stature, as it offered only one course of study, a ten-month master's program. Elsewhere at the university, the journalism program and its faculty were regarded with condescension. I have no concrete evidence that that was the case—and its reputation is better today with an added two-year master's and a PhD track—but this perception did reflect my own views of where I had gone to school. Cheshire was not in the first rank of elite prep schools; Brandeis was too ethnic to be really cool; and Columbia's journalism degree, for all the eminence of its graduates, was not thought on a par with political science, English literature, philosophy, or business.

I now realize that these three places provided experiences, skills, and a sense of the world that enabled my life choices. Let's say I had gone to Exeter (as I said, I didn't want to repeat a year), been accepted as an undergraduate at Columbia, and then had been, say, a Rhodes Scholar at Oxford (I don't think anyone from Brandeis had ever won one at that point)—what would my sense of entitlement be or my expectations of success? My education was clearly fine and perhaps, because it was not especially glamorous by the standards of the 1960s,

58

protected me from an excess of arrogance and later assumptions of success without effort.

Two Brandeis classmates and I rented an apartment on West 99th Street, just off Riverside Drive. They were Arnie Reisman, who was the other Brandeis graduate at the J School, and a philosopher in the PhD program. Marta had clearly hoped that I might move back home. When I was in college, my parents had moved from the Belnord to the Beresford on Central Park West. The move to this elegant building was the moment that my immigrant parents picked up the white-gloved-life thread they probably expected to have in Europe.

One rainy Saturday afternoon before the start of the fall term at Columbia, a girl who was a summer friend came to visit me in the Beresford apartment. Józef was probably playing bridge at his club. Marta disappeared and, after the girl left, came home damp from the rain.

"Mother," I said, "where have you been?"

"I didn't want you to think I was getting in your way with that girl," she replied.

Despite this not-so-subtle hint to make the home apartment irresistible, I moved to 99th Street.

The Columbia class was one hundred students, of whom at least twenty were women, plus a handful of foreign students. They were a cross-section of recent college graduates including some who already had professional experience, nearly all white. My only journalism had been those articles for *The Justice*, so I was very much at the low end of the learning curve. The shape of the courses was to help us to think and write like journalists. Most of our time was spent being trained to write stories based on reporting assignments. There was almost no element of technology involved—in contrast to today's requirements. We never even had a typing test. The broadcast training was minimal: a single small camera in a classroom. Under the direction of Professor William Wood, who had a connection to CBS Radio, I devised a live weekly panel show called *Counterpoint* that aired on a UHF municipal television station, channel 31, at 8 P.M. on Mondays. A panel of students (I think I was the only regular) would interview a guest whose qualification was that he or she was doing something provocative.

One fateful evening our guest was Jesse Gray, the leader of a Harlem rent strike. As we went on the air, Gray had not arrived. This being a live show, we started to interview our moderator, John Cooley, a postgraduate fellow who later worked for the *Christian Science Monitor* and ABC News in the Middle East. Gray did finally show up. To put it kindly, this was television at its most basic.

The assignment for the J School's final paper was to report and write a magazine-length article. I chose the Gray rent strike and spent time in Harlem reporting. My adviser was Penn Kimball, one of the most colorful of the J School faculty, who had been sidelined from the big news organizations by the McCarthy-era blacklist of anyone thought to be left-wing. He had a wonderful elastic face, a little like Tweedledee, wore bowties, and was considered a tough grader. I worked hard on the story and did well enough on that assignment and elsewhere in the course to graduate with honors, my only academic distinction of that kind, ever.

Most of the professors were middle-aged men who had journalism backgrounds. But being a teacher was not considered a pinnacle of the field, although they were all, in retrospect, impressive. The dean was Edward Barrett, who had been an assistant secretary of state for communications in the Kennedy years. The one woman I recall was Betsy Wade, a copy editor at *The New York Times*. She had newsroom swagger and later was a leader in women's demands for greater standing in the *Times* news department.

It was, on the whole, a very good year. I had a small group of friends, several of whom remained close for years thereafter. A handful of us eventually made it to *The Washington Post* and two—Larry Meyer, an ex-Marine, and Marilyn Berger, who became White House correspondent for NBC News—are still in touch. At one point, I was considering the possibility of working at NBC; Marilyn, memorably, told me, "On television you look like you are doing something important, but you are not." The chance to become a celebrity in newspapers and earn a big paycheck from a journalism career seemed remote in those days.

My "social" life at Columbia was, by my standards, very placid. Nina and I had split up and my dalliances were marginal. I guess I was too busy learning to be a reporter to think about much else.

In the spring of 1965, the focus was on getting jobs. This was before the Vietnam buildup was in full effect, so the draft was not yet a significant factor. Two members of the class were hired by *The New York Times* (I was envious), but the only newspaper to which I remember applying was the *Providence Journal*, which then had bureaus in every town in the state, making it a good place to get on-the-ground experience with all kinds of stories. In its way, I think the appeal was that you were a mini correspondent, choosing what to write about aside from town council meetings.

I moved to Benefit Street in Providence, Rhode Island, just off the Brown campus. This was a good enough job, but not as prestigious as the *Times* or the summer internship at *The New Republic* that my friend David Sanford got.

My first slot at the *Journal* was in the North Providence bureau. All I can recount of those weeks was a story I wrote about a local figure that began: "Despite his Italian-German ancestry, Dante J. Giamarrco is the 'Young Turk' of North Providence town politics." The lede of the piece was read literally by Greeks in the town (the tensions in Cyprus having created Greek-Turkish friction), and Giamarrco had to explain himself. North Providence was a working-class town and group identities were strong.

After eight weeks I was transferred to be the Bristol reporter in a bureau run by a crusty veteran named Sid Jagolinzer. Bristol was a cultural step up from North Providence. It was across the bridge from Newport and had much more of an old New England vibe than the grittier North Providence. My workday was roughly 2 to 10 P.M., and I got paid a few cents per mile for use of my Valiant. I churned out small news stories and features that appeared in zoned sections of the paper. I cannot remember a single one.

My life in Providence was lonelier than I liked. I was, after all, working nights. In any case, that period was short. David Sanford was offered a full-time writing job at *The New Republic*, based on his excellent work over the summer. He had been planning to start as an assistant at *I. F. Stone's Weekly* and let me know there would be an opening. I was excited at the chance to go to Washington. I made a quick foray to DC for lunch with the legendary I. F. Stone himself. I had only spent eight weeks at the *Providence Journal*.

Chapter 6

Izzy

IN THE LATE SUMMER of 1965, I. F. Stone, on David Sanford's recommendation, took me to lunch at a restaurant in Washington, DC's small Chinatown. We had, as I recall, fish with ginger, wrapped in paper and dipped in boiling water. I must have passed the audition, because Stone offered me $100 per week and said I would earn every penny. I stayed until the following summer and got a raise to $110 and an education in journalism (of what Stone would have called "being a newspaperman") worth millions.

Izzy Stone (as everybody called him) was a rare character in Washington—an independent journalist, beholden to no editors or publishers and free to investigate and express opinions as he saw fit. He had once worked for the *New York Post*, *The Nation*, and *PM* (all then liberal or left-wing publications), but after finding opportunities constrained during the McCarthy era, he started his own independent newsletter, *I. F. Stone's Weekly*, which at its peak had 70,000 subscribers (Izzy and his wife, Esther, mailed them personally) and an outsize influence on political debate in Washington.

I arrived on Izzy's doorstep at a particularly good period, personally and professionally, for him and his four-page *Weekly*. After years of being so hard-of-hearing that he had to wear an elaborate headset with antenna, making him look like a bespectacled Martian, Izzy's ears had been repaired by a doctor who had performed the same operation on Chairman Mao. Many people would still talk to him as though he were deaf, especially on the phone, so speaking and listening habits of years' duration were being relearned. Even news gathering was different. Izzy was especially well known for poring through transcripts of hearings and speeches and finding nuggets other reporters would miss. Now he could actually hear what was being said at events like press conferences. Izzy was naturally gregarious and excited to be part of any and all conversations. But he needed to also retain his relentless pursuit of news, hidden in the recesses of papers and documents. His restored ears were both a thrill and a distraction.

The political tenor of the time was also working to his benefit. In the first half of the 1960s, the youthful idealism of the Kennedy years—as expressed in such ways as the Peace Corps, the Freedom Riders, and sit-ins—was evolving into what soon became the campus-based anti–Vietnam War and civil rights movements. This also coincided with the emergence of what was known as the New Left. The Old Left of the 1930s, '40s, and '50s was exhausted by the alliances and battles of that era: the Popular Front; the Nazi-Soviet pact of 1939 and the Anglo-Soviet-US partnership of World War II's later years; the sour loyalty tests of the Cold War and McCarthyism; the Soviet invasion of Hungary in 1956. Six months before the Hungarian upheaval, Izzy visited Moscow and wrote what turned into one of his most famous citations: "I feel like a swimmer under water who must rise to the surface or his lungs will burst. Whatever the consequences, I have to say what I really feel after seeing the Soviet Union and carefully studying the statements of its leading officials. This is not a good society and it is not led by honest men."

History's view of the Soviet regime would later harden considerably, but at the time, for a left-leaning journalistic icon to break with Moscow in this way was a radical move—all the more so because Izzy did not veer sharply to the anti-communist right as did so many other apostates of that era. He held to his convictions about free expression, human rights, and the dangers of using anti-communism as justification for war in countries with nationalist aspirations—like Vietnam. These positions made Izzy especially attractive to the New Left, whose manifestos, like the Students for a Democratic Society's Port Huron Statement of 1962, rejected communist orthodoxies but argued for profound social change at home and around the world.

Izzy was decades older than the students and civil rights leaders like Martin Luther King Jr.—he was fifty-seven when I began working for him—but his writing was so vigorous, fresh, and clever that he appealed to this new generation with humor as well as insight. Despite the generational divide, he was able to identify with the instincts of the young.

As Izzy's assistant, I was expected to have read thoroughly by 7:30 A.M. *The Washington Post*, *The New York Times*, and several other out-of-town newspapers—though, mercifully, not *Le Monde*, the Paris paper that Izzy seemed to most admire. In the course of my day, I would swing by the Capitol and the State Department to collect handouts, read the wire services, attend hearings and press conferences, and generally cover the beat that extended, as did Izzy's interests, very widely. He liked to say, "There is a great story hanging from every tree," but to me it seemed that there were a great many trees. I worked in the basement of Izzy's home on Nebraska Avenue, where I maintained the enormous clip file and was summoned upstairs by buzzer to Izzy's office. The kitchen was on the way, where Esther, who as circulation manager was the *Weekly*'s only other employee, kept a supply of peanut butter and other snacks that maintained my stamina as the day wore on. In the evening, I digested the *Congressional Record* and other formidable official publications in search of revelations. Izzy also encouraged me to write my own pieces and gave me a fistful of bylines, an honor rarely accorded an apprentice.

Izzy would take the finished *Weekly* to his printer on Wednesdays and then celebrate with dinner out and a movie. Sometimes Izzy and Esther went dancing, which they both adored. (For years their summer routine included traveling across the Atlantic on ocean liners because they especially enjoyed the nightly *dansants*.) By Sunday morning Izzy was in full stride again on the next week's issue and so, therefore, was I. In retrospect, I recognize the enormous benefits and experience I derived from my year with Izzy, but at the time the long-term gains were obscured by the torrential work load and the fact that I was too busy to satisfy a growing urge to kick up my own heels a bit.

Working for Izzy was, as much as my master's degree, a foundational course in journalism. I rented a townhouse on Capitol Hill with a J School classmate, Larry Aaronson, who was able to defer the draft—by then an issue for young men—by working as a teacher, a calling that turned out to be his lifetime career. My other close friend in Washington was David Sanford, now a staff writer at *The New Republic*, which was in an especially good period of excellent writing and influence. Both fellows turned out to be gay and were active advocates for the gay rights movement.

Little of that year was spent dating. I was not a person to go to bars or networking events. The job working for Izzy did not come with a workplace community. In any event, I was way too busy chasing around DC on the *Weekly*'s behalf. Izzy had told me he was a taskmaster, and he wasn't wrong. After only a week or so, I heard him on the phone with Robert Silvers, the editor of *The New York Review of Books*, and say (or at least I think he said) that his new assistant hadn't yet shown him much of, well, anything. I was dismayed, of course, but held on making my rounds, huffing and puffing through the workweek and weekends. This was a kind of boot camp: arduous, humbling, and very valuable. And I was not happy.

I can't recall who recommended I see a psychiatrist whose name I remember, improbably, as Felix Von Mendelsohn. After a session or two, he said he had a solution for my mood. "I'd like to introduce you to my daughter," he offered. I don't think that ever actually happened. The point, however, was right on. I was lonesome and would certainly have benefited from more fun. I was, after all, just twenty-two years old. This was my first direct foray into psychological counseling.

I was so immersed in my work and so wary of Izzy's wrath that I had two indelible meltdowns. The first came on a piece that I wrote (signed with my initials) making the point that military use of "non-lethal" gas in Vietnam was actually lethal when the gas was in tunnels, where the Viet Cong and North Vietnamese were hiding. A day or so after the *Weekly* was distributed, Izzy received a call from a scientist who said my analysis was nonsensical. Oh boy. This would have to be the first correction in the history of the *Weekly*, I thought. I was terrified. I raided the refrigerator and consumed large amounts of peanut butter and a box of crackers.

In my reporting I had talked to a professor at Harvard named Matthew Meselson who confirmed that in high concentration, gases fired into closed spaces would be lethal. Of course, anything that restricted breathing in a tunnel would eventually be lethal, including peanut butter. The *Weekly* escaped unscathed.

But I remained anxious and unhappy, and the second meltdown had me bemoaning my fate on a phone call to my parents that spring. Józef, for the one and only time this happened, came to Washington and spent the day with me. There was a wonderful couple in Bethesda, Stan and Judy Frosh (Stan was a lawyer and Judy a dancer), who had invited me to their home many times on a Sunday. Józef and I spent the afternoon there. I recovered my bearings and went on to finish the *Weekly*'s publication year, which ended in July, after which Izzy and his wife, Esther, would sail off to Europe on vacation.

At some point I received a notice to report for a draft physical. We were taken by bus to the appointed base. I shared seats with Bill Lynch, a deep-voiced radio reporter. We went through the inspection together. I received a 1-Y deferral because of the visible damage to my right-hand medial nerve and a doctor's letter. Lynch was drafted and worked for Armed Forces Radio. I can't help but wonder all these years later what I would have done had I been drafted. I cannot imagine that I would have gone to Canada or to jail.

Also, that spring Izzy went to Vietnam to report on the escalating war. He had skipped a week and was planning an eight-page special. His readers were poised to get a definitive account of the scene in

Saigon. Izzy was, by his standards, uncharacteristically intimidated by the task to which he had set himself. He paced the neighborhood. His first drafts were too soft; too much on the beauty of Vietnamese women's *ai dao*, a tunic and flowing black trousers. Esther and I sat in the backyard and wondered whether the great I. F. Stone could write his way out of the block. Inspiration finally arrived and Izzy's piece was so good it was included in a collection of classic reporting published years later.

My own writing was intermittent. But I was the only one of Izzy's assistants who was ever given a byline. One full-page piece began with a description of Attorney General Nicholas Katzenbach as "not a bad man." Izzy revised that to say Katzenbach was actually "a good man." I. F. Stone was never shrill. He made the facts—and a sense of humor—tell the story.

On the last issue before the summer break, Izzy thanked me for my services and gave me a send-off as a colleague. It was an honor.

When Izzy died in 1989 at the age of eighty-one, I wrote a piece for the op-ed page of *The New York Times* headlined "A Journalist's Journalist."

Marta and Izzy had one especially memorable encounter, at least to me. In 1965, an English translation of the extremely erotic and acclaimed French novel *The Story of O* was published. There was a French language bookstore in Rockefeller Center, and one afternoon a year or so later my mother stopped by to purchase the novel in its original language. As she stood at the register, a shortish bespectacled gentleman was standing next to her. It was I. F. Stone. I don't know what he was buying or even if he recognized Marta. I am, however, aware of the fact that she told me that story.

PART TWO

~

Words, War, *and* *Autocracy*

Chapter 7

Swinging London

MY SOJOURN IN LONDON, from the early fall of 1966 until June 1968, was proof of two things that come in handy in journalism (and life): being in the right place at the right time, and luck.

During my year in Washington working for Izzy, I had met a woman named Sari Gilbert, another aspiring journalist. I told her that I planned to go to London later that summer, and she told me to look up her friend Bob Mott, who was working in *The Washington Post*'s London bureau.

Before arriving in Britain, I spent a month in Poland visiting relatives. They were a fascinating group; many were intellectuals and writers. I stayed with Marta's cousin Karolina Beylin, a very prominent cultural critic who shared her apartment with her sister Stefa, who wrote about film, and a former beau of Karolina's known as Pan (Mr.) Stanislaus. They would gather for every meal together but otherwise I never saw any signs of residual intimacy.

I also visited Auschwitz, chilling for its austere evil.

I arrived in London in September with a plan to stay for a week or two. The *Providence Journal* had offered to take me back in the Pawtucket bureau, and I expected to accept. Someone had given me the names of two recent graduates of Oxford who had a flat in Islington, then a working-class borough near central London. They were part of a Trotskyite group of International Socialists at Oxford. My association with *I. F. Stone's Weekly* gave me entrée and some cachet. Also in the apartment was a young woman named Hazel Brimley. She had been the girlfriend of Wynford Hicks, a dashing former president of the Oxford Union, a political radical who wore the required tailcoat over his jeans. I never met Wynford, whose red bushy hair apparently made him especially visible in a crowd. He had just left for Australia and Hazel remained behind.

Hazel had attended Central School of Speech and Drama, a leading British acting school. She had grown up in a middle-class family in Manchester, was less political than her flatmates, and had a small part in *Coronation Street*, a long-running British television serial. She was also working in marketing at Radio London, which was known as a pirate radio station. At the time, Britain had no commercial radio broadcasting, so popular music—rock and roll in the era of the Beatles and the Rolling Stones—was mostly broadcast from ships anchored off the coast. The biggest ones were Radio Caroline and Radio London.

I moved into the apartment and in a matter of days was sharing Hazel's room. By the end of the second week I decided to stay in London. I sent a telegram to the editor of the state desk at the *Providence Journal* to report that I was unavoidably detained overseas and would be unavailable to take the job in Pawtucket. My new plan was to stay in London and look for a job in journalism there.

My left-wing friends put me in touch with Richard Clements, the editor of the socialist weekly *Tribune*, and I also looked up Michael Lydon, a *Newsweek* correspondent whose older brother Chris had been a Justice Department employee, a great admirer of Izzy, and later a reporter for *The New York Times*. I asked my flatmates what I could be expected to be paid as a starting weekly salary in journalism. They said eight pounds a week—at the time the pound was valued at $2.80, so less than $25 a week. Off I went.

The *Newsweek* and *Washington Post* offices were in New Zealand House, a modern high-rise on the Haymarket near Piccadilly Square. As befit the publications' shared ownership, the offices were together on the eleventh floor, and I showed up unannounced at the receptionist desk and asked for Michael Lydon. He was not in. But as I was about to leave, I remembered Sari Gilbert's friend Bob Mott, and asked if he might be in. He was and agreed to see me. Bob was in charge of the London headquarters of the Los Angeles Times/Washington Post News Service, which handled incoming copy from those two newspapers' correspondents as well as stories from *The Guardian* and *The Observer*, a Sunday paper. Bob was also sort of the manager for the office, which was led by *The Washington Post*'s London bureau chief, Karl E. Meyer.

Karl was an extremely sophisticated PhD from Princeton who had written editorials for the *Post* before being assigned to London, considered a particularly posh job. Karl was in his late thirties but had the bearing of seniority, highlighted by his pipe-smoking. He had been the Washington columnist for the weekly *New Statesman*, then the leading British political weekly, so he was very well known. He appeared so often on British television shows that the satirical magazine *Private Eye* called him "Karl J. Pipesucker." He had a fabulous corner office with a panoramic view of London and lived in an elegant flat on Thurloe Square with his glamorous wife, Sarah, and the first of their children.

Mott was a bachelor. He very much wanted to be a *Post* correspondent, but Karl's light shone very bright, and Bob was in its shadow. I presented myself to Mott, who said that by amazing coincidence he was looking for a night assistant editor for the news service and asked if I might be interested. Of course I was. Bob asked what my salary requirements might be. The flat had said eight pounds a week. I asked for fifteen. Bob said that was ridiculous and offered me thirty to start right away working Tuesday to Saturday from 2 P.M. on and to handle incoming stories. That came to $84 a week. Izzy had been paying me $110 when I left, but by London standards $84 was a fortune. I had been looking for a job for no more than a couple of days and was already making almost four times the minimum starting pay for a reporter.

The *Post*'s reporting stringer was Robert Kaiser, a graduate student at the London School of Economics who had built up a formidable collection of clips under Karl's tutelage. He and his wife, Hannah, were moving to Washington, where Bob was to join the city desk. He would stay for almost fifty years and become managing editor.

Karl especially liked my connection to Izzy and could imagine my becoming the new Kaiser. But for now, Mott needed an assistant. So, on that very first day of job hunting, I was at the start of an eighteen-year stint at *The Washington Post*. Overnight I went from being an unemployed roommate of Trotskyites to a well-paid member (by local standards) of a major American newspaper's London bureau.

Within days after I started at the *Post*, an assistant foreign editor in Washington named Lee Lescaze asked me to go to Oxford on Sunday to do a story on Lise Meitner, a physicist who was receiving the Enrico Fermi award, a major scientific prize and unusual for a woman to be so honored. I took a train to Oxford and covered the story. Returning to London I was very nervous about this first story for *The Washington Post*. I finally sent it in telex bursts of 1,500 words a minute.

The next morning there was a message from Lescaze telling me that the story was on the front page. And, he added, it had been "re-jiggered to make it less dry if not more wet." What that meant was that I had made my first appearance in the most visible place in the newspaper with a story that had been pretty much rewritten from top to bottom with my name at the top. It was like that first paper at Brandeis. ("Not a stupid paper, Mr. Osnos, but an ignorant one.") I particularly remember a congratulatory telex from a Columbia classmate already at the *Post*. There I was at a pinnacle and feeling like a fraud. In any case, it was a beginning.

The Kaisers were in their last months in London. They were my age and had married in 1966. Bob had the manner of a successful young Yale man in every respect: self-confidence, a watch fob, and an elegant cape. Hannah was a superb partner for Bob, assured enough to hold her own with this estimable fellow. Decades later she received a doctorate in anthropology, published her thesis, taught in colleges, and started using her maiden name, Jopling. They were then and remain a great tribute to the benefits of a good marriage. I was later to follow Bob in Saigon and Moscow and eventually work alongside him in Washington.

I particularly remember an early lunch in the penthouse of New Zealand House on a visit from Katharine Graham. This was my first encounter with the truly extraordinary proprietor of the Washington Post Company. It was an elegant occasion. There were waiters serving us in proper attire. We were joined by the *Newsweek* correspondents and by Alfred Friendly, the longtime managing editor of the *Post*, a Graham family retainer who had been unceremoniously bumped aside by the arrival of Benjamin Bradlee as managing editor. Friendly had opted to come to London as a roving foreign correspondent in what became known at the paper as "returning to his first love" in situations where editors were ousted from prominent positions.

I have no recollection of the conversation at the table but was acutely aware that Bob Kaiser addressed Mrs. Graham as "Kay" and Alfred Friendly as "Al." It never occurred to me that I would ever be of sufficient stature to address these very grand personages by their first (and shortened) names.

The *Newsweek* bureau was headed by Henry T. Simmons, a former defense correspondent for the magazine, a gruff sort who was an odd choice to lead coverage of what *Time* magazine had already dubbed in a cover story "Swinging London." That's not to say he couldn't be colorful. In a pub with several of us from the office after the Arab-Israeli Six-Day War in June 1967, Henry described the conflict as "The Yids got the Gyptos by the Ying-Yang." The youngest reporter in the bureau was Kevin Buckley, a gregarious ladies' man and a recent graduate of Yale who became a lifelong friend.

The *Newsweek* business staff and advertising salespeople were British and took long boozy lunches and then broke out the drinks again in the late afternoon. This was an unusual pairing of the two sides of journalism—stories and sales—in tandem offices.

Hazel and I took a furnished apartment together on Parliament Hill, just off the spectacular Hampstead Heath, a sprawling park of scale and hilly beauty. The rent was twelve pounds a week. Having set up house, we were a couple throughout that fall of 1966, and as I recall we were having an excellent time. After that first story for the *Post*, I was told by the paper's foreign editor, Philip Foisie, that for some reason—I think it was about paying me a stringer fee on top of my salary—I would not be able to write for the paper. Kaiser was scheduled to leave, and Mott wanted to be more than an office factotum and angled to write, although Karl never really recognized him in that regard.

Somehow (I can't remember how) I pitched myself to Murray (Buddy) Weiss, the editor of what was then called the *New York Herald Tribune*, an English language paper published in Paris in a collaborative partnership between *The New York Times* and *The Washington Post*, a collaboration that lasted for another thirty-five years as the *International Herald Tribune*. Weiss had been an editor at the *Herald Tribune* in New York until it closed. He landed the job in Paris although he spoke no French and had to deal with press room unions with sign language and an interpreter. Buddy encouraged me to submit pieces and I did. One, in particular, was a reverential description of a prix fixe Chinese meal in a North London restaurant, at that time my favorite food ever.

After running several pieces, Buddy invited me to visit the *Trib*'s offices in Paris and stay with him and his wife. The paper was based at 21 rue de Berri, off the Champs-Elysées and across from the Hotel Lancaster, which had a bar made famous by the presence of mid-century celebrities like Ernest Hemingway. The newsroom was a classic. The staff, mainly copy editors and a few reporters, was very colorful: American and British expats with a fair number of eccentrics. They sat at desks surrounded by Gauloises cigarette fumes as waiters from the bistro downstairs navigated the room with trays of espressos and other beverages. It could not, not, have been better.

There was a British pop group called The Move that was promoting a song with a postcard featuring a drawing of Prime Minister Harold Wilson sitting on a bed naked with his rumored mistress, a Downing Street aide named Marcia Williams. Wilson sued for defamation and the case was settled with The Move making a contribution to a charity of Wilson's choice. The prime minister said that if anything like that was ever said again, he would take the perpetrator to the proverbial cleaners financially. On the very day that story appeared inside the *Trib*, there was a back-page feature by the columnist Flora Lewis all about the rumors of Wilson's dalliance with Williams, including a photograph of the two of them together. The result was a major suit against the paper. What that meant was that Buddy Weiss was unable to come to London, lest he be slapped with legal papers.

So it was that Buddy arrived late on a Friday night in a snap-brim fedora and sunglasses and slipped out of town at dawn on Monday. At least he had a glimpse of London's glamour. The suit was finally settled with, as I recall, the *Trib*'s entire year of profits going to Wilson.

My daily duties involved monitoring incoming copy from *Post* correspondents and those of the *Los Angeles Times* and sending them to clients in Europe, cutting some in most cases. There was a French translator in the office to serve clients in France and Belgium. I was also handling nightly packets of mimeographed stories delivered from the newsroom of *The Guardian* courtesy of its syndication man who I knew as "Jimmy" who began every conversation with "Hi Ho!" He would summarize the incoming output. There was, for instance, the indomitable diplomatic correspondent Hella Pick—he called her "the dreaded Hella." Years later, when I was posted to Moscow, Hella was a regular visitor and became a good friend.

There was also Victor Zorza, the London-based Kremlinologist who sat in a corner of *The Guardian*'s newsroom behind what was known as the Kremlin Wall of Soviet newspapers and had an assistant known as Trotsky. Victor was in a constant struggle with Phil Foisie for better use of his stories in the *Post*, and I became the designated mediator. Victor's Kremlinology was legendary, but his writing was arduous. Later he moved to Washington and wrote a celebrated book about the death of his young daughter. We were, by the end, somewhat improbably, friends.

The most difficult editorial challenge was to decipher the work of
The Guardian's Calcutta correspondent. He wrote his stories in what
was known as "cablese" to reduce the number of words and thereby
save transmission costs. A typical sentence might read, PRO FORNDESK
EX MALHOTRA GURKHA GARRISON UPBLOWN INDOPAK BORDER,
meaning "For the foreign desk, from Malhotra: A garrison manned
by a detachment of Gurkhas was blown up on the border between
India and Pakistan." He wasn't much of a writer under the best of
circumstances, but rendering his style into acceptable English was a
major chore. Even when cablese was no longer really necessary, correspondents used it to signify, metaphorically, their membership in the
correspondent clan.

Aside from being told I couldn't write for the *Post*—and grum-
bling because Kaiser had made a considerable name for himself with
his London-bylined stories—I had a dream job for an aspiring
twenty-three- and twenty-four-year-old newsman. What I remember best about the halcyon Hazel period was how it ended. She invited me to her home in a Manchester suburb for Christmas. That
turned out to be an unfortunate collision of cultures. The family's
modest row house was heated by small appliances that worked when
you put in shillings. The whole time we were there the telly was on
and the atmosphere, for me, was exceptionally dreary. My guess is I
was not at my best and shortly thereafter Hazel moved out. But all in
all, my time with Hazel was short, sweet, and a fine adventure.

Finally that May, I received a letter from Foisie with this welcome
news: "Our partners on the newservice have formally, and not unwill-
ingly, agreed that you may report and write for *The Washington Post*
and the newservice.... at the present time, it will not be possible for
me to pay you for your efforts." I couldn't have cared less.

At the center of the office was a glassed-in hub called Comcen,
which around the clock served the transmission needs of the global
bureaus with buzzing telex machines and long printed-out story files
and messages. The staff was four gents with appealing cockney accents, our Beatles. Comcen is, of course, as gone as hot type in

printing plants. Today a reporter can send stories from his or her phone almost anywhere.

Michael Lydon, the man I originally looked up at *Newsweek,* left to be the first employee in San Francisco of a new publication called *Rolling Stone.* His wife, Susan Gordon, would later become famous as the author of a piece about female orgasms for *Ms.* magazine, at the time a breakthrough in candor. When Kevin Buckley was assigned to Saigon as *Newsweek*'s bureau chief, he went to Carnaby Street and bought himself a stunning green suit that was entirely inappropriate for war coverage but nonetheless memorable. Arriving in London as a *Newsweek* stringer was Richard Blumenthal, a Harvard graduate on a Marshall Scholarship. Richard was a person of extraordinary intelligence and dignity. Anthony Lewis of *The New York Times* described Richard to me as "the kind of young man who pleases his elders," not something that was said about the majority of young men at the time. Richard devoted his later career as a lawyer to public service. He was Connecticut's attorney general for multiple terms and elected to the US Senate twice. We were neighbors for years in Greenwich and both married into the same extended family. Small world.

My junior job at the *Post* was good enough for me to encounter a succession of celebrities passing through London. I particularly remember taking the poet Allen Ginsberg to a restaurant in Chinatown for dumplings. Someone had given me a list of what to order and so I displayed unearned expertise. I had dinner with Alex Haley, who had written *The Autobiography of Malcolm X* and later was author of *Roots.* I interviewed a very young Liza Minnelli at a restaurant called the White Elephant. The television host David Frost was just beginning to be a star in the British satire boom of the 1960s. Later he was immortalized in the play and movie *Frost/Nixon.* I got him on the front page of the *Post*'s Sunday arts section.

On the personal side I found myself in some unlikely venues. One of the best was the home of Ella Winter, the widow of the great twentieth-century muckraker Lincoln Steffens. Her husband was Donald Ogden Stewart, the brilliant screenwriter of such films as *The*

Philadelphia Story. He had been blacklisted in the McCarthy era and left the country. They had a large home in Hampstead, and Winter convened a salon of interesting people, of whom I was almost certainly the least well along in age and accomplishment.

I met a fellow named Robert Cassen, a sociologist who was going to spend a year in India. He had a terrific furnished flat on Thurlow Road in Hampstead and I leased it for ten pounds a week. My neighbors in the basement were two elderly sisters, both called Miss Grundy, who had charge of the immaculate garden. Upstairs was an actor whose major recent role was as a corpse in that year's hit film *Blow Up.* The Beatles released their album *Sgt. Pepper's Lonely Hearts Club Band*, which I played over and over on my small phonograph. I still can conjure the comforting aroma of coal from furnaces in the alley, at a time before it was considered a polluter.

In the spring of 1967, life was to take a major turn. I made a trip to New York, the first since I had left Washington the year before. For some reason I called my Brandeis girlfriend Nina, although we had not been in touch. She was living in her parents' apartment on West 96th Street, off Central Park West. All I recall was that in a few days we ended up back in "a relationship." And before I left it was agreed that Nina would come to London to join me. She entered a master's program at the Courtauld Institute of Art and eventually had a part-time job at a Bond Street gallery.

Travel was inexpensive, and we visited Egypt, Israel, and an idyllic spot called Side on the Turkish coast, which was the villa of Alfred Friendly and his wife, Jean. We also went to Spain, where over a meal my cousin Monica Holmes, daughter of Uncle Gustav, advocated very strongly that Nina and I should get married. Fifty years later, I asked Nina why Monica got the notion that it was a good idea. Apparently, Nina had talked admiringly about decorative dinner plates, and Monica concluded that Nina was really expressing a domestic desire. Marriage, in that era, was a logical result of cohabitation.

Monica had a very forceful presence and so Nina and I sent off telegrams to our respective parents announcing our engagement. The wedding was in October 1967. I had just turned twenty-four, and Nina was twenty-two. My recollection of what was a meaningful occasion, after all, is vague. Nina's is better. We were married in a synagogue at Marta's request. Karl Meyer was best man. Izzy and Esther were there by coincidence. Nina remembers that when the rabbi asked her to say something in Hebrew (about which she knew nothing), she began to giggle, as did her sister Annie. The rabbi covered over the embarrassment by saying that Nina was just nervous. We registered at the Hampstead Town Hall, and on the marriage certificate Nina was described as a "spinster." The reception was at our flat and the food came from the same Chinese restaurant I had written about for the *Trib*. I know that fact because Arnie Kanter, one of my Brandeis housemates, happened to be in London with his wife, Carol, and they were invited to the reception—and not, Arnie says, the wedding.

Given that it was a marriage—really, as Nina and I agreed all those years later, playing marriage—I remember little about the nature of our home life. Nina does remember that since I was working nights she would come to the office and study while I worked. She didn't like all those nights at home alone. It was all certainly fun. Józef, for reasons unfathomable, had shipped me my car, the 1962 black Valiant convertible with red upholstery. The steering wheel was on the wrong side for Britain and why I needed a snappy convertible is a mystery.

We were young and newly married with smart jobs in what was London's postwar heyday of rock and roll, miniskirts, and loosening standards when it came to sex—openly acknowledged as opposed to the traditional British way of considering anything other than procreation to be naughty. Joan Bakewell, a television presenter for the BBC, wrote a review in *The Spectator* in 2019 of a book about the era under the heading: "It was pretty good for me . . . We strode through the decade as if clothed in gold—enjoying new loves, clothes, music, drugs and opportunities." Now eighty-five, she is the Right Honorable Baroness Bakewell (DBE), a Labour Party peer. Looking at photographs of her from the sixties, I can see why I had a crush on her from a distance.

My work at the *Post* was going well. I placed stories in many sections of the paper, including prime space on the front of the Sunday Outlook section for a piece based on a British article entitled "50 Works of English Literature We Could Do Without." I wrote something like "The mere thought of *Lorna Doone* makes my head hit the pillow."

I caught the admiring eye of the foreign desk by deciphering the British press sufficiently to enable the *Post* to run a story on Prime Minister Harold Wilson's secret and unsuccessful effort to broker a peace deal on Vietnam with visiting Soviet prime minister Alexei Kosygin, which was otherwise barely deducible. And I was not surprisingly focused on the possibility of advancing at the *Post*. I was transfixed by a letter to Bob Mott from Ben Bradlee. I held it up to the brightest available light and saw that it said the *Post* was absorbing new reporters "Not to mention Osnos." Which indicated that I had managed to register on the top editor's radar.

In the early spring of 1968, Nina and I went for a weekend in Cornwall at the southwestern tip of England. It was a glorious April weekend except that the papers were dominated by the aftermath of the assassination of Martin Luther King. On the front page of *The Observer* was a picture of heavily armed soldiers on the steps of the Capitol. I told Nina that I thought it was time to go home. And two months later we went to Washington (along with the Valiant) and took a furnished sublet on North Carolina Avenue on Capitol Hill ready to embark on the next phase of our lives.

For the summer I was a fill-in on Phil Foisie's foreign desk under the direction of Harry Rosenfeld, a boisterous New Yorker and another refugee from the late *Herald Tribune*. I must have had New York cred with Harry because he kept a supportive eye on me thereafter at the paper, although I didn't realize it at the time.

Chapter 8

Metro

THE WASHINGTON POST was Ben Bradlee's newsroom. His presence was palpable even when he seemed to be doing crossword puzzles in his glass office, and there was an unmistakable aura about him. He had arrived just three years earlier from *Newsweek*, first as deputy managing editor and very soon thereafter taking the top job, which led to Alfred Friendly's move to London. Upon my arrival in June 1968 as a summer fill-in on the foreign desk, I became acutely aware of how much Ben meant to the paper's energy and momentum. Ben had the ultimate in editorial élan. With his sleeves rolled up to his forearms and his voice—a good-natured growl—he left an indelible mark on the daily contest for prominent space and play that was the core of the newsroom's distinctive rhythm.

Ben's authority was complete when he chose to deploy it. But his editorial genius wasn't about rewriting ledes or changing adjectives. It was his unfailing sense of what made a story stronger. His questions were precise and invariably to the point. His credo for the front page was that stories carry impact, preferably were exclusive, and were written with flair. He had particular admiration for intrepid reporting, especially when it was connected to good writing. If a piece was a dud, Ben would let you know one way or another, but he rarely held a grudge as long you came roaring back with a better version or some breakthrough on a running story.

Ben was in the process of creating the *Post*'s Style section (it would debut in January 1969), which became the *ne plus ultra* destination for major profiles and features that changed the character of what readers could expect to find in newspapers. The edgier writing of the kind that had previously been found in magazines like *Esquire* would make the section hugely popular and influential. Style was as closely read in Washington as the front page and leading columnists. It is generally acknowledged now that Style revamped the way celebrities were covered—particularly politicians and the public figures whose reputations depended on their visibility. Ben liked the sassy tone that Style set, and the rest of the paper benefited from the readers it attracted.

His loyalty to the newsroom's best interests was total. He had an exceptionally close relationship with *Post* publisher Katharine Graham, whose confidence in him enabled him to make decisions that more than occasionally irritated the powerful people in the capital who were Mrs. Graham's friends. This was one of the ways Ben Bradlee's *Washington Post* enlivened the stodgy national capital. His newsgathering instincts were superb; his commitment to journalism of excellence was total; and the whole enterprise reflected Bradlee's inimitable persona and integrity. He was truly everything a great editor should be, and I was proud to work for him.

That first summer job's main virtue was to establish me in the newsroom as a young man with an interest in foreign news. The big stories were domestic, such as the uproar in Chicago at the Democratic National Convention. But the night of August 20, my colleagues and I returned from dinner after the close of the first edition to learn that the Soviets had invaded Czechoslovakia to take down the government of Alexander Dubček, who was establishing "socialism with a human face." The *Post*'s correspondent, Anatole Shub, was on vacation in Maine. So, over the next few hours, the foreign desk put together accounts from Prague of the evolving realization among citizens there that their hopes for major political change were being crushed.

In September I was assigned to the Prince George's County bureau. As in any professional ecosystem, there were status markers. On the "local" staff, as it was called, being a city reporter was a higher tier.

I was being sent to the suburbs, which was considered less impressive. That turned out to be wrong. PG, as it was known, was a great assignment. Prince George's County bordered the south side of the District of Columbia. It was decidedly working-class, blue-collar, and rural, as distinct from Montgomery County to the north, which was upper-middle-class (and dull). The invisible line separating north from south cut through these Maryland counties.

PG was southern in attitude and character. It was a sprawling mass stretching from the outskirts of the Black neighborhoods in Anacostia and ending at Charles County, which was closer to Mississippi than geography would indicate. PG had the twelfth-largest school system in the nation. In College Park was the University of Maryland, but most of the close-in towns were made up of small houses, affordable developments, and storefronts. Farther out, including Upper Marlboro, the county seat, was a culture of virtually all white families, still living with tobacco fields, and in ways that were largely unchanged from decades past.

There were terrific characters to write about. Sheriff Bill Kersey got me on page one when he decided to form an air corps division. Jesse St. Claire Baggett was a bulbous-nosed county commissioner eventually indicted twice and convicted once for corruption. He spent time in the Leavenworth federal prison. When he died in 1983, the *Post*'s obituary was headlined: "Last of P.G.'s Movers and Shakers." Gladys Noon Spellman was the county chief executive, elected as an insurgent to the longstanding county political machine, but able to hold her own with the good ol' boys. She was elected to Congress in 1975 but had a heart attack and never recovered consciousness until she died eight years later.

State Judge Richard Painter took a drug overdose after he was accused of a crime. The police released no details, but I confirmed his condition by announcing at the PG hospital that I was checking on the status of "the patient Painter."

There was a small press room on the ground floor of the county courthouse where the *Post* reporters and one from the evening paper,

The Washington Star, were based. Reporters would cruise the halls in search of news. I quickly learned to read papers on desks upside down. For using my car, I earned eight cents per mile, which came in handy.

One weekend *The Washington Star*'s intrepid PG reporter, Martha Angle, had a scoop on the indictment of a number of prominent PG politicians, including Baggett. I was mightily chagrined and ran around to match her story for the next day's paper. From a phone in the downtown newsroom I commanded the operator to "get me a lawyer" to clear my piece for publication.

"Hi. Osnos here from PG," I said to the man picking up the phone. "Who is this?"

"Bill Rogers," he replied.

"Hi Bill, I've got this story I need to get cleared right away . . ."

"Okay, but I need to tell my dinner guests that I'll be right back."

I put my hand over the phone and said to an editor nearby, "This guy is giving me a hard time." He was not.

We finished the conversation. The story ran and the saga ended. Bill Rogers's full name was William P. Rogers, senior partner of the *Post*'s law firm, Rogers & Wells, who had been attorney general in the Eisenhower administration and would soon become Richard Nixon's secretary of state. I do not recall ever apologizing to him.

On another weekend I was in the newsroom when a triple ax murder was reported in Montgomery County. I was sent off to get the story. When I phoned in from the scene, Bill Brady, the night editor on duty, greeted me with "Give it to me, ace, the blunt end or the sharp end." I dictated my notes to a rewrite man named Harry "The Doll" Gabbett, who wore a fedora at his desk and could turn out an immaculate piece in minutes. Gabbett may sound like a stereotypical cliché, but he was as real as can be. One of his most famous stories was the report on Bill Brady's wedding. After describing the bride's dress, Gabbett wrote, "Brady was natty in a gray suit with a crease down the front of the pants. But in truth it was the same suit he wore to the press club ball." The story was checked out of the *Post*'s "morgue" of old stories so many times that the paper crumbled.

Perhaps my most important story was the unrest at Bladensburg High School. PG was undergoing a profound and very quick change from majority white to majority Black. Palmer Park (later famous as the home of boxing champ Sugar Ray Leonard) flipped almost completely in a year or so as the whites fled further into the county or further south to Charles County. These blue-collar whites were being replaced by middle-class Blacks, mainly government employees who wanted to take advantage of better schools and housing. The result was racial tension and some violence at Bladensburg High School and elsewhere. The story I wrote called this the new American front line, where the inner city meets the suburbs. That was an early call on a phenomenon that led to Prince George's becoming the largest majority middle-class Black county in the United States.

The other *Post* reporters in Upper Marlboro, by chance, had both been classmates of mine at Columbia and were talented. But I was a dervish in constant motion, and they were not, well, as frenetic, so I led the way in PG, except when Martha Angle of *The Washington Star* combined her skills and charms (I know that this is no longer an acceptable term) with the cops and the district attorneys and got stories we could not. She later worked for *Congressional Quarterly*, married a great *Star* investigative reporter named Robert Walters, and for a time we were neighbors on Capitol Hill.

The PG year sounds like a set piece of newspaper nostalgia, but these are not gauzy recollections. Coming from my background, PG was exotic, an almost foreign land. And I had loads of fun. I returned to Upper Marlboro for a visit in 2019. PG was no longer at all rural. The courthouse was now a vast government edifice, although the facade of the old courthouse was preserved. Nearly everyone in the courthouse was Black and so are the great majority of PG's residents. The area's largest casino and convention center is in the county. By chance, I encountered one of the *Post*'s reporters. When I told her who I was, she seemed more dumbfounded than awed. And then she rushed off.

I started writing book reviews for the paper beginning with one about a Beatles book, given that I had recently lived in London. The

Books editor was Geoffrey Wolff, who himself was to become a major writer. When Herbert Marcuse, a leading left-wing philosopher, published a book called *An Essay on Liberation* (a follow-up to his classic book *One Dimensional Man: Studies in the Ideology of Advanced Industrial Society*), I was assigned the review. It ran in the *Post*'s new Style section. A *Post* operator called me at home that day to say that Marcuse was on the line. A high-pitched voice with a clearly faux German accent complained about what I had written. It was Izzy, affirmation in his way that he was watching me.

When Wolff was leaving to become the book editor of *Newsweek*, he recommended me to the managing editor of the *Post*, Gene Patterson, to be his successor. Patterson, a blunt-speaking southerner who had been a courageous editor in Atlanta in the civil rights battles of the early sixties, called me in and told me I'd be crazy to take the job. I wasn't qualified, he said, and he was, of course, right. But that was an early indicator of my penchant for what would become, decades later, my life's work.

A year in, I was promoted to the Maryland state beat, as the number three behind Peter A. Jay, a patrician descendant of John Jay, the first chief justice of the United States, and John Hanrahan, one of the best investigative reporters on the paper. Our editor was Barry Sussman, a droll and clever fellow who guided his reporters with a superb mix of leadership and lessons. Barry later was one of the key editors of the Watergate stories and frustratingly did not get the credit he clearly deserved.

My role on the state beat wasn't well defined and tended toward features. I visited every penal institution in Maryland and profiled them. I also went to a three-day retreat in Annapolis for judges, probation officers, DAs, cops, and inmates who changed places in role-playing exercises, including sending the judges to jail for a day. The high point of that assignment was that the *Times* sent one of its most revered reporters, Homer Bigart, who had desk number one in the *Times* newsroom. He was a former war correspondent of distinction and was famous for, among other things, an endearing stammer. In a bar one night I asked to what he attributed his longevity as a newsman.

"Very easy," he replied, "I never read my own stories in the paper." This was his way of not losing patience with copy-editing changes or other desk depredations that drove reporters nuts. I found that advice helpful and put it to good use when I was a foreign correspondent. By the time the paper arrived by mail to, say, Saigon or Moscow, the stories were at least a week old. Complaining to the desk about a re-written lede would be a pointless exercise (the editors had long since moved on), and I used the Bigart rule to my benefit in a variety of ways and still try to do that whenever I write. I do not, however, always succeed.

After six months or so, there was a major shake-up on the Metro desk. The top editor was replaced for, among other things, having a dalliance with one of his young reporters. The new Metro editor was Harry Rosenfeld, my boss from the summer stint on the foreign desk. Harry's mandate was to up the metabolism of local coverage. There was a murder: a teenage girl and her boyfriend in suburban Virginia killed her father. Her nickname was "Muffin." Harry mobilized us to cover the story like the kidnapping of the Lindbergh baby. When I resorted to the phones for interviews, Harry, who had nice things to say about me otherwise, told me to get out into the streets. A star reporter who asked for an additional day to do his piece was reminded that the *Post* was a daily newspaper and deadline was in an hour. Philip Geyelin, the editor of the editorial page, finally wrote a piece that chided Metro for its overcoverage of this crime story. Harry was incensed and threatened to resign. The morning after the editorial, Bradlee sent Harry a note, a classic of the genre: "Harry Baby: You getting mad at me is like the guy who beats a dog for not giving milk. If that editorial is aimed at anyone, it is aimed at me. I think it's a horseshit editorial and I intend to move on to serious problems. B."

Harry decided that I was being underused as a Maryland feature writer and decided to send me to one of the liveliest beats on the city staff, the federal courts, including the US Court of Appeals for the

DC Circuit, considered the second most important court in the country after the Supreme Court.

All felony offenses originating in the District of Columbia were sent to federal court. The local courts of that time only handled misdemeanors. One of the best cases was two brothers who set themselves up as doctors in Anacostia, lacking any medical training. In their fraud trial, their defense lawyer, a New Yorker with a splendid and appropriate accent, said the "per-perted perpetrators" were praised by people in the community for making house calls. They were convicted. Years later, when I returned to Washington from Moscow, I encountered one of the brothers selling Hondas at a local dealer. I bought one, although not from him.

Because of its standing and location, major civil cases went through the appeals court. There were judges of great distinction on the bench. The leaders were J. Skelly Wright, whose civil rights opinions were considered classics of progressive thinking, and David Bazelon, who created the framework for the classification of the mentally ill in criminal cases. I came to know Bazelon well. He seemed to enjoy young reporters.

My favorite among the colorful roster of lawyers in the courthouse was Seymour Glanzer, the head of the white-collar unit of the US attorney's office. He appealed to my appreciation of New York mannerisms, which in Washington were still unusual. It was correctly said that you could not get a decent bagel in the District. Glanzer and his small team were a source for a stream of entertaining stories, and a few years later they were prosecutors during the Watergate period.

The district court and appeals court also were the setting for major public policy issues, including the building of a trans-Alaskan oil pipeline, which was stopped by a group of young environmental lawyers. This was an era in which the courts became a major factor in the significant issues of the time, setting precedents that are still relevant today.

Covering the court was for me, at least, relatively easy. Over time I could produce several stories a day, dictating them off the top of my head to a person typing them out for the copy desk. I compared this skill to push-ups. You start with one each day and added more as you got stronger. Harry was right to send me to the court to teach me the fastest way to write news stories combined with once a week (on Saturdays mainly) doing a feature piece.

One memorable Saturday, we learned that *The New York Times* was planning a major story on political corruption, with indictments coming from a federal grand jury in Baltimore. We didn't know what the story was, but we had to find out. Calling around was not working so we were desperate. I concluded that the only way to match the *Times* piece was to have someone buy the first edition of the Sunday paper in Times Square at about 8 P.M. on Saturday. We decided that the only reliable person we could ask was my mother. She dutifully went to Times Square and from a phone booth called to report that the only story from Baltimore was in the travel section. The *Times* had kept its scoop out of the first edition. I couldn't ask my mother to hang around further, so we gave up that idea. Fortunately, Carl Bernstein, a fellow young Metro reporter, had yet another idea. He called the *Times* loading dock and persuaded the fellow answering the phone to read him the opening paragraph of the second edition's front-page story. A congressman was being indicted for graft involved with the construction of the Capitol garage. *Voila*, we had the story in our third edition later that night. (I can't remember whether we acknowledged that the *Times* had it first.)

In the late spring of 1970, Bradlee called me into his office to say that he and Phil Foisie wanted to know if I would go to Vietnam when Bob Kaiser finished his tour there in the fall. In seconds I said yes, never considering how Nina would feel about that assignment. What was interesting is that Bradlee never asked me about my views on the war even though I had worked for I. F. Stone, or what I knew about the military, which was next to nothing. As I wrote, I carried a 1-Y deferment from the draft. Bradlee would not have known that. Yet, he never asked about my draft status or whether I would have gone if I had been called up.

That was Bradlee. The assumption was always that you knew what to do to meet his expectations for energy, output, and accuracy, or he would not ask you to meet them. A young writer named Jeff Himmelman was later given access to Bradlee's papers for a book called *Yours in Truth*. Here is an excerpt of a letter Ben wrote to Katharine Graham explaining his decision to run a controversial story:

> Katharine . . . Our duty is to publish news when it is news and when we have checked its bona fides . . . Often, in this town, to a President or his representatives . . . a newspaper that yields . . . to pressures sacrifices one of [its] most precious assets—the vitality and commitment and possibly the respect of its reporters.

To be tasked at age twenty-six to cover an American war was a compliment that Ben did not need to gild with praise. And he did not.

There were ex-Marines in the newsroom (vets from World War II and the Korean War) who probably scoffed at the appointment of such a neophyte. But Bradlee's standards were not challenged. Will this reporter knock himself out? I met that test. (A note: the *Post* never sent a woman reporter to Vietnam. A freelancer named Elizabeth Becker was hired in Cambodia after that war started. She became the preeminent chronicler of that conflict with her book *When the War Was Over* and was a great success at the *Post* and later at *The New York Times*. Today the notion that only young men can qualify to cover combat seems truly antediluvian.)

When I told Nina about the assignment, she made it clear almost immediately that she wasn't going. She had a very good job as a curator at the Corcoran Gallery of Art, a leading museum whose director was one of the most influential specialists in the contemporary art scene. For perhaps the only time it had ever happened, the Washington art community was one of the country's most exciting, and Nina had very much the ideal job. Nina was happier in her work, it seemed, than in our marriage.

When she and I talked about this period decades later, we agreed that there wasn't anything particularly wrong in our relationship, except that we were both obsessed with our work. The cadre of young male *Post* reporters spent most social evenings analyzing newsroom status markers and Nina, probably like most of the other women in our lives, felt marginal. In fact, I think I was proud of Nina's role at the Corcoran and was more interested in art than perhaps she realized. But we were on parallel tracks rather than a joint one. I asked Nina if I remembered rightly that she had an abortion that year. She said she had. She had gone to the hospital by herself. We were too young—and I was clearly too insensitive to be a married man.

In the summer I began to prepare for Vietnam. I enrolled in a Berlitz immersion course to learn French, which was still thought to be a political second language among the Vietnamese. I did reading and reporting on the war and military jargon to prove to the sceptics that I could tell the difference between a battalion and a brigade. In November, I made arrangements to fly through Paris and arrived in Saigon just before Thanksgiving. The next phase of life was underway. I had just turned twenty-seven.

Chapter 9

Vietnam

MY FIRST MEMORY of Saigon was the Thanksgiving dinner at the villa of my old friend from London, Kevin Buckley. The notable memory of that occasion was the presence of a stunning twenty-three-year-old redhead named Susan Sherer. Susan had recently arrived to assist the Lawyers Military Defense Committee, a group of civil liberties lawyers with funding from philanthropists in Boston, who provided free counsel to GIs. She sat elsewhere at the table and I don't think we spoke. But she noticed me, too, she later said, along with the fact that I was wearing a wedding ring.

In the hierarchy of Vietnam correspondents, status was determined by experience and swagger. As a first-time war reporter and the number two in the bureau (my old Maryland colleague, Peter Jay, was the bureau chief), I was treated, on the whole, with condescension by those with notches already on their belt. In an early signal, I had been told that there was a terrific apartment I should get because it had a balcony/veranda that would be great for parties. *Time* magazine's bureau chief, Jonathan Larsen, the scion of a founding Time Inc. family, and his wife, Wendy, said they wanted the apartment and were more likely to give parties, so I was told to back off, which I did.

Instead I took a much less glamorous apartment on Ngo Duc Ke, off Tu Do Street, not far from the office, one of two apartments rented by the *Post*. Local craftsmen made rattan furniture, and somehow I also acquired a cat. I moved in after a few weeks in the great Continental Palace Hotel, the quintessential establishment in the colonial style where people gathered in late afternoon for cocktails on what was known as the Continental Shelf. The other *Post* apartment was over a garage on Nguyen Hue, a broad nearby boulevard. Perhaps because it had a large living room with high ceilings, this was considered better than my place on Ngo Duc Ke. I soon had a housekeeper named Ngyuet, who was helpful but not much of a cook. Nguyen Thi Tam, the housekeeper at the other apartment, certainly was. Years later after she fled to Washington, she would come to our home and make spectacular Vietnamese meals. The last time we saw her was at a party she gave for her eightieth birthday.

One of the first projects Peter Jay and I devised was that he would go to the most embattled province in the country, Quang Tri, just across the DMZ from North Vietnam; I would go to An Giang province in the Mekong Delta, essentially untouched by the war because the local religious sect, the Cao Dai, had a pact of some sort with the Viet Cong, the communist guerrillas inside South Vietnam. We decided that I would drive the office car, a Mazda sedan, to An Giang. For several reasons, this was an astounding decision. I had never driven a car with a standard transmission (a clutch) and took a lesson from our morning office person, Joyce Bolo, whose husband, Felix, was the Agence France-Presse bureau chief. In the memoir of Harry Rosenfeld, who had spent several months on an assignment in Vietnam for the *Post*, he revealed that he too had gotten a lesson in standard transmission from Joyce. For us New York boys, driving a standard as distinct from automatic transmission was a bit of exurban manliness. I spoke no Vietnamese and was not planning to travel with an interpreter. I would be traveling through Kien Hoa province, a Viet Cong stronghold, oblivious to my surroundings. You could correctly say that I was very naive.

Off I went and made it to An Giang. I did have a fender bender in the provincial capital, but a local mechanic fixed the car in a day or two. I made it home with a story about what Vietnam would be like if it were at peace.

Another early story involved a trip to Quang Ngai province, headquarters of the Americal Division. The division had been the focus of major criticism following the My Lai massacre, for which soldiers from this unit were responsible. My Lai was one of the worst cases of US abuse of Vietnamese civilians.

To get to Quang Ngai from Saigon, I hitchhiked my first ever trip in a helicopter, a two-seater with a jump seat in the back. The pilots were two young warrant officers. We lifted off and I realized that the doors were open. I was strapped in but found our trajectory over the treetops disconcerting. I tapped one of the GIs on the shoulder and asked him to explain. "Hey, fella," he said, "how else would we attract ground fire so we can call in strikes on the VC below?" I distinctly remember thinking that I was a very long way from the Upper West Side of Manhattan.

The Americal base was a sprawling, classic US Army outpost. There were places to relax (bars, fast-food joints, a PX) and incoming artillery at night resonated at a distance. Reporters in Vietnam carried Defense Department identification designating us as officer equivalents for the purpose of priorities in quarters and transportation. It did occur to me that were we to be captured by the Viet Cong, it would be hard to explain that despite our Defense Department cards, we were, in fact, civilians. I rarely went anywhere in fatigues and was never armed.

The story from the Americal was about booby traps as a danger to US troops; at the time, they were a greater source of casualties than firefights. On that trip, I didn't feel especially endangered even by the helicopter ride (despite my initial trepidation) or the surrounding sounds of artillery exchanges on the base perimeter. But at least I really knew I was covering a war.

The *Post*'s bureau in Saigon was over an art gallery open to Tu Do Street, a main downtown thoroughfare, across from the Continental. Next to us was the office of the Lawyers Military Defense Committee, which meant that Susan Sherer and I were neighbors. The *Post*'s office was a good-sized room with an entry hall and a bathroom where we stored supplies and our weapons, which as far as I know were never used. Peter Jay and I each had a desk. There was also a desk for our superb Vietnamese reporter Vu Thuy Hoang, who had excellent political connections. He didn't travel with us because he had a family and a part-time job as a journalist on a local paper. Hoang understood the whys and wherefores of Saigon and made us seem knowledgeable about them. Our messenger was a petite young woman named Bui Van Lam who made her way around the city on a motorbike with her *ao dai* flowing behind her, performing errands and delivering copy to the Reuters bureau where teletypists transmitted our stories via telex to Washington. She was later replaced by her brother, who called himself Peter Lam because the *Post* correspondents were also called Peter. Lam was a draft dodger who was eventually caught and sent to the front. I wrote several stories about him using a pseudonym. He was eventually killed in Quang Tri.

Aside from Joyce Bolo, Jolynne D'Ornano helped us in the afternoon. She was married to a Corsican businessman. Joyce and Jolynne were invaluable mainstays of our never-ending need for arrangements. It was a small but very well-functioning operation. Down the hall was the *New York Times* office, which was twice our size with four correspondents and several Vietnamese reporters. The bureau chief was Alvin Shuster, by our standards an older man, maybe forty. Alvin had come from London, where he had been the number two. His wife, Miriam, and their three children lived in Hong Kong. Alvin was not the image of a swashbuckling war correspondent. He was small in stature and looked unlikely in military-style garb, but he was an irresistible presence with an unforgettable laugh and intrinsic wisdom, reflected in his writing. Alvin wasn't and didn't need to be a part of our generation of young hard chargers. He and Miriam became beloved lifelong friends. Also in the *Times* bureau was the incomparable Gloria Emerson, known as "long lady" by the Vietnamese because she was very tall. Gloria was by any standard a great character, hyperkinetic yet elegant in a way given her past coverage of Paris fashion. Gloria made a significant mark through her coverage of the effect of the war on the Vietnamese people and foot soldiers from all sides. Gloria was pro-civilians and pro-GIs, but defiantly not a friend of war.

Her relationship with Alvin was the kind that would make a great 1930s movie. "Alvin! Alvin!" she would proclaim, unleashing on that day's news, lest he miss her meaning. At the first sign of any trouble in Saigon, Gloria would don a gas mask because of the likely tear gas and rush to the scene. Alvin made sure that her extraordinary passion was successfully channeled in a continual stream of stories that had enormous impact on readers when they were published. In 1978, Gloria wrote *Winners & Losers* about Vietnam, which won the National Book Award. The book was dedicated to her *Times* colleague Craig R. Whitney, her friend and ours.

Craig arrived in the same week or so that I did. He and I had met briefly in Washington when I was working for Izzy and he was a clerk to the *Times* columnist James "Scotty" Reston, a position comparable in those days to a top-tier fellowship or a clerkship at the Supreme Court. Craig had served in the Navy as a speechwriter for Secretary of the Navy Paul Nitze and had spent a year in Saigon as a lieutenant junior grade assigned to the Seventh Fleet. He was also a magna cum laude graduate of Harvard in French literature.

Craig had the résumé of an aristocrat but came from a middle-class family in central Massachusetts. He had attended prep school and college on scholarships and was as unpretentious as he was dignified. In forty-five years at *The New York Times*, Craig was a correspondent in Germany (twice), Moscow, London bureau chief, Paris bureau chief, Washington bureau chief, foreign editor, and an assistant managing editor. He was an accomplished organist, and among the many books he wrote is *All the Stops*, a history of the American pipe organ that is considered a classic in that exotic field. He wrote stories for the *Times* about great organs the world over, and the foreign desk could not resist responding to those stories with messages like "Shorted your organ" or "Your organ squeezed out on a tight night."

Gloria dedicated her book to Craig for a number of reasons, including the fact that when she had an automobile accident and needed a bit of cash, he loaned it to her, a fact that I remembered more vividly than he did. When Gloria, physically and financially constrained, committed suicide in 2004 at the age of seventy-five, one of the first calls from the family was to Craig.

For years Gloria would say that Susan had made a mistake ending up with me when Craig was also on the scene (although not, as far as I know, in the running). Craig did marry Heidi, whom he met in Bonn, where she worked at *Newsweek*. They had two children of identical ages to ours and when we eventually moved to New York, we chose to live in Brooklyn Heights, because that is where the Whitneys lived. In October 1971, for our respective twenty-eighth birthdays (the 12th for Craig, the 13th for me), we threw a party at Saigon's Cercle Sportif, a club remnant of a gracious French past. The press corps, diplomats, and even a few Saigon-based military people showed up. When I submitted my expense account for that period, I was asked to justify the $80 I had spent on it. It was approved.

The work pattern for Peter Jay and me was that one of us would be somewhere in the countryside with troops or visiting provinces while the other stayed in Saigon to cover Vietnamese politics and diplomacy. My arrival in the fall of 1970 coincided with what was as close to a high point for the United States in the war as there ever was. Before leaving Vietnam, Bob Kaiser had written an important series called "The New Optimists," which captured the sense that, after all, the conflict might end for Americans more favorably to our interests than was thought possible. The series was right at the time, but ultimately the story did not turn out that way.

President Richard Nixon had declared a policy of "Vietnamization" under which the South Vietnamese Army would acquire more responsibility and US forces would be drawn down from a peak of 500,000. This was six months after the invasion of Cambodia by Americans and South Vietnamese with the goal of clearing out North Vietnamese forces from their bases there. The ultimate consequence of that operation was to trigger what became a brutal civil war in Cambodia that in time would lead to the Khmer Rouge and its reign of brutality, and to the death of probably 2 million Cambodians.

I always thought of the Vietnam War as a pendulum, with the Americans gradually taking control of the country from 1965 until the early seventies as troop strength and air strikes grew. Then, as those forces withdrew and Congress limited American assistance, the Viet Cong and North Vietnamese moved back and established full control of the entire country as the last US officials were lifted off by helicopter on April 30, 1975.

All things considered, our lives in Saigon were comfortable. There were French-style restaurants, an officers' mess where we could get a good steak, and a steady stream of socializing with other young reporters from newspapers and news magazines. The wire services and television networks had more of their own circles, with TV correspondents generally sent in on short tours to establish their bona fides.

Though a few of the reporters (including Peter Jay) were there with their wives, many of the "bachelors" took advantage of the free-flowing availability of marijuana and opium, and some dated the glamorous Vietnamese women. In Phnom Penh, there was a popular opium hang-out called 482 (for its address) where I would spend occasional languorous nights after curfew. But in Saigon, my life was spent at the office, writing, preparing for field trips, at dinner, and falling into bed after midnight. I had a small black-and-white television to watch AFVN (Armed Forces Vietnam Network) but rarely did except for the news broadcasts, highlighted by the fetching "weather girl" Janie, married to an NBC reporter. AFVN Radio, made famous by Robin Williams as Adrian Cronauer in the film *Good Morning, Vietnam*, provided a soundtrack of sixties rock and early seventies tunes.

There were very few women reporters. Aside from Gloria Emerson, one of the best was Judith Coburn, the *Village Voice* correspondent. She and Susan were friends because of their age and stage and because they didn't live in the relatively high-rolling way of representatives of well-endowed publications. In fact, Susan lived in a small hotel, the Royale, with a ceiling fan and a Corsican proprietor who held court on the ground floor pretty much always stoned on opium. Years later, Susan would say that one of the reasons she took up with me was that I had an air-conditioner. Susan and Judy were close to two very talented young photographers, David Burnett and Mark Godfrey, freelancers who shot mainly for *Time* and occasionally for *Life*. Susan and David were together so much that I assumed they were a couple. But they were just close friends in that vaguely raffish ecosystem.

Photographers, in particular, were largely a class of their own because outside of Saigon they could do their jobs only by taking the significant risks of getting up very close to the action, and few of them were supported by an infrastructure like the one Peter Jay and I had at the *Post*. The movie star Errol Flynn's dashing son Sean, a photographer, was killed somewhere on a Cambodian highway riding his motorcycle, the sort of death that inspires glamorous obituaries. Similarly, the diplomats and spies in Saigon and the "contractors" (engineers, construction workers) tended to stay within their own cohort.

In our office Peter Jay and I kept a tie on a hanger to wear when one of us went to the US Embassy. And we were occasionally invited to visit senior diplomats in their villas. Most of the "dips" were wary of dealing with reporters even in social settings, although younger ones less so. The military brass, MACV (Military Assistance Command Vietnam), was headquartered on Saigon's outskirts. The basic stance of the officers there was inherently suspicious of the motives of reporters, especially ones like me from the "liberal" *Washington Post* and without a military pedigree. Older correspondents like Jack Foisie (brother of Phil) of the *Los Angeles Times* and Keyes Beech of the *Chicago Daily News* had covered Korea and were considered a safer bet for the colonels and generals. I thought these reporting "elders" were savvy in the best sense: they didn't let their experience make them any less critical when it was necessary than were reporters my age.

After I had been in Vietnam for about a year, I was invited to appear on an hour-long broadcast of William F. Buckley's *Firing Line*, to be taped in Saigon. The other panelists were George MacArthur, who had been in Vietnam for seven years (with the AP first), and Stan Cloud, the *Time* bureau chief, who smoked a pipe. Watching that show nearly fifty years later, I was struck by my own youth and the nuance of most of my comments. I expressed little of the sense that the war was hopeless, although I probably intuited that it was. I talked about what I saw around me, not what I felt. I certainly had empathy for Vietnamese civilians and was drawn to the distinct jargon and "grunt" culture of the GIs. And I smoked.

It is fun now to watch YouTube clips of the Bob Hope Christmas shows I attended in Da Nang and Saigon, with young draftees in the sweltering heat thrilled to see performers like Lola Falana in a tight white pantsuit belting out "Reach Out and Touch Someone." Gauzy memories of those soldiers all these years later are not surprising, but I had a sort-of man crush on those GIs even then.

There were a number of main story lines we pursued:

The first was progress in the war itself. In February 1971, the ARVN (South Vietnamese forces) sent troops into Laos to cut off North Vietnamese movement along the Ho Chi Minh Trail. US forces provided air support and logistical backup. On the night before the invasion, Craig Whitney and I and a few other reporters and photographers, including Larry Burrows of *Life*, one of the true greats of his generation, camped on the Laotian border. We built a small fire and basically hung out until the next morning when the ARVN troops passed us in armed procession on their way into Laos. News of the impending operation had been under embargo so once it began, I hitchhiked back to a US installation a few hours away to file my story. There was no possibility of doing anything from the scene. There were no phones or telex facilities at the front. The next day Burrows and a few other photographers caught a chopper ride across the Laotian border. They were shot down and all died.

The Laotian invasion ended after a few weeks with a South Viet-namese withdrawal. Whatever progress had been made in the early going was nullified as the battles went on. That was a pattern in the war: victories were temporary with the outcome at best a stalemate.

The major military action of the "Vietnamization" period was a North Vietnamese countrywide offensive in the late winter and spring of 1972. There were some main unit engagements and one

South Vietnamese province, Quang Tri, was for a time overrun. But the ARVN, with American air support and advisers, held off the North Vietnamese, which led to a sense that the worst of the conflict might be ending. That was, again, a premature judgment.

The offensive followed Richard Nixon's visit in February to China and his meeting with Mao Zedong and Zhou Enlai. After the meeting with Mao, a leading Saigon newspaper published a front-page cartoon of the two leaders performing fellatio on each other. My instinct was that Nixon in China was the ultimate signal to the South Vietnamese that America would eventually abandon the effort to protect the Saigon government and military. Nonetheless, the ARVN's performance in the spring offensive was good enough to provide cover for the United States to continue pulling out troops. The last were to leave a year later, in March 1973.

Then there were the "sideshows" (as they were called) in Cambodia and Laos. The situation in Laos was especially murky. The CIA was deeply involved on the side of the Royal Lao government against the communist-backed Pathet Lao. "Our side" was supported by the Hmong warriors in mountainous northern redoubts. Landing by chopper in the valleys surrounded by morning mists and shadows was surreal, a twilight zone of military encampments. Vientiane, the Laotian capital, was sleepy. Reporters there tended to take advantage of local pleasures, including a club called the White Rose, where young women would perform amazing feats with cigarettes in their body orifices. It was a war in which there were deaths and civilian suffering, but it was still hard for outsiders to take it completely seriously because of its remoteness and eccentricities, which of course was wrong. The spokesman at the American embassy in Vientiane was vulnerable because when he would say things that were clearly not true, his ears would turn bright red. Yes, that was the case. The ambassador, G. McMurtrie Godley, was notable for his off-putting zeal in choosing bombing targets from maps arrayed in his bunker-like office.

We would also regularly cover the situation in Cambodia, where a coup before the US-backed invasion in the late spring of 1970 unleashed what became a decade-long civil war. Phnom Penh in the early seventies was a respite from the cacophony of Vietnam and the American presence, which was still confined to the US embassy. Aside from the brief foray into Cambodia's Parrot's Beak in May 1970, there was no American military engagement on the ground in Cambodia, reflecting the extent to which this was an outsourced war against communists with Khmers doing the fighting on both sides. The United States provided air support for government troops and economic support that was gradually cut back and ended before the Khmer Rouge victory in 1975. Our best political source was a diplomat at the Israeli embassy, who was astute and had nothing to lose by talking to reporters. His ambassador once joined us at 482 and after a pipe or two exclaimed about the Cambodians, "How can I express it . . . the zeroness of these people." The massacres between 1975 and 1979 when the Vietnamese invaded and ousted the Khmer Rouge was for Cambodians an appalling tragedy for which the United States never recognized its responsibility.

In Phnom Penh the correspondents stayed at the Royale Hotel, which had been a center of activity for French expats and retained a residual old-style flavor with a pool and sunset aperitifs. There was a small resident press corps, the most famous of whom was a young Australian, Kate Webb of UPI, who was soft-spoken but a fiercely focused war correspondent. She spent time as a prisoner of the Khmer Rouge. Our help in Phnom Penh consisted of Dith Pran and his driver-sidekick Mouv. Before the war they had worked assisting tourists in Siem Reap visiting the temples at Angkor Wat. They would meet us at the airport and provide indispensable guidance and interpretation. Pran became famous when Sydney Schanberg of *The New York Times* moved to Phnom Penh full-time and hired him. Their relationship, including Pran's years in Khmer Rouge captivity and his escape, were made into a book and movie called *The Killing Fields*. Sydney, as we all knew and as portrayed in the movie by Sam Waterston, was intense and highly competitive. Pran told the *Post*'s correspondent H. D. S. Greenway that Sydney would dispatch him to the filing office to check on Greenway's stories to be sure he wasn't being scooped. When Pran finally made it to the United States he became a successful photographer for the *Times*. He died in 2008.

Another story line was diplomacy and Vietnamese politics. The peace negotiations were taking place in Paris well beyond our reach or even much interest. Events in Saigon had their own rhythm. There was a presidential election in the fall of 1971 that after some manipulation re-elected President Nguyen Van Thieu with 94 percent of the vote. The opposition was symbolic and even that was harassed. Corruption was widespread at every level because nominal official salaries were small, and bribes were essential—and taken for granted—in getting things done.

The US embassy was led by Ambassador Ellsworth Bunker, a senior and esteemed diplomat of the old school WASP type. We saw him only rarely. The deputy ambassador was Charles S. Whitehouse, also a patrician sort who had his initials on velvet slippers he wore at cocktails. One of the best observations on Whitehouse came from Larry Stern, who was a visiting *Post* correspondent. Watching Peter Jay, descendent of John Jay, meeting Whitehouse for the first time, he said there was a "chromosomal salute" of class peers. Jay, it needs to be said, was emphatically no snob despite his august heritage. He later owned a few small local Maryland newspapers and took over the family farm.

The CIA station chief, Ted Shackley, avoided us completely, although he did see Alvin Shuster of the *Times* occasionally, picking him up on a street corner in a sedan with shrouded windows. Shackley doubtless thought Alvin was old enough to be taken seriously. He was succeeded in 1972 by Thomas Polgar, who was accessible, talkative, and insightful. I can't isolate what I learned from him, but he was very much a source on broader themes. My top-level contacts at MACV were rare, but I did get to see the commanding general, Creighton Abrams, and his successor, Frederick Weyand, as my time in country earned me some credibility. After Peter Jay left in early 1972, I became the bureau chief, which in the hierarchal military jargon qualified me for greater access. Abrams managed, improbably in a losing situation, to emerge with his reputation for leadership essentially intact. By contrast, the standing of General William Westmoreland, the US commander in the late 1960s, deteriorated as his misjudgments and dissembling became clear over time.

I also had good relations—other reporters did as well—with John Paul Vann, the legendary retired colonel and subsequent civilian leader in two of South Vietnam's four regions. The only way to describe him is to refer readers to Neil Sheehan's *A Bright Shining Lie*, the epic history of America's years in Vietnam, which correctly portrays Vann as a metaphor for a misguided but essentially well-intentioned commitment to elusive victory, somehow driven by a belief that the United States could give South Vietnam a sustainable anti-communist government. Vann came to know that this would not happen, but he sought to meet the goals set before him despite his private doubts. His most indelible insight was about why the United States was failing in Vietnam—"not because we only had ten years of experience there," he said, "but because we had one year of experience ten times." Vann died in a helicopter crash in the highlands during the 1972 spring offensive.

Another officer who gave me access was General John Cushman, the senior military commander in the Mekong Delta. He was extremely forthcoming with me on issues of GI morale and drug use, serious problems in his region. (One of my stories on that subject made it into the movie *The Post*, about the paper's reports on the Pentagon Papers. Tom Hanks as Ben Bradlee growls that "Osnos has a story tomorrow on GIs and heroin in Vietnam.") As American forces withdrew and were less engaged in frontline actions, the grunts and especially the support troops—the "rear echelon mother fuckers," or REMFs—were buying small, cheap vials of heroin on the streets and rolling the drug into cigarettes.

This was a striking reflection of the attitude that draftees, in particular, had. They were in a war they believed was probably unwinnable in a place very few of them knew anything or cared much about. They knew that "in the world," as America was called, returning GIs were far more likely to be hassled than welcomed. Draft resisters, including those who moved to Canada and Sweden, tended to be admired. Soldiers were not, and that made them cynical or worse. There were frequent cases of "fragging," with soldiers placing grenades under officers' beds and other defiant behaviors. The Lawyers Military Defense Committee, where Susan worked, provided its free legal assistance, more often than not, to GIs involved in infractions of discipline. Peter Jay and I contributed to a *Post* series and a book called *Army in Anguish*, an accurate framing of what we were seeing in the war zone.

And we wrote about Vietnamese lives. There was a young boy on the street outside our office who was crippled and walked on his hands. Passersby called him "the Crab." I wanted to know what his life was like, and so I went to his home in a neighborhood of ramshackle huts. He was a bright and handsome boy of maybe twelve. When I asked him what he most wanted in the world, he said "a wheelchair." After the story appeared in the *Post* and was picked up by *Stars and Stripes*, the military daily distributed in the region, the boy received a wheelchair. I have a photograph of the presentation with an air force sergeant who organized the gift. A fund was set up from donations that was sufficiently large to support his family. I cannot say for certain, but my recollection is that when I left Saigon for the last time in March 1973, the boy was back on the street, on his hands.

Local life went on from the Delta villages to the Cercle Sportif, where I once saw a Davis Cup regional quarterfinal, while a few blocks away an artillery strike landed. A great many of the Vietnamese, despite decades of conflict, still managed lives of family, education, and culture. I wrote a long story about what Vietnamese read for pleasure, mainly novels steeped in mythic lore. The tendency to condescend to these "little brown people" on our side or, worse, "gooks"—while (probably) exaggerating the patriotism and commitment of the enemy—was one of the many reasons that the United States proved so completely unable to prevail in what was really a civil war.

As I said, our lives in Saigon were comfortable, but this was a war zone and there were at least three times in the two years I was there when I could easily have been killed—not counting the helicopter over Laos that was shot down the day after I left the front, killing Larry Burrows and others. In February 1971, Ben Bradlee traveled to

Asia en route to visiting his son, who was living in India at the time. Ben was scheduled to arrive on a Tuesday, and so on Sunday evening I arranged to meet François Sully, a *Newsweek* correspondent, at 8 A.M. the following morning for a trip by helicopter to the Cambodian border with a Vietnamese general, Do Cao Tri. At some point that night the bureau received a telex saying that Ben was coming a day early and would arrive at Saigon's Tan Son Nhut airport in the late morning. I let Sully know I wouldn't be making the trip with him and joined Peter Jay in picking up Ben at the airport. When we got back to the office, Joyce Bolo was ashen. She said that the chopper with Tri, Sully, and others had blown up on takeoff and everyone was killed. My legs went out from under me and I fell into a chair. Incredibly, the moment passed immediately, and we had a busy few days with our boss. I don't remember talking or even thinking about what happened until years later when Ben was writing his memoirs. His researcher called me to ask about Ben's Saigon trip. I told her about the Tri incident, and it ended up in Ben's book. Retelling that anecdote and the fact that it had faded so quickly still amazes me. I asked Peter Jay in 2019 what he remembered, and he confirmed my recollection that what was, after all, a near miss, had made no impact on us—although he remembered that another reporter, Michael Parks, said he had also been scheduled for that trip and decided not to go. He told Peter that he was shaken. The mind can be unfathomable.

The second incident was in a provincial capital somewhere in the Mekong Delta in 1972. I was traveling with Martin Meredith, the Reuters bureau chief, and Chuck Benoit, a former staffer at the US Agency for International Development and at the Ford Foundation whom we had hired as an interpreter to replace our assistant, Ron Moreau. (Ron had worked in a Vietnamese village as a conscientious objector. We paid him $50 per week plus $25 for every photograph that ran in the paper. Ron soon came back to Vietnam as a *Newsweek* correspondent.) Benoit spoke fluent Vietnamese like an army officer. On a street lined with little shops in early afternoon we were confronted by several ARVN soldiers who were either drunk or high. Benoit said something that set them off. They lifted their M-16s and started waving them around and shooting over our heads and at our feet. The blast shutters on the shops went down. We took off, making it to a near corner, and rolled into the ground and to safety. The shooting stopped. I recently checked with Chuck about what had happened to be sure the danger was real.

The third incident happened when the Paris Peace Accords were signed in January 1973. Craig Whitney and I went to Quang Tri to observe the moment of the cease-fire at the Demilitarized Zone between North and South Vietnam. At dawn we saw the North Vietnamese soldiers waving at us from across the border. We got into a van heading to Hue for filing. On the road it was clear that there were still firefights underway as the ARVN were seizing whatever land they could. As we encountered one of these exchanges, an ARVN officer stopped us, outraged that we had come upon this violation of the cease-fire. He proceeded to shoot our tires with his pistol. Our driver was terrified. Craig's excellent interpreter, Luong, did his best to mollify the officer, who drove away leaving us at the side of the road surrounded by intermittent gunfire. We flagged down a passing military truck and scrambled into the back, pulling the tarp over our heads. I don't know what happened to our Vietnamese driver. In Saigon, Susan was covering the phones and received an alarming call from someone saying that Craig and I were missing near the DMZ. We did make it safely to Hue and filed our stories.

What is most striking about these episodes is that, superficially, at least, we took them in stride. Did these near-death experiences have any lasting impact on us? I really have no idea. I asked Peter Jay recently if he ever felt scared. Not really, he said, although being under fire in a helicopter was unnerving. We were war correspondents, but our roles as reporters and perhaps our youth meant that we made it home wiser, perhaps, but spiritually unscathed, at least as far as we could detect. Later in the book, I will try to explain what I considered "deflection," the fact that we somehow minimized whatever danger there was in our minds. Because the number and role of American troops had been reduced, their frontline combat missions were fewer than they had been earlier in the war, and that meant we were less exposed, on the whole, to bloody GI battles. Nonetheless, in a war zone threats to life and limb are inevitable.

In the spring of 1971, Nina came to Vietnam for a visit. We went to Bali on a holiday. The Indonesian island hadn't yet become a major tourist destination, and we had a simple cabin on Kuta beach. We then spent a week in Saigon, and I went to Hong Kong with her for a weekend at Repulse Bay, the most charming of colonial-era hotels. And then Nina left. She did not intend to stay or return.

Back in Saigon, I needed to come to terms with this prolonged separation and our different lives. Alvin Shuster and I had lunch at an officers' mess. His characteristically "menschy" (Yiddish for warm and sensible) advice was to ask if I could imagine a lasting marriage like his and Miriam's. And the answer was no. I wrote Nina a letter saying that it was time to recognize that we should not try to stay together after Vietnam. I wish I had kept the letter or Nina's response, but when I returned to Washington we got divorced. My lawyer was Stan Frosh, a prominent attorney who had been so friendly to me the year I worked for Izzy. He didn't need to be paid, but as a stamp collector asked me to get him an entire year's output of postage stamps from Laos. That cost me about $90. In the divorce settlement I kept our record collection and Nina got several pieces of contemporary art we had acquired.

Nina became a notable figure in the curatorial world when she started to organize a union at the Corcoran and was fired. She sued and won the case against the museum. She then went on to have a successful curatorial career at Wesleyan University's art museum and as an adviser to wealthy collectors. She never remarried but had a long-term relationship with a prominent New York-based music entrepreneur.

When we met in 2019, Nina and I agreed that by the standards of these things, our relationship had been much more of a young couple's adventure than the basis for a long-term marriage. Nina said she realized that she was not really the marrying kind. The long-term consequence of our years together were valuable experiences in life rather than a legacy of regrets.

I was now a bachelor in Saigon. In the midst of an August afternoon tropical storm, I offered Susan Sherer a ride to the police station on the Mekong River, where she needed to renew her residency card. Something clicked. A few days later I asked Susan to join Craig and several others for dinner at a Chinese restaurant specializing in Peking duck. The duck was delicious, and by the end of the evening Susan and I were a couple and never spent a night apart again for the next forty-nine years and counting, unless one of us was traveling. I asked her recently what she had thought might happen that evening—August 29, 1971—after the dinner. She smiled and said she had brought a toothbrush.

In February 1972 I received a letter from someone in the *Post* newsroom that carried the revelation that it had been announced in Washington that at the end of my tour I would be returning to the Metro desk. I had not heard about that from Foisie and was devastated. In my mind, being sent back to Metro rather than the National desk or to prepare for another foreign assignment meant that I was not considered a success in Vietnam. When I read my personnel file in 2020, I found the draft of a letter he either never sent or I never received, dated January 23, 1972. This is the gist of what it said:

> A hasty note and one long overdue . . . You are scheduled to go back to Metropolitan for a time, whence you came. There are lots of reasons for this—all good. Harry needs you and wants you . . . I must say that you have done well abroad and have also shown steady improvement. I see you going abroad again . . . and I want you, therefore, as time allows and keep up your interest and your studies . . . we are trying to advance plan 2–3 years ahead and you are on that list . . . Thanks for doing so well, and for being a trouble free and hardworking correspondent.

I will never know why I didn't see that letter. Nor did I remember a letter I later wrote to Harry Rosenfeld, Metro editor, I found in my personnel file asserting that I would approach the new assignment with enthusiasm . . . I can only imagine how differently I would have felt about my return to Washington. At a distance, everything from the home office is magnified. I could well have asked about this reassignment. I did not. As the saying goes, it doesn't change a thing but it's nice to know.

Harry Rosenfeld had been one of my newsroom mentors and in his memoirs had very good things to say about me. Peter Jay had also gone to Metro after he returned from Saigon, but as Harry's deputy. The failure to give me notice of the move and a qualifying explanation was a lesson in leadership that I never forgot.

When the 1972 spring offensive began, my tour was extended. By now Susan was working at *The New York Times* as office manager. She had shocked her family that Christmas when she told them on a visit that she was returning to Vietnam and was dating a journalist. When she had first left for Saigon, her father had said, "Whatever else you do, stay away from those foreign correspondents," highlighting our unreliability as a group. Susan never presented herself as a rebellious sort, but she was guided then and forever after by instincts of extraordinary clarity.

That spring period was probably the most intense of the war in many years. But in contrast to the late 1960s, it was mainly a Vietnamese-fought war with American support. The number of American troops was now relatively small, perhaps 25,000 in country with air force and naval units deployed in the region for what was primarily air cover.

There were two stories that caught for me the significance of Vietnamization when it came to the respective role of the US military and the ARVN.

When an air force unit pulled out of a base in the Mekong Delta, they left behind the dogs that guarded the perimeter. After a few weeks the few remaining US advisers noticed that the dogs were looking skinny and weak. The advisers determined that the daily food ration for the dogs had been higher under the Americans than the food ration of the Vietnamese soldiers who became their handlers. So the dogs' ration was adjusted downward. And they died of starvation.

In the second case, a base outside Pleiku was transferred to the ARVN, and the US military took everything away, including the air-conditioners in a fortified bunker. When the North Vietnamese attacked, they sent artillery through the holes left behind where the air-conditioners had been. The facility was overrun.

One morning a telex came from Howard Simons, the *Post*'s managing editor—Ben Bradlee's number two. Simons wrote that a very respected defense correspondent for *The Baltimore Sun* had called him and said that Osnos is doing an outstanding job in Vietnam and, he added, we agree. I remember that message because for the first time I felt real thrills going through my body. A few words made a big difference for reporters far away, another lesson I took with me for later use.

In mid-June, after a night with 482's relaxing opium in Phnom Penh, I left Indochina for what I thought was the last time. I was more experienced at opium by that point than Craig. He said that the next day he was so debilitated by a hangover that he was unable to properly cover whatever story he was supposed to be reporting. Nearly fifty years later that memory still makes us laugh.

I flew to Vienna to meet Susan and, for the first time, her parents. This was not your typical "meet the boyfriend" dinner. Susan's father, Albert W. Sherer Jr., was the US ambassador to Czechoslovakia, and her mother, Carroll, was a formidable woman of many talents. We drove to the palace in Prague where Ambassador and Mrs. Sherer lived. The setting in the Czech capital was in every way grand. On June 19 there was a small item inside the *International Herald Tribune* about a break-in at the Democratic Party headquarters in Washington two nights earlier. Little did we anticipate what that would become.

But I was far from done with Vietnam. On October 26, 1972, on the eve of the US presidential election, National Security Adviser Henry Kissinger declared that "peace is at hand," based on his secret deliberations with North Vietnamese negotiators in Paris. Peace at last. I was told to go back to Vietnam to cover this very welcome turn of events. Susan, who by then was working for the ACLU's military rights project, agreed to go with me—a very distinct plus. Except that the day we arrived in Saigon, the United States began the most sustained heavy bombing of Hanoi and environs of the whole war. The North Vietnamese had balked at elements of the supposedly all-but-finished treaty. Less known to us at the time was that President Thieu was opposed also because the pact envisioned substantial North Vietnamese troops remaining in the South.

In any case, with peace again off, the resident Saigon press corps flew off for the Christmas holidays in more pleasant places. Susan and I were staying in the guest room of the *Post's* apartment over the garage on Nguyen Hue. The correspondent who had replaced me, Tom Lippman, and his wife, Sydney, left behind their dog. In the middle of the night the phone rang with a very unusual direct call from the foreign desk about the bombing story. I rushed out to the phone and stepped right into the dog's poop. Rather than feel the exhilaration of being back on this great story, I identified myself with the dog shit at that moment.

But after the holidays, the negotiations over the treaty resumed. Moods quickly improved. The treaty signing in Paris was on January 27, 1973. I have told the story of Craig and I returning from the DMZ that day and barely escaping alive. The most memorable event of the days after the treaty was the return of the American POWs at Tan Son Nhut. Amid the floodlights late at night, the prisoners came off the plane in sprints of dazed exuberance. They were a very welcome symbol that this corrosive conflict was ending, at least as far as Americans were concerned.

Susan had already left to return to her job in Washington, and at the beginning of March I left also with a brief stop in Hong Kong, where I had a three-piece suit made that I kept for decades. Only now do I realize that having a custom-made suit was an echo of my father's suit in Bucharest in 1940, which was so instrumental in saving my mother and brother.

Chapter 10

Echoes of Vietnam

VIETNAM WAS TO BECOME a very important element of my life, especially as an editor and publisher. Aside from whatever personal impact the experience had, the war—on the ground and at home—shaped my views about politics, human nature, and storytelling. Among the books I published were a volume of elegiac poetry by Wendy Larsen and a Vietnamese friend (I recruited the assistance of Jonathan Galassi, a real poetry editor, for that one), and narratives by Morley Safer, Malcolm Browne, Jack Laurence, and Stanley Karnow—actually on the Philippines, a follow up to his classic history of Vietnam. Ours won a Pulitzer. William Prochnau's *Once Upon a Distant War* recounted the superb early work of the young David Halberstam, Neil Sheehan, and Browne. I reissued Ward Just's prescient book *To What End*, written after his 1966–67 tour for the *Post*. And I published three books by Robert Brigham, a leading historian of the war, including a devastating appraisal of Henry Kissinger's role called *Reckless*.

Dan Weiss, the president of the Metropolitan Museum of Art, wrote a biography of Michael O'Donnell, a young helicopter pilot and poet who was shot down in Cambodia and whose body was not recovered for thirty years. As Dan said, the story could have been one of 58,000 for all those young people who had died in what was a pointless conflict. Presenting this book to the salespeople who would be handling it, I asked how many in the room had been in Indochina in any way between 1965 and 1975. No hands went up. That war was history without the gauzy cloak of victory in World War II.

The most important book about the war I was involved with was *In Retrospect: The Tragedy and Lessons of Vietnam* by Robert Strange McNamara. As secretary of defense in the Kennedy and Johnson administrations, McNamara became identified as the leading figure in Halberstam's portrait in *The Best and Brightest*—the men responsible for the Vietnam debacle, both the misguided mission and the failure to publicly assess the war's destiny for failure. I had probably met McNamara by the early nineties because he was close to Katharine Graham (we were occasional guests at her dinners) and he was active on the Washington social scene as president of the World Bank.

McNamara's name was anathema to a great many in Washington's political and journalism circles. Cynics said he was at the World Bank to atone for his actions as defense secretary. He was the target of particular contempt because he appeared to be so self-confident about the war's progress as defined by data, when in fact he had recognized early on what the war's trajectory would probably be. Bob was in his midseventies when his literary agent, Sterling Lord, sent a proposal for his autobiography to Harry Evans, the publisher of Random House. Given my Vietnam background, Harry brought me into the acquisition meeting and said the book would be mine if we took it on. An advance was negotiated, and I brought the project to Times Books, the imprint where I was now the publisher.

Bob's intention was to tell the full story of his life, including his time as the president of the Ford Motor Company and at the World Bank. He only planned a chapter or two on Vietnam. In our first meeting I told Bob that his book would be read most closely for what he had to say about Vietnam and urged him to write that chapter first. He agreed. From the outset, I found Bob to be responsive to my role despite his reputation for bullheadedness. We never had a disagreement about the approach he needed to take. He went to work and came back in a matter of months with 100,000 words on how the war had escalated and why the Kennedy and Johnson administrations had driven policy in the way they had. He provided a strikingly nonjudgmental portrayal of his views.

The team on the book also included a young historian, Brian VanDeMark, and Geoff Shandler, a young editor at Times Books. We had many sessions with the developing manuscript and transcribed interviews with Bob to get the cadence of his voice and ideas. For all the progress we made, I still felt we hadn't broken through to Bob's private despair over the conflict itself and how it had divided the nation. In one of our last sessions, under careful prodding from Geoff and me—"How do you feel when you visit the Vietnam Memorial on the Mall with the names of every American killed in the war?"—Bob said, "We were wrong, terribly wrong, and we owe it to future generations to explain why." Geoff recalls that I was already gathering my papers to leave when McNamara said that, and I sputtered something akin to "That's it!" All these years later, I have listened to hours of our interviews with Bob as we went over and over the thought processes he had at the time.

Once we settled on the title, we designed a cover of Bob sitting alone in the East Room of the White House, which conveyed a sense that he was a solitary figure with a reputation for public arrogance. We published the book in April 1995, shipped about 100,000 copies to start, and designed an extensive publicity rollout and travel schedule.

The release of the book was explosive. It became the leading news story in the country for days because of the level of outrage it provoked. Many people felt emphatically that McNamara's silence about the war for a quarter century disqualified his right to explain it and to explain himself. An editorial in *The New York Times* said, in effect, that McNamara deserved to suffer nightly torment for his crimes. This was before the age of social media, but Times Books was bombarded with faxes denouncing Bob for acknowledging in 1995 that the war was wrong when he had known in the 1960s that this was the case and that victory was impossible.

There were many reasons—largely inaccessible—why Bob had not openly discussed his views earlier, although those who knew him well in Washington were aware of his anguish over the war and saw that he would tear up in talking about it. He was of a generation that was not given to openly sharing feelings, preferring instead to have a few alcoholic "pops" to ward off emotion. National Security Adviser McGeorge Bundy, whose role in the war was comparable to McNamara's, escaped ignominy by maintaining what was regarded as a dignified silence and was hailed for his progressive leadership of the Ford Foundation.

If there were any people who saw the revelations in McNamara's memoirs as an act of courage—literally no other major architect of the war ever admitted that it was "terribly wrong"—they were drowned out by the attacks. Bob's tendency toward rhetorical bluster meant that his public appearances were insufficiently contrite to satisfy his critics. Still, the book immediately went to number one on every bestseller list.

Perhaps the most notable evening of the publicity tour for the book was at Harvard's Kennedy School of Government, where the atrium was packed with reporters and television cameras on hand to gauge the response. Bob was introduced by his friend, the economist John Kenneth Galbraith. He was holding his own until near the end when a Vietnam vet began to harangue him, to what seemed the approval of much of the audience. McNamara snapped: "Shut up." We knew of course that there would be widespread coverage of the incident. It was awful. My son Evan, then an undergraduate at Harvard, was sitting next to me and squeezed my knee hard, reflecting the tension he felt with me and the rest of the room.

The evening ended and we all went back to the Charles Hotel nearby. Very early the next morning there was a knock on my door, and there was Bob in a raincoat and running shoes preparing to take a brisk walk along the Charles River. I thought he was going to tell me that he wanted to terminate the book tour because of the stress on him and so many others who came to hear him speak. He said the opposite. "I know what makes people so angry," he said. "But I have to do this. I need to talk about the war and its lessons so we can prevent anything like it happening again." Bob continued to travel, flying alone from city to city. Given the level of indignation the book had caused, we offered him security if he wanted it. He did not. The book was number one on bestseller lists for a month and sold hundreds of thousands of copies.

In a perhaps surprising way, Bob felt he had achieved the purpose of the book: to let the country know his innermost thoughts—as best he could express them—as a cautionary tale.

I would go on to publish two more books with Bob, assisted by Robert Brigham and foreign policy expert James Blight. *Argument Without End* was based on meetings McNamara had been instrumental in organizing among leading Americans and Vietnamese who had been involved in the conflict. The final book was *Wilson's Ghost*, Bob's perspective on the way to avoid a twenty-first-century repeat of the bloody twentieth century.

One day while we were working on *Wilson's Ghost*, Bob called and told me that a filmmaker named Errol Morris wanted to make a movie based on interviews with him. Knowing that Morris's films were darkly revealing about their subjects, I asked Bob what his capacity for further excoriation and humiliation would be. Bob went ahead with the film, *The Fog of War*, which was on the whole a fair portrait of an old man struggling to convey his thoughts about the past, as far back as World War II, when he had been an army bombing officer who chose civilian targets in Japan. "We burned to death 100,000 civilians in Tokyo," he said, noting that had the United States lost the war he might have been tried as a war criminal for that. The movie was a critical and commercial success and probably did more for Bob's redemption than the book—and was certainly seen by a far larger audience. It also won an Oscar for best feature documentary.

Two moments stand out for me as emblematic of the distance that Bob had traveled. One of the most celebrated antiwar protestors of the 1960s was David Harris, the president of the student body at Stanford University. He later married the singer Joan Baez and went to prison for a year for his protest activities. In the 1990s, Times Books commissioned him to go to Vietnam and write a book exploring his impressions of the country and his own experiences. He was in the office one day when McNamara also was. I recently asked David what he remembered of that encounter; he responded that Bob gave him an inscribed copy of *In Retrospect*, writing, "To David Harris. With Admiration. Robert McNamara." David said that he was stunned, and all these years later still was.

And at *Time* magazine's seventy-fifth anniversary celebration in Radio City Music Hall in March 1998, chosen guests were asked to pay tribute to someone they greatly admired. John F. Kennedy Jr. chose McNamara and said this: "After leaving public life and keeping his own counsel for many years, Robert McNamara did what few others have done. He took full responsibility for his decisions and admitted he was wrong. Judging from the reception he got, I doubt many public servants would be brave enough to follow his example. So tonight, I would like to toast someone I've known my whole life not as a symbol of pain we can't forget, but as a man. And I would like to thank him for teaching me something about bearing great adversity with great dignity." Bob was not present.

Robert McNamara would never be forgiven by the vast majority of Americans, but when he died in 2009 at the age of ninety-three, he was, at least, better understood.

His family sent out a card to those who had written condolences that said, in accordance with his wishes, "there will be no funeral or memorial service and his ashes will be placed in Snowmass, Colorado, and Martha's Vineyard." I wrote at the time, "I can hear McNamara's gravelly voice and picture him waving his hand to lend emphasis to his determination not to be extolled—or denounced by a protestor—at a posthumous event. In different circumstances he might have been persuaded otherwise . . . But it would be inconceivable, I suppose, for his survivors to overrule McNamara's fiat that the scattering of his remains be the only ceremonial recognition of his very full, very long, and very controversial life."

Only recently did I learn that his widow, Diana Masieri Byfield, apparently authorized the placing of a headstone at Arlington Cemetery, but when McNamara's son Craig was told about it, he said that he had not known that his father's wishes had been countermanded. Such was the complexity of the McNamara family dynamic. Byfield did release Bob's letters to his beloved first wife, Margaret, for a "re-evaluation" of McNamara by brothers William and Philip Taubman, two distinguished historians.

The family condolence acknowledgment contained these parting thoughts by Bob, written in 1999: "I will hope, as well, to see others continuing to pursue the objectives which I have sought (very imperfectly at times): to move the world toward peace among peoples and nations and to accelerate economic and social progress for the least advantaged among us."

Chapter 11

The Gap Years

THE TRANSITION FROM war correspondent to general assignment reporter on the Metro desk was bumpy. Instead of the momentum and visibility of Indochina coverage, I was just a cog in a newsroom, or so I felt. On the opening day of the DC school system I was assigned to go to some elementary schools and phone in a report on the children's arrival.

Susan and I had a short-term rental near the office that we called "Cockroach Corners." At the end of the summer of 1972 (during the period before I was summoned back to Saigon), we were driving down 4th Street on Capitol Hill when Suze (as I had come to call her) spotted a very cute attached townhouse on a corner slightly elevated from the street. 401 D Street would be a great place to live, she said. The next day I checked and found it was available. It was the perfect place for us at that stage: cozy with a fireplace in the living room, a bedroom, a study, and even a small backyard with a fig tree. It was really a country cottage and remains one of my favorites of our many residences. We were settled. Suze went to work at the ACLU's military rights project. We had a cat. That aspect of life was excellent.

But my professional self was troubled. On about October 1, Suze pointed out to me one morning that in fifty-four weeks I would be thirty! That realization gave me chills to compound my angst. I was assigned to write a series on "The Loneliness Industry," the rise of services for singles, primarily among the Baby Boom generation, slightly younger than we were. I was sharing the series reporting with LaBarbara Bowman, a talented young African American woman whom I did not know at all. Notably, our stories were divided by race. I don't know why this subject caught the editors' attention, but off I went. I was not a person who had any interest in a "singles scene," bars, or mixers. I was not a single parent. I was living with a woman who would be my beloved wife. I had proposed one weekend that fall and she had accepted. I was getting a divorce to be paid in stamps.

The weirdest experience was a singles weekend that I attended at the Concord Hotel in the Catskills. When I said that I was a reporter for *The Washington Post*, the reaction among the women was "sure, good story." I was also geographically undesirable, since I was from Washington and not New York. I had a serious mind freeze trying to write that piece, the first time that had ever really happened. I doubtless overreacted and assumed that I would never be able to write again. The piece finally got done, and it even won a local journalism award for feature writing. Suze said that my weekend at the Concord seemed to be more upsetting to me than being shot at on a road near Quang Tri.

I also did a major investigative report on the use of methadone to treat heroin addicts in Washington. A friend of my brother's from medical school was overseeing drug policy for President Nixon and became a valuable source of information. And the piece was, in its way, a tribute to Robert's own work on addiction, which was significant.

I was restless enough that I got in my head the notion that I should consider leaving the *Post* and move to Vermont to start a career in public radio. What was especially strange about that fantasy was that public radio was still in its very earliest stages. I knew somehow that I would find that reporting and the audience appealing. Years later my radio connection proved to be significant and I was a regular on NPR's *Morning Edition*. But Vermont was definitely not going to happen, then or ever.

The fall of 1972 was notable for the landslide reelection of Richard Nixon and the simmering Watergate scandal. That story belonged to the Metro desk because the national staff thought the break-in at the headquarters of the Democratic Party was a peripheral issue. So my colleagues Bob Woodward and Carl Bernstein took on the story under the direction of Metro editors and with the spiritual and personal endorsement of Ben Bradlee—a relationship that would become one of the great sagas of journalism history.

The Woodward-Bernstein story (an odd-couple of Bob, from Yale and the Navy, partnered with my friend Carl, a colorful college dropout) has been told in books and movies and needs no reintroduction from me. There was a time when Carl had completed reporting on a piece about American draft dodgers in Canada but couldn't get the series done. He and another friend from the *Post*, Richard Cohen, came to my row house, spread out Carl's notes on the floor, and tried unsuccessfully to put the story together. Why do I remember this? Because Carl's pre-Watergate life became so legendary that the anecdote turned up in David Halberstam's epic portrait of journalism, *The Powers That Be*.

It turned out that I was to be a bit player in the Watergate epic. In late October, with the wretched loneliness series finished, I was told one evening to write the story about the only time the Watergate duo got a story wrong, an assertion by a witness to the grand jury that had not been made. It was a low point of their coverage and I had the dubious honor of turning it into a front-page story. That earned me a cameo in Carl and Bob's splendid book *All the President's Men*. When the Senate Watergate hearings began, I drew the enviable assignment of watching them on television, assuring me daily front-page bylines with my J School pal, Larry Meyer, who wrote the lede after attending the hearings in person.

After my winter foray in Vietnam to cover the cease-fire, I returned to the newsroom and my undefined status. My only significant article that spring was how one small bedroom community, Riverdale in Prince George's County, had come through the war. There had been soldiers from Riverdale who had died in the conflict, but no memorials or other recognition of the casualties, in a town where the fallen in previous wars were honored with plaques. It is striking to realize that service in the Vietnam War was so thankless. Disdain and disinterest were the norm.

Growing increasingly frustrated, I decided to apply for a year-long journalism fellowship being established at the University of Michigan with support from the National Endowment for the Humanities. Ann Arbor was not a place I knew anything about, but it was across the state from Lakeside, Michigan, where Suze's family had their summer home, making it somewhat familiar territory.

Everyone at the *Post* knew that my goal was to be a foreign correspondent again, but I could not get a reliable signal on that from Phil Foisie. I declared my intention to study Russian in my fellowship year and the *Post* topped off my NEH grant to match my salary. It was assumed by the fellowship's judges that I was being sent by the paper to prepare to go abroad, and I was almost rejected on the grounds that the *Post* should be paying me to study and not the government. This was ironic given that I still had no commitment from Foisie. The foreign staff came to call him "la foise" (made up and not a compliment) because of his seemingly inscrutable demeanor when, in fact, he was a determined newsroom calculator exercising power by withholding information or praise from his reporters. In my personnel file it turns out he was consistently positive about my work.

When he died at age seventy-three in 1995, the *Post*'s obituary hailed Foisie's role in establishing foreign news at the *Post*, which was true. I always thought Bradlee found him intriguing because he had gone to Harvard, was an improbably good tennis player in black oxfords, and would disappear most afternoons for a mysterious rendezvous that Bradlee concluded involved a hotel room across the street. This was never confirmed.

On Friday, July 14, 1973, Suze and I packed all our belongings into our Chevy Vega mini station wagon and a rental car and headed off to Lakeside, where we would be married in August. Then we would move to Ann Arbor.

In midafternoon, listening to the Watergate hearings on the car radio, I heard Alexander Butterfield testify that there was a taping system in the Oval Office, the revelation that eventually led to President Nixon's resignation. Suze was driving behind me and said that I began swerving on the highway. I was driving away from the biggest political story of the era, voluntarily pulling back from the center ring to spend a month on vacation, get married, and go to school. For all my ambition, I don't remember being especially troubled. In my mind, a new chapter was starting, and I was right about that.

Suze and I were married on a sunny Saturday afternoon, August 18, 1973, on a patch of sod carved out of the woods above the septic tank in Lakeside by Suze's father, Ambassador Sherer. The spot was forever after known as "chapel on the cess(pool)." Suze and I wrote the ceremony. My name was then entered on a tablecloth only used over the Christmas holidays, dating back five generations. Our formal nuptials were in the home of a justice of the peace in St. Joseph, Michigan. We have a snapshot of Suze, beautiful, and the largish officiant, smiling warmly. Suze has always said, looking at the picture, that she likes the fact that she looks positively petite. There is a photograph of us at the end of the afternoon ceremony, dressed in white, beaming with joy.

We arrived in Ann Arbor in late August and rented a house on Orchard Hill Drive, an unpaved side street to Geddes Road, one of Ann Arbor's main residential thoroughfares. The house belonged to a professor of Nordic myths on a year's sabbatical in Scandinavia. It was wonderfully eccentric, furnished with pieces from northern churches. Once we got it cleaned up it was just right for us. Suze and I signed up for courses in Russian, one spoken and one designed to enable us to read a newspaper after a single semester. We also took courses in Russian history and culture from the excellent Michigan faculty.

Neither of us knew Ann Arbor or the culture of a great big, state-based university city on a par with Berkeley and Madison. We soon dubbed our environs "Cambridge without the pretensions." We had season tickets to Michigan football games. I loved the scene—cheering crowds of 100,000, the great Michigan fight song "Hail to the Victors," and the football on the field. Brandeis had no football team and the Columbia team set a record for Ivy League losses. Suze was less interested but joined anyway, bringing a book. In the midst of her reading *Doctor Zhivago* one Saturday, an old grad indignantly, but mercifully in jest, told her to put the book down or risk assault.

I was in the first class of what later became known as the Knight-Wallace fellowships, endowed by the Knight Foundation and Mike Wallace, the legendary CBS journalist who had attended the university and donated a comfortable headquarters house. Along with the Nieman program at Harvard and a Knight program at Stanford, the fellowship gained prestige. With brilliant fundraising by its longtime director Charles Eisendrath and the eventual support of the university, our fellowship found a meaningful and apparently permanent place in journalism circles.

The Michigan academic year ended in April, so our main recollections were of fall and winter. We were young newlyweds in a setting that suited us. It was, all in all, a very good sojourn. At some point in early spring, Phil Foisie visited and conveyed that I would, in fact, be going to Moscow that summer to replace Bob Kaiser. So, it was now the case that I would follow Bob in London, Saigon, and Moscow. There were some people at the *Post* who thought we were one person.

One early hint of what Moscow would be like came when Georgy Arbatov, the head of the Soviet Institute for US and Canadian Studies and an influential figure with an unusually open mind (and a sense of humor) for a senior Communist Party official, paid a visit to Ann Arbor. Suze and I arranged a small lunch for him with relevant faculty and students at a "natural" food restaurant. He was entirely flummoxed by the menu until I came to his rescue. He would become one of the few official Russians I saw regularly in Moscow. He confided to me later that I had been his "favorite" Moscow correspondent (I'm not sure why), and at Random House I eventually published a very good book by him about the Soviets called *The System*.

Our short Washington stay in a hotel en route to Moscow was memorable for two encounters. The first came when Katharine Graham was invited to attend a dinner in honor of a visiting member of the Soviet Politburo. She told the Soviet embassy that she would attend if she could bring the *Post*'s new Moscow correspondent. Because they wanted Mrs. Graham, they agreed. Suze and I cleaned up our little Chevy Vega, and I drove to "Mrs. G's" very grand home in Georgetown to pick up my date. It was an amazing experience, not because of the dinner, but the fact of Mrs. Graham's gesture. In fact, I can say that to the extent it was possible, we were friends for the rest of her life. Suze and I were invited to occasional dinner parties at her home, which were legendary affairs in Washington to which only a few of the *Post* staff were included. She once joined us on a Sunday night at a small bistro in London and wrote us a note afterward telling us how much fun she had. In the late 1970s she and her friend Joseph Alsop, the columnist grandee, invited us for a weekend at her farm, but as the parents of two toddlers, we declined. Later she hosted, by my count, four book parties for my authors at her home, a very big deal in DC terms. They were even covered by C-SPAN. Katharine Graham was truly an amazing person.

The second encounter of note came on my first visit to the newsroom in nearly a year. This was during a very glamorous period when *All the President's Men* was being turned into a film, which generated excitement and envy from anyone even remotely connected to the project. I was standing at the foreign desk when Carl Bernstein came over to say that someone wanted to meet me. The next thing I knew I was shaking hands with Robert Redford. "Peter," he said, "I so enjoyed your movie." Redford was referring to a documentary called *I. F. Stone's Weekly* that had been released the previous winter to much acclaim. Vincent Canby, the *New York Times* film critic, said the modest black-and-white picture made him feel the way other people felt about *The Sound of Music*. I had been interviewed for the movie (as had Carl) and described colorfully what it was like to work for Izzy. Redford had noticed.

So, there we were, rested and ready for the Soviet Union. We began by visiting Suze's parents in their baronial residence in Prague. It is safe to say that we were probably the only US correspondents in

Moscow who chose to spend occasional "outs," as they were known, in the Czech capital. The US ambassador's residence had been one of three palaces owned by a rich Jewish family who escaped with a train-load of their possessions as World War II started. The house was taken over by the Nazis and it was still possible to uncover a bit of paper in German under a book or in the pantry. Albert and Carroll Sherer were the very best of the Foreign Service, devoting their entire careers to representing the United States in difficult assignments: Morocco, Hungary (from which they were expelled), Poland, Czechoslovakia, Togo, Guinea, and Equatorial Guinea, as well as postings at State Department headquarters in Washington. Albert (Bud) had been a navigator in the Pacific theater during World War II; he served his country for forty years. Carroll was equally accomplished in her way. In Togo, she started a business called Togo-A-Gogo, making garments from the beautiful local fabrics and returning the profits to the artisans. Even *The New York Times* was impressed. Bud (Albie to his grandchildren) died at seventy in 1986 from cancer. Carroll became a highly respected interior decorator and, as MaMere to us, built an elegant suite onto our house in Greenwich, where she spent the last years of her long life. She died in 2012, still as glamorous and savvy as she was when she arrived in Tangier in 1946, a young bride in heels and with a feather in her hat. She wrote a memoir, privately published, called *A Great Adventure*. And so it was.

Chapter 12

Kutuzovsky 7/4

WE ARRIVED IN MOSCOW in mid-June 1974 for an overlap with the Kaisers. After three very active years in the Soviet Union, Bob and Hannah had a strong sense of understanding and skill in navigating the world of the *Washington Post* correspondent. In Vietnam your status among colleagues tended to be determined by how close you were to completing your tour, measured by your DEROS—date estimated return overseas. In Moscow, status was based on a different principle, measured from your date of arrival rather than your date of departure. The longer you had been there, the more it was assumed you would know. We were at the beginning of an assignment and inevitably made to feel slightly ignorant by Russians and other reporters, which in fact we were.

Our arrival coincided with a summit visit by Richard Nixon, only two months before he resigned in disgrace. The prevailing mood was by Cold War standards upbeat. Moscow had been spruced up. The disabled and dissidents had been removed from the streets. At official occasions, warm toasts were shared by the principals. *Détente* was the operative term.

Bob and Hannah were great hosts. They took us on a full round of their contacts among writers, artists, refusenik Jews, dissidents, and a handful of official Russians, including my acquaintance Georgy Arbatov and top editors from the leading Soviet newspapers, *Pravda* and *Izvestia*. The Kaisers' Russian was excellent. I had a grip on the language and often spoke with problematic grammar and Polish inflections (from what I had heard at home). This actually came in handy because with a name of imprecise ethnic origin and blue eyes, I was often mistaken for a Pole or Lithuanian, instead of an American and a Jew. Even so, when it became useful after we'd been there for a while, the KGB found ways to denounce me as a Jewish activist and a spy. Suze said little but it was always grammatically perfect.

Our first trip out of Moscow was to Alma-Ata, the capital of Kazakhstan, to cover the all-Soviet Spartakiad, a kind of national youth Olympics. We were so inexperienced that at the airport we didn't realize that foreigners were exempt from the boarding scrum. We did manage to squeeze our way on to the plane. In a way this was a repeat of my first trip in Vietnam, setting out on a journey by trial and error rather than experience. Alma-Ata was pretty much a classic of the Soviet-era provinces: shoddy high-rises that had moved the residents out of traditional yurts and cottages and into apartments, along with the full array of Soviet ideological paraphernalia and exhortations. There was some local ethnic flavor from the Asian physical characteristics of many of the people and the mountainous surroundings. Everyone spoke Russian as distinct from Kazakh. It was July and very hot, 40 degrees Celsius, which is about 100 degrees Fahrenheit. There was no air-conditioning in our Intourist hotel room (that I remember) and to cool off we bought a bottle of local "champagne," chilled it in toilet water, and sat on a balcony at sunset. I really don't remember the sports event at all—mainly the heat and the sense of learning how to work in this daunting place.

In that first summer Suze and I did lots of travel around the country. One of the best trips was an overnight train to Murmansk, the largest city north of the Arctic Circle, which took thirty-six hours. In the summer months, the sun never sets there, which creates an oddly addled sense of time. In the winter it is essentially dark from November until February. The buildings were all painted festive colors, and children were exposed regularly to sunlamps. We were treated to significant amounts of fish and vodka in our reporting rounds. The train trip up and back was fun. We said it was like being sick without being sick. All you could do was recline, eat a bit, read, and engage with other passengers. The train was a very good place to talk to ordinary Russians. On other trips I wondered whether people had been planted near us for one surreptitious reason or another. But the Murmansk trip didn't seem to us especially monitored.

We settled into the *Post* apartment in Kutuzovsky, a broad boulevard near the city center, one of two compounds set aside for foreigners. The apartments were fine by Soviet standards. Their main distinguishing feature was a militia stand at the entrance to track who came in and out. Our apartment, furnished by a long line of our *Post* predecessors, was midcentury Scandinavian modern and tidy. A key feature was our stacked washer-dryer in the bathroom. There was a living room, a smallish kitchen, a dining room, two bedrooms, and a small balcony where, in later years, our daughter Katherine was bundled up in her carriage to get some of the frigid Moscow air during naptime.

We were told to assume that the apartment was thoroughly bugged, and we adjusted to the standard practice of using pseudonyms for our Russian contacts ("Beard" for Lev Kopelev, a writer; "Round" for Victor Pivavarov, a painter). We avoided saying anything in our home that might be damaging to friends or used to embarrass us. We wrote notes on Etch A Sketch pads, which like magic slates left no record. I always wondered whether anyone listening to our conversations could make sense of them. A couple's dialogue tends to be sentence fragments rather than complete, or explanatory declarations with identifying details. The building's infrastructure was a little shabby. The elevator was constantly "under repair," and the hot water had to be turned off for the entire month of August for "cleaning" of the pipes. That, too, made me wonder whether the listening devices worked. On the other hand, a recently dismantled US embassy apartment disclosed eleven hidden devices in just the living room.

The *Post*'s office was across the courtyard in a small suite: two rooms, a telex room for files, a toilet, a kitchenette. Regina Kazakova was the translator and general assistant. Regina was in her thirties and married to a famous Russian actor. She was assigned to us by UPDK, the KGB-supported agency that put staff into foreign correspondents' homes and offices. It was assumed that Regina was expected to report on us to keep her job and to maintain her access to special stores for hard-to-get food and clothing. But Regina was always very much her own person.

Our driver was Ivan Fyodorovich. The Kaisers called him their "roads" scholar. Ivan was a proud Soviet citizen. One of his favorite sayings was "*Sovietsyaka znachet otlitchnaya*" (Soviet means excellent). Ivan was responsible for driving the office Volvo and performing the essential tasks of office maintenance. Suze and I soon decided to buy a small Zhiguli, modeled after an Italian Fiat 124, which we could use for informal purposes, as much as that was possible. All correspondents' cars had a license plate of some size with K-4 as the opening digits. Anyone really determined to track us could do so. Our housekeeper and later babysitter was Irina Stepanovna, another familiar Russian type: sturdy, friendly to us, but not a friend. We never met her family, though we did learn that her son served in the army and was killed in a helicopter crash that was never officially acknowledged.

A favorite Irina story came after we'd been in Moscow for a year or so when a supposed dissident (who turned out to be a KGB informer) gave me what he said was the Ministry of Meat and Milk Production's confidential recipe for sausages, which showed that the actual meat content was reduced by adding roughage and even sawdust. This was probably an exercise to gain my trust for later use and abuse. The document was legitimate from every indication. I wrote a story about it that ran deep inside the *Post*. It was picked up, as so many of my stories were, by the Russian language service of Voice of America, which people managed to listen to despite regular jamming. The next day, for the one and only time this ever happened, Irina asked Suze if the sausage really was so corrupted, acknowledging that she listened to VOA—a no-no in principle. The death of Irina's son profoundly affected her in ways that I, at least, could never reach. But Suze knew how very sad she was.

Our night help was a very formidable lady named Varya. She would clean the office, sometimes babysat, and walked the dog—for protection, she once said, against Ivan Fyodorovich's unwelcome advances.

Suze was and is a committed dog person. So, in a matter of weeks we had a puppy purchased in what was called the "bird market"— at the time as close as you could get to capitalism on the streets. Suze called it the "perfect pooch." One weekend we were invited to a picnic at the dacha of Walter Stoessel, the US ambassador, and his wife, Mary Ann, who were friends of Suze's parents. The occasion was memorable, first because Mrs. Stoessel was wearing a sweatshirt that said "Fuck Communism," and second because the dog was off the leash and hit by a car. Before long we added a new dog, a fox terrier mutt we called Rumple because of his behavior, which included on one occasion humping Ambassador Stoessel's pants leg at our apartment, which he diplomatically ignored. Rumple also "made love" to the leg of the Chinese news agency correspondent having lunch in our dining room. He smiled politely.

Rumple eventually emigrated to Lakeside. At the airport where we were sending him off, the babushkas gathered around me and declared, "You are sending that dog to America? What will they think of us? We have so many beautiful borzoi."

Our domestic situation was comfortable enough. We would order food from Stockman's in Copenhagen and shop for perishables, such as they were, from hard-currency stores where rubles were not accepted. Ordering from afar could be tricky. We once received a carton of an unneeded corn chili condiment that could easily have lasted through our tour and that of our successors. Our menus were simple. Irina's specialty was tuna casserole. We used to say that even at the hard-currency stores the meats came in two variants unspecified as "with bone" or "without bone." We were so eager for fresh corn that we once stood on line in Tbilisi, Georgia, for what turned out to be pig corn. Caviar, on the other hand, was readily available from the cook at the US embassy snack bar, who had a bustling black-market business on the side. Distinguished visitors, including Averell and Pamela Harriman, feasted on this delicacy at our table. Vodka and brown bread were relatively easy to get at stores across the street.

This is perhaps the place to stress that the entire assignment in Moscow was a shared responsibility. I got the *Washington Post* bylines, but Suze was expert beyond measure in handling the complex unofficial Russians we dealt with, among many other things. Whatever else they may have felt about us, there were a great many "small favors" they would ask in return for our friendship, and Suze would navigate acquiring Western medicines, for example, and generally deal with their issues. I tried to maintain a bit of professional distance, which caused at least one dissident, Andrei Amalrik, to maintain that I was unsympathetic to his cause. The truth was that Suze thought he was boorish to his wife and said we would not see him socially.

We went on most of our trips together. Usually Suze's presence was enough to minimize provocations. There was, however, one memorable occasion in Moldavia, on the way to Romania, when in a hotel restaurant (as our firstborn baby, Katherine, snoozed in a stroller) a middle-aged couple sat with us and then told the local *Pravda* that as a Jew myself, I said they should emigrate. The attack on us in the newspaper said that during this episode I "danced on ruble notes." Then, when our train approached the Romanian frontier, we were carefully inspected and in Katherine's carrier, under a pillow, the Soviet border agents found Suze's contacts book. It was returned but doubtless copied. I never saw Suze so much as flinch at the personal hassles or, it needs to be added, what were in retrospect dangers. I think her parents' years of diplomatic service in the Soviet bloc gave her a baseline for endurance that was unusual among Americans.

But she was determined for us to maintain a reasonable schedule. I could return from the office whenever I was done. But then I had to stay home, allowing no late-night forays to check the telex machine. That meant we very often ate at 9 or 10 P.M. Suze would put candles on the table and wear a long dress in some lively print pattern. This commitment to routine and style was part of her (successful) effort to make our daily lives less grim. We followed the Kaisers' suggestion to accept every invitation in the first year no matter how dull it might seem. Then we were qualified to choose what was worth the time. Our mail was delivered through the American embassy's APO (military address) to avoid Soviet interference. The highlight of each week was Friday afternoon, when the magazines would arrive. Phil Foisie limited the mailing of the *Post* to just the news sections, a money saver. Our friend Lee Lescaze, then based in New York, would surreptitiously send us the Style section and, at Suze's specific request, the comics. We would savor these publications in a way that could never again be matched.

Another daily highlight was the arrival of a three-day-old *International Herald Tribune*, usually at lunchtime, through the Soviet mail. In today's relentless onslaught of information, the joy, the simple pleasure of reading a newspaper printed in Paris in English cannot be exaggerated. Unless I was having a business lunch or a meeting with someone, I would come home for lunch. I wore a tie and a jacket to the office. We bought heavy fur-lined coats and wool hats for what seemed like a very long winter. Our music came from a phonograph and a cassette player. We listened to records like the Broadway cast album of *A Chorus Line*, sixties and seventies rock, and, after Katherine arrived, *Sesame Street* music. There was a television (Russian channels only, of course), which we very rarely watched except for the tedious evening news when it was necessary. Overseas calls, even to the *Post*, were so rare that I would advise the foreign desk days in advance that I was planning one. Overall, it is now striking how remote we were from the Washington rhythms. Years later, when I visited Moscow after the fall of the Soviet Union, the Moscow bureau was on the *Post*'s switchboard in Washington. I was stunned. For better or worse (and I think better), we were very much on our own when it came to work and life.

We made some close friendships in the diplomatic and journalist communities. There were the Mallabys, Christopher and Pascale. He was the political counselor in the British embassy, later ambassador to Germany and France. They were as smart as they were fun to be with. At the British Foreign Office, Christopher was known as "old laser brain." One of his colleagues was Nigel Broomfield, a retired army officer with traditionally correct English style. Whereas Christopher was completely comfortable in conversation with a reporter, Nigel found it much harder. But he and Valerie, his lovely wife, were classy if not informative. Benoit d'Aboville was a handsome young Frenchman, a bachelor we thought, although it later turned out he had a daughter in Paris, which explained his immediate attraction to Katherine when she was born in 1975. Benoit would return from courier trips to Paris with artichokes, French cheese, and *saucisson* in his briefcase. We would revel in the fact that we were probably the only people in the thirteen time zones of the Soviet Union eating artichokes at lunch. At the American embassy, Warren Zimmermann was the political counselor and would later be the last American ambassador to a unified Yugoslavia. His wife, Teenie, was clearly not a fan of Russia, but she did plan an excellent scavenger hunt that took us all around Moscow.

Among journalists, *Newsweek* correspondent Alfred Friendly Jr. and his wife, Pie, were especially fun to be around. Pie, an irrepressible Virginia belle, made every occasion festive. On July 4, for instance, she would bring out bunting and mosquito coils for their apartment on a high floor in Kutuzovsky. The Friendlys were from Washington aristocracy—Alfred's father, whom I had met when Katharine Graham visited London in 1966, had been the managing editor of the *Post* before Bradlee arrived—which meant that very fancy folks would always call on the Friendlys when passing through Moscow. They played bridge with the visiting Harrimans, to take one small example.

Jacques Amalric was the correspondent for *Le Monde*. His wife was a film critic. Their son, Mathieu, became a famous French film star. Paolo Garimberti was the correspondent of *La Stampa*, an Italian with an American's zeal for reporting. He later was editor of several Italian newspapers and director of a national television network. He and his wife, Daniela, had two sons, known as Frederico and Perchik.

There were other Americans—at *The New York Times*, the *Chicago Tribune*, and *Time*—along with a visiting British journalist, Jonathan Steele of *The Guardian*, and his wife, Ruth, who became lifetime friends. Jonathan was what is known in the UK as an "Old Etonian," a graduate of the country's top "public school" (that is, private school) for boys. He was an ardent leftist, however. Once, we were covering the KGB's disruption of an unofficial art show in a Moscow park. Jonathan waved his finger at the bulldozers and shouted, "Lenin would have been ashamed of you!" Another colleague, Lynne Olson of the Associated Press, would become a major historian of World War II.

The networks' coverage of Moscow in those years was erratic. Richard Roth was CBS's youngest correspondent. He used to quip that the only stories he could get on the air ended with this line: "Havana cigars they have plenty, but the Russians have never tasted Coca-Cola."

The four-person Reuters bureau was very good. I arranged that for fifty rubles a month, Ivan Fyodorovich could each day pick up their outgoing file of stories, which were valuable for my files.

At the first early sign of spring (when there was still a smattering of snow on the ground) our core group of friends would go on Sundays to a field outside Moscow that we called the cabbage patch, distinguished mainly by its proximity and some grass. What splendid Sundays they were. Benoit's cheeses, caviar by the spoonful from jars. We were in a place that fascinated us all and, for those afternoons at least, outside the sphere of work pressure and clumsy Soviet efforts at intimidation. After Katherine was born I had a personal revelation that working every day (with breaks for social activities and meals) was not in anyone's interest, so I decreed that from Saturday afternoon until Monday morning, I would stay away from the office except for a quick telex check, given that there was virtually no other way for me to know if anything was happening in the country or the world. A regular break made a real difference.

Suze had a complementary social network among Russians and expats and would set off in the Zhiguli to see them. As has always been the case, her reserved warmth and smile made every encounter better. I was the assertive one and Suze softened the edges. Years later, after I had become a publisher, I was ushered into the presence of the outgoing head of Britain's MI6 intelligence agency, who was planning to write a book. We had met before, he said, when he was undercover in the embassy. What do you remember about me? I asked. You were "very energetic," he replied, with British cool.

As I said, our contact with Washington was minimal. Foisie wanted to save on telex charges, so our messages from the foreign desk were terse: "held file" was one of the very worst. You would send a story with intensity in every word and that would be the home office response. It was a stupid policy and when I became foreign editor, my first pronouncement was to mandate warm greetings in reaction to every story. I understood, as I was told by a veteran correspondent, that "paranoia begins the minute you turn off 15th Street," where the *Post* was then located. From afar, reporters assumed that the foreign desk was a grumpy assemblage who considered the people far away as ne'er-do-wells, which was unfair to both parties.

Our arrangements, in addition to our short trips to Prague for R&R at the US ambassador's residence, included two annual "outs" in which the *Post* paid for us to travel to western Europe for a week or so as a break. We visited Craig and Heidi Whitney in Bonn, along with trips to London, the Côte d'Azur, and twice to Italy in the spring, which we especially loved. "Hopeless but not serious" was the affectionate description of Italian politics in the seventies, when the Italian Communist Party was the country's largest while everyone who could do so continued to have a very good time. The Gritti Palace, the swankiest hotel in Venice, would not allow us to bring Katherine to the restaurant or patio because the few remaining guests awaiting the communist takeover might be irritated. I made a démarche to the hotel manager, who then arranged a banquet for us and his family in a private dining room.

In the last weeks of Suze's pregnancy with Katherine, she went to Lakeside and I was to follow from Moscow. Her due date happened to coincide with a joint US-Soviet space mission called Apollo-Soyuz. The *Post* had an expert space correspondent, Tom O'Toole, but Foisie wanted me to stay on station for the link-up (which Bradlee memorably called the Americans finally sticking it to the Russians). I wanted to be on hand for the birth of my first child. Foisie said that my presence at the hospital was unnecessary; fathers, he said, were a "fifth wheel." I went anyway and arrived a day or so before Katherine did, on July 22, 1975. When I passed through Washington on our way back to Moscow, the word around was that "Foisie was down on me," a potentially lethal criticism in newsroom lexicon. Once again, the personnel file contained an unexpected memo written by Foisie to Mrs. Graham on July 18.

> Dear Kay:
> Thank you for spending so much time with Osnos on what must have been a busy day for you. It was a great boost to his morale. As you know, we send some of our very best abroad, including some of the bright young ones on whom the future of the Post may depend . . . I think it important for the Post and that you especially be alerted whenever one of the really good young correspondents comes to town so you can reacquaint yourself briefly and factor him (or her) into your thinking about the future.

This discovery decades later made me wonder again why or whether my impression was so wrong. Another mystery of human nature that cannot be solved.

For Evan's birth a year and a half later, we were scheduled to be in London for the Christmas holidays. We stayed in the senior Friendlys' townhouse on fancy Cheyne Walk. (They were away.) To add to the sizzle, on the day before I left I had been summoned to the

Foreign Office in Moscow and rebuked for "systematic anti-Soviet" journalism, apparently because I had written a piece at the time of Soviet leader Leonid Brezhnev's seventieth birthday, making jest of the fact he was being hailed as "middle aged" when his predecessor, Nikita Khrushchev, had been ousted at that age as too old.

The warning was serious and unusual enough to be reported by other news outlets in the United States. I received a telex of support from the foreign desk that said: "Meanwhile, eye [cablese for "I," so as not to be misunderstood as the number "1"] want to reaffirm what you already know. We think you are doing a magnificent job and we back you all the way. Your father called after hearing the news on the radio and eye reassured him that you are okay."

And I was, especially when Evan was born on Christmas Eve 1976 at Queen Charlotte's Hospital.

A few days later, Suze's mother arrived to help. The temporary nanny we had hired left a note saying that she did not intend to be a "factotum." I remembered there was an agency called "Solve Your Problem," and on very short notice they produced Marion Gales to help us, arriving with a suitcase and bearing a striking resemblance to Mary Poppins. She later accompanied us on our return to Washington in the summer.

Over our three years in Moscow, there were a half dozen or so themes to the coverage:

Relations between the United States and the Soviet Union. It was necessary every so often to take the temperature of superpower status rivalry. Our first year was the détente period, with the high point being a summit between President Gerald Ford and Leonid Brezhnev in Vladivostok in November 1974. Within a month, however, Brezhnev slipped out of sight with what turned out to be the first open evidence of his mental and physical decline, although he lived on until 1982.

By 1977, with Jimmy Carter in the White House elevating human rights as a core issue, the Soviets chose to crack down in a variety of ways on all the symbols in their view of détente—arresting dissidents, harassing Western reporters, turning the tap up and down on Jewish emigration, and asserting that those who left the country were "traitors." All this would prove to be the start of the last decade or so of the Cold War, but we did not know that at the time.

Soviet politics and the economy. We could not in any conventional sense cover the Kremlin. We did get signals about the prospects for various Soviet players among the geriatrics running the country and lesser figures. Vadim Nekrasov, a senior editor at *Pravda*, and I became sufficiently friendly for him to extend an invitation to his daughter's wedding. Then he abruptly disappeared. I never knew exactly what happened, but the suggestion was that Nekrasov had become a "heavy drinker." I doubt that was the reason.

Another contact in the Soviet press corps was Melor Sturua of *Izvestia*. (His unusual first name was an acronym for Marx, Engels, Lenin, October Revolution.) He was by any standards a flamboyant fellow of Georgian origins. He had a red Plymouth convertible with large fins, purchased on a trip to the United States, that was enough to stop traffic when it was parked near his downtown office. He wore a Rolex-type watch. Melor managed to hold on despite his penchant for the good life. After the collapse of the Soviet Union, he moved to Minnesota and became a college professor. The last I heard, he was still writing for *Izvestia*, at age ninety-one.

I've already written about Georgy Arbatov, a seasoned observer and the head of the Institute for US and Canadian Studies. What little we knew at the time about the inner dynamics of the Central Committee and KGB would likely have been gleaned from these "official" Soviets. What were their motives in dealing with me? Unlike dissidents, they never asked me for favors. Someone must have authorized seeing me, and in the case of Nekrasov, shutting him down.

I covered the economy by comparing reality with claims. The consumer market for ordinary Russians was crude. Eastern bloc goods were of especially poor quality. As for services: I once took a pair of shoes to be resoled and they came back with nails in them through the bottoms. And a suit sent to a "dry cleaner" was returned folded all wrong and without buttons. Suze cut my hair. She took care of her own. In having the Zhiguli repaired, we were advised to remove anything that wasn't attached to the machinery. We lost the windshield wipers, and the steering wheel of our little car was replaced by something from a truck. We were advised that we probably hadn't left enough vodka in the car to satisfy the mechanics. I did get a "Letter from Moscow" for the paper out of the experience, which was doubtless read more closely than my political thumbsuckers.

Fresh food was hard to find. All Russians carried what were known as "just in case" string bags on the chance that they might see oranges or bananas briefly for sale.

My lasting insight of those years was that the verb "to buy" was not the common term for shopping. Instead it was "to obtain" or "to acquire with difficulty." An extraordinary statistic I heard from Professor Stephen Kotkin of Princeton University was that at its peak, the Soviet economy was one-third the size of the American one, but by 2018, the Russian economy was one-fifteenth the size. So much of what the Soviets claimed for their economic achievements were what was widely known as *pokazuka* (for show), the Potemkin villages of facades that covered up widespread conditions from third world poor to shoddy first world style. The exception were the czarist-era palaces in Leningrad, the Bolshoi Theatre in Moscow, and the amazing and lavish metro stations.

Dissidents and defectors. The role of dissidents in our era was significant, not for their numbers or apparent impact on the Soviet citizenry but because Western reporters covered them so extensively, including me. There is no doubt that Andrei Sakharov, the great scientist, was one of the most important figures in the country, first for his work developing the hydrogen bomb and then for his outspoken belief in democratic reform. But in 1975 (when I met him) he was virtually unknown outside a small circle of intelligentsia and foreigners. And yet there is equally no doubt that it was his spirit and courage and those of others in his circle that highlighted the corrosiveness of the Soviet system. Sakharov and his fiercely determined wife,

Yelena Bonner, led a crusade in our years from their kitchen table in a small apartment where Sakharov wore cardigans and slippers.

There were many strands of dissident activity. There were ethnic groups like the Crimean Tatars who resisted Moscow's dominance; Jews who wanted to emigrate to Israel or the United States; progressive writers and artists navigating censorship; some religious fundamentalists. Like most assemblages of disruptive humans, the dissidents had noble qualities, but they were also complicated and often difficult. They were dissidents, after all. I have described Andrei Amalrik, brave and prescient in predicting the demise of the Soviet Union in 1984. (He was off by seven years.) But I didn't like him, personally, although reporters and dissidents were supposed to be friendly. Having decided that I was insufficiently sympathetic to his cause, he wanted to organize a petition denouncing me in the *New York Review of Books*, something he had done before his arrest about a *New York Times* reporter. Thankfully, he did not get a response from others he could use. It never happened.

After our Moscow tour I wrote an article for the *Columbia Journalism Review* making the point that our great admiration and access to the dissidents may have overstated their role in the country. What we now know is that the republics of the USSR were a much more varied group than we doubtless realized. The world would have better prepared for the many conflicts in the post-Soviet era in that vast empire—wars, nationalism, and oppression—if we had spent more time in the Central Asia and Caucasus states.

Amalrik wrote an indignant letter to the magazine. He died in exile in a car accident in 1980 in Spain.

The writers we came to know were an especially interesting group. Lev Kopelev and his wife, Raisa Orlova, were at the center of Russian "liberal" literary life. They had been especially close to the Kaisers and, while they certainly welcomed us into their orbit, I always had the feeling that we were considered more useful as suppliers of hard-to-get items and conduits for mailing material to the West—which we could do through the American embassy's postal system—than we were soul mates.

Vladimir Voinovich and Vasily Aksyonov were successful and popular authors despite being on the outer edges of doctrinal acceptability. Both left for the West but came back at least part-time after the fall of the Soviet Union and were widely read. At Random House I would publish three books by Aksyonov in English translations that were wonderfully well reviewed in the United States and Great Britain. The first was a nonfiction American travelogue called *In Search of Melancholy Baby*, for which I was the editor. Vasya and I had what was, in retrospect, a fascinating cultural clash over his chapter about the Washington, DC, motor vehicles bureau, where most of the staff were Black. I told him that his account of the DMV was racist and would seriously impact how his book would be received.

He said, "You are censoring me."

"No," I replied, "I'm protecting you."

"That's what they always say," he bristled.

As the editor I prevailed. The incident reflected how difficult it sometimes was to connect our different sensibilities. Vasya was a very fine writer. Critics compared his fiction to Tolstoy and Dostoyevsky. Suze and I nicknamed him Tolstoyevsky.

I will write a good deal about Natan Sharansky later in the book. Our relationship turned out to be the most important and lasting of my time in Moscow.

Looking back I now recognize the truly incredible courage it took for dissidents to challenge the Soviet state at its apparent pinnacle of power. Yet because these people were accessible to us and so much else about the Soviet Union was not, our perceptions of the situation across the country were not as deep or informed as our interactions in Moscow. We spoke Russian. We were able to travel (with permission and generally under surveillance). How different would our judgments have been if, for example, we lived in a village or provincial city for a month?

Soviet life and memorable travel. Despite the restrictions I tried as much as possible to write about the specifics of daily life. We attended a full week of what was available in Moscow theaters, for instance. This turned out to be more extensive than generally realized. Mikhail Bulgakov's daring *The Master and Margarita* was at the Taganka theater with more than a touch of subversive politics. There was a Russian translation of the Don Quixote musical *The Man of La Mancha*. Socialist realism there may also have been, but the takeaway of the week was more than that.

I wrote extensively about what Russians were reading, aside from dissident literature in the photocopied form known as *samizdat*. Besides Aksyonov and Voinovich, who were eventually banned, there were a number of writers of note who were able to skirt censorship by narrowing their scope to country life or carefully drawn historical themes. There were what was known as "thick" magazines like *Novy Mir*, which contained literary forays that were intriguing even when they were a bit dense or obscure. In a culture where there were so many formal limitations, part of the pleasure of reading was to see how far the boundaries could be moved.

I spent several months attending a local court in our neighborhood to gauge how the Soviet system of justice worked. I had a very difficult time writing the series until I came upon a concept put forward by Harold Berman, a professor at Columbia Law School: *Cannot the tyrant do justice?* Even tyranny needs a system of order. Much of European justice was based on the Napoleonic code, imposed by the French emperor in the early nineteenth century. Also, I concluded that in the United States, at least then, the more important a case was to the state—for example, Vietnam-era protest cases involving the great Dr. Benjamin Spock—the more likely it would be that the nuances of protocol would be followed, and justice ultimately done. But at the lower levels of American courts, defendants tended to be shuffled through without much regard for the niceties of the law. In the Soviet Union, a person stealing a loaf of bread would likely be chastised by the local court and ordered to do community service. From what I saw, there was in fact order, if not fairness. In political cases, like the dissident trials, the system was completely compromised by party control.

I wrote about the most important feature in the lives of urban families, what was known as *zhil ploshad*, living space measured in meters. Because of the history of communal apartments in shabby buildings, finding a place of habitable size was a major objective unless you were a member in some form of the Party hierarchy. In most apartments, as at the Sakharovs, the kitchen was the center of family life. The evening tables carried an array of herrings, pickles, and potatoes, accompanied by vodka or Georgian wines. These were the evenings we most enjoyed with the Russians we knew best.

When Suze was pregnant with Katherine, we undertook to try what was called the Lamaze method of preparing for delivery with the wife of a visiting American doctor. This turned out to be the basis for a great story: a Ukrainian-Jewish doctor working for the Ministry of Railways in the mid-twentieth century developed something he called "psychoprophylactic" childbirth in some way connected to the Pavlovian principle of "mind over matter": breathing exercises designed to minimize pain in delivery. In early 1950, the doctor, Ilya Velvovsky, was summoned to Moscow in a round-up of subversive Jewish doctors. Somehow, he persuaded his captors that his methods were pure Marxism, because the Bible says women should suffer in childbirth and his approach was natural and pain-free. So impressed were the authorities with this explanation that on February 14, 1951, they declared that henceforth all babies in the Soviet Union would be born according to psychoprophylactic standards. Velvovsky's work became known to Dr. Lamaze in France, and he traveled to Ukraine to study the method and popularized it in the West. In his books, he credited "Russian" innovations for the practice. Eventually a French biopic about Velvovsky was made and called *Red Doctor*.

Is every detail of this story verifiable? A quick contemporary Google check shows a number of scholarly citations, with a footnote about my story. Our guide was a Russian friend, Yuri Sokol, and his wife, an ice-skating coach. Piecing it together in a credible way was the fun of it, and since reliable information was so hard to get, reporting from Moscow on stories of this kind was an adventure.

We had considered the possibility of Katherine being born in a Moscow hospital, but decided against that when we read the report of an American diplomat's wife that leeches were being used to clean blood. As far as we could tell, the requirement that babies all be born according to Velvovsky's method was systematically ignored, although the box was always checked by nurses on official forms. Suze went to Lakeside for the birth, as I already described, and Evan was born in London. There were limits, it turned out, to our desire to immerse ourselves in Russian life.

Most of our trips in the Soviet Union left us with at least one indelible memory. In our first summer Suze and I went to Lithuania and the other Baltic republics. In Vilnius we met a young pianist at a recital who invited us to his home for supper and to meet his wife. It was a fun evening discussing American politics in what was the summer of Richard Nixon's disgrace. The pianist told us he would be giving a performance at a major Moscow concert hall in September and that we should come. He said he would arrange tickets for us. But to be sure, I ordered two tickets from the box office. On the night, we arrived to find that no tickets had been saved for us, so we used the ones we had bought. We went backstage but our "friend" had already left (fled). Somehow years later I found out (I don't remember how) from someone in Washington who knew the pianist that his sister had warned him off any contact with the dangerous American correspondent and his wife. It was one of those occasions when we never really could be sure of whether the KGB was involved or whether it was just a Soviet citizen's instinct for survival in a culture of fear.

A favorite trip came in our last winter, when David Shipler of *The New York Times* and I decided to go to the coldest place in the Soviet Union in February and describe life there. We flew to Yakutsk, a city in Siberia where the temperature was routinely 40 degrees below zero. It was so cold that if you took a cup of water outside with a plan for tossing it into the air, it would freeze before leaving the glass. I was wearing L.L. Bean boots with thick soles, which immediately cracked. The hotel was well insulated, which meant double- and triple-thick windows. Yakutsk life, as I remember it, was relatively relaxed by Soviet standards. A local journalist invited us to join a picnic in the taiga, the frozen woods outside town.

We made our way in a Russian jeep and unloaded in a clearing. Among other pleasures of the evening was a fish soup boiled over a campfire of gathered wood. Considerable amounts of vodka were consumed for warmth. This subfreezing evening was considerably less ambiguous than other evenings with "officials" when there was a risk that alcohol could be a prelude to some sort of provocation.

The Trans-Siberian Railroad is one of the great voyages of the globe, running all the way from Moscow to the Far East, a journey that takes a week. Suze and I decided to go halfway, to Novosibirsk, Siberia's most important city. The train was comfortable enough. We had a sleeping cabin in what was called "soft class." We soon made the acquaintance of a man returning home from Moscow and talked about many things with him. We gave him a copy of *Time* magazine. He said he was an engineer. I gave him my card and a few weeks later he called me at the office to say he was in Moscow and wanted to meet at a café up the street. After the opening exchange, he said he had lost his ticket home and asked if I could advance the cost of the trip. I understood that a photograph of me handing money to a Russian for nefarious purposes would have been a serious problem. Was he just a jerk who had squandered his cash on booze? I'll never know. I told him that asking an American for money could get him in big trouble. We parted ways and that was that. I did write a piece about this, among others, of what I called "chance encounters"—innocent or arranged? Bradlee was in that weekend, loved the piece, and stripped it across the top of the Sunday front page. The overnight telex telling me that was, well, beyond welcome.

Harassment. In Vietnam the major risks were those expected in a war zone. In Moscow the risks were harassment and bullying. I never

felt we were in real physical danger, although there were cases of reporters being drugged or caught in a staged car accident. As time
went on, the public pressures on us increased (as I said, we routinely
factored in surveillance). I was identified as Natan Sharansky's CIA
contact in *Izvestia* just before he was arrested, and again afterward. I
was called a spy in the weekly *Literaturnaya Gazeta*. A document I
later obtained from a Freedom of Information Act request shows that
the CIA did a check of whether I did, in fact, have any intelligence
connections. All they found about me in the files were clips and, in
another report, two occasions when I had apparently and unknowingly met CIA agents. One seemed to be at a roadside urinal in
Maryland. These things could be tricky. An occasional visitor to Moscow was General Sam Wilson, head of the Defense Intelligence
Agency. He would invite me to meet with him in the embassy's secure
"bubble," a safe place to talk. He was forthcoming. So, doubtless, was
I, although I had no "inside" information to share. I never thought of
this as collaboration with what the Russians called "special services."
But you never know what might end up in the files and how my role
might be described. I could have been considered an "asset" by American intelligence, although I certainly did not intend to be one.

The campaign reached its crescendo in the spring of 1977, when
the Soviets decided to crack down hard on the incipient human rights
movement that had followed the signing of the 1975 Helsinki Accords, which among other things committed the Soviets to respect
human rights. President Jimmy Carter's principled stance on the
issue added to the incentive to attack reporters and dissidents. After
the second major *Izvestia* attack on me while Suze and I were on a
break in Italy, I wondered whether we would be allowed back into the
country. We were.

A short time later, Maynard Parker, a top editor at *Newsweek*,
visited Moscow and said he had a message for me from Katharine
Graham. It was a little vague, but the essence was that she had been
told by a high-level Washington official that I was likely to be the
target of a major KGB provocation and should consider leaving the

country for the safety of myself and my family. Suze and I discussed this seriously and consulted with Christopher Mallaby, our closest friend among the diplomats. I felt that leaving or being expelled would be a short-term relief followed by a sense that we had somehow failed by giving in to intimidation and giving the KGB a pretext to disclose that we had helped dissidents by mailing packages for them and getting them medicines, which, as I have written, we did. I recently asked Christopher what he remembered of that conversation. Very little, he said, because his standard advice to his own staff with a KGB problem was, if at all possible, to find a way not to be intimidated or blackmailed. And that is probably what he said to me. He added that his wife, Pascale, remembered talking to Suze, who told Pascale something along the lines that the worst thing they could do is to expel us, and we were close to the end of our tour anyway. Admirable sangfroid.

Suze and I discussed the matter during a walk around the Kutuzovsky compound, to avoid listening devices, and we decided to stay. From then on, until our scheduled departure in late June, I did not drive, and whenever I was outside I kept my hands in my pockets so that nothing could be thrust into them (a standard KGB ploy). I'm sure we were being followed, but neither Suze nor I remember being especially unnerved by the tension. Why was that the case? Perhaps we thought that we were protected by being Americans. Perhaps it was the fact that I had had no contact on the subject with my editors in Washington that I can recall and found none in the personnel file. If my bosses—except for Mrs. Graham—were not especially concerned, why should we be? And finally, Suze's father was the chief American delegate to the Helsinki follow-up conference in Belgrade, where working conditions for journalists were a topic of discussion, although we hadn't—then—spoken to him on an open phone line about what was being said about me.

As our departure date approached, we made plans to take the office Volvo to Helsinki to trade in for a newer model, part of a regular arrangement. I was to take the train to Leningrad where I would meet our driver, Ivan Fyodorovich, and cross the border. One after-noon, my assistant Regina told me to go outside with her and said that she had strong reason to believe that I would have a problem at the border and should not go. I didn't ask her how she knew. We did want to exchange the car, so Suze asked the wife of a US diplomat to make the trip with her, which would assure some measure of protection. That is what happened.

Only in 2019 did I discuss this with Regina. We assumed that anyone working for us had an obligation to report from time to time, and Regina's employment as our office interpreter was overseen by UPDK, a KGB agency. Regina came to the United States in the late 1980s, invited by the actor Robert De Niro because of her extraordinary skill at simultaneous translation to work in theater and ballet productions. So, I asked, how did she know that an incident was in the offing? She said it was a conclusion she had reached because of the level of attacks on me in the press. In fact, Regina told me that she had always refused to be an informer. With a Latvian Jewish father and a Tatar mother, Regina was, by Russian standards of the time, exceptionally attractive. She was married to the famous Russian actor Mikhail Kozakov. Her refusal to cooperate, she said, apparently led the KGB to assume that she had some form of high-level "cover," as the Russians called these things. In 1980, when it was apparently clear that she did not have a protector, she was fired from UPDK and told she would never work for the government again.

One evening we finally called Suze's father in Belgrade and os-tentatiously said to him that we were being assailed and that he might want to tell his Soviet counterpart, Ambassador Mendelevich, that with working conditions for journalists on the agenda, harassment of his daughter and son-in-law was a mistake. I don't know what he did, but almost immediately—like a water tap—the attacks stopped. Meanwhile, Robert Toth, the *Los Angeles Times* correspondent, was also preparing to leave at the end of his tour and had just returned from a final trip to Siberia. He received a call from a contact who suggested they meet on the street where he would give him some documents about parapsychology, a field of interest for Toth. As soon as the documents were handed over, a car pulled up and Toth was hustled off to Lefortovo prison for interrogation.

That went on for several days. Toth was allowed to go home in the evening but was not permitted an American diplomat to accompany him in the prison. I have a photograph of a few of us reporters standing outside Lefortovo as the questioning went on inside. Bob had limited Russian but was required to sign the pages in Russian of his interrogation, which focused on his relationship to Natan Sharansky. Toth was a science specialist, and in one story (with Natan's help), he listed Soviet secret installations based on the places where Jews had been turned down for visas on security grounds. The headline on the story, which Toth did not write, of course, made this sound more revealing than it was. In any case, this "evidence" was used against Sharansky at his trial. Toth and his family were allowed to leave on schedule. Natan was sentenced to thirteen years in the gulag, of which he served nine, including three years in "punishment cells" and several long periods of being force fed.

After the former Supreme Court justice and UN ambassador Arthur Goldberg was brought in over Albert Sherer in Belgrade that fall—we had already left the Soviet Union—my spy identity was revived. A Soviet television documentary (which I managed to see) showed us with Katherine in a stroller on the way to visit Russian friends. The voiceover said that this looked innocent but was in fact a meeting to exchange espionage information. Even more bizarre, in 1979, when there was a cult incident in Guyana in which almost a thousand people died from poisoned Kool-Aid and a *Washington Post* reporter covered the story, a book published by the Soviet foreign ministry carried a picture of me (from an old visa) stating that I was the reporter's CIA handler when I was, in fact, foreign editor of the *Post*.

A report by the KGB on the Sharansky affair was eventually shown to Natan, who shared it with me. The tone was exuberant, calling the case against the Moscow Helsinki Group a complete triumph. Natan's principal accuser, a supposed dissident named Sanya Lipavsky, who had been recruited by the KGB in part because his father was facing a lengthy prison sentence for commercial crimes, was given a high Soviet award. The only mention of me was that a year after the arrests, I had written in the *Post* that the Lipavsky-Sharansky affair was a major story in the United States. So, the same fellow they were calling a spy was now cited as a source for their claims of success.

When I next visited the Soviet Union in 1987, accompanying Robert Bernstein, the founding chair of Helsinki Watch who by then was also my boss at Random House, I swept through customs while Bob was subjected to a thorough search.

After the fall of the Soviet Union in 1991, there was a brief period when the Kremlin's files were open to outside researchers. Fred Coleman of *Newsweek*, working on a book, came up with a lengthy document dated March 21, 1977, labeled "Top Secret" that reported in detail the Politburo's deliberations about what to do in response to President Carter's advocacy of human rights. Sharansky was designated as a major target for action. He was already in jail. And then there was consideration about what to do with "correspondent" Osnos and a young embassy political officer, Joseph Pressel, who maintained contacts with dissidents. They decided against my expulsion because of a likely US retaliation against a Soviet agent under cover as a journalist. Instead they approved a campaign to vilify me—*disaccreditatsia*—which was already underway. The document was signed by Yuri Andropov, the head of the KGB and later the general secretary of the Communist Party. The document is framed and on my wall at home. There was a clumsiness to the KGB campaign against correspondents like me: Sharansky said that KGB documents he was shown in preparation for this trial listed three American journalists as his collaborators—Shipler, Toth, and me—and said all three were Jewish. In fact, I was the only Jew. How serious was the danger to us in 1977? Sharansky and I decided the answer is "maybe." Had the Soviets wanted to make an indelible point about Carter's support for human rights, they might have made me an example by arresting me and forcing a confrontation. They did not. However, Toth's interrogation at Lefortovo was a sample of what might have happened.

In 2020, I tracked down a man named Vladimir Osnos in Moscow, the son of one of Russia's great chess masters. As I've noted, I have concluded that Osnos was a rare but not unique name in Russia. Once, at the height of the attacks on me, I had a call in the office from someone who said he was my cousin from Krasnoyarsk, the Siberian city where my father's brother had been exiled after serving in the Red Army. A call to me on an open phone from a "relative" at that time struck me as unlikely, so I said I had no relatives.

When I made contact with Vladimir and asked him whether in the 1970s anyone with the family name Osnos had been contacted by "authorities" about me, his response was classically ambiguous. In response to whether he had received my query, he wrote: "Yeah, I received your message. But I can say nothing concerning that."

A final note. All in all, the Soviet tactics seem crude in retrospect, at least as far I was concerned. I was glad we stayed and left on our own accord. For all that happened, those three years in Moscow were completely engrossing. In nearly every respect, I cannot imagine a better way for a reporter and his young family to spend the time than in so compelling a country.

Chapter 13

An Astonishing Cast of Russians

MOST MOSCOW CORRESPONDENTS aspire to finish their tour with a book addressing the question, "What are Russians really like?" I devised my own book plan: a portrait of the Litvinov family. Maxim, the patriarch, was a dapper (high-button shoes) diplomat who represented the Bolsheviks in London and was later Stalin's foreign minister. Surprisingly he was never purged, though he did sleep with a gun under his pillow in case the secret police came to arrest him, his widow, Ivy, told us. The Litvinovs were sent as envoys to Washington during World War II. Ivy was British and managed in the Stalin era to contribute stories to *The New Yorker*.

Ivy later moved to Brighton on the English coast. The rest of the family stayed in Russia, and her grandson Pavel was an early prominent dissident. Ivy was in her eighties when I visited her in Brighton and got shards of what was to be her memoir. I wrote a major story about the Litvinovs for the *Post*'s Style section, offering a hint of Ivy's less than completely conventional personal story. The family did not like my article and gave access instead to a British journalist who wrote what I thought was a mediocre account of a fascinating family.

Before I could regroup around another book topic, I was promoted to be the *Post*'s foreign editor and plunged into that job instead of taking the customary after-Russia leave. As I think about it now, all those stories in the newspaper reached a wide circulation of potential readers, whereas a book's circulation was likely to be limited. But the appeal and stature of a book remains the goal of a journalist, even today, in the digital age.

In the decades since leaving Moscow as a reporter in June 1977, I have stayed more engaged with Russians than I could have anticipated. As an editor and publisher I amassed quite a list of Russian authors: Boris Yeltsin (twice); Vladimir Putin in an early and misleading and nonetheless revealing self-portrait; Anatoly Dobrynin, the long-term and strikingly approachable Soviet ambassador in Washington; Georgy Arbatov of the USA institute; and some of the most significant Soviet dissidents, including Andrei Sakharov and Natan Sharansky, with whom I published four books.

Dusko Doder, one my successors for the *Post* in Moscow, wrote a particularly astute book about the Soviet Union called *Shadows and Whispers*. Dusko, with a Yugoslav background and fluent Russian, had a Slav's understanding of the late Soviet mindset and broke political stories no other Western reporter could get. I remember thinking when I saw a *Pravda* photograph of Konstantin Chernenko, the last in the succession of very old men ruling the country, that Dusko could reckon with those types because (no offense intended) they had the same "tailor," meaning, of course, much more than a fashion sensibility.

Years after leaving Moscow, an article published in *Time* magazine accused Dusko of having KGB connections that enabled him to get his scoops. He once drove past the Soviet defense ministry at night, saw that the lights were on, and calculated—correctly—that the country's leader, Yuri Andropov, had died, a full day before the official announcement. In Washington, a senior State Department official dismissed Doder's report, saying that the reporter must be smoking dope. The charge about the KGB was preposterous but personally hurtful and professionally damaging. Dusko had to use Britain's tougher libel laws to sue and eventually won the case. The whole episode took what seemed to me, at least, a considerable emotional toll. This was before the age of the internet, when this kind of scurrilous accusation has become routine.

At the height of the mania over Mikhail Gorbachev in the late 1980s I made several unsuccessful attempts to acquire a book by him, which was published elsewhere. The closest I came was to be a book coauthored with the Columbia professor Seweryn Bialer, who had access, he said, to the charismatic Soviet leader. We launched the project, but then sadly and mysteriously Bialer disappeared from public life. He died in 2019, and I never found out what had happened.

But I did publish two books by the first post-Soviet president of Russia, Boris Yeltsin. The first book, published in 1994, was called pompously *The Struggle for Russia*. The origins were characteristically murky for a Russian project. The actual seller or owner of the book was a Russian trading company based in New York that had secured the rights from we knew not where, but my colleagues and I made sure, as nearly as we could, that they were real. The book was Yeltsin's political vision for Russia as it emerged from the Soviet era. I would have to read it again to see whether his mission bore resemblance to the actuality. We published the book with some fanfare, and it was called "astonishing" by *The Wall Street Journal*, "intensely observant" by *The New York Times*, and "extraordinary" by *The Washington Post*. The Russian version was called *Notes of the President*, reflecting the fact that the book was meant to be a diary of his thoughts from 1991 to 1993. Sales were modest, which was okay because whatever it was the Russian businessmen wanted from the project they had probably gotten.

Andrew Nurnberg was Yeltsin's London-based (and very legitimate) literary agent and friend who had developed a close relationship with the Russian president. Andrew had studied Russian and was by any measure one of the most imaginative and endearing characters in the book business.

To mark the book's worldwide publication, Andrew arranged for a French restaurateur (who was a client) to stage a lavish multicourse meal for the various publishers in a ceremonial hall at the Kremlin. This annoyed the Kremlin chefs sufficiently for them to insist on matching every French course. The result was that the diners— including Yeltsin, his wife, Naina, and the other guests—consumed a great deal of food, wine, and vodka. A blonde in white mini boots entertained with an accordion. Yeltsin ordered his defense minister, Pavel Grachev, to make an adulatory toast to the president. We knew and Grachev did not that he was described in the book as a limp figure destined to be fired. If you have seen the film *The Death of Stalin*, a brilliant farce about events surrounding Stalin's demise, our Kremlin banquet had quite the same feeling, although no one was ultimately shot.

The morning after the banquet, the guests were escorted to a stone villa stained green on the grounds of the compound where we were staying. This was Stalin's dacha, where he collapsed and died in March 1953. A docent in a dark blouse with a white lace collar and virtually no affect let us look around.

This was definitely not a customary tourist destination. The feeling I had was that aside from emptying the ashtrays and occasional dusting, nothing had been touched since the day Stalin died more than forty years earlier. The dictator did not have a conventional bedroom. He would sleep on couches around the house and on the porch. We stared, mouths agape, at the divan covered in a Persian rug where he expired. Hitler killed himself in a bunker. Standing at the place where Joseph Stalin drew his final breath left us awestruck. The most famous photo image of the dacha had been taken outside, with Stalin's young daughter Svetlana sitting on the lap of Lavrenty Beria, the KGB murderer of the 1930s purges.

Yeltsin's second book was called *Midnight Diaries*, and it was published in the fall of 2000, after he had turned over the presidency to Vladimir Putin. Yeltsin's daughter Tatiana and his close adviser Valentin Yumashev (they later married) were in charge of this book's progress. When they came to New York to work with us, they stayed in a boutique hotel on the East Side, took taxis, and enjoyed a family-style dinner with us at a Vietnamese restaurant. The point was that if the Yeltsin family and his cronies had enriched themselves as so many had in the post-Soviet years, they restrained their profligacy at least on that trip.

On a Sunday afternoon as this second book was completed, Andrew Nurnberg and I were invited to Yeltsin's dacha outside Moscow. It was spacious, but not grandiose. There were children's shoes and boots in a pile by the front door, along with a stack of videos on a table. Yeltsin greeted us warmly in his library, and we spent a casual hour or two discussing his book and his decision to step down from the presidency. In my somewhat labored Russian I told him that Americans thought that the way he came to power—declaring for democracy—and how he left, by his own choice at the turn of the millennium, were symbolic of an honorable career. He said he had anointed Putin as his successor because in the scrum of potential leaders, Putin was the one who had shown the most spine while the others were sycophants. He felt Putin had the kind of self-confidence that a new Russian leader would need. It has been said and widely believed that Putin promised Yeltsin that he and his family would not face criminal penalties for their activities in the 1990s. And it is also said that Yeltsin stashed vast sums in overseas accounts. I have no idea if any of this is true. But there was no sign of excess luxury in what I saw of his personal lifestyle. After his death, Tatiana and Yumashev moved to Austria, I read, and went into the real estate business, among other things.

When *Midnight Diaries* was published, Yeltsin came to the Frankfurt Book Fair, the largest international gathering of publishers. He seemed somewhat dazed. His speech was slurred. The prevailing view was that Yeltsin was succumbing to years of alcohol abuse and old age. He was in his late sixties. There was no doubt that Yeltsin was a very heavy drinker, and he acknowledged this in his book. I never saw him again, but Andrew told me that he had an operation on his heart in Germany that involved some rewiring and in his last year or so he seemed much improved. His mind and speech were clear.

Was Boris Yeltsin a great man? He did guide Russia through a nearly bloodless revolution. In the chaos of the first post-Soviet years, he really had no idea or template for how to reinvent a nation as vast and complex as Russia. The freedoms enjoyed in that decade were genuine. There was a lively cultural and media scene. But the flip side was what might be called severe discombobulation. There was no coherent environment for economic stability. State-owned enterprises were sold off for ridiculously low prices, enabling the rise of what became known as the oligarchs, Russians who made billions in those years every which way. They used graft, corruption, bullying, and ingenuity to take control of vast industries and resources. My view was that there was no real possibility that the upheaval that demolished the Soviet Union could evolve smoothly into a modern democratic nation. And the triumphant Western nations were too satisfied with the Kremlin's downfall to create a system of economic assistance to assure the development of a true market society.

Perhaps someone else could have made that happen—Gorbachev, maybe—but Yeltsin was not the one to succeed. I do believe that at his core, Boris Yeltsin was a good person, a human in the round. And his failures were not exclusively his.

While Andrew and I were in Moscow for the Yeltsin visit, we stayed in what had been a KGB guest house, which had a world-class sauna and no other guests. Over a meal we discussed with Yumashev—a media adviser to Putin as he had been to Yeltsin—how the new Russian leader might introduce himself to the West. Should he write a book? Yumashev asked. I said no, because everyone would know that he did not actually write it. Instead I suggested that Putin sit for open-ended interviews with several major Russian journalists for what would be a self-portrait complete with family photos. This would provide a sense of the man that was not just rhetorical bluster. Putin agreed and the book was published as *First Person*. It appeared all over the world. I felt it showed a measure of Putin's personality that was candid enough to be believable. That was the general reaction to the book. Bob Kaiser's review in *The Washington Post* said that the book revealed a much less attractive image of Putin than I thought it did, despite smiling pictures of his wife and daughters and his description of himself as a solid reformer. History has proven Kaiser right.

In the American market the book's sales were modest. As an aside, a startup digital publisher decided to invest $500,000 in marketing an e-book with large ads in *The New York Times* and *The New Yorker*. This idea was very, very far ahead of its time and as I recall, the net sales were thirty-seven copies.

As I write, Putin has exceeded Stalin's time as Russia's *vozhd*—supreme leader. Through his wiles and guiles, he has restored Russia's place as a major power in the world, flush with oil revenue, devoid of principles that were the hope, at least of the dissidents, for genuine democracy.

My only encounter with Putin was at a dinner at "21" in New York hosted by Tom Brokaw in 2002 or 2003 for a group of journalists. My takeaway was Putin's bluntness and dry-eyed approach to every issue. He sneered rather than smiled when he said that Boris Berezovsky, a prominent oligarch, "doesn't pay taxes to us and he doesn't pay taxes to Israel either. Why should he get away with that?" Berezovsky eventually died in the UK under mysterious circumstances, a broken man. One by one, the Yeltsin-era moguls and leading political figures were driven into exile, sent to prison, or murdered. It's Putin's show now.

Those cozy family pictures in *First Person* seemed ironic when Putin left his wife for a young ice skater; his daughters, it was said, became vehicles for securing a fortune abroad. I often wondered, what could Putin possibly buy with all those billions? Russia is much smaller than the Soviet empire was. But it is still a formidable factor in the world, a complex mix of sinister, shrewd, and oafish. There is much about Russia to admire in its history, its culture, the bravery of its people in war, and their stoicism. And much to deplore.

Anatoly Dobrynin was the Soviet ambassador in Washington from 1962 to 1986 and certainly had the most enduring presence of any Russian in the United States during the Cold War. He knew everybody and was involved in every great event of that very long period. Dobrynin had the kind of personality that made him seem more pragmatic and accessible than his association with the Kremlin would suggest. After leaving the ambassadorship, Dobrynin retained the high-powered literary agent Morton Janklow, and I acquired and edited his book. Given that Dobrynin arrived in Washington in 1962 as the youngest-ever Soviet ambassador and the book was published in 1995, the full range of his experience was vast.

Dobrynin's draft was written in Russian and the translation was diligently worked over by Larry Malkin, a long-time writer for *Time* magazine and the *International Herald Tribune*. He is a journalist of skill and exuberant energy, demonstrated in the number of books he and I worked on together. To be sure we had the history right and an appropriate tone, we asked the longtime *Washington Post* diplomatic correspondent Don Oberdorfer to help us with verisimilitude. I remember days of working with Dobrynin, Larry, and Don at the Malkins' dining room table in a Murray Hill apartment. Dobrynin was a pleasure to deal with. He understood what we needed without resorting to dissembling, prevarication, or defensiveness. Did we get a full story? Probably not, but I believe we got as close as anyone could. The closing paragraphs of the book are full of optimism about the democratic consensus (after the fall of the Soviet Union) between the values of Russia and the United States. Today those comments feel ironic in many ways—hope deferred at best. Dobrynin was featured on *60 Minutes* and had a full publicity launch for the book, which was titled *In Confidence*. It was a *New York Times* Best Book of the Year, and one reviewer wrote, "No other ambassador in modern times has played such a prolonged and crucial part in international affairs and has been prepared to write about it so uninhibitedly . . . The most revealing account of 40 years of the cold war to come out of Russia." I don't recall whether it was published in Russian, but I expect it was.

I consider three European men of the twentieth century to be especially instrumental in bringing about the fall of the Soviet empire in the 1980s. There were, of course, many others who played significant roles, but my three are Pope John Paul II, George Soros, and Andrei Sakharov. I saw the pope only once, from a distance, on his trip to Poland in 1979. I watched him as one of a very few reporters who were allowed in a cell at Auschwitz where he prayed on behalf of Maximilian Kolbe, a priest who had died there and was beatified by the pope. John Paul showed the fallacy of Stalin's remark that popes had no "divisions" to send into battle. In those sunny spring days in 1979, virtually the entire Polish nation turned out to see John Paul make his way through his native country. That outpouring showed the extent of his charisma, and it was easy and correct to conclude that the fall of Polish communism was inevitable. The Solidarity movement led by Lech Walesa was launched a few months later, and in 1989 the communists were overthrown. Though John Paul was very conservative on most doctrinal matters, he was also an icon of resistance to communism, the most powerful force to take on the Soviets. Sadly, that did not ignite a lasting affinity for humanitarian values and openness in his world. In Poland, the church that was a symbol of opposition in the Soviet era has aligned with the right-wing forces that have dominated Polish politics in recent years.

George Soros was in many ways the beau ideal of all latter-day communists—a very, very rich man. What the Soviets and Eastern Europeans did not understand about Soros was that his genius for making money was matched by his passion for the "open society," as described by the philosopher Karl Popper. In the years of *glasnost* and *perestroika* and the early years of the post-Soviet era, Soros created an infrastructure of civil society organizations and support for democratic ideals and artistic creativity. What the communists and their early successors missed was that George was subversive to their ideology, a radical as well as a billionaire.

In effect what Soros did was establish the sorts of enterprises that the communists and their repressive counterparts elsewhere abhorred. But because Soros was breathtakingly rich, he was able to do it. Increasingly after 2000 as the politics in these countries deteriorated from early hopefulness, pressure on the open society enterprises grew and many had to be curtailed or shut down. Still, an entire generation of people saw what was possible in progressive reform and that impact had some indelible qualities.

Suze and I first met George through our mutual involvement with Human Rights Watch. George used his early involvement with what started as Helsinki Watch in the early 1980s as a tutorial in the language and practice of human rights advocacy. My long-term engagement with him began in 1998, soon after the launch of the first season of my new publishing house, PublicAffairs. We had just published *The Starr Report*, an instant reprint of the independent counsel's investigation of President Clinton and a number one bestseller. A few weeks after that, I received a call from Kris Dahl, a literary agent at ICM, who said that George Soros had written a book called *The Crisis of Global Capitalism*, about the international financial melodrama then unfolding. The book was under contract to Random House to be published in April 1999, but Soros wanted it out sooner. Random House said they would move the book up to January, but he was not satisfied. Kris suggested I contact George and offer to publish the book.

"How soon do you want it out?" I asked him. *How about a week from Monday* was his answer, to coincide with the World Bank/IMF meetings scheduled in Washington. There was a finished manuscript. Our editor, Geoff Shandler, took it home for the weekend. On Monday morning, our managing editor, Robert Kimzey, found a copy shop that said it could produce 5,000 bound pamphlets in five days, one of which was Yom Kippur, when the shop was closed. I said to George that it really wasn't necessary to give the whole book away at the meetings. How about putting the first chapter on everyone's chair instead? He agreed, and that is what happened. We published the full book in hardcover in November, by which time we had licensed the foreign rights in thirty-seven countries. In the United States it was a national bestseller with about 60,000 copies sold. Perhaps most astonishing, George decided that his conclusion had been wrong about the scale of the crisis, and we published a revised version the following year. My thought then and since was that the way to deal with George Soros when it comes to books is "Say yes. Cope later."

Suze's and my relationship with George has lasted ever since, and I published another half-dozen hardcovers and several paperbacks. In them he continued to pursue and clarify his guiding philosophical thesis called "reflexivity"—the way events and trends influence how markets sway—often with unintended consequences. Knowing how to make the right calls was a source of Soros's genius and vast wealth.

George's writing was treated with condescension by some reviewers and philosophers until the great international recession of 2008–9 turned out to be a validation of his sense of how market distortions such as subprime mortgages can convulse economies. George was very pleased to be rich, very engaged, and proud of his open society philanthropy and activism. But I think he took exceptional pleasure in finally being vindicated as a philosopher.

Every summer, Suze and I were invited for a weekend at George's Southampton home. These were invariably fascinating. The vibe managed to be elegant and yet surprisingly informal. At lunch, he tended to be barefoot, having just returned from a swim in the Atlantic. George was an excellent host and particularly after he married his third wife, Tamiko, seemed to be having a good time, jousting over long meals with his guests. He did not appreciate the vagaries of age affecting his hearing and eyesight. These new limitations challenged him but did not slow him down. He continues to be a completely engaged and expert citizen of the world.

George has become a major nemesis to the global right wing, which deploys a mix of conspiracy theories and anti-Semitic tropes to discredit his activities on behalf of progressive causes and civil society. The reality is that George is influential because of his beliefs and his money. But the notion that he is a mastermind of everything the right-wingers around the world reject is nonsense. The attacks are not easy to ignore, especially when a bomb was placed in the mailbox at his home in Bedford. Yet George has shown extraordinary equanimity (at least as I could measure it) in almost every way. Michael Vachon, Soros's very savvy longtime adviser on media and politics, said one evening as we sat at dinner, "George, no one is ever going to feel sorry for you" having to endure the slings and arrows of fame and fortune.

What did bother George, I thought, was that in his homeland of Hungary, the autocratic leader Viktor Orbán, who had once studied at Oxford as a Soros-funded fellow, made George the focus of his nativist political strategy. This also included the completely spurious suggestion that his father's protection of the family in World War II somehow involved a glancing Nazi contact. This was too personal an affront for George to ignore. He sued several times to stop the defamation. In time, I came to understand that George's father, Tivador Soros (born Schwartz), was the most direct influence on his character—as George would say explicitly. His father's successful protection of the family when the Nazis were rounding up Hungary's Jews was, George believed, the basis of his own daring and risk-taking in finance and life generally. How "great personages" relate to family is almost always a valuable insight to them.

George has been married three times. As I said, from what I have seen, he and Tamiko are as close as any outsider can imagine a couple to be. His son Alexander, whose mother Susan Weber was George's second wife, has emerged as his heir in philanthropy, serving as deputy chair of the Open Society Foundations, founded by George after the collapse of communism in Eastern Europe. Now in his midthirties, Alexander has a PhD in history from Berkeley. His siblings have forged their own way in finance and philanthropy. Bearing an illustrious name and vast wealth across generations is almost always a challenge, but I think George Soros's family and friends recognize what an extraordinary man he is.

I met Andrei Sakharov in 1974. He was already a dominant figure in the Soviet human rights movement. As a physicist responsible for so much nuclear research, he had received every honor the Kremlin could bestow. The depth of his courage and integrity in defying the Soviet system cannot be overstated. His base was a small apartment (by any Western standard) in central Moscow that he shared with Yelena Bonner, his second wife and as much a "La Passionaria" as Sakharov was outwardly reflective and scholarly. In 1975, Sakharov received the Nobel Prize for Peace but was not permitted to travel to

Oslo to accept the award. Yelena was out of the country being treated for eye problems, so she accepted the award on his behalf. A few weeks later we invited the Sakharovs to our apartment for a small dinner. The only other guests were our Italian friends the Garimbertis. Yelena wore the same outfit in which she had accepted the Nobel Prize. Andrei wore a suit and a tie Yelena had brought home from abroad. It turned out that this was, if not the first time the Sakharovs were in an American journalist's apartment, the first time they were free to explore all the fixtures that would not be found in an ordinary Moscow flat.

The dinner was fine. But the part of the evening that I remember best was Sakharov's fascination with the stacked washer/dryer in the bathroom. He stuck his head inside and carefully examined the wiring. "Nobel-winning Physicist Encounters Washing Machine" could have been the headline. In the Moscow years I was always respectful of Andrei, a little wary of Yelena's wrath.

In the fall of 1976, Robert Bernstein, the CEO of Random House, who as a publisher and a person was becoming increasingly interested in issues of human rights, came to Moscow, accompanied by his wife, Helen, who shared his devotion to these principles. Suze and I were among the names they had been given to look up. Over the next week, as they met Sakharov, Sharansky, and others, we became friendly. Their curiosity and charm were immensely appealing to us, and I certainly was aware that Bob was one of the major figures in the publishing world. On one of their last days in Moscow, Bob said to me, "Journalism is not a fit profession for a grown man. If you decide to get serious, call me." He was sort of joking, I think. But I heard him and remembered that offer.

Over the decades, until he died at age ninety-six in May 2019, Bob had more influence on me than perhaps he realized. As was the case with Izzy Stone and Ben Bradlee, I had absorbed lessons from him he may not have realized he was giving.

Bob grew up in a comfortable New York family. His grandfather, a businessman, supported Jews escaping from Europe in World War II. Bob went to Harvard and served as a noncommissioned officer in the army in South Asia. He started in sales at Simon & Schuster, and when he moved to Random House he earned the confidence of Bennett Cerf and Donald Klopfer, the company's founders. He became CEO in 1966 and led Random House's extraordinary growth until a different owner, Si Newhouse, decided in 1989 to replace him with Alberto Vitale, who was running Bantam Doubleday Dell.

At Random House Bob was regarded with a mix of respect for his authority and some bemusement that he would open every sales conference not with a discussion of profits and losses, but rather with a speech about human rights.

In his way, Bob was a philosopher. He would say that if you have to fire someone you had hired, it is at least 50 percent your fault for the mistake. He was about six-foot-four and counseled me that whenever he and I were in a photograph together, I should lean forward a bit, so the height discrepancy would be less notable. After I joined Random House in 1984, Bob kept an eye on me but essentially let me find my own level of acceptance in the company.

Bob was one of the founders of Helsinki Watch in New York and became the chair of Human Rights Watch as it developed into one of the world's most influential nongovernmental organizations. He shocked his colleagues at Human Rights Watch in 2009 when he published an op-ed in *The New York Times* attacking the organization's criticism of Israel. He said that because Israel was a democracy under permanent siege from its Arab neighbors, its actions and policies should be treated in a different fashion from other countries in the Middle East. Human Rights Watch had the view that all countries should be judged equally when the issue was human rights. For the next decade his relations to the organization were frosty.

In 2019, I persuaded Bob that he could take the same position with Human Rights Watch that he had taken in an earlier difference of opinion with the American Civil Liberties Union: that while he disagreed with the organization on some matters, he was still very much a supporter of its mission and goals. Robert Kissane, the chair of Human Rights Watch, invited Bob to sit at his side at the annual

New York dinner, and Bob was recognized and applauded. This gesture made it possible in obituaries three months later to say that Bob had reconciled with the group he had founded.

My relationship with Andrei Sakharov moved into another phase a decade after our first meeting, when the Alfred A. Knopf division of Random House was preparing to publish Sakharov's memoirs, which Bernstein had secured with a handshake on one of his visits to Moscow. By then I was working at Random House and was recruited to help on the complex project.

In the years since agreeing to write the book, Andrei and Yelena had been sent into internal exile in Gorky, where their lives had been difficult, including the forced feeding of Sakharov when he went on a hunger strike. When Yelena later wrote a book of her own about that period, she called it *Alone Together*, the right metaphor.

As Gorbachev launched the perestroika process, he allowed a phone to be installed in the Sakharovs' apartment in Gorky. By phone, with a KGB guard still outside, Gorbachev invited Sakharov to return to Moscow to "resume your patriotic work." The security immediately was withdrawn, and Andrei and Yelena resumed their activism, as Gorbachev had promised they could.

I was not Sakharov's main editor; that was Ash Green of Knopf, who was a master of editorial skills and specialized in serious nonfiction. I was brought in to move what had become an intractable process along: to be the enforcer. The tenacity that makes you a Nobel laureate, a scientist, and a leading dissident in the Soviet Union made Sakharov a difficult person to persuade. And Yelena was even tougher. My role did not make me popular with some members of the Sakharov family and others in America who saw me as a crass commercialist. Ash had called his experience trying to get the Sakharov translation finished his Vietnam. He, Sakharov, and I once spent an hour wrangling over the difference between describing scientists working "furiously" and working "with abandon," the phrase we finally settled on.

In October 1987, when Bob, Helen, Ash, and I traveled to Moscow, we were joined by the Bernsteins' close friend, the great actress

Claudette Colbert, who had not visited Russia before. We spent a memorable dinner in the Sakharovs' kitchen with Claudette and Yelena's mother, Ruf Grigorevna, a wiry, spry woman of the same vintage as the movie star. Ruf had spent a decade in the gulag, smoked cheap Russian cigarettes, and had a hacking cough that shook the bench she and Claudette were sitting on—a cozy yet broad spectrum of twentieth-century women's experience. After three days, Claudette had enough of the Soviet Union and we managed to get her aboard an Air France flight days ahead of her planned departure. At customs she could not produce a piece of jewelry that she had declared and had gone missing from her hotel room. The customs officer threatened not to let her leave. I was escorting her. She was in tears. I grabbed her elbow and rushed past the desk to a waiting Air France official. Fortunately, I was not then detained.

(Two months later, Gorbachev was on a state visit to Washington, and Claudette was invited to the state dinner at the White House and seated at the head table. Bob remarked that she was there representing the "room service constituency.")

The Bernsteins, the Sakharovs, and I went to Leningrad for the weekend. I was the translator. My Russian must still have been good enough. I had a chance to watch the great Andrei Sakharov in repose. For all his global stature, Sakharov was unrecognized on the street. His picture had rarely been published. We went to museums, a palace, a concert, and most memorably had dinner at what was probably the first "private" restaurant in Leningrad. Our other guest that evening was David Cornwell—aka John Le Carré (also a Knopf author), who was researching the book that became *The Russia House*. I had met him in London in the early eighties and we were all in the same hotel. There is a photograph of us all at the table. What a night! Sakharov and Le Carré talked about spies, particularly Klaus Fuchs, a scientist who was a Soviet agent in Britain and the United States after World War II.

At one point, the Soviet government allowed Sakharov to travel to the United States, which made everything less cumbersome. Knopf put him up at the Regency Hotel on Park Avenue. I once saw the great physicist emerge from a closet with the luxury hotel–supplied fabric covers for shoes on his hands, wondering what they were for. Really.

I asked Andrei what he found the most impressive thing he had encountered in the United States. His scientific counterparts at MIT was his first thought. Then he added that the second most impressive thing were Yelena's grandchildren and their classmates at Phillips Andover, one of the country's best boarding schools. It was their curiosity and optimism he so admired—in contrast, I suspect, to elite students in Soviet schools.

Finally, the book was ready to be published when the Sakharovs decided they wanted to add a detailed description of the time since their return from their exile in Gorky, which would have meant another delay. So, we agreed to begin work on what became a short second volume. I felt that his memoir was of great importance, but the front-page review in *The New York Times* reached a different conclusion. The reviewer was James Billington, the librarian of Congress and a Soviet expert. Here was his devastating quote: "The result is a bulky volume likely to incline most readers to settle for the excerpts already published in *Time*."

Sakharov died in 1989, at the age of sixty-eight, but Yelena lived on until 2011, when she died at eighty-eight in Boston. She did what was possible to preserve Sakharov's legacy, although, alas, it is no longer a theme of contemporary Russian life.

Natan Sharansky and I worked on four books together, starting with his prison memoir that we titled *Fear No Evil* from the Twenty-third Psalm, which he would repeat when he was subjected to torture of mind and body. Natan is the bravest person I have ever known. We all ask ourselves how we would react to terror. Sharansky decided on his first day in captivity, charged with treason, a capital offense: They cannot humiliate me. Only I can humiliate myself. Over time he and I came to understand each other better than we possibly could have at the outset. My sense is that for much of the time we worked together he was too embedded in his own life to truly value our friendship. As we both became grandfathers with a clearer sense of our joint past, I think he recognized the nature of our relationship—two men of common Jewish heritage with sharply different lives. Natan is as close to being a personal hero of mine as I have ever allowed myself to have, for his courage, his demonstrated integrity of conscience, an unusual wit for so public a man, and—selfishly—for our being linked forever together in that top-secret Politburo/KGB document acknowledging at the highest level that we were a problem. Only he went to prison.

I met Natan shortly after arriving in Moscow. At the time he was known by his Russian name, Anatoly, and his friends called him Tolya. He was introduced to me at a going away party for Alec Goldfarb, who had received an exit visa after acting as the contact between Jewish refuseniks and the Western media. Tolya was to be Alec's successor. My first impression was of meeting a man in his midtwenties, short and balding who did not seem to have the natural presence of Goldfarb, who, among other things, had a way with women. *You're the spokesman?* I thought. I quickly understood, however, that Tolya had an inner spirit that I would like. I had encounters with him in the first two years, as did other reporters, but it was in the third year when our relationship became significant.

Tolya's beloved wife, Natasha, had left for Israel the day after their wedding, but the Soviet government refused to allow him to join her. She was not born Jewish but converted, and over the years became more observant than Sharansky, who had an embedded secular side. For Natan (as he was to become), emigration was as much about freedom and cultural identity as about religion.

Because he was so smart and inherently politically astute, Sharansky also became a link to the "Helsinki" dissidents, people like Sakharov and Yuri Orlov, another scientist. They saw in the Kremlin's signature on the Helsinki Accords a means of leverage to reform the Soviet Union, particularly its respect for human rights. No other figure of the time so straddled the two strands of Moscow-based dissent—the right to emigrate and democratic change.

This unusual position made Sharansky an almost inevitable target of KGB wrath. It would not be enough to get rid of him with a visa, as they did with Goldfarb and other Jewish activists. His relationship to Sakharov and the reform movement was especially vexing to the Kremlin, because he was so good at what he was doing.

At some point in the fall of 1976, Natan moved into an apartment with Sanya (Sasha) Lipavsky, who as I mentioned earlier turned out to be a KGB informer and the principal witness against Sharansky in his trial. He was a doctor from Central Asia who said he had applied to emigrate and had been turned down. Lipavsky was a warm, ingratiating fellow. He provided medical care to refuseniks and had a job in a clinic until he was fired. Lipavsky was the person who had given me the highly revealing document on the meat content of sausages. Suze and I met Lipavsky at the home of another dissident as he made his way into the core of the dissident movement.

In early February, Lipavsky and Sharansky came to our apartment for dinner. Lipavsky brought roses, not a common sight in a Moscow winter. Evan was only a month old. Natan held the baby very carefully and said, "I wonder if I'll have one of these . . ." That was the last we saw of them before Natan was arrested. A few weeks later *Izvestia*, the government newspaper, published an excerpt from Lipavsky's "open letter" asserting that Sharansky was a spy and that I was an envoy of American "special services." Natan's arrest and imprisonment followed. And I was in the crosshairs of the *disaccreditatsia* process the Politburo had decreed for me.

Years passed. When Natan was finally released from the gulag in 1986, he immediately emigrated to Israel and secured a very prominent literary agent, Marvin Josephson, the chair of ICM. Bob Bernstein, Marvin, and I flew to Israel to make the deal. For me that first encounter after nine years was emotional. For Natan, I believe he was still too dazed to absorb the reunion. On some level Natan may have felt that I and others, both Russian and Western, had left the Soviet Union unscathed while he endured the cruelties of a long prison sentence. But he never said a word about that.

We made a million-dollar deal for US rights, a very expensive acquisition. Natan wrote the first draft in Russian. Each day in his new life, he would spend several hours immersing himself in the gulag years. In a matter of months there was a full draft. In the first of what became many sessions, he read the Russian to me and I tried to edit as we went along. Next, the manuscript was given a literal translation by an Israeli writer, Stefani Hoffman. I realized that we would need an expedited process to take this first draft to a finished manuscript for a Western, particularly American, audience. At that time Bill Novak was the hottest name in book collaboration (ghostwriting), having worked with Lee Iacocca on his blockbuster autobiography and with Speaker of the House Tip O'Neill on his memoir *Man of the House*, which became one of my first big Random House bestsellers. Novak told me that his two dream projects were to write a book with Paul McCartney of the Beatles and one with Natan Sharansky.

I told Bill that I could arrange for him to work with Sharansky on what was surely a below-market rate for him—$100,000 would be the most I could pay. He agreed, and together with Natan we rendered the book into an exemplary narrative. That said, I do remember one particularly animated editing session in a Jerusalem hotel room. I tried to get Natan to do some pruning of the text for purposes of clarity. He refused and finally declared: "The KGB couldn't break me, and you won't either." He was right, although the book did get shorter.

Fear No Evil was scheduled to be published in the spring of 1988. My colleagues and I chose a dust jacket with slightly rough paper suggesting a prison wall, and no other adornment other than the title.

We planned a major rollout. I sat for several hours as Natan was interviewed by Diane Sawyer for *60 Minutes*, the top-rated news program. Natan was invited to be a featured author at the annual convention of the American Booksellers Association, which was a signal that this was going to be a major title. Random House hosted a lavish cocktail party. The ABA convention that year was in Anaheim, California, and my favorite memory of the occasion was watching Evan, age eleven, and Natan together in a small boat in Disneyland's "Pirates of the Caribbean" ride.

As the publication date drew near, Ronald Reagan and Mikhail Gorbachev were in a courtship of superpower leaders. Reagan scheduled a trip to Moscow in what was to be our publication week. The Sawyer piece was dropped as insufficiently startling. The *New York Times* review by the novelist Robert Stone was fine, I thought, but dryer than I would have liked. Reading it again now, I realize that it was beautifully written; Stone concluded that Sharansky had "advanced the cause of all humanity."

I was nervous. The cancellation of *60 Minutes* was an ominous publicity setback. The images of Reagan and Gorbachev strolling through Red Square together were not the right backdrop for a dissident's description of Soviet repression.

The book did respectably well yet fell well short of our commercial expectations. I was in full-on grief. With years of reflection, I realize I was contrasting the massive success of Donald Trump's *The Art of the Deal*, which I had edited without passion and published the year before, with Natan's book, for which I felt very deeply.

Years later I asked Natan how he felt about the experience of writing and publishing the book. His response was that our big advance and other foreign rights deals made it possible for him "not to bend" to the financial challenges of his new life, a marriage, children, a home, and a career.

When I started PublicAffairs in 1997, I licensed the paperback rights to *Fear No Evil* and reissued the book. Over the years since then it has sold thousands of copies in print and ebook formats. For that edition, I asked Serge Schmemann, a former Moscow and Jerusalem bureau chief for *The New York Times*, to add a commentary about Natan's life in Israeli politics, where he had led a party of Russian immigrants and became close to Prime Minister Benjamin Netanyahu and his right-of-center policies. Thankfully, Natan was unfazed by this addition. "In prison," he said, "I was an inspiration. In politics I am a disappointment" to American Jewish liberals. What I did not understand then, but do now, is that Sharansky's views were not ideological. They were based on his commitment to democratic reform, which he said was necessary if the Palestinians were to be true partners in peace.

All of Natan's later books, including the one he is writing as I write this, were published by PublicAffairs, without agents. In that sense, our trust was mutual.

It is amazing to consider now the range of my engagement with the Soviet Union and then Russia: Sakharov, Sharansky, Yeltsin, Putin, Dobrynin, Arbatov, Aksyonov; William Hyland, the editor of *Foreign Affairs* magazine who wrote a superb small book called *The Cold War Is Over*; Dusko Doder's *Shadows and Whispers*; David Hoffman's *The Oligarchs*, a defining book about the mogul billionaires who emerged in the madcap Yeltsin era.

As a reporter and as a book person, I was able to engage Russia in full. I never did write my big Russia book, as so many other correspondents had. But I was certainly able to make a literary contribution, drawing on the years that Suze and I spent in Moscow.

Chapter 14

Thornapple

WE RETURNED TO the United States in the summer of 1977 no longer a young couple, but a young family: Katherine was two and Evan was six months. We soon acquired a large mixed-breed black Labrador retriever called Max and a cat whose name I can't recall. I imagined we would buy a largish house with a circular driveway in one of the tonier parts of northwest Washington, which I associated with having arrived.

Instead we bought 4005 Thornapple Street in Chevy Chase, Maryland, a house on a perfectly nice block in the suburbs. Nothing fancy—a wood-framed two-story, three-bedroom structure with a largely unfinished attic and basement. We painted it gray with a red door, and it looked exactly like what a child's vision of a house would be, including a chimney with curly smoke coming out of it on cold days. The most distinctive feature was a spacious deck overlooking the backyard with a spectacular oak tree in the middle for shade. Washington's weather made it possible to use the deck much of the year. The attic was sufficiently habitable for a succession of free-rent babysitters and short-term nannies. In the basement we set up a cave-like office for me to write in. The kitchen was simple. The doggy door wasn't big enough for Max to squeeze through, but our cat could, as did the occasional raccoon (set free in the woods when captured in a cage approved by the Humane Society).

My salary as the foreign editor of the *Post* was certainly respectable, but we had none of the extras and tax benefits we had overseas, so every penny was being spent. Suze made the choice not to look for work while the children were so small. In retrospect, I understand that was a move as bold as her foray at twenty-three to a war zone. In Washington, where the operative measure of status was "What do you do?," a stay-at-home mom was low on the totem pole. So, on both counts—the house and our income, net of taxes and mortgage—our homecoming was less grand than I imagined it would be. Decades later I realize how clear Suze's vision was for our lives, and she was absolutely right.

At the *Post*, the foreign editor was actually number two in the hierarchy. Foisie was the assistant managing editor for foreign news, and my immediate boss. My predecessor was Ronald Koven, who had worked for years at the *International Herald Tribune*. He was efficient but, in my view, charmless. In preparing to take up the job, I talked to my good friend Lee Lescaze, who had also served as foreign editor. He either said, or I heard him say, that I should not pattern myself in any way on Koven's approach to the job. I followed that advice probably to a fault. Koven, now back in Paris as a correspondent, certainly noticed. Foisie saw my energy and independence as a lack of respect for his seniority, which it was. I was brash and determined to make my mark in the newsroom. I was a comer, as my personnel file confirmed, and Foisie, while recognizing my commitment to the job (and a certain skill), must have thought I was too ambitious for his taste. Foisie had never been a foreign correspondent himself, and though he was responsible for establishing the *Post*'s first-rate foreign coverage, he didn't really understand what it meant to be essentially on your own multiple time zones from the home office. I did. Enough about Foisie. The truth is that he was the person who managed my years on the foreign staff of the *Post*. I should have been more grateful than I was.

Coming from Moscow to the visible and prestigious-sounding position of foreign editor, Suze and I were welcomed into what was thought of as Washington's social elite of that time. A hostess named Maida Mladek, a friend of the Sherers of Czech background, organized a major welcome-home dinner for us at her Georgetown home.

Among the guests were Arthur Burns, the head of the Federal Reserve, and David Bazelon, the chief judge of the US Court of Appeals, whom I had met as a reporter on that beat. Suze and I were astonished that so many "important" people would venture out on a fall Sunday evening to greet us. We used to joke about the propensity in Washington to put a pork chop in the right window to draw a crowd.

I was welcomed into a full range of establishment entities. I joined the Federal City Club, the slightly raffish alternative to the staid Metropolitan and Cosmos Clubs. I was nominated and admitted to the Council on Foreign Relations. Sally Quinn, the arbiter of style at the *Post*, told *Washingtonian* magazine that I was the best-dressed man at the paper, admittedly not a high bar. That description was more important than just an aside in a magazine. From then on, for better or worse, my newsroom presence was either enhanced as a figure of note or resented by those who thought "well-dressed" meant arrogant and cocky.

Over time we were invited to dinner at some of the more exclusive homes of that era. Mrs. Graham's close friend Polly Wisner Fritchey had an impressive salon. Her daughter, Wendy, had been a close friend of Suze's at Sarah Lawrence. Tom and Joan Braden's Sunday night dinners had cachet. We saw the actor Rex Harrison there one evening. The British ambassador, Sir Nico Henderson, and his wife were top of that heap, living in grandeur on Massachusetts Avenue. As a once and forever watcher and sightseer, I was more drawn to the Georgetown sizzle than Suze was, but she certainly held her own. She did notice that very often she was seated behind a potted plant.

We were in our early thirties with a young family and a very standard income, so there was a bit of two-track living. We had a Chrysler station wagon that had no air-conditioning. We bought a secondhand Volkswagen Beetle, but it had serious mechanical problems and we gave it back. Instead we got the cheapest car we could find with air-conditioning, the small Honda Civic, which is what I used to commute.

I really enjoyed being foreign editor for the right reasons. I stayed in close and empathetic contact with the correspondents. Several of the older ones initially concluded that since I was now part of management, I was not to be trusted. The best example of this was Bernard Nossiter in London. As a visiting fellow correspondent, he had taken me to dine at expensive restaurants. When I turned up in London as foreign editor, we had sandwiches in a pub. I had to remind him that every foreign correspondent since the legendary nineteenth-century scribe Richard Harding Davis had to file timely and accurate expense reports. As the British would say, he was not amused. Bud later went to *The New York Times*.

For all its success, the *Post* was always insisting that we look to cut costs. We only had twelve bureaus, about a third as many overseas reporters as *The New York Times*. Bradlee thought that with the end of the Indochina wars, interest in foreign news would be reduced. He took the budget of one of our overseas offices and established what was called the "Dulles bureau," meaning that its correspondents could be based in Washington and fly out to places when events required. I had what I thought was a better idea, something called "the World's Majority," to send reporters for extensive looks at places we rarely covered. The first assignment was for Bill Peterson, a national desk reporter who had never been out of the country. His mission was to visit Guatemala, Indonesia, East Africa, and Pakistan and describe his encounters with that degree of poverty. I asked Bill if he wanted to go before running the idea past his editor, my good friend Larry Stern, who was not surprisingly pissed. This was a mistake I vowed never to make again; I would abide by the doctrine of "no surprises." At home and in the office, it is much easier to deal with preemptive reactions than to calm indignation after the fact.

The big stories during my first year were the upheavals in Soweto, the sprawling Black township outside Johannesburg; the election of the first Polish pope; Egyptian President Anwar Sadat's trip to Jerusalem (which incorrectly made it seem as if peace in the Middle East was finally possible); and a civil war in Ethiopia and Eritrea. The

Africa correspondent, David Ottaway, was immensely productive, to the point that Bradlee wondered how many readers really cared about a civil war in a distant land.

The work schedule was midmorning to early evening. I would come in most Saturdays, late mornings, because that is what the section editors were expected to do, and to be available for a "relaxed" lunch with Bradlee or Mrs. Graham when they were in. Larry forgave me for the Peterson brouhaha and would on Fridays consult with me, given my sartorial reputation, on proper dress, cool casual. Larry taught me that a key measure of presence is "Dress British. Think Yiddish. Look Irish." Neither of us could ever master that last requirement.

This six-day work week meant less time than there should have been for weekend activities with my children. I did cherish driving Katherine to Montessori school in the mornings, singing our version of Elizabeth Cotton's "Freight Train," and visits to Chinese restaurants for dumplings. I was not an absent dad and was much more involved than my (indomitable) father, who in European style never played catch with me. But time was crowded, and Suze ran the household show. In her memoir, my mother called her my "secretary of state."

A major perk of the job was to visit the *Post*'s bureaus abroad. Particularly unforgettable was traveling to South Africa, Rhodesia, Saudi Arabia, Jordan, and Israel in one whirlwind month. Another notable trip was to Nicaragua in the midst of its civil war and Cuba, which was mostly off-limits to Americans. For that trip I was guided by our Central America correspondent, Karen DeYoung, who had started at the *Post* as an occasional stringer in West Africa and forty years later is still at the paper, having done major work as a reporter and editor, winning a Pulitzer among other distinctions. Being a woman in what was a highly competitive, predominantly male newsroom never fazed Karen, she says, as it did so many other women in those years, who endured condescension and more.

In 1979, as I've mentioned, I returned briefly to foreign reporting, covering the first visit to Poland by Pope John Paul II. It was thrilling to observe and was the precursor to the end, a decade later, of Soviet hegemony in the region.

Our family's money was tight, or it felt that way. During an eighty-eight-day newspaper strike in New York, the PBS station WNET started a nightly newscast hosted by Marilyn Berger, my friend from the J school and later the *Post*. She invited me to be the foreign affairs commentator for the show. I would take the 8 A.M. shuttle to New York (which then cost only $18), grab a taxi to the midtown studio, read my commentaries, catch the 10 A.M. shuttle back to Washington, and arrive in the office at 11:15. I doubt I had asked for permission. The $200 I received each week (plus air and taxi fares) came in handy. If it sounds frantic, it was.

In those years, people like us typically did not have weekend houses, and there were regular Saturday and Sunday night dinners with friends, real and intended. A feature of ours was to have dinners prepared by Nguyen Thi Tam, our Saigon cook and housekeeper. We would call Tam, and she would arrive with pots, pans, and all the necessary ingredients for a dinner that was memorable, I still think, to all present.

The *Post* also extricated the family of Vu Thuy Hoang, who had been our esteemed resident political reporter and translator. Hoang worked in the *Post* library until his retirement twenty-five years later. His elegant wife, Trang, started as a cocktail waitress at a Hilton and later ran the cosmetics section at a large Nordstrom's department store in suburban Virginia. When she was laid off at the Hilton on a spurious allegation about errors on checks, she got a lawyer from the National Labor Relations Board and successfully sued, calling the assertion "a wound to my honor."

On August 11, 1979, while jogging on Martha's Vineyard, Larry Stern had a heart attack and died instantly. We were on vacation with Suze's family in Lakeside when I was called with the news. Larry was fifty years old and beloved for his wit, charm, savvy, and a sense of all things worth knowing. He was Bradlee's closest friend in the newsroom and his long-time neighbor in a townhouse on 21st Street. They

were an unlikely pair. Stern was proof that charisma does not necessarily come from an imposing physical presence. When I was preparing to go to Vietnam, from which Stern had recently returned after a
short-term assignment, his cryptic advice to me was: "Take lots of
naps." (It was tropically hot and, after all, a war zone.) Larry's one
completed book project was about negotiations over the future of Cyprus, a narrow subject. The United States always seemed to support
the wrong side in this never-ending dispute between Greece and
Turkey. He called the book *The Wrong Horse*.

Larry was married twice. I never met his first wife, the mother of
his four children—a colorful quartet, as I recall. His second marriage
was brief and possibly a rebound after the end of his relationship with
Felicity Bryan, an English journalist and literary agent. Felicity was
fifteen years younger than Larry, and their perfect match was, alas,
never to be made. Felicity did marry later and had three children. She,
along with her wonderful husband, Alex Duncan, remained close
friends until her death in 2020. (As an aside, Felicity shared with me
a few letters she had exchanged with Larry in their years as a couple,
and I fell in love with them both all over again.) Felicity's name was
perfect for her personality. She endured tragedies—in particular, the
suicide of her daughter Alice, who was bipolar, and the death of her
siblings from cancer, a disease that also afflicted her multiple times.
She was the quintessence of resilience, and one day in 2019 we talked
at length about what made that possible. There are inherent qualities
in our personas that we do not ultimately control. Resilience was one
of hers. She was brave and beautiful as well as exceptionally gifted
and was in my private pantheon of greats.

After Larry's memorial service in a Quaker meeting house, all the
attendees gathered on the veranda outside Mrs. Graham's office in
the *Post* building. After a few "pops," as Bradlee called them, Ben
threw his glass against a brick wall and it shattered. Then everyone
else threw their glasses, leaving a large pile of debris. Ben hung a
photograph of Larry outside his office, and the *Post* established a
summer fellowship for young British journalists that is still regarded

as a valuable asset to the best of each generation of reporters from Larry's favorite foreign country.

Larry was the assistant managing editor for national news when he died. Dick Harwood, a grizzled ex-Marine who was the deputy managing editor and Bradlee's enforcer, was appointed in the interim. Shortly thereafter, William Greider was named to replace Larry. Bill was a brilliant reporter who was privately a political radical by any standard, with an extraordinary skill for writing and thought. Even in his new position he continued to write regular columns for the *Post*'s Outlook section called "Against the Grain." He and Harwood had both worked at the Louisville *Courier-Journal* and shared a common disdain for Washington social elites, although by virtue of their positions and talent, both could easily qualify. Their personal politics, however, were very different. Harwood was the *Post*'s hard-ass conservative. H. D. S. (David) Greenway, a pedigreed long-time Asia correspondent for the *Post*, hired from *Time*, was doing an obligatory six months in the newsroom. Harwood confronted him (I was nearby) with the fact that "the GAO was out with a report on the GOP and Dole." Greenway looked at him wide-eyed and asked, "Dole, dole. Who's on the dole?" I thought David was in career trouble, not instantly knowing who Senator Bob Dole was. Two years later, when Greenway received the Marines' highest decoration for civilian valor in the 1968 Viet Cong assault on Hue, Harwood was in the stands at the Marine barracks ceremony. I felt especially good for David.

Bill Greider's entire career had been in the United States, and as assistant managing editor he would be responsible for coverage of diplomatic and national security issues as well. He decided that he needed a national editor as deputy, with a background in foreign news. At someone's suggestion, he approached me. Having already described my cool relations with Phil Foisie, I'm sure my boss was not altogether sorry to see me go. My successor was Jim Hoagland, a superstar foreign correspondent and Pulitzer recipient.

What I didn't know was that Harwood had already effectively offered the job to two other people. One was Peter Milius, who had been national editor, had returned to reporting, but now wanted his old job back. The other was Dan Balz, a very smart political reporter. But instead Osnos, an interloper with no experience on the national staff, was appointed. The very highly regarded national staff had many factions covering the full range of domestic affairs. Only the reporters known collectively as "diplo" fathomed my selection. They were a formidable team—Don Oberdorfer, Mike Getler, Murrey Marder, John Goshko, and George Wilson. Lee Lescaze at the White House had extensive foreign experience and was, as I said, a good friend.

Balz was made politics editor and Milius returned to the desk as day national editor, the number three job. I must have known that Dan and Peter would reasonably resent my presence, but it quickly became clear that Peter, in particular, was furious. My job came with a small glass office in the newsroom across from Greider's windowed office. Somehow, I sensed that if I sat next to Milius on the national desk as deadline approached, he would likely explode. Balz was mellower and popular with the staff. For months I did not take my seat at the desk and would instead roam the floor and stay in close consultation with "diplo." I heard a rumor that I was considered slow in taking on my role.

One day in the fall I had lunch with Meg Greenfield, the *Post*'s estimable editorial page editor, and described to her the differences I had found between being foreign editor and national editor. On the foreign desk, I said, you could discuss the tensions between the Fangs and the Bubis, the main tribes in Equatorial Guinea, and no one would challenge your expertise. But talk about Ted Kennedy and the incident at Chappaquiddick in which a young woman died, and everyone was knowledgeable. My point was about the more rarefied world of foreign news versus the homespun character at national. Meg, who had a mischievous sense of humor, said that this was a column I should write for her. I did, and the piece was called "No More Champagne." The day it ran I found a vituperative note in my typewriter from Hoagland denouncing me for writing so blithely about my former colleagues. I was stunned. Hoagland was a certified star and I was a newbie national editor with, doubtless, appropriate insecurities. Maybe I apologized and said that treason had not been my intention. Maybe not.

So, there it was: the editors on the national desk wanted to marginalize me and the editor on the foreign desk was for the moment my self-appointed nemesis. I could have taken to bed with the covers over my head but apparently did not. I stayed the course. My relations with diplo were fine. Greider, as admired as anyone in the newsroom for his integrity and style, gave me his support. I gradually became tolerated and even substituted running the regular national staff weekly meeting when he was away. Years later I asked several former colleagues why they thought I got away with being an outsider. I never got a good answer, but I came to realize it was part of the pattern in my career: the curious blend of being a participant but also enough of an observer to be able to maintain my equilibrium in periods of unusual pressure.

If you were young and ambitious at the *Post* in those years, your relative standing in the prospective contest to succeed Ben Bradlee as executive editor was a big deal, especially if you were one of those whom Ben called "the papabile," on the analogy of those in the College of Cardinals who were considered worthy of being chosen as pope. Incredibly, the first story about Bradlee's potential successors appeared in *Washingtonian* magazine in 1979, when Ben was not yet sixty and more than a decade before he stepped down. Among the photographs in that story was mine, along with Greider, Kaiser, Hoagland, Woodward, and Leonard Downie Jr., the paper's London bureau chief, who would be the eventual choice. Len had come to the *Post* as an intern and over time succeeded in every position he was given. Because he had gone to Ohio State, some of the Ivy Leaguers called him "Land Grant Len."

Being in that portfolio was helpful outside the newsroom with people who were easily impressed. You can cash checks more easily, I thought. Inside the paper it was a sort of parlor game. Jay Mathews, a witty *Post* correspondent in Los Angeles, kept photos on his office wall of the "contenders" and moved them up and down according to what he thought was happening to them.

On Thornapple Street, matters were in hand. Suze was managing the home front with customary grace. We loved our deck. Katherine made a lifelong friend of Julia Von Eichel across the street. Now in their forties and living on opposite coasts, they seem to talk or text every day. Evan was charming, small, and we thought a little hard of hearing. Doctors took out his tonsils and adenoids and the problem cleared up, although he told us coming out of surgery that he was "completely mad."

One major development of that period was our friendship with David and Edie Tatel. David, a brilliant civil rights lawyer, had been Suze's first boss in Chicago at the Lawyers Committee for Civil Rights, and he and Edie lived nearby. David had a condition called retinitis pigmentosa and was slowly going blind. He was also in a daily running group and invited me to join. I became a regular, along with a handful of others from the neighborhood, my first-ever team. On weekends there were as many as a dozen of us going for long runs along the scenic C&O towpath on the Potomac. David went on to serve as a distinguished member of the US Court of Appeals for the DC Circuit and presided over Katherine's and Evan's weddings.

Our group had no official name but was dubbed by Michael Kinsley, the editor of *The New Republic*, the "Greater Chevy Chase Conventional Wisdom Running Club"—which among Washingtonians of a certain category was a gentle put-down. The group, especially David and Edie, were an important addition to Suze's and my life.

My friend Barbara Cohen had become news director of National Public Radio and had the idea of starting a weekly foreign affairs program called *Communique* with a revolving group of hosts, of which I was to be one. We aired after the Friday edition of *All Things Considered*. NPR was relatively new but had already established itself as a source of reliable and thoughtful news coverage. When *Morning Edition* was launched in 1979, Barbara suggested I have a weekly on-air conversation with the host, Bob Edwards, at 7:10 A.M. each Monday. This involved preparing what was essentially a roadmap of questions and answers on topics agreed on in advance. I would arrive at the studio on M Street shortly before 7 in running clothes and be home by about 7:45. Suze said that listeners would throw their clock radios across the room because I sounded too perky for that early hour. I soon understood NPR's impact from the number of people who would say they listened. I received $100 a week for the pleasure and continued the spot for the next five years.

I also did some television, including occasional stints on the PBS program *Washington Week in Review*. That visibility led the Harry Walker lecture agency in New York to offer to represent me for speeches. I was cheap, about $2,000. My line was that I would be invited to address the "Society of Industrial Polluters" in assemblage in Marco Island, Florida, so they could listen to me for forty-five minutes and then deduct the fun time as a business expense. (There was, of course, no such organization.)

I gradually came to realize that while these media appearances and speeches were satisfying for the "stature" they provided, they were considered corrosive to my commitment to the job I held at the *Post*. Newspaper journalists who became regular television personalities found it much easier to be on camera than to do the hard slogging of real reporting or editing, or so I believed. When I was leaving the *Post* in 1984, Don Graham (Katharine Graham's son and successor as publisher) said he thought that I was doing all these things because I didn't really like my job; they were not in his mind a plus. In fact, the money was welcome, and it was nice to be recognized. And what was unusual when I did it forty years earlier is now a major part of the allure of being a Washington reporter—a sort of glamour and a lucrative contract to appear regularly on cable news: the reporter as "brand."

After Katherine and Evan were in school, Suze went back to work. One of her jobs was as a producer for a weekly PBS show called *Inside Washington*, which was actually taped outside Baltimore in a place called Owings Mill. It was far enough from Washington that

Senator Paul Tsongas, on his way to an appearance, quipped, "Now I know what happened to Jimmy Hoffa," the Teamsters boss who had disappeared years before. The host was Mark Shields, later to become a beloved Friday evening mainstay of the *PBS NewsHour*. In 1982 when we moved to London, Suze was replaced, somewhat improbably, by Lynne Cheney, the firebrand conservative who was the wife of Congressman (and future Vice President) Dick Cheney.

The title of national editor sounded prestigious despite being a deputy's job. Inevitably, in Washington style, I would be asked whether I missed having a byline. If I had still been a reporter, I would doubtless have been asked whether I aspired to be an editor. I sensed a bit of personal restlessness. At one point, David Tatel and I considered going to Port Gibson, Mississippi, where the local NAACP had mounted a boycott of discriminatory stores. We liked the fact that when General William Tecumseh Sherman arrived there in the Civil War, he said the town was "too beautiful to burn." Great title for a book, but we never moved beyond it.

A highlight of those years was that I developed a good relationship with Brigitte Weeks, the editor of *Book World*, the *Post*'s weekly book review section. Her expertise was fiction, so she would regularly ask me for suggestions on who might review upcoming nonfiction books. In return, she would let me choose books to review myself. I had started subscribing to *Publishers Weekly*, the trade magazine of the industry. I didn't really know it yet, but I was moving in a direction that was still a few years away.

I started to wonder whether my daily reporting career was really over, and whether I would be primarily an editor from then on. A rumor circulated in the newsroom that I would become Paris correspondent. Bradlee gave it some credibility when he started calling me Pierre. In fact, the plan in the works was that Len Downie would come back from London to become national editor and I would take his place. Suze and I were happy to go to London, but I also understood that the switch was a signal of Downie's eventual ascendency as Don Graham's choice to succeed Bradlee.

That spring of 1981 was a difficult one at the *Post*. A Metro reporter named Janet Cooke won a Pulitzer Prize for a story about an eight-year-old heroin addict, but within days the truth came out that she had made it all up. Bradlee and Woodward, who was her editor, were profoundly embarrassed. Most of the journalism world, it is safe to say, found some (private) pleasure that the paragons of Watergate celebrity had been knocked down a peg. Not long after, Bill Greider upended his career at the *Post* by writing a major article for *The Atlantic* about what he had learned in secret weekly meetings on administration policies with David Stockman, the boy-wonder head of the Office of Management and Budget. Bradlee couldn't understand how Bill would have scooped his own paper. Bill had provided a steady stream of insights from those breakfasts to the staff, but no one knew that he would write a major piece elsewhere. This was a classic case of forgetting the doctrine of no surprises. Bill left and became successively the national correspondent for *Rolling Stone* and *The Nation*. He wrote bestselling books and was able to fulfill, I think, his role as a brilliant and completely independent writer and thinker. He was also a great boss.

Our move to London was set for June 1982. We were putting the Thornapple Street years behind, a happy time in most respects, but with a tinge of retrospective awareness of the challenges in trying to combine parenting, ambition, and managing in a semi-fast lane. In your twenties, I thought, marriage was new and exciting. In your forties, marriage and family had either found the right path or not. It was in your thirties, with small (much loved but demanding) children and wanting to balance the right mix of career and home, that life, even as privileged as ours was, poses tests.

Chapter 15

The Brits

DAYS AFTER ARRIVING IN LONDON, I had my first big story: the birth of Prince William, the son of Charles and Diana, who would one day become heir to the throne. The royal show was still in the full glow of Diana's charms. Then on July 9, less than three weeks after the prince's birth, a mentally disturbed man named Michael Fagan made his way into Queen Elizabeth's bedroom in Buckingham Palace while she was sleeping. That was followed on July 20 by an IRA bomb that killed four mounted members of the Queen's Household Cavalry on their way to the Changing of the Guard at the palace. That same week the Queen went into the hospital to have a wisdom tooth removed.

In Len Downie's last months as the correspondent, Britain had waged a successful war against Argentina to reclaim the Falkland Islands. My tour was clearly beginning on a very different note. Our friend from Moscow Christopher Mallaby invited me to attend a ceremony at Buckingham Palace where he would be receiving a KCMG, a very high honor (known, unofficially, as "Kings Call Me God"). Despite the distractions of the previous weeks, the Queen was completely herself, and I wondered (as people often did) what was in the purse she held while also being regal. Even a queen, it seems, has to be prepared to blow her nose.

The small orchestra on hand played "Strangers in the Night," the Frank Sinatra classic. Did they know the irony of that choice of music so soon after the dramatic episode of the intruder?

Before leaving, Downie had been informed that he would be getting the first-ever American journalist's interview with Prince Charles. That was now to be mine. On August 5, it took place and my coverage appeared at great length in the *Post*. In my color sidebar I wrote these fateful words: "He is only a few years younger than I am. Some people say we look a little alike. I longed for the opportunity to say directly, 'Look, let's be friends. Tell me how it really feels to be the Prince of Wales. Would I like it?'"

The interview itself was revealing. The prince said he wasn't sure of what his proper role should be and made a number of introspective comments. The transcript was reprinted in the British papers. The *Sunday Mirror* put out posters across the country calling it "Amazing."

Suze told me to leave out the sentence about our supposed physical resemblance. I should have. The line reverberated in the *Post* newsroom. *Washingtonian* ran a picture of my press card with Charles's face.

We were invited to a dinner that fall at the US ambassador's residence in honor of the prince and princess. According to protocol, we were clustered with another couple waiting to be introduced. They turned out to be Julie Nixon and her husband, David Eisenhower. Although I was representing the newspaper whose reporting had led to her father's resignation, Julie and David were friendly. Her father was not mentioned. When Suze and I were presented, the prince said jokingly, "It was so nice to meet a serious journalist."

In 2018, at a reunion of *Washington Post* alumni, David Maraniss, one of the paper's great writers, told me, unsolicited, a story so striking that I asked him to confirm it in an email. This is what he wrote:

"I was in the Austin bureau, sometime in the late 80s . . . Prince Charles paid a visit to Dallas for some reason and I went up to write about it. Largely forgettable event, I think. But I was introduced to him and said I was with *The Washington Post* and he lit up and said, ah, Peter Osnos. People say he looks like me, or I look like him. He was smiling when he said it, though drolly."

No further comment seems necessary.

Through the Kaisers' friends Peter and Sybil Pagnamenta, we learned of a townhouse on Elgin Crescent in Notting Hill, a fashionable neighborhood with a large communal garden behind the surrounding homes, all of which were painted in lively colors. The owners were Michael Howard and Sandra Paul; he was a Queen's Counsel attorney and she was a former top model. They were moving to Kent, where Michael was going to run for Parliament as a Tory. (He would later become the leader of the Conservative Party.) We could have their beautiful and stylishly cozy house for three hundred pounds a week—a far cry from the ten pounds a week I'd paid for my flat on Thurlow Road fifteen years earlier. I worried that I would not get approval for such an expense—more than $2,000 for a month's rent, a huge number at the time. I did get the OK, although we paid a share.

So, we got a fully furnished, elegant three-story house. It could not have been better in all respects. Next, we needed to find schools for Katherine and Evan. He was five and enrolled at Hill House, the school made famous when Prince Charles went there before becoming a boarder at Gordonstoun. It was run by a retired colonel whose mantra was "You cannot teach small boys unless they are a little bit tired." So, he kept the students on the move all day. They could be seen in and around the buildings in Kensington in their rust-colored knickerbockers. Evan was so small that his size was 000. For most of the two years he was there, Evan would compete with another boy, an Iranian, to get a weekly sticker on his sweater awarded to the "best boy."

Our first school visit for Katherine was to Faulkner House, a ritzy all-girls school. At the intake interview I asked the headmistress what the racial composition was. "We had one once," she replied. "It was a disaster." She was referring to the daughter of a Nigerian tribal chief whose seventh birthday was celebrated at the Dorchester Hotel with pink champagne. I asked about the religious makeup. "Most of our girls are C of E [Church of England]. We do have the occasional Catholic and the odd Jew." Katherine went instead to Hampshire House, located next to the Libyan embassy, which meant walking past armed police on surrounding rooftops. The second year she went to Glendower. She had some trouble keeping her beret on straight and her socks pulled neatly up to her knees.

This was London life in the eighties.

I found a compatible running group that would circle Hyde Park and Green Park in the mornings. There were two other Americans, lawyers, and several Brits, one of whom would run in his Wellington boots. Suze managed the household, which involved time-consuming daily school pickups, and she worked part-time as a salesperson in a small, posh neighborhood bookstore. We already had a group of good friends from Washington, Saigon, and Moscow now living in London. We went to the theater. I joined the Reform Club, which, to avoid being stiffed by members, had a pay-as-you-go policy for food and drink.

With little major news to report, I conjured my subjects. I went to Oxford and wrote about what it meant to be a Rhodes Scholar, the program then celebrating its seventy-fifth anniversary. Being a Rhodes then and to this day was a forerunner of later professional success, Bill Clinton being a prime example. One Rhodes Scholar characterized the group to me as an assemblage of American "over-achievers" proud and lucky to be headed toward elite status. I spent Nobel week in Stockholm writing about the strangeness of being a wonky professor thrust into the limelight. On the day of the ceremony I had lunch with the chemistry awardee and his wife, who warned him not to eat anything that would give him indigestion later. I rented white tie and tails for the banquet. I wrote about the British institutions that interested me: *The Economist* magazine, the BBC, the Reuters news agency (which had started by sending news around on carrier pigeons), and the brilliant satirical magazine *Private Eye*. I interviewed the actor Alec Guinness and the novelist John Le Carré. I was made *persona non grata* at the American embassy when I wrote about our ambassador John Jeffry Louis under the headline "At Least Our Envoy in London Gives Good Parties." We somehow became acquainted enough with Carol Thatcher, daughter of Margaret, to be invited to the family quarters at 10 Downing Street.

I interviewed Michael Foot, the Labour Party leader, a scholarly left-winger who said that he had not been to the United States in thirty years—a revelation that was a news story in the UK. Had he won election as prime minister, Foot would have been a very unlikely partner for Ronald Reagan, I thought. My political reporting was immeasurably assisted by my friendship with Jim Naughtie of *The Scotsman* and Peter Riddell of *The Times*. Brits were given "lobby" access in Parliament to MPs and ministers. Americans were not. Their help made me look better in the *Post*.

Every Monday morning, I would go to Bush House, the headquarters of the BBC World Service, to continue my weekly appearances speaking with Bob Edwards on *Morning Edition*. My friend Robert Siegel, NPR's London correspondent, would assist me in the process. I would sit in front of a large hanging microphone of the kind used by Edward R. Murrow reporting from London in World War II. British broadcast media would call regularly for me to appear and send a cab for me. After a while I realized that London traffic made the journeys too time-consuming. I would have been better off taking the Underground.

My beat included Scandinavia, which enabled me to visit the headquarters of Lego on a Danish island where I accepted a gift of Lego blocks, which was then Evan's favorite pastime. In Iceland, I discovered that this member of NATO had no army of its own and wrote a story calling it the ultimate American "client state." The Icelanders were furious.

It was on one of those Scandinavia trips that I had a personal epiphany. A Soviet submarine had been spotted in waters near Stockholm, and depth charges were being dropped. Bradlee thought this was a great spy story and I was sent to cover the search. Standing on the shore with binoculars, hoping to get a glimpse of the sub, I was next to the young Stockholm stringer for UPI. After spending the night on the floor of a local church, I wondered, "What am I doing here?" We never saw the Soviet sub. I knew that questions like that reflected a restless attitude. It reminded me of the observation that Bob Bernstein had made to me in Moscow some years before, that "journalism was not a fit profession for a grown man." A year after this epiphany, I would take him up on his invitation to call.

It is clear to me now that while our personal and even professional situation in London was excellent, there was a significant undertone of what I thought of as thwarted ambition getting in the way of my satisfaction. When I would tell Brits that I had given up the position of national editor at the *Post* to become a foreign correspondent again, the response was invariably some version of "What did you do wrong to be sidelined from ascending the greasy pole of achievement?"

By 1984, I had spent four years in London—two years in my early twenties, footloose, and two years in my late thirties, with a family and on the edge of a change.

I am an Anglophile when it comes to significant elements of British style, and as the saying goes, "Some of my best friends are Brits." I like droll humor and antic irony. I later published a book called *A Great Silly Grin* about the genius of *Monty Python*, *Fawlty Towers*, and *Beyond the Fringe*. I am a fan of British kitsch like *Chariots of Fire* and *Downton Abbey*. But in my years as the *Post*'s London bureau chief, I saw other aspects of Britain's latter-day character. There is "pickled Britain"—bowler hats, stately homes, the royals, high tea, Ascot, Eton, Harrow, Oxford, and Cambridge. The effort to maintain these institutions in the modern world was impressive, somewhat authentic, and yet occasionally comical. On the other hand, there was what I thought of as the "still syndrome." As in "Britain can still mount a naval task force to take back the Falklands" or "You can still walk most streets at night and feel safe" or "You can still have shirts made at Turnbull &

Asser on Jermyn Street," which I do. The point of "still" is that the days of whatever is under review are numbered.

The tradition of "stiff upper lip" and "keep calm and carry on" remains the standard goal, although class identities remain strong, especially among the upper tiers where attitudes range along a spectrum from excessive self-deprecation to clueless arrogance.

Americans used to call the whole business "England" just as we incorrectly called the Soviet Union "Russia." Now it is Great Britain or the United Kingdom, finally recognizing that the Scots, the Northern Irish, and even the Welsh are not necessarily on board with all things English. The Brexit fiasco, a self-inflicted crisis to break away from natural European partners in economics and continental security, has rendered Britain a second-tier power that can still be classy in some ways and so tawdry in others. The same, of course, can be said of the United States, which is much bigger, much wealthier, and still very much an ethnic and social work in progress.

And what of the "special relationship"? It does have its place in American appreciation of the English language, culture, and, pre-Brexit, of London as a major center of finance. There is also a strategic partnership in intelligence and defense. But in the Trump era and regularly in the past, the United States regards itself emphatically as the senior partner in any alliance. We very much like the Brits, but we don't need them.

In the summer of 1983, on the way to our summer vacation in Lakeside, Suze and I stopped in Washington, and I picked up the rumor that I was a finalist for the position of assistant managing editor for the Style section, a prime job. I spent the visit with the necessary people but didn't directly advocate for myself. One evening in August I got a call from Shelby Coffey, the deputy managing editor, telling me that the new editor of Style would be Mary Hadar, who had been the deputy and was a great choice. In a sense that conversation struck me as "case closed," although I was not especially disappointed, as I recall. Whether I knew it or not, I was beginning to separate myself from the *Post*. That fall in Reykjavik I got a call from the foreign desk to say that I was getting a $25-a-week raise. If I said thank you, I did not mean it.

In December I went to Oslo to cover the awarding of the Nobel Peace Prize to Lech Walesa, the founder of Poland's Solidarity movement, who was not allowed to travel and would be represented by his wife, Danuta. I noted the echoes with Andrei Sakharov eight years earlier. The trip was notable for two reasons. R. W. Apple Jr., the legendary *New York Times* bureau chief in London, who was so profligate that the *Times* gave him his own expense line in the newsroom budget, arranged for me to join him for dinner at Oslo's best restaurant on one of the busiest nights of the year, two weeks before Christmas. The meal was amazing.

The second reason was that by the time I returned to London I had resolved to call Bob Bernstein and ask about a job. As I think about it now, it was the only time in my career that I actively pursued a real change. I had been at the *Post* for seventeen years. Bob's invitation to consider Random House had been made seven years earlier. He was interested enough when I called to send the formidable editorial director of Random House, Jason Epstein, to London to talk to me. Jason was one of the most important (self- and otherwise) figures in publishing. Bennett Cerf, the founder of Random House, used to quip about Jason, "He is the bear I cross."

Jason had refined taste, so our dinner was at the Connaught Hotel, London's finest, with a bottle of wine beyond my palate's capacity to judge. The next day we went to the Gay Hussar, a modest establishment in Soho that was a favorite of mine but was suitable because of the artsy crowd that ate there. I slightly overreached by asking Jason if I could join him for a visit with his friend Diana Phipps, a leading British interior designer who lived a few doors down from us on Elgin Crescent. After all I hadn't been invited. When Bob reported to me on Jason's trip, he said his only concern was that I might be "too aggressive." I later learned that Jason had rejected the appointment of British publisher Sonny Mehta to a senior job at Random House. Mehta later became publisher of Knopf. My insight was that Jason thought I was insufficiently qualified to constitute a challenge to his authority. (I should add here that Jason and I got along extremely well once I had been hired.)

After Christmas I was asked to come to New York to continue discussions with Bob and other senior executives. Oddly, I don't remember much about that visit except that I came home with a firm job offer and slept eleven hours straight. The position was senior editor at the Random House imprint with a significant improvement in salary. All moving expenses would be covered. We would have a car and a mortgage from Advance, the Random House holding company, at the lowest possible rate. At Bob's recommendation, Aryeh Neier, the director of Helsinki Watch, hired Suze to be its first press director. Altogether those terms were more than a doubling of what I was earning at the *Post*.

At lunch with Tony Schulte, Random House's executive vice president, I conjured the request that after six months, if I was still employed, I would be named associate publisher, although I had no real idea what that title meant. In keeping with Bernstein's approach to matters of that kind, he told Schulte to agree. After all, it would be up to me to figure out what the job required. It was a fateful request because it put me on a path of aspiration that most editors didn't have. It was decided that I would begin work in New York at the beginning of April.

I called Karen DeYoung, who was now foreign editor, and said I wanted to come to Washington to talk about a move I planned to make. She got the point and told Bradlee that something was up. She didn't know what the job would be but the assumption in Washington was that it was going to be something like banking because I must have implied that the salary improvement would be too big for there to be a discussion about a match from the *Post*.

Ben and his wife, Sally Quinn, invited me to stay with them. When I gave them the news, they seemed happy for Suze and me. Among other things, my departure resolved the nettlesome issue of the future of one of the cadre in the newsroom angling for a top-tier position.

I have been asked a million times why I left the familiarity and glamour of *The Washington Post* for the unknown terrain of Random House. The closest I can come to an answer is that I didn't think I would learn as much at the *Post* in the next ten years as I had learned in the past decade. I was drawn to books and, although I didn't realize it, I liked the challenge of business. Richard D. Simmons, the *Post*'s president, wrote me to say that he was sorry I was leaving because he had planned to offer me a job on the newspaper's business side.

And yet, a new career at forty with a family? Suze was, as always, indomitable. What if it didn't work out? Thankfully I'll never know the answer to that question.

I have now been gone from the *Post* twice as long as I worked there. And yet my association with the place remains strong. A person I was dealing with in 2020 on a publishing issue asked me if I was that fellow who worked at the *Post*. Evan's prominence in journalism is usually combined in people's minds with my years in the fray. A standard line is "Now you're known as Evan Osnos's father," a compliment to be sure.

The *Post*'s hold on me comes from many factors. I was young and so was the paper, in its way, with an exuberance it had not had in its past. Ben Bradlee was irresistible. A leader is more important in newsrooms than, say, in law or dentistry.

I once wrote a piece for the Outlook section about Henry Kissinger's memoirs that made gentle fun of his vituperative criticism of a South Vietnamese official he called "egregious; outrageous; obnoxious"—to which the Vietnamese Hoang Duc Nha responded, "He gives me too much credit." Kissinger sent a complaining letter to his friend Katharine Graham that his serious book was being treated so lightly in her newspaper. She sent the letter to Ben, who forwarded it to me with a note that said, "Here's one for your baby book."

My eighteen years at the *Post* were a succession of master classes in the world, in which I was able to indulge my curiosity and my instincts for observation. The managing editor, Howard Simons, the Jewish yin to Bradlee's WASP yang, told me as I started my tenure as foreign editor to "be a spectator," or don't become overwhelmed by the contest for standing and too dependent on outsiders' misplaced awe at a high position at the *Post*. He may not have thought I had heard him, but thinking about it now, I mostly did.

Somehow, as the story about the tensions of my arrival on the national desk suggest, I was able to stay clear, for most of the time, of the internal politics that were inevitable in a newsroom of so many talented and ambitious men. (They were mostly men, though two of the three most important people to the newsroom, Mrs. Graham and Meg Greenfield, were women.) In all my years at the *Post*, I had the feeling that I was aspiring to get better at my assignments and in the view of my editors not quite making it. If I had known, as my personnel file showed, that I was better thought of than I realized, would I have stayed? Probably not.

Today's *Washington Post* is a vastly different place, owned now by Jeff Bezos, the world's richest man. It is a 24/7 technological juggernaut with global readership, overwhelmingly online. For what it was like in the Bradlee-Graham era, I recommend watching *All the President's Men* or *The Post*. And then I advise reading Ben's memoir *A Good Life: Newspapering and Other Adventures*, Katherine Graham's *Personal History*, Meg Greenfield's *Washington*, Harry Rosenfeld's *From Kristallnacht to Watergate: Memoirs of a Newspaperman*, and Leonard Downie's *All About the Story: News, Power, Politics, and the Washington Post*.

PART THREE

~

Books and Books

Chapter 16

The Eleventh Floor

ON MONDAY, APRIL 2, 1984, I arrived at Random House. The company's offices had once been in the Villard Houses on Madison Avenue, a collection of stately townhouses across from St. Patrick's Cathedral that was also the residence of senior Catholic clerics. But that colorful setting had been replaced by a generic high-rise on Third Avenue. I was given an office on the eleventh floor of 201 East 50th Street, on Editors Row where all the senior editors were arrayed. I had a furniture catalog from which to choose my chair, desk, and couch. I had a Royal typewriter. Outside my office at a small desk sat Derek Johns, a young Englishman who had been the assistant to my predecessor, who had just left. Fired. His predecessor had also left (too much time playing cards with other editors, I was told). So, I was to be the third strike in that space, an outsider in the higher ranks of the otherwise illustrious editorial team.

In late morning, I was asked to come up one flight to Bob Bernstein's office, where Bob introduced me to a smallish, unassuming fellow, dressed casually. He was S. I. (Si) Newhouse, the chair of Condé Nast and the owner of Random House. Si must have been aware of my arrival, although there was nothing in his manner that suggested he was curious about this recruit. If I was supposed to be unnerved or impressed by that introduction, I don't remember that I was either.

Afterward I chatted with Derek and asked whether he would be interested in being my assistant. He was no longer working with anyone else, so he agreed. His salary was $12,000. I promised him that I could do better and got him to $18,000 within a year.

Derek knew all the jargon and procedures of publishing and just enough about navigating Random House to get me started. In a few days I understood the essential difference between journalism and book publishing. In journalism, you got the story; it was printed, and you went home. In publishing, you got the story, the books were printed, and then you had to sell them. I recognized that there were three phases to the publishing process: acquisition, which involved identifying projects and working with literary agents on the financial terms; supporting the writing and editing of the book; and figuring out how the book should be published. Because I didn't know what an editor did, I undertook to do everything until someone told me not to. I carried my notebook from floor to floor and interviewed publishers, business staff, and sales personnel at all levels. I accompanied two senior sales reps on their rounds of Madison Avenue carriage trade stores and jobbers/wholesalers, two ends of that cultural spectrum.

At my first meeting of Random House editors with the sales team to discuss upcoming books, Mario Cuomo, the governor of New York, stopped by to tout the publication of his new book, which would be published that summer. When questions were solicited, I had to stop myself from asking why he was pitching a book instead of doing the people's business. Fortunately, I realized that this was no longer appropriate.

An editor with a stammer started describing the narrative of a book he was presenting. Jason Epstein snapped, "Cut the plot." The novel was *Blood Meridian* by Cormac McCarthy and it got a dismissive response. Years later, when McCarthy was published by Knopf, he was a major and highly regarded bestseller.

Then, and this was an especially tricky moment, Bob Loomis, one of the true greats of the editing field, started talking about a book called *A Bright Shining Lie* by Neil Sheehan. I had been in Vietnam when Sheehan had started work on the book in 1972 and knew that it was about John Paul Vann, the former Army officer and early sceptic of the war who had become a senior civilian official in the country and was killed in a helicopter crash. Bob said that a defining secret of Vann's life was his love affair with a Vietnamese woman. Among those of us in Vietnam it was thought that the real story of Vann was that he was a metaphor for America's well-intentioned, hopelessly misguided mission in Vietnam. I very carefully presented my bona fides as the only person in the room who had known Vann and shared my opinion about the real meaning of the book. My recollection is that I got away with that early display of brashness. It turned out that despite Bob's optimism that Sheehan would complete his work in time for the book to be published later that year, it was not to be. But when the book was finally published it received the 1988 National Book Award.

The only editor in the building who I had known previously was Ash Green at Knopf. As I've said, he worked on Russia-related books and other nonfiction that matched my sensibilities. One morning Ash brought me a list of books he had published in recent years so I could see their sales history. I was surprised to see how low the numbers were. Moshe Dayan, the Israeli war hero, had written a memoir. It sold about 9,000 copies. This was an essential reality check. Serious nonfiction is important and can have great impact, but it does not necessarily sell in bestseller numbers. Editors had to recognize that the advances they offered needed to be calibrated to a book's sales potential and not to their personal enthusiasms. Ash was singular in reaching out to me. If any of the other senior editors invited me to lunch or dinner, it was rare. They were not hostile. They were just not terribly interested.

Joe Fox, who had edited Truman Capote, Philip Roth, and other great novelists, was the friendliest. Among his biggest successes was Jim Fixx's *The Complete Book of Running*. (Soon after I arrived at Random House, Fixx died of a heart attack.) Joe would offer Suze and me the use of his house in the Hamptons for our kids' spring break in the following years.

The Random House of 1984 was a much smaller enterprise than the company is today. The Newhouse family had bought it from RCA in 1980, as the conglomerate began to unravel. RCA sold Hertz car rentals and Banquet Foods the same day. The sale price of $60 million or so was reported on the front page of the *Times*. That included, aside from the Random House Trade Division (which was known without affection elsewhere in the company as "Little Random," to avoid confusion with the corporation as a whole), Alfred A. Knopf, Pantheon, Random House Children's Books, Ballantine and Vintage paperbacks, and a relatively small reference department.

As now a private company, its finances then and going forward were never public. But with James Michener at his peak, Dr. Seuss, the Babar catalog, Richard Scarry, Kahlil Gibran's blockbuster *The Prophet*, Audubon bird guides, and an impressive backlist on the Vintage trade paperback list, the company was solidly profitable. This was the first year of *Fortune* magazine's list of the one hundred best companies in America to work for, and Random House was one of them.

The imprints were led by strong publishers. Robert Gottlieb at Knopf was considered a brilliant book editor, and his publishing team led by Jane Friedman was superb. Andre Schiffrin at Pantheon had a sophisticated list and, like Gottlieb, no lack of self-regard. Susan Petersen ran the paperback divisions with fierce charisma and discipline. She was so intense that Bernstein told me he would have to order her to take vacations. And the children's list managed its superstars efficiently. I think Ted Geisel (aka Dr. Seuss) was Bernstein's favorite author.

At Random Trade, Jason Epstein had the title of editorial director rather than publisher. Jason was a genuinely esteemed figure in New York publishing. He was one of the founders of *The New York Review of Books*, had pioneered the concept of "quality" paperbacks, and was thought of as a great intellectual. Jason provided me with an invaluable response to all authors complaining that they or their family could not find their book on bookstore shelves. When Mario Cuomo called the morning after delivering the keynote speech at the 1984 Democratic

National Convention to say that his wife had looked everywhere in San Francisco for his book without success, Jason replied: "Governor, no author since Homer has ever found his own book in a bookstore."

Everyone recognized Jason's standing and stature, but he was never intended to be a team leader or an empathetic counselor. If he thought you were smart (for young men) or attractive (for young women), he made time for you. Otherwise he was busy. One day years after I had come to Random House, Jason stopped by my office and mentioned, casually, that over the weekend he was going to marry a famous *New York Times* reporter named Judy Miller. She is very smart, he said. Nearly thirty years later they are still together, a distinctive pairing of talent and personas.

Most of the business side was managed by Tony Schulte, the tweedy and amiable person who was executive vice president of the whole company. He was busy and always late to meetings. I thought, for all his charm, that he was symbolic of what then appeared to be a relaxed relationship to process and the bottom line at Random House. When Geraldine Ferraro became the first woman ever to be nominated to a major party presidential ticket that summer, Schulte authorized the interested editor—Charlotte Mayerson, who said she knew Ferraro—to offer as much as $50,000 for the inevitable book. It eventually sold for $1 million. Tony was definitely old school in an industry that was moving into a new era of mega advances.

One of the younger editors was Jonathan Galassi, whom Jason, for some reason, underestimated. Jonathan wanted to sign up Pat Conroy's *The Prince of Tides*, which would become one of the major novels of that decade. Jason said no. Galassi left Random House a couple of years later and went to Farrar, Straus and Giroux, where his first acquisition was Scott Turow's *Presumed Innocent*, a hugely successful, classy commercial novel of the kind that the Random House trade list of the 1980s needed and didn't have. He later became the publisher of FSG and a renowned poet.

The three senior women on the floor were Anne Freedgood, in charge of Vintage paperback reprints and at perennial loggerheads with Jason over one thing or another, fussing without fury; Charlotte Mayerson, who seemed angry to me, apparently with good reason, as she sensed (correctly) that women at the imprint were marginalized; and Carol Schneider, the publicity director, as skilled in the profession as she was in sidestepping the political complexities of the group and what by contemporary measures were those misogynistic tendencies on the floor. There were several gifted younger editors—of whom Derek became one after a year helping me—who went on to be established figures in the business. Most shared a preference for evening fun, cocaine, booze, and shrewd awareness of the trends in publishing for younger readers. Vintage Contemporaries, with authors like Jay McInerney, Richard Russo, and Richard Ford in original paperbacks, was the most exciting corner of the imprint.

The managing editor (who was responsible for the publishing process) was Tony Wimpfheimer, the stepson of Donald Klopfer, the Random House cofounder who would still come in from time to time to brief new employees on the company's history. Tony was an avid golfer.

There were a half-dozen in-house copy editors in windowless offices, all women, who were indispensable but essentially ignored. Barbé Hammer, Wimpfheimer's assistant and later Bob Loomis's, wrote mystery novels under a pseudonym.

There was an art director, interior designers, and an advertising director. Jason's idea of the best place to advertise most books was in his own *New York Review of Books*. There were no regular editorial meetings. One small scandal on the floor came when a young female assistant complained to Personnel, as it was then called, because an editor had a pair of wind-up testicles on his desk.

This was, of course, before the digital age, and everything was done on paper. There were typewriters and telephones. Smoking was permitted. Editors tended to "work from home" on Fridays as they made their way to the Hamptons or similar weekend locales. The longish publishing lunch was still the norm, although Bob Gottlieb at Knopf made a noticeable point of having everyone come to his office for a sandwich. Jason had more expensive tastes and was a major gourmet. An invitation to have Jason's home cooking was rare and coveted. I got one, but only after I had left Random House.

As for me, Derek told me recently that Jason had described me as a "very exciting man" in anticipating my arrival. But no one told me that Derek had already been assigned as my assistant. Because I was known to be Bob Bernstein's friend before being hired, I was thought to have high-level cover. It is still, all these years later, amazing to me that I was given no significant briefing on how to do the job and didn't realize that I should have had one. Ever since I have adopted the maxim that "jobs are 10 percent given and 90 percent taken."

The best advice I got on this topic was from Bernstein himself. After a few weeks (it must have still been April because it was on the day of my mother's Passover Seder), I complained to him that I had not been included in some meeting of senior people in the company. He looked at me without a smile and said, "Peter, keep your eye on the books. If the books work, everything will be fine. If they don't, nothing will save you." If I had taken a two-month course in management, I could not have gotten better guidance. On my last appearance on NPR before leaving the *Post*, Bernstein was invited to describe my new job. When he was asked what he would tell me on my first day, he replied, "Listen." Listening when I needed to and keeping my eyes on the books turned out to be my guiding principles at Random House. Those two mandates were for me, at least, as valuable as months of training might have been. I did focus very firmly on the books. I didn't even realize that I had not been given a vice president title, which was technically meaningful in corporate terms. When many years later I was named one, it no longer mattered.

The first book I acquired was *America's Health Care Revolution* by Joseph Califano, a prominent Washington lawyer who had been in the White House under Lyndon Johnson and had been Jimmy Carter's secretary of health, education, and welfare. Joe's prescience on health care was, in retrospect, amazing. The advance was modest, but I was now handling a substantial author on a topic I knew little about.

The next book I considered was by Tad Szulc, a senior *New York Times* correspondent, represented by Morton Janklow, a top agent, who I came to realize must have liked working with me because we did a lot of business together. Szulc said he had an understanding with Fidel Castro to write a biography with complete access to the Cuban leader.

My instinct was that unless Castro was planning to retire or defect, Tad was going to have a hard time really getting the goods. We sidestepped that one and years later it was published elsewhere, long before Castro passed from the scene. I don't think anyone ever did get as deeply into Castro's life as a writer would like. These early acquisitions were all arranged by Bernstein, who clearly knew that getting me launched was essential. The rest of the editing and publishing job was up to me.

One of my first personal buys was a book by Stanley Karnow, who had been a distinguished *Washington Post* correspondent in Asia and had written the definitive history of the Vietnam War that coincided with a major series on PBS. He now wanted to write a history of the US presence in the Philippines. Given his stature, this one was likely to be expensive. I got a partner from Ballantine, one of Random House's paperback imprints, and we made a successful offer of $250,000. The book won a Pulitzer Prize when it was published in 1987, although Karnow and I had many a tangle. He was my first publishing diva and a great journalist.

Going over this list now, I realize that these were all authors I knew and who knew me from Washington or elsewhere. Gary Sick, the Carter administration's chief expert on Iran, contracted to write a book on the 1979–81 hostage crisis. That book, *All Fall Down*, got my first front-page review in *The New York Times Book Review* and was later selected by the *Times* as one of the best books of the year. The book that Wendy Larsen, whose husband Jonathan had been *Time*'s bureau chief in Saigon, wrote with a Vietnamese friend did exceptionally well for a poetry book, was widely reviewed, and sold about 11,000 copies. It would be many years before I tried my hand at poetry again.

Elisabeth Bumiller was a *Washington Post* reporter whom I admired. Her husband, Steve Weisman of *The New York Times*, had been assigned to New Delhi, and the *Times*'s policy was that *Post* and *Times* reporters could not cohabit. Really. So Elisabeth had to give up her job. I called her to say that I didn't know what she would do in India, but whatever it was I would like to be involved. I gave her $5,000 as a down payment. Elisabeth wrote *May You Be the Mother of a Hundred Sons*, about the women of India. She gave us the fabric for the jacket design and took all the photographs. Her writing was completely clean. All these years later, the book is still in print. I always say that Elisabeth is the kind of writer who gives editors a bad name because she does it all. As I write, she is the Washington bureau chief of *The New York Times* and an assistant managing editor. Quite a run for a reporter who started by covering parties in Style. That *Times-Post* cohabitation policy has long since been abandoned.

And then there was the downside of being new and untested. In every editor's drawer there are the troubled projects. These were handed to me—a form of hazing, although it certainly wasn't designated that way.

These were:

A book by the attorney and Harvard law professor Alan Dershowitz about his representation of Claus von Bülow, who was on trial for allegedly giving his wife, Sunny, a drug overdose so he could have an independent private life and access to her money. With Dershowitz's efforts, von Bülow was eventually acquitted. And *Reversal of Fortune*, Dershowitz's victory lap (and his good title), was now mine. Dershowitz had written a previous Random House book, *The Best Defense*, about his legal career, which had been a success. And yet, Dershowitz was at the top of the sales department's least favorite author list for what can be called, with understatement, his nasty belligerence. No further description is warranted.

Alan took an early dislike to me because, among other things, when I visited Martha's Vineyard that summer of 1984, where he had a house, I hadn't called him. His verdict was that I was a snob.

After the manuscript was completed, it somehow (I have no idea how) ended up in the hands of Sunny von Bülow's children. They hired Michael Armstrong, a prominent, tough lawyer, and accused Dershowitz of violating attorney-client privilege. That meant weeks in an airless lawyer's office with Lesley Oelsner (a former *New York Times* reporter who was now a Random House lawyer), Dershowitz, and Armstrong, haggling over language in the book.

The book was finally published. Nora Ephron's review in *The New York Times* eviscerated Claus and Alan. The end was "I see that Random House has just honored Mr. Dershowitz and Mr. von Bülow with a champagne toast at The Palladium. That seems a logical enough place for the von Bülow case to have ended up. As for me I'd rather be in Rhode Island," where Claus had allegedly poisoned Sunny, who lived on for years in a coma. I do not recall being invited to the Palladium.

Dershowitz was indefatigable, and with his son's assistance *Reversal of Fortune* was made into a respectable movie. We sold the paperback rights. The last time I saw Dershowitz was at a cocktail party in the Vineyard years later, where he introduced me as the only person who had ever edited a book of his that failed.

Next up was a book by a writer on Cape Cod named Leo Damore, who claimed to have the full story of Senator Ted Kennedy and Mary Jo Kopechne, who drowned when the car she and Kennedy were driving went off a bridge at Chappaquiddick Island in 1969. The book had been acquired for $250,000 from Lucianne Goldberg, an agent who was later famous for her role in exposing Bill Clinton's dalliance with Monica Lewinsky as an adviser to Linda Tripp. That was Goldberg's line of work.

When the manuscript arrived, many of its revelations about Kennedy's behavior came from a Kennedy cousin, Joe Gargan, who had been paid $15,000 for his version of the story. My reading of the manuscript, I concluded, was that it was 85 percent clips, 10 percent marginally new, and 5 percent dynamite if true. When I met with Damore and Goldberg and gave them my judgment, Goldberg, dressed all in leather, said that Damore needed a good spanking. I said we would have to see transcripts or tapes of the Gargan material and would put the entire manuscript through a legal read.

On reflection, Goldberg decided to withdraw the book, refusing to pay back the advance, and successfully planted items in places like the *New York Post* that this Random House editor was a stooge of the Kennedys. I was even knocked in a *Spy* magazine piece on the Kennedy family influence.

In keeping with my early experience at Random House, no one really told me how to handle this situation. I said we should sue Damore for the money and we did. Robert Callaghy, a lawyer on retainer for Random House, and I showed up in a New York City courtroom on a Friday afternoon for the case to be heard. "TGIF," the judge said as he took his seat. When I was called to testify, the judge asked me to describe Random House's policy for factual accuracy in books. When I finished, noting that I had come from *The Washington Post*, the judge asserted that the *Post* could not meet that standard.

"Your honor," I replied, "the *Post* is not on trial."

"Oh, lighten up," the judge quipped.

Nonetheless, we won the case. The book was resold to Regnery, a right-wing publisher. It became a bestseller when released. As far as I know, no one ever raised the issues I had, then or ever. And in 2018, the book was the basis for a movie called *Chappaquiddick* and was reissued. Damore, however, died in 1995.

There were other challenges, including a book on John DeLorean, a colorful rogue who had manufactured cars until he was busted on a drug charge. That book's extended legal read was as daunting as the Dershowitz fracas. And there was an expensive investigative biography of Jesse Jackson, then in his prime, by three writers who never delivered a manuscript.

In the summer of 1984, Jason asked me to accompany him to dinner at "21" with Roy Cohn, the notorious New York fixer/lawyer and a close friend of Si Newhouse's from their schoolboy days. When we arrived at the restaurant, Cohn was not yet there, and the maître d' told us to wait in the bar. Jason turned on his heel and said we would meet Cohn at another restaurant. Recognizing what had happened, the owner chased us down the street and settled us into Cohn's prime table. Cohn, as was his preference, ate what looked like a can of tuna fish. Fortunately, that book, which was a pallid account of his life, was published elsewhere after he died.

For a newcomer, I was getting unusual attention in the press, especially in *The New York Times*, which then covered developments in publishing closely as a major New York industry. I was described as a possible heir to Bob Bernstein as CEO of the company. That was ridiculous, of course, because I was almost literally still finding my way to the restroom.

My approaches to agents and editors from other companies were mixed. As a representative of Random House, I had some cachet but realized that everyone was aware I was new and therefore probably ignorant. One of the most prominent agents, still very much in the business today, told me that if a publisher made money on one of his books, he had failed his client by having asked for too small an advance. Another leading agent, with whom I had many social friends in common, would chastise me for one thing or another. On one occasion the attack was such that she even called the next day to apologize, in tears.

My most logical competitor among editors was Alice Mayhew of Simon & Schuster, who was the revered steward of many of the great journalists then and until her death (still on the job) at age eighty-seven in 2020. I had met her briefly at the *Post* because she was the editor for the Woodward-Bernstein books. When I called to ask her to lunch, she said, "You must be kidding." We never did dine.

(She may not have noticed but in 1987, only three years after I got into the business, she and I were both named in an *Esquire* portrait of the publishing "universe" as leading nonfiction editors. If she did see it, it would not have helped in our relations.)

I had another early insight when I signed up a book by Sam Donaldson, ABC's White House correspondent, who was especially well known for his animated questioning style. He had covered both the Carter and Reagan presidencies. Three months after he started writing, he sent me a few listless pages—"stool samples," a friend helpfully described them.

This was clearly a problem. I went to his Virginia home and somehow, we devised a solution. You are a talker, I said, so talk to the word processor (as they were then called) rather than "write." Tell your stories with your colorful broadcast voice. I realized that journalists think because they are reporters, they should be able to work in any form of delivery. On the other hand, if you can play a violin you may not be able to handle the tuba. Michael Jordan was a great basketball player but only middling in baseball.

A few months later a stack of papers arrived, really a stream of consciousness memoir. I handed them to my new assistant, Lisa Kaufman, who had arrived after having worked as James Michener's assistant in Texas, and together we fashioned a book that became my first national bestseller, even being tied for number one on the *Times* list. Sam credited me in his acknowledgments, but I am herewith giving Lisa the recognition she deserved.

We got needling but good-humored quotes for the dust jacket from people Donaldson covered for the jacket. Ronald Reagan's was: "Sam Donaldson is the Ayatollah of the press corps," a reference to Iran's supreme leader, the sworn enemy of the United States. The best quote was from Sam's mother: "Sam was always an obedient child until he went back East."

Away from the office, Suze and I bought a co-op in Brooklyn Heights, in a building that was known to have had the borough's first elevator and to have been home to the playwright Arthur Miller's mother. The building was a hybrid of renters and owners, and the other two apartments on our floor were rent-controlled. One was home to an elderly but indomitable woman who outlasted us in the building and the other housed a couple who let their dog poop in the apartment and were generally smelly.

Our apartment was being renovated by the building developer. The process was going slower than expected, so at one point I appealed to him, tugging on his faith as an Orthodox Jew. "Do you really want us to mark Yom Kippur living on the street?" I asked. We moved in on time.

With my father's help, Airvel installed a state-of-the-realm central air-conditioning system. We had expansive views of lower Manhattan and, from the bedroom, of the Statue of Liberty. There was an ample master bedroom, two child-size bedrooms, and a spacious living room with room for a dining table. The kitchen had a large window, something of a luxury in New York apartments.

We enrolled Katherine and Evan at Packer Collegiate, one of two leading private schools in Brooklyn Heights. The other was called Saint Ann's School for Gifted Children, which was considered the tonier of the two schools, but Suze and the children sensed that there was something self-congratulatory about the vibe that they didn't like. So, Packer it was.

Under the terms of my employment, Random House provided a car to be exchanged every three years. Having just come from Europe, I chose a Peugeot station wagon, an unusual choice but impractical since the servicing had to be done at a garage almost an hour away in a remote part of Brooklyn.

Brooklyn Heights was just over the Brooklyn Bridge and considered an enclave of upscale "carriage trade–style" living in the otherwise working-class to ethnic middle-class neighborhoods of the borough like Flatbush, Fort Greene, or Williamsburg. Our Manhattan-based friends, on the whole, considered the journey to Brooklyn almost exotic. It took us time to understand or appreciate how rich the cultures of Brooklyn were. Next to Brooklyn Heights was Cobble Hill, a largely Italian-American neighborhood with a great stock of row houses and wide sidewalks. Atlantic Avenue had restaurants and shops that were owned by Arab merchants. Ultra-Orthodox Jews lived nearby. Park Slope had the beginnings of what became one of the most desirable neighborhoods in the city for young professionals.

With both of us now working in midtown Manhattan, daily logistics were complicated. Every day had to be organized from early morning send-offs to afterschool activities and longish vacations. We rotated part-time nannies (no live-ins) and deployed the children to afterschool programs. Many weekends we spent at a small outbuilding on the grounds of Suze's family home in Greenwich, Connecticut; the main house had been rented out. The kids slept on a roll-out. We were upstairs. There were hot plates and a small black-and-white television. We loved it, especially the trips out and back listening to Shel Silverstein reading his poems on cassettes and cast-recordings of musicals. Evan had a thing about running out of gas and kept us posted on the need for it. His best friend was a boy called Jocko. Katherine had school friends, among them Alexandra Whitney, Craig and Heidi Whitney's daughter. Evan was close to their son Stef. Sunday nights we would all gather at their apartment or ours. The kids paired off and we compared notes on our respective lives.

In its way our home life was idyllic, and yet we soon discovered that despite having twice the income as when I was at the *Post* and despite the fact that Suze was now working as well, we felt strapped. Private schools, year-round activities for the kids, the monthly maintenance on the apartment all added up, it felt, to barely what we could afford. I joined the board of our hybrid co-op, in which we and other owners had paid top dollar to share space with tenants whose lifestyles and resources were different from ours.

The co-op issues tended toward the absurd. To deter pigeons from noisily landing on his windowsills, one owner installed barriers and nets, sending the pigeons one floor up, to the outrage of that owner. We had lawyers living in the building, and the correspondence became so intense that, as (somehow, I was) the president of the board, I threatened to have it published, causing acute embarrassment to all involved.

There were disputes over what to do with the lobby to make it spiffier and enhance the value of our apartments, versus more mundane work on the elevator. There was no freight elevator. The Whitneys lived around the corner in a superbly run white-glove-doorman building. I can now confess I was envious and made a private resolve never again to share ownership of housing with people who were strangers. When we moved back to New York in 2014, we took a rental.

We joined the Casino, an elegant establishment across the street, a squash and tennis club for the gentry of the Heights. I worked out in its small gym and also began running in the neighborhood. The children took dancing lessons there. The Casino was featured in the film *Trading Places* as the quintessence of WASP style. Suze's brother Tony had a small part in the film, by coincidence.

As the first press director of Helsinki Watch and its new companion Americas Watch, Suze was responsible for shaping the strategy of human rights advocacy, very much a new concept. The most established organization was Amnesty International, whose members would launch letter-writing campaigns on behalf of political prisoners. The Watch committees were developing a different approach, a combination of Executive Director Aryeh Neier's focus on investigation and research and Bob Bernstein's skill at singling out leading dissidents—like Sakharov, Orlov, and Sharansky (called, for short, "SOS")—and turning them into global causes célèbres. I would later join the board of the organization, later renamed Human Rights Watch, the world's most important organization of that kind.

Whether the choice was strategic or instinctive, the Watch committees did research so thorough and impeccable that it could be the basis for advocacy that would be taken seriously. The media—and this was true at *The Washington Post*—considered advocacy of dubious credibility and rarely covered the reports and appeals that accompanied them. Many nongovernmental organizations used their work to raise money. By contrast, the Watch committees emphasized the investigation results. They did not have members but instead needed to have a handful of major donors willing to support what was still a little-understood concept. Whereas the civil rights and antiwar movements of the sixties had clear constituencies, the human rights agenda was less clear. In the Soviet bloc, national security conservatives and human rights liberals were aligned in opposition to the Kremlin. In Central America, human rights liberals were at loggerheads with conservatives who favored the autocratic leaders. In this way the Watch committees straddled ideology.

Aryeh's record of hiring women as key figures at the committee was impressive, although it needs to be said that because Suze left at five thirty or so, he thought, at least according to his demeanor, that she was working part-time. He once jokingly said that he employed women because they were cheaper than men. But thirty years later, when Aryeh was leaving the chairmanship of an organization called Center for Civilians in Conflict, he recommended Suze as his successor. And the role of women at what became Human Rights Watch was indispensable to its growth with a staff of nearly five hundred, an endowment of $150 million, and a peerless reputation for accuracy.

Chapter 17

Breaking Through

IN LATE SPRING OF 1984, very soon after my arrival, Bob Bernstein called me into his office to say that Howard Kaminsky, the publisher of Warner Books, would be coming to Random Trade as publisher. Jason would remain editorial director, technically reporting to Howard. Kaminsky, who was brash, smart, vulgar, and a personal favorite of Si Newhouse, was first cousin to the great comedian Mel Brooks and had a comparable persona.

Howard's style was clearly going to shake up the tweedy old-school vibe of the Random House imprint. Howard and I had never met, but by contract, I was to be named associate publisher after I finished six months on the job. Even so, Howard had no apparent use for me. Why would he? Nonetheless, my ascension was reported in *The New York Times* the same day as the story about Howard's appointment.

When Howard arrived after Labor Day, he organized the first-ever editorial meetings for the imprint and set out to jazz up the list with expensive commercial fiction. Vintage, the respected trade paperback list, added books on juggling, firehouse cooking, and other pop projects that made the editors wince. Howard was also responsible for the new Villard Books imprint, run by a savvy young editor named Peter Gethers, whose mandate was also popular culture and fiction.

Later that year, *The New York Times* decided to unload its book imprint because it was more trouble than it was worth persuading *Times* reporters to publish with this in-house company. The imprint's

greatest asset was crossword puzzles, although its list was more distinguished than its reputation. Random House purchased the imprint's contracts and licensed the Times Books name, and Jon Segal
soon became publisher, reporting to Howard. The great story about
the acquisition (which I confirmed with parties on both sides) was
that Random's opening offer was $1 million. The *Times* said that this
was too low. Somehow the figure of $4 million was said to be the
price. But the *Times* negotiators misunderstood the bid and the price
was settled at $1.4 million. Business in that era could clearly be
casual.

Howard then hired Carolyn Reidy, a very gifted subsidiary rights
director, to be associate publisher. (She later was CEO of Simon &
Schuster for twelve years before her death from a heart attack at age
seventy-one in 2020.) I was asked if I wanted to be associate editorial
director to Jason instead of associate publisher. I dodged that, recognizing that being Jason's deputy would be a problematical proposition. Howard soon set up a cabinet of Gethers, Segal, and Reidy. He
told me to look after the in-house copy editors. I knew that in the
imprint hierarchy, that role was peripheral. But I liked the scholarly
nature of what they did and hired Mitchell Ivers, with whom I worked
very closely because he was a much better line editor than I was. I
didn't realize it at the time, but others have now told me that Howard
was perfectly ready to see me rise or more likely fail on my own. I did
not ask him for help, other than approval of my acquisitions, and
never got much that mattered.

It soon became clear that Si Newhouse had Howard in mind to
be Bernstein's successor. Howard called himself the CEO of Random
House Adult Trade Books, which created confusion with Bob's title
as president of Random House, Inc. Bob's formidable assistant, Anne
Johnson, had Bob's letterhead changed to "Chairman, President and
CEO" after Bob complained that people were asking why he had
been replaced by Kaminsky. This was not a partnership destined to be
smooth.

I had internalized Bob's early advice to stay focused on the books and not the bureaucracy. I essentially shrugged off Howard's sidelining of me, which, in retrospect, was the right strategy.

After my acquisitions of Donaldson and Karnow, I cooked up two books on my own. When the space shuttle *Challenger* blew up in 1986, the most celebrated astronaut killed was a schoolteacher from New Hampshire named Christa McAuliffe. I recruited a reporter from her hometown newspaper to write a biography of Christa called *I Touch the Future*, on her role as teacher, mother, wife, and astronaut. It sold well. An excerpt appeared in a women's magazine, for which we were paid $75,000, a great deal of money for a serialization.

Around the same time, I read a profile in *The New Yorker* by Calvin Trillin of the *Miami Herald*'s ace police reporter Edna Buchanan, who was so well known that everyone in town called her just Edna. We called her book *The Corpse Had a Familiar Face*, one of Edna's legendary story openers. She was a wonderful character who lived in a small house on a Miami island cooled by ceiling fans. She kept a pistol in her glove compartment and boots in the trunk for use at bloody crime scenes. We got along but could never really get past the sign over her typewriter that read, "Never Trust an Editor, Never Trust an Editor, Never Trust an Editor." Edna became a successful crime novelist.

My breakthrough year turned out to be 1987. My biggest acquisition going into that year had been the memoirs of Thomas P. (Tip) O'Neill, the great speaker of the house who planned to retire after the 1986 midterm elections. I prevailed over Simon & Schuster in an auction because Kaminsky must have been directed by Newhouse to buy the book. Newhouse was apparently frustrated because the previous week S&S had prevailed in buying former UN ambassador Jeane Kirkpatrick's book for $975,000, and he believed Random House should be trying harder for commercial hits. Because the O'Neill auction was on a summer Friday when the office closed at one o'clock, I was alone. Bernstein was not involved. Howard relayed messages to me by phone. My competitor was Alice Mayhew, who had trouble reaching her boss, Dick Snyder, who was on the road to his weekend house and must not have had a car phone. So, I prevailed at Tip's $1 million. At the time that was considered a very large number. In the years that followed advances for prominent public figures and popular novelists routinely measured in the seven and even eight figure sums.

The auction was rich enough to justify a story in the *Times* with a front-page key. It said I was the acquiring editor, a very high-profile squib. That was relatively early in the process of politicians getting such lucrative advances for their memoirs. Tip's comment to critics was that he had spent a lifetime in public service and wanted to enjoy his retirement. That seemed to be a satisfactory response. Tip later did an ad for American Express on a beach with his feet in the sand under an umbrella, with a wide grin.

Tip chose as his coauthor Bill Novak, the sought-after cowriter of Lee Iacocca's multimillion-copy bestseller (and who would later work with me on Natan Sharansky's memoir of the Gulag). Boston-based journalists and politicos scoffed at the choice: although Bill lived in the area, he was not one of them. The word was that unless Tip talked in detail about Jack Kennedy and women (Kennedy had been his predecessor in representing that congressional district), the book couldn't be taken as truthful. He was after all writing a million-dollar book. Ridiculous? Afraid not. After all, salacious sells.

After acquiring Tip with some fanfare, I started to receive proposals for other big names. Lynn Nesbit, a prominent agent with a reputation for only handling upscale clients, sent me a few paragraphs from former President Jimmy Carter and his wife, Rosalynn, about how improvements in health care and other factors had added a decade to the life of twentieth-century Americans, which was to be a focus of the Carter Center, established in Atlanta.

For years after Carter lost reelection in 1980, his national reputation was blurry to negative. After writing his presidential memoir, *Keeping Faith*, Carter wrote a book about the Middle East called *The Blood of Abraham*. I was surprised to see how well it had sold.

So, I began to think about how these earnest paragraphs about health might form the basis of a book that people would want to read.

As I had done for Stanley Karnow's book on the Philippines, I enlisted the financial support of Ballantine to help pay the advance and set off for the Carter family home in Plains, Georgia. The simplest way to describe the home is to quote a Japanese philanthropist, who remarked when he saw it, "Not much of a house for a former president." (He became a major donor to the Carter Center despite a reputation in Japan for connections to gambling syndicates.)

The house was a single-story ranch house with a smallish kitchen, a work room for Carter's woodworking hobbies, a master bedroom where the Carters watched the evening news, and a dining table where we did the editorial work. What made it distinctive was the small Secret Service outpost at the end of the driveway. I once asked the agents there what it was like, and they said they had a lot of time for weightlifting and other activities, including following Carter on his morning runs. I joined him a couple of times. The pace was fine. I wish I had a way of remembering what we talked about.

(In Atlanta, at the headquarters of the Carter Center and presidential library, the couple had an apartment small enough to require a Murphy bed, to be lowered from the wall at nighttime.)

The idea we devised for the book was to be called *Everything to Gain: Making the Most of the Rest of Your Life.* The Carters were still in their fifties when they went home to Plains in defeat, with financial troubles at the family peanut business. It was never publicly reported at the time, but Rosalynn took the loss harder than Jimmy did. She had all the symptoms of advanced rheumatoid arthritis and needed help going from room to room. The symptoms subsided. Jimmy devoted himself to what was destined to become the most impressive postpresidential career in American history, including building houses with Habitat for Humanity and winning the Nobel Peace Prize.

The theme of the book was to combine social responsibility with a healthy lifestyle to take advantage of those extra years of life. The Carters wanted to write it jointly. It soon became clear that the process was not going well. Jimmy was a fast writer and Rosalynn was slow. I went back to Plains, stayed in a nearby motel, and the three of us ate our meals, after grace, in the kitchen, served by a housekeeper in a sweatshirt. My suggestion was that they write alternate paragraphs. His would have a J at the start and hers, an R. They did the writing and a researcher provided the supporting data. The book then flowed to completion.

One evening in the fall of 1986, as we were finishing our work on the book, Jimmy Carter's successor, Ronald Reagan, was confronted with the biggest scandal of his presidency, known as "Iran-Contra." I sat with the Carters in their bedroom watching Reagan's attempt to explain himself. Carter didn't say much, aside from noting that Reagan looked "very bad." I thought, with amazement, that I was watching a president brought low by Iran seeing his successor struggling with the same country.

Everything to Gain was published in the spring of 1987 and became a solid bestseller. Sam Donaldson's book was out at the same time. I suddenly had two *New York Times* bestsellers. Even more incredible, President Carter started to say in interviews that the effort to write the book with Rosalynn was the most contentious period in their marriage. At first I thought he was joking, but he said it often enough and so specifically that I think there really had been a problem. He even wrote somewhere that an editor came down from New York and saved their marriage.

Carter's next book was about his outdoor activities. He published that one with Bantam, which had published his presidential memoir. He came back to Random House for *Turning Point: A Candidate, a State, and a Nation Come of Age*, about his first run for office, for the Georgia State Senate in 1962. It was edited by Paul Golob, a young editor with exactly the right touch for Carter and other formidable authors. We then published a children's book, *The Little Baby Snoogle-Fleejer*, with illustrations by his daughter, Amy Carter.

Then Carter sent me a collection of his poetry for consideration. I was baffled. I wrote him that he was likely to be judged not as a former president but as an amateur poet, and the reaction might well be harsh in what is a cynical world. A few months later he sent me a page of paper headed "To Peter Osnos." (Carter never used "Dear.") On it he had pasted a poem torn from *The New Yorker* called "The Sea of Serenity" and underneath it wrote:

> *Poems editors seem to buy*
> *Don't make sense, lack rhyme and rhythm*
> *If they don't amuse or edify*
> *What else should we do with 'em.*
>
> Jimmy C.

Who am I, I wondered, to tell a former president of the United States that he couldn't publish a book of poetry if he wanted to? Carter had taken lessons from Miller Williams, a prominent poet who had appeared at his inauguration. I asked for the poems and sent them to three people in the Random House building for their judgment. Knopf had a proper poetry editor, Crown had just published poetry by Jimmy Stewart, and Villard had had a huge success with a book of bromides by Robert Fulghum called *All I Really Need to Know I Learned in Kindergarten.*

We came out somewhere between genuine poetry and the cachet of a celebrated author. One of our copy editors was herself a poet and she took on the book. Carter asked a sixteen-year-old named Sarah Elizabeth Chuldenko to do the illustrations. The book was called *Always a Reckoning and Other Poems.*

Here is the start of one called "Rosalynn":

> *She'd smile and birds would feel they no longer*
> *Had to sing, or it may be I failed*
> *To hear their song.*
> *Within a crowd, I'd hope her glance might be*
> *For me but knew that she was shy and wished to be alone.*

The book went on the *New York Times* bestseller list as nonfiction and stayed there for two months. Carter inscribed my copy, "Best wishes to Peter Osnos, our publisher, editor, referee, and friend."

On a Carter roll, I noted that he gave the homily every Sunday at the Maranatha Baptist Church in Plains and that these were being recorded. I asked Lynn Nesbit to send them to me, thinking that it would be an easy enough task to collect them into a book. Realizing that I had no experience in liturgy, I recruited two people to work with me. Nessa Rappaport had been the editor of Carter's presidential memoir at Bantam Books and was an observant Jew. Karl Weber, a Times Books editor specializing in business, was a faithful Episcopalian and asked to be on the team.

When the collected material arrived, it became clear we had a problem. The homilies were based on Baptist scripture and if Carter thought they made personal points, that's not how it read to us. We sent him a version designed to emphasize the more accessible material and scheduled a visit to Plains to discuss the process going forward.

It was a Saturday morning in the spring of 1996. Suze's brother Peter and his wife Marilu were visiting. We were lingering over brunch when the phone rang, and an agitated former president was on the other end. His message was blunt: we had turned his heartfelt religious teachings into bland and, to him, meaningless pap. There was no point in our coming to Plains, he said, and we should call off the book.

I managed to persuade Carter that Nessa, Karl, and I should still make the trip because it was all arranged. And finally he said okay. The next day we assembled at the dining room table in Plains, and I spent forty-five minutes, as I recall, explaining to Carter that while he may have thought the book was deeply personal, his use of the Baptist playbook actually created a barrier to real feeling about what he was saying. A better test, I said, would be explaining to readers why he called himself born again and how that came about. Mercifully, he seemed to understand our goals.

After a day or so, Nessa and I left, and Karl stayed on. When he and Carter finished, we had the makings of a book to be called *Living Faith*. In the acknowledgments Carter wrote, "After discussions with my publisher . . . it became clear that it would be better to describe how these Bible texts have helped to shape my Christian faith and how these religious beliefs have affected my life." He then credited Karl and Nessa for their "probing questions and suggestions," helping him to relate his interpretation of Scriptures to "some of the most interesting and controversial issues of modern society." It was a major success, selling about 250,000 copies. And there was enough left to say that Carter wrote a follow-up book called *Sources of Strength*.

Two final points about working with Carter, who went to Simon & Schuster for the rest of his writing career, which eventually numbered about twenty books. Every one of our books included a national tour in which Carter would sign copies at bookstores. He had a contest with himself to see how many books he could sign in an hour. Only he would know the actual count, but it probably was close to a thousand. He would not look up and would scribble *J. Carter* in a flash.

For one of the books, he was making an appearance at the 92nd Street Y, a major venue in New York for authors. I invited Evan, then a teenager, to come along, and we met Carter at the Waldorf-Astoria's presidential suite. The three of us then got into the back seat of a sedan with the Secret Service in front. It was around the time of the 1992 presidential debates and we discussed how it felt to have that much pressure in a campaign. Evan, sitting between us, sat straight and never moved his head to whoever was speaking. After Carter got out, I asked Evan why he had been immobile. He explained that the back seat was so tight that he was sure that if he turned to face the president, their noses would collide.

Working with a past, present, or future president tends to be unforgettable. A Speaker of the House can be unforgettable, too.

The collaboration with Tip O'Neill and Bill Novak was a master class in the editorial process, especially since I had only been at Random House for a year or two when I acquired the book. Bill did his research and met with Tip in Boston and Washington, as he was finishing his final term as speaker. I joined them whenever I could and read all the transcripts of their interviews.

Recently Bill shared a couple of his memories that added texture to my own recollections. On the vexed question of Kennedy and women, Tip's view (the only person who did not call him Tip was his wife Millie, who used Tom) was that he had nothing to say "while the widow, Jackie, was alive." Finally, Novak recalled, Tip got a little angry: "That guy would screw a skunk. Okay, are you satisfied?" We eventually concocted a line like: *There are a lot of stories about Kennedy and women. I'm just not going to repeat any of them.*

When we finished a full draft of the manuscript, Tip and I had lunch at a Capitol Hill club. I presented him with the thought that the publication of his book would be a lot like a political campaign in which he'd have to get booksellers and readers to "vote" for him. I could tell that Tip now understood how to handle the book going forward. "I'm asking you," he bellowed to a gathering of thousands of booksellers in the spring of 1987, "sell my book and I'll do everything I can to make it worth your trouble." They did. The book became a major bestseller.

Every book has its challenges. For Tip O'Neill, choosing a title was one of them. I was flummoxed until one day, after trying and rejecting a long list, *Man of the House* popped into my head. Done. Another challenge came when I shared the manuscript with a sales executive at Random House, who responded that it was enjoyable but lacking in gravitas. I hurriedly recruited a policy aide of Tip's and they crafted an epilogue called "What I Believe." A third came when we learned that *The New York Times* had asked William Safire, a former Nixon speechwriter and now a conservative columnist for the paper, to review it. "Tom," said Millie, "he's going to wipe the floor with you." Instead, the review featured on the front page of the *Book Review* with a smiling photo of Tip in a tam-o'-shanter, as Safire spoke admiringly of Tip's use of Boston speech. Safire was also the *Times's* language columnist.

When the first finished copies arrived from the bindery, I flew to Tip's cozy house "down the Cape" (as he called it) to present one to him. With Millie watching on the porch, I talked to Tip about his upcoming media schedule. "Not doing Phil Donahue," he said. "He'll just be asking me about abortion and I'm not going there." Donahue had a top-rated daytime show, and I must have shown how worried I was about Tip's stubbornness.

Millie looked up from her knitting and said, "Tom. He's begging you, Tom."

Tip said okay and went to Stamford, Connecticut, where the show was taped, with Mary Beth Murphy, a young publicist with the perfect Boston Irish-Catholic pedigree. Donahue did not ask about abortion.

A few years later we compiled a list of Tip's anecdotes in a book under the banner of his famous saying, *All Politics Is Local.* I remember two things about that project in particular. Tip gave us a cassette of Irish ditties he sang with his longtime assistant Leo Diehl, who for years (in a wheelchair) had been the guardian of who got into Tip's office on Capitol Hill. Jon Karp, a young editor (and later the CEO of Simon & Schuster), and I went to the Cape for an editorial session and stayed in a bed-and-breakfast near Tip's house. In the morning, Tip showed up and joined us for a very hearty repast of pancakes, bacon, and probably pastries. Millie, he confided, would be furious. Alas, Tip died just as that book was released. What a wonderful man he was, and a great politician, so sorely missed nowadays. The book is a classic of savvy.

Bill Novak and I proved to be a good match. As I've discussed, he helped me take Natan Sharansky's first draft of *Fear No Evil*, translated literally from the Russian, and render it into a polished manuscript. Bill reminds me that I told him that he would have to do the project at somewhat less than the top-tier payment he deserved. When we were done, Bill told me he would have done it for nothing. "Now you tell me?" I replied.

I would often say that Bill had the attributes of a great character actor, like Alec Guinness. His writing face was fine but generic. That enabled him to adopt the persona of the individual with whom he was collaborating. He would do the background research and tape his interviews and, as we did with Tip, I would read the transcripts and join in interviews wearing my reporter's robes. I had enough background in most of these areas to help Bill with the context of the stories. He said that he was surprised in our first project with Tip how much I seemed to know about Congress, which I must have learned as national editor, although I didn't realize at the time how much I was absorbing.

One instance of Bill's process that really stands out was for a book I didn't publish. I recently asked Bill for his recollection of an episode involving Oliver North, the Marine lieutenant colonel who as a White House aide was at the center of the Iran-Contra scandal during the Reagan administration, in which North and others sold arms to Iran and then gave the money from those sales to the Nicaraguan Contras in direct defiance of Congress. The episode was the most serious threat to Reagan's presidency—I mentioned earlier watching Jimmy Carter seeing Reagan on television struggling to explain himself.

As so often is the case with scandal celebrities, North got a lucrative book contract and Novak signed on to write it, apparently without any public announcement. Here's Bill on what happened:

"You said to me one day, 'I realize you can't confirm this, but I know you are working with Oliver North. It would be great if he could say, "Reagan knew everything."' I know a good line when I hear it, so I discussed it with Ollie, and he said, 'Sure.' Those words appeared on the cover of *Time* magazine . . . Your brief comment may have been the most helpful editorial advice I ever received and was for a book you even weren't working on."

I remembered suggesting that North add "I think," but when I consulted the book there was no conditional wording. I got a note from North on Marine "Semper Fi" stationery saying, "Your words were right from the start!" At trial, North was acquitted, and the book did very well. What did Reagan really know? I have no idea.

The next project I worked on with Bill was the memoirs of Nancy Reagan. Random House had acquired the book from Mort Janklow for about $2 million. Kate Medina, a very highly regarded editor who had joined Random House from Doubleday, was handling the project, and a female writer was selected as the collaborator. After a few months it became clear that Nancy (as we were told to call her) was unhappy with the writer and wanted a change. Our publisher, Joni Evans, suggested that Novak be brought in, and he was retained. Bill said he wanted me to work with him. An awkward but eventually successful tag team was created whereby Kate was Nancy's editor and I was Bill's. I did spend a good amount of time with Nancy, and it was memorable.

Our first meeting was at the White House a year or so before Ronald Reagan's term was ending. We met on the second floor in the family quarters. Nancy—in a red dress, her preferred color—sat on the couch with her legs tucked under her, a girlish posture for so exalted a personage. She had a small dog next to her. Kate, Bill, and I were arrayed around her. Nancy's soliloquy was startling. She said that her life in the White House had been harder than anyone realized. Only seventy days after they moved in, Ronnie (as she called him) was badly wounded by a would-be assassin. She said she never again felt comfortable watching him leave her side.

She described her frustration at the media's smirking about her dishes, her clothes, her devoted gazes at Ronnie. She added that she had been publicly embarrassed by critical comments from her son and daughter. Both she and Ronnie had been treated for cancer. Her beloved stepfather died. "You think this is fun?" she asked. My unexpressed thought was that this would be a fascinating book if what she was telling us was in the narrative.

We asked for a very thorough tour of the White House, from attic to basement, and got it. We learned that the Reagans shared a bedroom and watched television in the evening with food trays in front of them. We saw their exercise machines and Nancy's dressing room, complete with her array of scents and cosmetics. We went into the Lincoln Bedroom at the far end of their floor. Upstairs was the glass enclosed solarium where Nancy learned that Ronnie had been shot and which she avoided from then on.

Walking through the White House in that way, recognizing who else had lived there, was thrilling, and I marked it down in the same category as, over the years, being in Prince Charles's private library; Margaret Thatcher's sitting room at Downing Street; dinner at the Kremlin; the room where Stalin died; the Carters' bedroom; and many other venues that do not feature on any tourist itineraries.

Over the next eighteen months we would meet with Nancy in swank places like the Carlyle Hotel in New York and the Bel-Air in Beverly Hills. Nancy seemed to enjoy the process. She'd put her heels on coffee tables and I never recall her showing impatience with us. In our Bel-Air suite, she told us that when she and Ronnie were courting, the movie fan magazines were recording their romance in detail. I observed that she was a starlet and he had just gotten divorced from Jane Wyman, who had called him the most boring man in the world.

The next day Nancy arrived with seven scrapbooks of clips about her and Ronnie. What was especially noticeable about them was that every reference to Jane Wyman was crossed out in ink. Mrs. Reagan was fierce when she wanted to be.

A major issue about the president was the widespread belief that for all his geniality, he was personally very remote. Reagan's letters, when later published, showed connections to people that were not apparent in his dealing with staff and even friends. One description was that people always left encounters with him feeling a bit frustrated at not really reaching him. The Reagans had friends from their California life, but these were mostly maintained by Nancy. Vice President George Bush and his wife, Barbara, served with the Reagans for eight years and, I was told, were never invited to a dinner upstairs with just Ronnie and Nancy.

The most famous example of Reagan's inaccessibility was the experience of his chosen presidential biographer, Edmund Morris. Based on his brilliant biography of Theodore Roosevelt, Morris was given complete access to the president and those around him. The book was Random House's and I was one of those auditioned to be the editor. Bob Loomis, the distinguished fiction and nonfiction editor—the year Sheehan won the nonfiction National Book Award, a novel Bob edited was the fiction winner—was selected.

When the book was finally published in 1999, it was called *Dutch* (Reagan's nickname) and featured a fictional character telling the story. Morris said he found Reagan "inscrutable." His view was that Reagan was, at his core, too hollow to be properly portrayed. Critics of the book were not impressed, saying that Morris, for all his access and writerly skill, had punted.

Almost a decade before, in working with Nancy, the question always was, what was Nancy's real relationship with Ronnie? Was their closeness her delusion? Bill, Kate, and I needed to come up with the answer.

Here is what appeared in the book: "Although Ronnie loves people, he often seems remote, and he doesn't let anybody get too close. There's a wall around him. He lets me come closer than anyone else, but there are times when even I feel that barrier."

Looking at the book now, I see that some of Nancy's observations were truly sad, reflecting the pain she had described in that first meeting we had: "What I wanted most in all the world was to be a good wife and mother. As things turned out, I guess I've been more successful at the first than at the second."

Bill was finding the writing harder than he expected, thinking that he had somehow missed too much of the story to make it work. We took all the transcripts to my home—by then we had moved into the main house in Greenwich—spread them out on the floor, and pieced them together. He later wrote me, "I flew to Connecticut in despair and you showed me there really was a book there. I wasn't quite persuaded. But I came home with some hope."

When Nancy's book, *My Turn*, was released in 1989, she was still vulnerable to attacks of one kind or another. The best word to describe the reviews is snarky. One biography published around that time said that she had had an affair with Frank Sinatra during her White House years. I very much doubt that. Her devotion to Ronnie was real and deep. As time went on, the public view of Nancy seems to have softened and her commitment to her husband and her stance against narcotics stopped being mocked. *My Turn* did very well in spite of the reviews. The last time I saw her was at a big dinner a year or two before she died. She was frail and couldn't see well, but when I introduced myself, she brightened and said, "We did have fun, didn't we?" And we did.

In my circles, working with Nancy was not admired. There was an undercurrent that for all my supposed seriousness of purpose, I was making someone who was not popular look better than she was. Editing Nancy, however, was not nearly as consequential in defining my early editorial legacy as the work I was doing with a New York real estate figure named Donald J. Trump.

Chapter 18

The Art of the Deal

IN THE FALL OF 1984, a few months after my arrival at Random House, I was at lunch with Si Newhouse and Bob Bernstein. We were in the Bahamas at a sales conference, and dining with the owner and the boss was, I'm sure I thought at the time, a big deal. I had been told that Newhouse was ordinarily phlegmatic, but on one subject he was animated: Donald Trump, a glamorous young New York real estate mogul who had completed construction of a shimmering tower on Fifth Avenue with his name embossed in large gold letters. This Trump fellow, Newhouse said, was more than a comer. He had arrived. At the suggestion of Si's close friend Roy Cohn, Trump had recently appeared on the cover of *GQ*, one of the Newhouse-owned Condé Nast magazines. The issue had flown off the newsstands.

By 1984, Trump had been around for a decade. In 1976, a first profile in *The New York Times* said: "He is tall, lean and blonde and he looks ever so much like Robert Redford. He rides around town in a chauffeured silver Cadillac ... He dates slinky fashion models ... and at only 30 years of age estimates that he is worth $200 million." The story noted that he was New York's "number one" real estate promoter of the mid-1970s.

This was my first encounter with Newhouse on a book issue. Word was that he was hands-off when it came to acquisitions, although I learned that he could make his point absolutely clear when he wanted to. On this occasion, he said emphatically, let's do a book with Trump.

Newhouse said that he would arrange to see Trump and propose a book. It was decided that Howard Kaminsky and I would go along with him.

It has been said that it was Newhouse's idea, or maybe Kaminsky's, to mock up a cover of a Trump book with shiny black paper and big gold letters. I'm pretty sure the idea was mine because I put the cover on a Russian novel that I had on my shelf.

The meeting date arrived, and we were led into Trump's twenty-sixth-floor office by his personal assistant, an elegant woman named Norma Foerderer. The office had a spectacular view of Central Park and the Plaza Hotel, which Trump coveted. The walls were covered with his picture on magazine spreads and some plaques. There was a large phone console, but Trump summoned Norma and others with a shout.

Newhouse made the pitch. Trump liked the cover but said his name should be larger. I never figured out whether Trump was engaging in self-parody making that observation or ones like it later. There was sarcasm in Trump's manner but I never spotted irony. By the end of the meeting, it was clear that Trump was ready to do the book. Either then or immediately thereafter we learned that a writer named Tony Schwartz, who had worked at *Newsweek* and the *Times*, had already come to Trump with the concept of a book they would write together, to be called *The Art of the Deal*. All the pieces were in place. I don't remember dealing with either an agent or a lawyer. The advance was $500,000, to be split evenly from the first dollar with Schwartz as the coauthor.

The Trump process was not like the other books I was handling. Tony Schwartz was not a ghostwriter: his name got full billing on the cover, and he did a masterful job on the book. He shadowed Trump, channeled his stories, and made the narrative very readable. He framed Trump in the best possible light. I did not watch that process closely and was impressed by the results. There wasn't much for an editor to do and I doubtless told Tony so. (Tony has repeatedly and very publicly said that he now deeply regrets being Trump's coauthor. I have no reason to doubt that he is sincere in his chagrin.)

Instead, my responsibility became all the publishing elements—how the book looked and how it would be marketed and publicized. I became the Random House sponsor of what we thought would be a significant seller in the holiday buying season of 1987. I don't recall that Newhouse was involved in any way; signaling his interest in the book with the sales department, for example. They may not have known. Kaminsky would logically have been at the helm of our efforts, but somehow, he was not. And in October 1987, just a month before Trump's publication date, he was fired by Bob Bernstein. His successor was Joni Evans, who came from Simon & Schuster in the wake of her divorce from Dick Snyder, who was that company's CEO. She was as street-savvy as Kaminsky, with additional assets of tact and charm. She spent the fall getting her bearings. That meant I was the point person on *The Art of the Deal*.

In the months leading up to the book's release, I accompanied Trump to meetings with the heads of the major chain retailers, which were led by Waldenbooks, with well over a thousand stores in malls and storefronts around the country. The CEO was Harry Hoffman, a big man with an equally large ego, who tended to think book publishers were fusty and way behind in understanding how books should properly be sold. At some swank French restaurant, I watched Hoffman and Trump bond. They agreed that they could make *The Art of the Deal* a number one bestseller. Hoffman was even a larger man than Trump, and I could sense a mutual swoon as I observed, probably very quietly, from the other side of the table.

The design team devised a snazzy dust jacket for the book, with Trump's photograph against a photo of Central Park in the background, the same cover that is on the book being sold today. Lining up media—the Random House publicity department was superb—went quickly. The top shows of the time, Phil Donahue in daytime and Larry King at night, as well as almost anyone else who asked, were each given a slot. Publication was scheduled for right after Thanksgiving.

In December, the big book party took place. It was in the Trump Tower atrium, festooned for the season. It was lavish. Black tie. Paparazzi. Spotlights outside with onlookers behind barriers. I was the Random House person on the receiving line standing next to Newhouse with Trump and Schwartz. I found myself shaking hands with a long line of movers and shakers including heavyweight boxing champ Mike Tyson, Barbara Walters, Barry Diller, and Norman Mailer (a surprisingly close friend of Roy Cohn). The book had already landed on the *Times* bestseller list in its first week, and I gave the celebratory toast. The mood was jubilant.

At that very moment my wife Susan was in Moscow with a delegation from Human Rights Watch, where she was meeting with prominent dissidents. Susan and I have been a couple since the early 1970s. Never in our marriage can it be said that we were further apart in geography or spirit.

Sales were enormous. The book went to number one and stayed there. Random House had shipped about 125,000 copies to start. They disappeared very fast. Reprints were ordered and shipped on an almost daily basis to keep up with demand. Trump was thrilled. Schwartz, on the other hand, was frustrated to learn that some booksellers were out of stock. He had stores on his speed dial and would report that fact in furious calls. I've always believed that of the two bylines on the book, Schwartz was the more frenetic. Given the 50/50 split in the contract, he was on the way to making a fortune in royalties. Trump, however, was definitely not passive.

Joni Evans would later tell me that she was at home during Christmas week when Trump called to say he wanted a thousand copies delivered to Aspen for his upcoming ski vacation.

Donald, it is Christmas, she said. All the warehouses are closed. He said to deal with it, and he would send the books out on his jet. Evans managed to reach Si Newhouse. The warehouse was mobilized. The copies reached Aspen and were sold.

There was a widespread and publicly gossiped-about belief that Trump was buying his own book to boost his bestseller numbers. The books were certainly being pushed at his casinos and other places with the Trump brand. But as people then, perhaps, did not understand, Trump doesn't spend money if he doesn't have to. The sales of *The Art of the Deal* were at a million copies in hardcover by mid-1988—and they were true sales.

My relations with Trump were smooth. He was so glad to have been solicited by Newhouse and had become, in what for him had been an easy climb, a national celebrity. The *New York Times* review ended with this notable sentence: "Mr. Trump makes one believe even for a moment in the American dream." Then there was this ambiguous closing line: "It's like a fairy tale."

Natan Sharansky's *Fear No Evil* was published six months later, and as I have mentioned, its sales fell below my expectations. At the time I thought my dismay had to do with the book's commercial shortfall. It had been one of my biggest financial bets since arriving at Random House. There was going to be a considerable write-off on the advance. But I gradually came to understand that something else was responsible for my sense of failure. I had really done very little to make Trump's book a commercial triumph and was not emotionally engaged with it. I had been tasked to the mission and pulled it off. Sharansky was to me a soulmate. After all, he had gone to the gulag and I went home. And his book's sales were disappointing.

It was probably the following fall that Evan expressed a fascination with professional wrestling of the scripted kind. He said he would like to go to a World Wrestling Federation extravaganza in Atlantic City and asked to bring a friend. This was a Trump-promoted event. I called Norma in Trump's office and was sent three tickets. Their ostensible face value was $10,000 each, clearly a phony price. What I noticed at the packed arena was that the wrestlers were very big and the referees were very small. When Trump arrived to take his seat, the crowd went wild with applause. He was at least as big a star as Hulk Hogan or whoever was in the ring that day. *The Art of the Deal* and the surrounding fuss had made him a hero to wrestling fans.

It was probably inevitable that either Trump or Newhouse would propose a sequel. And so plans for one were launched.

Newhouse and I were invited to lunch on Trump's yacht—the *Princess*, a 281-foot vessel he bought from a Saudi billionaire arms dealer—anchored in the East River. What I most remember was that by dessert, Newhouse had authorized a $2.5 million advance, five times what we had paid for the first book. Once again, I was to be the editor.

Schwartz told me that he was not available so I recruited Charles Leerhsen, a gifted *Newsweek* writer who had coauthored the memoirs of the legendary test pilot Chuck Yeager. Again, I don't recall Trump using a lawyer, although I am sure someone did review the deal for him.

As the work began, I sensed that Trump's world was starting to be troubled. In October 1989, three of Trump's top casino executives were killed in a helicopter crash on the way to Atlantic City. When I expressed my condolences to Trump he replied, I recall, "You know, I was supposed to be on that chopper." Chopper? Remembering my own close encounter with an exploded helicopter in Vietnam, I would have liked to know whether that was really the case.

In February, Trump's boxer, Tyson, was defeated in Tokyo by Buster Douglas despite being a heavy favorite. Instinct told me that was not a good sign.

Then word spread that Trump's marriage was going under, despite his wife Ivana's executive role in his acquisition of the Plaza Hotel. The new woman in his life was yet to be revealed. Trump was still opening casinos in Atlantic City, most notably the Taj Mahal. But there were whispers that he was overstretched.

By the end of May 1990, we had a manuscript in draft. The only time I ever saw Trump lose his temper came when we sent a photographer to do a cover picture in Trump's office at the Tower. Arriving early, the photographer attached black garbage bags to the ceiling to reduce glare. When Trump saw the bags, he demanded they be removed and tossed the photographer, telling him that he would be charged for any damage to the paint.

The photo we eventually chose was Trump tossing an apple in the air, which had been on the cover of *Fortune*.

The title we chose was *Surviving at the Top*. On the back of the dust jacket were these words: "This is Phase Two of my life, in which the going gets a lot tougher and the victories, because they are harder won, seem all the sweeter . . . I know that whatever happens, I'm a survivor—a survivor of success, which is a very rare thing indeed."

The annual gathering of publishers and booksellers was in Las Vegas in early June. Trump was invited to be a speaker at one of the main events, a breakfast at which roughly three thousand people would be in attendance. The night before, Random House hosted a reception for about a thousand people at the Mirage Hotel honoring Trump and the mega-bestselling novelist Jean Auel and her *Clan of the Cave Bear* series.

I was to be Trump's escort. I went to the airport in a stretch limo to pick him up. When Trump exited his jet and settled into the car, he said he had a surprise. And there was Marla Maples, the secret paramour.

At the Mirage, Trump and Maples were given one of the fanciest suites. At the appointed hour I went to pick him up for the party. Maples opened the door wearing a peach-colored bikini. She was gorgeous. The gala was a success. Then Trump, Si Newhouse, Alberto Vitale (Bob Bernstein's successor as CEO of Random House), Joni Evans, and I went to dinner in a private room with a small group of top-tier booksellers, including the owner of Barnes & Noble, Leonard Riggio, and Mr. and Mrs. Ingram, owners of the country's largest book wholesaler, based in Nashville.

As we were about to start, Maples appeared in a stunning pink suit she said she had bought in a hotel boutique. Given that she was still supposed to be incognito, her presence caused a stir. I can't be sure of what the guests thought, but it was hard to imagine they were not dazzled.

Early the next morning I picked up a copy of *The Wall Street Journal* and saw featured on the front page a major piece about Trump's finances. In short, they were a mess. He was billions of dollars in debt, of which a very significant part was his personal responsibility. It was, by any measure, a full take-down.

The other speakers at the breakfast were the novelist T. Coraghessan Boyle and Angela Lansbury, the beloved actress. Boyle went first. Then Lansbury, who far exceeded the fifteen minutes she was allotted. Trump gave a spirited talk. My assumption was that the only people in the ballroom who had read the *Journal* story were the Random House contingent. The audience was enthusiastic.

Trump left the stage and we were rushing off to his plane to fly to New York. Before I left, Vitale whispered to me, in effect, "Get this book out fast. He is a wasting asset." On the flight were Newhouse, Evans, Maples, Trump, and me. I was watching Trump carefully to see how he was doing. I couldn't spot any anxiety. I don't remember anyone mentioning the story or his finances. I do remember thinking that as we were flying across the country, Trump's public reputation as a mogul was being badly tarnished. And in fact, *The Wall Street Journal* was a major story of the day.

On board we had a lavish lunch of shrimp, charcuterie, and assorted rich desserts. And then over the middle of the country, Trump took Maples into his private cabin and did not emerge until about ninety minutes later. I would not have been surprised if he had opened the jet's door and jumped out. Instead, he seemed unfazed. We landed at an airport in Newburgh, New York, in early evening.

Our Random House team scrambled to get *Surviving at the Top* finished and distributed as soon as possible. The publication date was moved to mid-August. About that time, I learned that *New York* magazine was planning a full feature on the book, around the theme of Trump's troubles. I was asked for my picture to go with the story. My private dread was that the caption would be something like: *He edited this dog*. I called Ed Kosner, the magazine's editor, whom I knew slightly. I asked him if would leave me out if I could find a better picture than mine for the story. He told me to try.

Carol Schneider and I studied contact sheets of snapshots taken at the Mirage party. We found one of Trump, Newhouse, Vitale,

Evans, and John Updike, the venerated writer and obviously a guest. That satisfied Kosner and I was spared, although I was quoted about our positive expectations for the book.

I hadn't looked at the book for thirty years, and so I found a copy and discovered this paragraph included from *The New York Times* of June 8, 1990, right after the *Journal* story broke. It closed: "Arrogance? For sure. And yet in a world lacking individual heroes, even some of Donald's critics must confess to a sneaking respect for his insistence on being himself, however outrageous, and catch themselves hoping that he'll find the strength and luck to escape."

Random House shipped hundreds of thousands of copies. Typical of the criticism was the review by Michael Lewis, who said in the *Times* that the book "is a portrait of an ego gone haywire." The book started at number one on the *Times* bestseller list and lasted in the top fifteen for seven weeks. Warner Books bought the paperback rights for $1 million, helping Random House recoup some of its investment. Warner changed the title to *The Art of Survival* and released it in July 1991. It isn't really possible now to assess the book's results, but my recollection is that returns of unsold inventory were about 80 percent of what had been distributed—ten times the level of returns for *The Art of the Deal*.

With *Surviving at the Top* finished, my regular contacts with Trump came to an end. In 1992, Trump hired Stephen Bollenbach, a leading financial executive in the hotel business, with the mandate to straighten out his debts. It would be hard to penetrate how he did his work, but a number of Trump assets—the Trump Shuttle, the Plaza, the yacht—were off-loaded. At the time the word was that Bollenbach put Trump on a $400,000-a-month allowance. In two years, Trump was apparently out of the worst trouble. When I later asked Trump how he had found Bollenbach and persuaded him to salvage his finances and the standing of the Trump Organization, he told me he had read about him in *BusinessWeek* and called him. Like that.

I can resolutely affirm that when I was asked to edit book three in the Trump canon, it was one of the factors—the proverbial straw on the camel's back—that led me to leave Random House. That book was published in 1997 as *The Art of the Comeback*.

At a White House Correspondents Association dinner about a decade later, I spotted Trump and his third wife, Melania, making their way through the crowd. He saw me, too, and I think he gave me a thumbs-up.

In the time since Trump announced his presidential bid in 2015 with his infamous Mexican "rapists" speech, I have watched his trajectory with a mix of recognition and increasing horror. Today's Trump is in many ways the same person I knew in the 1980s. He lives "over the store" in the White House as he did in Trump Tower. He neither smokes nor drinks. He obsesses about his image in the media and always needs to "hit back harder," in Roy Cohn's parlance. Back then, though, he got very little significant negative press. His estimable assistant, Norma Foerderer, has died, but her number two, Rhona Graff, is now his executive assistant in New York. Something about Trump confounds his reputation as a complete misogynist. He clearly grabs at women when he can, but others have worked for him for years and remain on station.

What is different now is that all of Trump's characteristics have become exaggerated. His instinct to personally insult people, for instance. I doubt he needs help to devise all those withering nicknames. His bluster and his knack for inciting full-throated outrage from his rally supporters echoes the approach of the worst demagogues in history. He does not take advice from anyone who disagrees with him. He makes all the decisions. No setback is acknowledged.

The upsides I saw of Trump—his energy, his daring, and his ability to navigate New York's toughest businesses without getting into criminal trouble—have become subsumed in the demeanor of an old man swinging wildly from his shaky mountaintop. Too many people have made outsiders' diagnoses of his mental condition. All I can add is that I very much don't like what I see. More than thirty years ago, when I was in the Trump orbit, Norma Foerderer asked me to have lunch with Trump's niece Mary, then a graduate student with aspirations to write. She and I went to a Japanese restaurant, and as we were preparing to leave, I asked, "What's he like at Thanksgiving?" referring of course to Trump. "You mean crazy Uncle Donald?" she replied. In 2020, Mary wrote a smash-hit book about Donald and the family. A long time ago she had picked up on the traits that have been so visibly on display from the Oval Office.

In 2016, Trump lost the popular vote for president by 3 million votes but emerged victorious in the Electoral College. On January 20, 2017, he was sworn in as president. I considered that fact a metaphor for Trump's life and career until then. In nearly a half century in real estate, construction, gambling, boxing, wrestling, beauty contests, and reality television, he defied the odds against getting his persona visibly burned by corruption. He survived four bankruptcies. He fathered five children from three wives and paid off two of those and at least one porn star and a *Playboy* Playmate. His campaign manager and personal lawyer went to prison. Others in his orbit have been convicted or have pleaded guilty to crimes and corruption. He hired and fired four of this country's most distinguished generals. He emerged tarnished but intact from the Mueller probe of his Russia ties. He became the third president to be impeached and then acquitted. It was the coronavirus pandemic—a natural catastrophe—that turned out to be the challenge that defied Trump's ability to wave it off, although he certainly tried. In his final days in office, after refusing to concede a loss in the 2020 election, he was impeached again for inciting an assault on the Capitol.

I am often asked if I regret having been the editor of a book that made Trump a national figure. I do regret that it helped to make him the person he became. Yet I was trained in journalism, and Trump was a terrific story. I was tasked by Si Newhouse to manage him on that first book. On the second book I was acting as a professional with a successful repeat author. When the third book was proffered, I departed. And that is a fact that I do not regret, then or any time since.

Chapter 19

Bill and Barack

AFTER A STINT as a congressional aide and senior positions in the unsuccessful but honorable presidential campaigns of Eugene McCarthy, Gary Hart, and others, my old college pal Eli Segal turned up in Little Rock as the chief of staff for Bill Clinton's 1992 campaign. After Clinton and Al Gore were nominated, the campaign released a policy compendium called *Putting People First*. Either Eli or I had the idea of publishing a paperback edition of the book. By this time I had become the publisher of the Times Books imprint and was managing a small but talented staff of editors. I saw *Putting People First* as an opportunity for Times Books to bring a document of great public interest to a broad readership hungry to learn more about the Democratic ticket and what the candidates planned to do if elected. And we could do it without having to pay a cent to its authors. We designed a cover of these two young men that the campaign liked so much they used it as a poster and waved around the book at rallies. *Putting People First* was a major success, selling in the hundreds of thousands of copies and establishing our imprint as a master of the "instant book," or as I thought of them, "rabbits" to be pulled out of hats. They were also out of the regular budget cycle, meaning they produced revenue you hadn't had a glimmer you would have when you devised the budget, and could give a boost to an otherwise lackluster year.

Four years later, Eli was an assistant to the president, having launched AmeriCorps, the national service program that was one of Clinton's signature achievements. Meanwhile, at Times Books, I was concerned over what seemed to be a projected budget deficit in that year's trade book list. I suggested to Eli that the president might like to do a book about his plans for a second term. On February 12, 1996, Eli met with Clinton in the Oval Office and then called me to say that the president had not only agreed but was surprised that the process had not already begun. In my office my colleagues cheered. But I had a slightly ominous feeling about this, which turned out to be justified.

To begin with, how do you sign up a book with a sitting president? Clearly there could not be a contract in which he was paid for a political tract. So my colleagues and I devised a plan: Times Books would pay all the expenses connected to the book. The company retained a prominent Washington lawyer named Bruce Sanford who was experienced in book matters. A writer/researcher was identified, a fellow named William Nothdurft, and Times Books agreed to pay all his expenses including, I joked, "his futon." Then I managed to persuade the estimable Random House lawyer Lesley Oelsner that we could make this happen. Sometime in March a contract was signed.

It was agreed that the project would be kept secret, so it would not become a campaign issue. Don Baer, the White House communications director, was our liaison with the president. We also knew that some people in the White House considered the book a distraction and opposed Clinton working on it. One spring afternoon we had a meeting in a West Wing reception room attended by Clinton; Baer; Harold Ickes, a senior aide with a political portfolio; Steve Wasserman, our editorial director, who would be editing the book; and me. It was about four in the afternoon, and Clinton arrived in a tracksuit, looking relaxed. About halfway through our conversation on the book's contents, he took a call from Bruce Lindsey, one of his closest assistants. He moved to another part of the room, but we overheard him say, "She did?" and some version of wow. He then returned and we continued talking until we were interrupted after about forty-five minutes. I later learned from Eli that Lindsey had reported that Janet Reno, the attorney general, had referred Hillary

Clinton's activities in what was known as the Whitewater case to a federal grand jury. We had just seen what became known in the ensuing years of the Clinton presidency as his "compartmentalization" between scandal and substance.

From then on, I worried about the process, not without reason. We were not seeing pages. Eli was scheduled to meet with Clinton several times, but each meeting was canceled when something else intervened: Secretary of Commerce Ron Brown was killed in a plane crash and then later a TWA plane out of New York exploded. Finally, Eli called one night to say that one chapter had been concluded, to my vast relief. I was in constant and doubtless nagging touch with Eli and Don Baer. It wasn't just that I wanted the glory of the book, but Times Books was being pressured on the budgetary front, and I needed the revenue that this book would bring. I was also under a lot of stress that spring trying to convince Jimmy Carter to accept my team's editorial judgment about the book that would become *Living Faith*. I once told Suze during this period that I was having a very tough day with my presidents.

It was now early August, with the Democratic convention scheduled for later in the month. We needed to have the book in stores in September to ride the crest of the fall campaign. I was in Lakeside and the Clintons were flying to a vacation in Jackson Hole, Wyoming. Baer called to say, "He's done it, signed off on the additional chapters." There were four. I called Wasserman, who was alone in the Random House building, to relay the news. Then Baer called again to say the pages had been misplaced. This was still an age when edits were all on paper, so a lost manuscript would have been a catastrophe. When I reached Wasserman (he later told me), "I developed a migraine, went blind in one eye and took to the floor." Finally, the manuscript was located, faxed to New York, and rushed into production. The book was called *Between Hope and History: Meeting America's Challenges for the 21st Century*. It was to be published on September 1 at 178 pages. We had suggested a $14.95 paperback, but Alberto Vitale said it should be a $16.95 hardcover.

This is the place to say that Steve was especially good in a crisis. He told me recently that he and Baer were at the printers in Pennsylvania but could not order the work to start because the president had not yet sent in his dedication. I was touting the book at a sales conference. This was another breath-holding moment in the Clinton saga.

At the Random House sales conference I announced our secret book. The news was of sufficient interest to appear on the front page of the next day's *New York Times*. I went back to Lakeside thinking that the right number to print was 200,000 copies. Within days we had orders for 600,000. Given our revenue pressures and the fact that no one gave me different counsel, I went ahead with the larger number. On the other hand, I had read the book and knew that it was bland rhetoric, having been massaged by a political adviser, Dick Morris, whose brief ascendency in the Clinton orbit ended when he was involved in a sex scandal. (He later became a fierce Clinton critic, but he did get a lucrative book contract with Random House for his story.) I had retrieved enough pages of the manuscript with Clinton's distinctive handwriting to know that, ultimately, we were safe in saying that it really was his book.

A *Library Journal* review said, "This work is better than the usual puffery written to produce votes through a rosy assessment of one's performance." Richard Bernstein, the *New York Times* reviewer, was critical, calling it a *Cliffs Notes* for Clinton's ideas, and saying that "while there is a bit of vision, there is not much that deserves the word destiny and only the briefest sketches of history." The book had a brief stay at the top of the *Times* bestseller list and soon dropped off.

As Election Day approached, David Streitfeld, the *Washington Post* reporter who covered the book publishing business, wrote that the book was being returned by "the train load." In an interview with Brian Lamb on C-SPAN, Clinton was asked why the book had not done better. The gist of his response was that he had been too busy to promote it; he also said it should have been a paperback. I wrote Clinton that he was the first author in history to say that a book's disappointing sales were not the publisher's sole fault. I didn't get an answer. As I recall, the book sold about 175,000 copies, which means that my original instinct would have been right. The lesson: think hard before getting a president of the United States running for re-election to write a book—or, only do it if you have a friend like Eli, who alas is no longer available. And never print three times as many copies as you think you need to solve a business issue. It only tends to make matters worse.

As for Clinton, he is proof, if any is necessary, that human nature has many facets. He was a superb politician, a real thinker, and an advocate for many of the right values in public policy. He was also a jerk, especially when it came to a twenty-one-year-old intern. Like so many major politicians he could be thoughtless when it came to the people who worked for him. In the weeks after the first election in 1992, Eli, having been chief of staff for the winning campaign, was made to wait for a significant role. It was Eli, says Phyllis, who came up with the idea of being Assistant to the President for National Service, the program known as Americorps that was one of the best initiatives of the Clinton years.

When Eli was dying of cancer in 2006, Bill and Hillary went to Boston and met with him privately in the hospital. I don't know what was said, but I was told that it was what Eli had wanted, needed, and deserved.

Phyllis and Eli were still students and very young when they married. She had a major career in civil society and government. Nothing came close to her devotion in guiding the lives of service and success of Eli and their children, Jon and Mora.

∼

IF I HAD BEEN ASKED at the end of my time at Random House how many presidents I had published, I would have said two. It would be many years later before I realized that the answer was actually four.

In 1994 I received a call from the literary agent Jane Dystel, asking if my colleagues and I would meet with one of her clients, a young man named Barack Obama. Three years earlier, Obama had been elected as the first Black president of the *Harvard Law Review*. His ascension at Harvard merited a story in *The New York Times* about that accomplishment, after which Dystel contacted him and urged him to write a book. I presume Obama had loans and other expenses as he started a career in community organizing and law and he signed a contract for $125,000 with Simon & Schuster. The details are fuzzy, but when he missed a deadline for submission of the manuscript, S&S canceled the book. Now he needed to return the $40,000 that he had been paid.

Jane told me that if Times Books would pay Obama the $40,000 he owed to Simon & Schuster, the book would be ours. He and I spent an hour together, joined by Henry Ferris, a Times Books senior editor, doubtless a meeting more memorable to Henry and me than to him. Obama looked very relaxed, wearing a tweed jacket and khakis. He told us what would later become his well-known life story: that his mother was a white woman, an anthropologist, and his father (whom he barely knew) was a Kenyan who had studied at Harvard. He was determined, he said, to finish the book, which would involve a trip to Kenya for research about his father, who had died there in a car accident. Henry and I were impressed by his demeanor and his confidence, and the deal was done.

Barack and Henry worked well together, and *Dreams from My Father* was scheduled for publication in July 1995. My recollection is that we printed about 8,000 copies and were satisfied with positive reviews in *The New York Times* and *The Washington Post*. Barack worked with our publicity department on appearances around his work and the beginning of his political career in Illinois. We later sold the paperback rights for $10,000 to the Japanese publisher Kodansha, which was launching a multicultural list in the United States. And we all moved on.

Nine years later, in 2004, Barack Obama was the Democratic nominee for the US Senate in Illinois, and was chosen to be the keynote speaker at the party's convention in Boston, which nominated

John Kerry for president. The speech was a classic of oratory and vision and boosted his candidacy and his national visibility. By this time, Times Books had folded at Random House, and its books were now part of the Crown imprint. Rachel Klayman, a sharp-eyed editor there, relicensed the book from Jane Dystel. Obama added a preface, but otherwise the book was unchanged, including the cover by the Times Books art director, Robbin Schiff, who had beautifully captured the themes and mood. The book was rereleased in paperback and became one of the fastest-selling books in history, eventually topping 4 million copies in multiple formats. Publishers all over the world rushed to publish it, and it is fair to say that Obama became an international celebrity as much for his literary skills as for his personal charisma. Tributes to the book's writing came from such luminaries as Toni Morrison and Philip Roth. Michiko Kakutani, the book critic of *The New York Times*, later called it "the most evocative, lyrical and candid autobiography written by a future president."

In 2006, as the buzz for an Obama presidential run grew, Crown published a political book, *The Audacity of Hope*, which was also a huge bestseller. By now Obama had moved on from Jane Dystel to Bob Barnett, the Washington superlawyer whose client list reads like the invitees to a state dinner, and his books had made him a millionaire as well as a national phenomenon. I fussed about Barack's transformation to writing superstar, which I considered part of a process in which the instinct to serve the country so easily becomes a massive payday. It is now standard and accepted that political figures aspiring for high office, leaving one, or even watching one up close, can spin that time into enormous book contracts. Book publishers can make politicians rich. On the other hand, Barack is a real writer. If he were a movie star or an athlete at that level of skill, he would be entitled to the rewards that the market sets.

On Inauguration Day 2009 I rounded up all of us who had worked on *Dreams from My Father* to reflect on the experience of what was now a piece of history. The net of that conversation was pride and a small measure of regret. Barack had been so efficient and so smooth an author that our anecdotes were few. "We wish," I told my former colleagues, "he had been a bit more trouble."

In 2017, I located our family copy of the first edition of *Dreams from My Father*, and through Obama's close adviser David Axelrod asked the now former president to inscribe the book to our grandsons, Benjamin and Peter Sanford. In my letter I pointed out the exceedingly unlikely fact that I was responsible for publishing books by two succeeding presidents, who could not in every other respect be more different.

As a young *Chicago Tribune* reporter, Evan had covered Obama's first and unsuccessful race for Congress in 2000. The book came back inscribed to Ben and Pete, "Dream Big Dreams," with "P.S. Your grandfather helped to publish this book" below the signature. A separate note to Evan urged him to keep up his good work at *The New Yorker*.

On Christmas Day, Ben and Peter opened the package and were stunned to the point of tears. History, I believe, will regard Barack Obama as an outstanding president, and on a personal level, his stature in our family could not be higher.

For his presidential memoir and that of First Lady Michelle Obama, Crown paid a reported $65 million. I wrote to Bob Barnett that the arc of $40,000 for our book to $65 million for the memoirs may well be a publishing industry record. In the era of Trump, the Obamas seem all the more remarkable as representatives of the best aspects of America at a time when we are subjected on a relentless basis to some of its worst.

I still find it hard to fathom my engagement with these two people as with so many others of first-rank stature—always from a distance and yet close enough to have real opinions about them.

Chapter 20

Mr. Clifford and Mr. Jordan

CLARK M. CLIFFORD AND Vernon E. Jordan Jr. were two of the most illustrious figures in Washington in the second half of the twentieth century—as attorneys and, equally, as pillars of the capital's permanent establishment. As it happens, I published both their memoirs. For all their distinctions, stature, successes, and connections, each found himself in the harsh and demeaning light of scandal. Their life stories are justifiable accounts of accomplishment, yet with a subtext of peril even in the higher reaches of Washington's movers and shakers.

Clark Clifford came to Washington in the 1940s as a lawyer from St. Louis and very quickly became a synonym for classiness and access to power. He served as a close adviser to Harry Truman and John F. Kennedy, and later as secretary of defense in the latter years of Lyndon Johnson's Vietnam-vexed presidency, succeeding Robert McNamara. Clifford's presence was itself awe-inspiring; he was almost preternaturally elegant with a crown of wavy silver hair, and he was renowned for taking his lunch most days at a counter seat in a pharmacy-diner in his office building. He was also a favored guest at the pinnacle of Georgetown dinner parties, hosted by Pamela Harriman, a doyenne of Democratic Party society (who had her own colorful past). At one of those dinners, Clifford was quoted as saying that Ronald Reagan was "an amiable dunce," an epithet that tracked Reagan forever after.

In short, Clifford was a living legend and well worth the $1 million advance that Random House agreed to pay him. Clifford's coauthor was Richard Holbrooke, the once and future diplomat who was an object of fascination in his own right for his perfervid ambition. I was designated to be the editor of the book, since I knew Holbrooke well and was thought to be savvy in the ways of Washington. For Holbrooke and me, our goal for the book was verisimilitude, meaning a full portrayal of Clifford's decades as an insider.

The three of us had our first lunch at the executive dining room of First American Bankshares, which was one of the largest banks in Washington. As chair, Clifford was surrounded in the offices by portraits and paintings that displayed its American heritage. But when I looked at a bank report, all its holding company leadership were Arab notables. Later I learned that the institution was ultimately controlled by the Bank of Credit and Commerce International (BCCI), whose head was Agha Hasan Abedi, a Pakistani with global financial reach. When I asked Holbrooke about this, he said that Clifford's position was largely ceremonial and very lucrative. For all his years in law practice, Clifford was not, by the most exclusive standards, all that rich. Clifford's senior partner, Paul Warnke, also a distinguished public figure, was dubious about the Pakistani connection. Clifford's younger partner, Robert Altman (married to Lynda Carter, the actress who had played Wonder Woman on television), was ardently in favor.

The writing and editing proceeded smoothly. Clifford was a master storyteller, and Holbrooke was an excellent writer. My editing responsibilities consisted mainly in helping them shape the highlights of Clifford's work as an adviser to five presidents. We decided to give the book the straightforward title *Counsel to the President*.

A particularly memorable episode Clifford recounted took place in February 1965 at Camp David when President Johnson asked McNamara to argue the case for escalation in Vietnam and Clifford, the case for restraint. The president chose to expand the war. I asked Clifford how he dealt with losing that argument. He replied that he had been trained as a trial lawyer to make his argument with utmost conviction and then move on. Clifford was a man whose political identity over the decades was as a moderate Democrat, respecting the initiatives of responsible governance but without any especial ideological tinge. He was a Johnson supporter, including in the early years on the war, but his term as defense secretary came as the president and the country accepted that victory in that conflict was not going to happen.

Clifford also became Jackie Kennedy's personal lawyer after the death of President Kennedy. As with Tip O'Neill, he was careful not to betray her privacy, while making it clear that for Mrs. Kennedy there was a lot to be private about. At a dinner marking the publication of the book in the summer of 1991, a room full of notables at the home of the magazine editors Harry Evans and Tina Brown, Jackie was seated next to Clifford. She was in a way the ultimate celebrity, world famous but unknowable.

The publishing rollout went well. *The New York Times* said that *Counsel to the President* was "an important book resonant with authority." *The Washington Post* called it a "gold mine for scholars." The book landed at number three on the *Times* bestseller list. But then the trouble started. The criminal activities of BCCI—money laundering, massive payoffs, graft, fraud—emerged. My private view was that Clifford had been lured into a relationship he never understood. All those Middle Eastern and South Asian names meant little to this gentleman in his eighties. At first, the stories seemed to bounce off the book, but the controversy eventually took its toll. We went ahead with the celebratory dinners, and the subject of his problems was scrupulously avoided. I was struck that Mrs. Clifford never joined him on the circuit. It was also clear that Holbrooke's pride in the project receded until it became a minor item on his extensive résumé.

Clifford's self-description was poignant. "I have a choice," he said, "of either seeming stupid or venal." He was indicted on charges of fraud, conspiracy, and receiving bribes. He was never tried because the court decided he was too ill. The year he died, 1998, he and Altman settled civil suits and paid $5 million to the Federal Reserve. I never could reconcile myself to the notion of Clifford as crooked. And yet how could a man who defined sophistication and judgment for so long have been so clueless?

Vernon Jordan was as glamorous as Clifford, but what made him different was that he was, proudly, Black. He came from a simple background in Atlanta. I visited the modest housing project where he was raised. Jordan went to DePauw University on a scholarship, at a time when there were very few Black students in any white colleges. He received his law degree at Howard University in 1960 and went south to take on, among other things, civil rights cases. He received national attention when he escorted Charlayne Hunter as she enrolled at the University of Georgia in 1961, defying white student outrage and state government resistance.

Jordan, a natural leader, served as executive director of the United Negro College Fund, and from 1971 to 1981 he was president of the National Urban League, one of the major civil rights organizations of that era, with a reputation for determination but not one of the groups that became identified with the Black Power movement. He joined the Washington law firm of Akin Gump Strauss Hauer & Feld, later became a banker with Lazard Frères in New York, and has stayed in both positions to this day.

Jordan's arrival in any room was an occasion. He was very tall, extraordinarily handsome, and well attired, and in most places one of the only African Americans on hand as a guest. He told me he would always make a mental list of any other Black people in the room who were not wait staff, and the number was invariably small. His commitment to the civil rights cause was never doubted, and he was the eulogist or speaker at events where the most prominent African Americans of that time were either mourned or honored. Vernon Jordan could and did go anywhere, but he never forgot the color of his skin and what that represented in American history.

On May 29, 1980, Jordan was almost killed when he was shot outside a Holiday Inn in Fort Wayne, Indiana, in the company of a white local woman official of the NAACP. The shooter, a white racist named Joseph Paul Franklin, was acquitted but years later was convicted of murder in another case. In prison, Jordan told me, Black prisoners surrounded Franklin and knifed him repeatedly in the arms and legs. He finally admitted the attempted murder of Jordan.

Jordan amassed an array of corporate directorships, including American Express, Dow Jones, Sara Lee, Corning, and many others. His business successes were matched with his visibility in Washington and New York elite circles. And over time, he became close to the charismatic young governor of Arkansas, William Jefferson Clinton. When Clinton became president, Jordan was one of his closest pals and confidants, sharing golf, gossip, political insight, and the definition of a good time—occasionally, I suspect, to a fault.

Jordan could have had a major position in the administration but preferred the role of outside adviser. That turned out to be a problem when in 1998 he was caught up in the scandal involving Clinton and the intern Monica Lewinsky. Jordan had been tasked to find Lewinsky a job in New York and was generally caught up in the swirl of that tabloid saga leading to Clinton's impeachment. He testified in various proceedings connected to the scandal and was invariably portrayed as too close to Clinton for comfort on this matter.

That period ended, and Jordan returned to his extraordinarily successful business and active social life. In 1999, he decided he wanted to write a memoir. His literary agent, Mort Janklow, asked publishers for what I was told was a $1 million advance. Invariably, the publishers would ask Jordan whether he was prepared to talk about Clinton, Lewinsky, and other behind-the-scenes Washington tales. His response was to say that everything he had to say on that topic had been given in testimony and Kenneth Starr's report on the affair. He had nothing to add. The project found no takers.

Among Jordan's Washington friends and occasional investment partners was Frank Pearl, the chair of Perseus Capital, Perseus Books, and therefore the majority shareholder at PublicAffairs, the publishing company I founded after I left Random House. Frank suggested that I meet with Jordan. The book Jordan wanted to write would be called *Vernon Can Read!* The title came from the exclamation of the retired head of the Bank of Atlanta, who one day in the summer of

1955 discovered the twenty-year-old Vernon Jordan, a summer hire as driver and waiter, engrossed in a book in the banker's library. The banker had never seen a Black person reading before. Jordan wanted his memoir to describe his youth and his civil rights work and to end with his departure from the Urban League for his life in big-time law, banking, and business.

I said that we would be proud to publish that book and made an offer of about 10 percent of what Janklow had been seeking. We made the deal. One afternoon perusing the shelves at the celebrated Washington bookstore Politics and Prose, Jordan came upon Annette Gordon-Reed's book *Thomas Jefferson and Sally Hemings: An American Controversy*, which showed conclusively that Jefferson had had a long sexual relationship and children with Hemings, his slave. Jordan called Gordon-Reed, introduced himself, and said he'd like her to write his memoir with him.

She was then a young law professor and readily agreed. She later moved to Harvard Law School, and for another book on the Hemings family she won both the Pulitzer Prize and the National Book Award.

The editor for Vernon Jordan's book was Paul Golob, whose style and skill suited the two authors as it had suited Jimmy Carter and so many others. When the writing started to arrive, Paul and I agreed that it needed to more closely reflect Vernon's voice and personality and how he developed his stunning ability to transcend every social barrier without ever losing his core commitment to racial justice. The four of us would assemble around a table at the PublicAffairs offices and talk through each chapter. On arrival, Vernon would make his way past the desks with warm greetings to everyone by name. I was seeing charisma at its best. Over time we enlivened the stories, not by changing them but by making them feel personal rather than descriptive. We questioned Vernon about how he really felt about the experiences that needed texture and context, and as he began to trust us, the book took shape.

When the manuscript was finished, Vernon organized a celebratory lunch at the Rockefeller Center executive dining room of Lazard

Frères. The menu was embossed with the jacket art, and all those who had worked on the book were invited. To his right, Vernon seated Darrell Jonas, my longtime assistant.

On release, *Ebony* magazine called it "an inspirational life story." Other reviewers were more enthusiastic. Vernon's television interviews were excellent and his appearances, especially at his family's church in Atlanta, were dazzling.

The Clinton issues were never raised. The book made bestseller lists. It was in every way a pleasure. I later published a second book with him, *Make It Plain: Standing Up and Speaking Out*, a collection of his eulogies and speeches. When it was time to mark the twentieth anniversary of PublicAffairs with a televised panel at Politics and Prose, I invited Mr. Jordan to do the introduction. Here is some of what he said, which conveys the many strands of Vernon's personal philosophy:

> At the end of *Vernon Can Read!*, I tell a story about how I was invited to speak at the NAACP's National Convention in July 2001, where I would receive the Spingarn Medal, the organization's highest honor. I was honored and humbled to walk in the footsteps of such previous honorees as W. E. B. Du Bois, George Washington Carver, Mary MacLeod Bethune, Medgar Evers, and Langston Hughes . . . As I pondered what to say about the years of the NAACP's history I had witnessed, the phrase "Look what we have wrought" came to mind. There is a tendency these days to focus on what we have not yet accomplished without pausing to think of how much we have accomplished so far. It is important not to lose sight of our victories . . . So it is with that I give PublicAffairs the dispensation to "look what you have wrought" . . . But don't get too comfortable resting on your laurels. You've all got more work to do.

Thank you, Mr. Jordan.

Chapter 21

Superstar

BEING A SUPERSTAR HAS CACHET. Being a sports superstar is an apex of sorts. Over time the paydays have become enormous, along with lucrative endorsements and an adoring universe of fans. I was able to get close enough to the experience of that realm to sense its impact in two books and one that didn't happen.

Kareem Abdul-Jabbar of the Los Angeles Lakers was planning to retire after the 1988–89 season, and the idea was to cover that year in a book, a follow-up to his bestselling memoir *Giant Steps*. I flew to Los Angeles for a first meeting. At the appointed hour, a stretch limo pulled up to my hotel, and Kareem's agent got out. He told me Kareem had a migraine. No meeting. Superstars set their own rules.

Instead, Kareem came to the Random House offices in New York a few weeks later. He is seven foot two. I remember thinking that when he stood up it was like looking at the sheer face of a wall. Kareem is famously dignified and reserved, and he doubtless detected I was no expert in sports books or personalities. Nonetheless, we got the go-ahead. The writer on the project was Mignon McCarthy, who had been the coauthor of Jane Fonda's blockbuster workout book. Kareem went on playing. Mignon did the reporting and writing. And then word came that Mignon had contracted the writer's nemesis, a block. I'm guessing that she found it very hard to penetrate Kareem's persona for the material that would make a compelling book. Ordinarily we would look for ways to deal with that problem to support Mignon. But since this was a book about Kareem's final season, the schedule was very tight. It had to appear at the start of the next basketball season.

My solution was to ask Kenneth Turan, a friend from my *Washington Post* days, to step in. Kenny had experience in sportswriting and was now the highly esteemed film critic of the *Los Angeles Times* and NPR, and he had also been the coauthor on several celebrity bestsellers. (He was then finishing one with the Hollywood legend Ava Gardner.) I asked Kenny through his agent if he could pick up Mignon's notes for the last third of the book and grind it out in a few weeks to meet our deadline. Kenny and I went to Kareem's home in Bel Air, and he agreed to this arrangement. At first Mignon was relieved but then, understandably, began to resent that the project had been taken away. I don't recall details of the tension but we somehow got the manuscript done. Mignon received full cover credit for her work and Kenny got my forever gratitude.

And then, another crisis. On the back of the dust jacket was a photograph of Kareem's locker with a pair of sneakers hanging in them. Kareem's agent told me that these shoes were not the brand he was now promoting and had to be changed. With literally hours before our final deadline to get the jacket art to the printer, we Photoshopped in a pair of Top Gears (at a cost, as I recall, of $25,000) so that we would have the books in time.

The book, called *Kareem*, did well. George Plimpton reviewed it for *The New York Times*, calling it "a wonderful memoir . . . the shelf of worthy books about basketball is meager . . . *Kareem* belongs with them." Kareem came to New York for an appearance at the 92nd Street Y. I took Evan with me, and as it ended, I brought him over to shake the great man's hand. Kareem nodded but didn't smile. As we walked away, Evan said, "Well, Dad, I think Kareem considers you more of a business associate than a friend." Kareem went on to do many other coauthored books.

Earvin "Magic" Johnson was another of the Lakers' all-time greats, celebrated for his skills, his boundless charm, and his legendary rivalry with Larry Bird of the Boston Celtics. Magic was as effusive as Kareem was cool.

Then, shockingly, Magic announced in the fall of 1991 that he was HIV-positive at a time when the AIDS epidemic was at its devastating peak. Because the disease was so closely identified with homosexuality and intravenous drug use, the notion of an athlete at Magic's level with the illness was almost impossible to absorb. The origin of the virus in Magic was never publicly identified.

After the announcement, Magic became a celebrity on a unique scale, and a book was inevitable. He was represented by Creative Artists Agency, and the competition for the project was intense. Random House prevailed at a very high price, several million. I was the acquirer and editor. Once again, I recruited Bill Novak to work with me, based on our remarkably good collaboration in the past.

Magic and his wife, Cookie, lived in a home on a hilltop with expansive views of Los Angeles. Bill and I settled in well for our sessions with him, reveling in his good nature and accessibility. The book was to be called *My Life*, which was slightly and deliberately ominous given his diagnosis.

As part of the deal Magic also agreed to be the named author on a paperback called *What You Can Do to Avoid AIDS*, with all profits going to the Magic Johnson Foundation for Prevention, Education, Research and Care in the Battle Against AIDS. A Times Books editor, Betsy Rapoport, took on the project and in a very short time completed a manuscript so persuasive that the American Medical Association endorsed it, saying, "Everybody—especially teenagers and parents—needs to read this book. Magic Johnson's message is straight-talking, honest, and accurate. This book could help save lives." We got strong support from Marian Wright Edelman, the head of the Children's Defense Fund, and Mathilde Krim, the chair of the American Foundation for AIDS Research (Amfar), two of the most respected experts in the field.

The book opened with a caution: "You're going to read some very frank things about sex in the book. Sometimes I use words you'll hear more often in the locker room than in the classroom. I do because every reader—especially young people—understand exactly what I'm talking about. I'm not trying to offend anyone. I'm trying to educate everyone in the best and most direct way possible."

For all the endorsements and the undeniable value of the book, we ran into trouble with retailers. Kmart and Walgreens, citing "blunt language," refused to carry the book. I went public with a protest, but that didn't matter. The concern was that the book described sexual activity that could be medically perilous. This was a book that should have had readership that it did not, alas.

Then we embarked on the memoir. Following our usual procedure, Bill and I would interview Magic at his home and then work on the transcripts and other reporting to prepare a draft manuscript. Magic's engagement with the process was impressive, but as I think about it now, strikingly unemotional. And yet in public Magic's presence was magic. When he came to Random House, the staff packed a conference room to cheer him on. And when the book was released, Random House marked the occasion with a lavish party connected to that year's American Booksellers Association convention. A long line of booksellers and others made their way to him. A bookseller from Vermont greeted Magic, gave him for some reason her daughter's ballet slippers, stepped away, collapsed, and died on the way to the hospital. We knew that this had happened but made no public announcement of the tragedy. Instead, we guided Magic down the line shaking hands and smiling. It was surreal.

In time, Magic became a symbol of how the HIV virus could be suppressed, and he has gone on to a very successful career in business and public life. Cookie said that Magic's recovered health was a "gift from God." It was certainly a medical miracle.

And then there was Joe Montana, the star quarterback of the San Francisco 49ers, who had returned from a severe back injury and was considered the greatest of all time, at least then. After one of his Super Bowl victories, a literary agent told me that Joe wanted to write a memoir-type book. We quickly agreed on a $500,000 advance and prepared for the announcement. But the day before we were to tell the press, the agent said we needed to postpone and suggested I come for lunch where Montana was getting an award as player of the year.

At the event I asked Bob Wolff, Montana's sports agent, about our book. He replied, in effect, "Get lost." He told me that Joe could make more money in thirty minutes doing a Pepsi commercial than writing this book. I realized then that the literary agent had been engaging in wishful thinking, hoping that Montana would say yes to a *fait accompli*. Before departing without eating, I did get Montana to sign a cover of the magazine with best wishes to Evan. I also once got an autographed Larry Bird basketball from another agent, which Katherine gave to a school friend, who was ecstatic.

As I write in 2020, the Lakers legend Kobe Bryant has just died at age forty-one in a helicopter crash, along with his daughter and seven others. The outpouring of grief from players and fans reflects the intensity of devotion to the greatest of athletes. Kobe's death, Magic's illness, and Kareem's migraine and temperament reflect the fact that up close, even the greatest of the great are just people.

Chapter 22

It Takes All Kinds

AS FAR AS I KNOW, Peggy Noonan and Molly Ivins never met. Their politics were very different. Peggy leaned right, proud of her working-class background and her understanding of America's disaffected. Molly leaned left and had a kick-ass Texas accent, although she went to Smith College and spoke excellent French. What they shared was enormous charisma on the page, which connected with their respective constituencies. It helped that they were good in public appearances. My role was as the editor and publisher that took them through their rise to success as authors.

Peggy came first. In January 1986, as a White House speechwriter for Ronald Reagan, she wrote the president's remarks on the day the space shuttle *Challenger* exploded on live television. Her speech and Reagan's delivery were hailed for eloquence in one of those moments when the entire country shared a sense of grief. Peggy wrote several other important speeches for Reagan and then wrote George H. W. Bush's acceptance speech at the 1988 Republican convention ("a thousand points of light" and "a kinder, gentler nation"), continuing her run of memorable rhetoric.

Peggy had worked at CBS writing scripts for Dan Rather's radio broadcasts, but she was not in the conventional sense a journalist. She chose as her agent Esther Newberg of ICM, who had moved from the world of politics to the world of books, bringing along a feeling for both fields. I acquired Peggy's book, which was mainly an account of her time in the White House and her upbringing. It had wonderful style and fresh insights without sneering or indulging in cloying encomiums. Peggy was also stunning, with the kind of cheekbones that look especially good in photographs and blonde hair set off by black turtlenecks. She made it to the cover of both *The New York Times Magazine* and *The New York Times Book Review*.

In the closing lines of her introduction, Peggy wrote the phrase "what I saw at the revolution," and that became the title. Here is what she said about the president she served so well:

> Toward mankind he had the American attitude, direct and unillusioned. He figured everybody is doing as much bad as he has to, as much good as he can. He was a modest man with an intellect slightly superior to the average. His whole career, in fact, was proof of the superior power of goodness to gifts. "No great men are good men" said Lord Acton, who was right, until Reagan.

And of Nancy Reagan:

> She looked down at what I was wearing, which was, unfortunately, a wrinkled khaki skirt and a blue work shirt and heavy walking shoes with white woolen socks. She looked me up and down, and I swear her mouth curled. The next time I saw her, I hid behind a pillar.

The book became a solid bestseller.

But as Peggy, I suspect, would agree, she was more complicated than she might have seemed. Her working-class origins and politics made her a little defensive. Her first chapter was titled "I Am Often Booed Because of Who My Friends Are." For her second book, Peggy decided to write a novel and chose to work with Bob Loomis, one of Random House's illustrious fiction editors. I stepped back, probably a little offended.

Fiction was not her thing, it turned out. So, I stepped back in and we prepared a book of essays called *Life, Liberty, and the Pursuit of Happiness*. It did only okay.

That was our last book together. Peggy has moved on to write a number of books that have done well for other publishers. She admired Pope John Paul II and had very little regard for Hillary Clinton. She landed as a weekly columnist for *The Wall Street Journal*, where her distinctive voice and judgment made her one of its best-read features, including by me. She was awarded the Pulitzer Prize for commentary in 2017. When we had lunch recently after more than thirty years, she thanked me for giving her a start and I thanked her for making me look so good.

My experience publishing Molly Ivins picked up where Peggy Noonan left off. About a year after *What I Saw at the Revolution* was published, Random House brought out Molly's first book, a collection of columns called *Molly Ivins Can't Say That, Can She?* I was the editor, which is to use the term very loosely since I didn't change a word.

Molly was a columnist for the *Dallas Times Herald*. Her assessment of all matters Texan was strikingly acute and funny. She observed, for example, that a guide to state legislators showed photographs of the backs of their heads from the balcony so that lobbyists could identify them. Her writing cascaded into brilliant snapshots of the world she both mocked and adored.

"When I would denounce some sorry sumbitch in the Lege"— that is, the state legislature—"as an egg suckin' child molester who ran on all fours and had the brains of an adolescent pissant," she wrote in her introduction to the book, "I would courageously prepare myself to be horse-whipped at the least. All that ever happened was I'd see the sumbitch in the capitol the next day, he'd beam, spread his arms, and say, 'Baby! Yew put mah name in yore paper!' Twenty years and I've never been able to piss off a single one of them."

It turned out Molly had another constituency. She wrote freelance pieces for *The Nation*, *The Progressive*, *Mother Jones*, and pretty much whatever "lefty" magazine there was. The result was that Molly had a fan base that was bigger than my colleagues and I realized. The first printing was just 11,000 copies, but the book jumped onto the

New York Times bestseller list for twenty-nine weeks in hardcover, selling well over 100,000 copies and an equal number in paperback. That version is still for sale.

I had met Molly in the 1970s during my time in Moscow, when she arrived as part of a group of "young leaders" of some rubric or another. We hit it off, probably because one of her journalistic heroes was I. F. Stone, my first boss. She worked as a reporter at the *Minneapolis Tribune*, the *Texas Observer*, and *The New York Times*, where she always said with pride that she had written the memorable obituary of Elvis Presley. Molly was six feet tall with an imposing, big-boned presence. Her demeanor was folksy. She liked to walk around barefoot. Hers was not the expected decorum of what was then still thought of as the Gray Lady of the news business. She finally was fired, she believed, for describing a community chicken-killing festival as "a gang-pluck."

So, when Dallas called, Molly went. A few years later a friend from the *Times*, Eden Ross Lipson, introduced her to Dan Green, a publisher turned book agent, with whose help Molly developed the concept for a book about the wacky Texas state "Lege." Green sent the proposal to me, and Molly and I had lunch at a fancy East Side French restaurant, a glimpse of New York publishing style of the 1980s. There was an auction among five interested publishers, and my bid of $249,000 prevailed—a lot of money for a first book by, essentially, a local columnist. There was also to be a collection of Molly's columns. Dan said we should put that book out first. I was reluctant because books of previously published work can be a tough sell, but I agreed. The idea was that Molly would take a year off from the paper to write about the "Lege."

When the book of columns became an unexpected hit, Molly appeared on television and radio, visited bookstores, and started giving speeches. That led to a syndication agreement for her writing. I didn't check in much with Molly that year as she rode the bestseller crest. On the date she was scheduled to return to her newspaper job—now at the *Fort Worth Star-Telegram*, the *Dallas Times Herald* having folded—she wore a T-shirt that declared: "Don't Ask About the Book." I think there was an expletive also.

The "Lege" book never materialized. As a writer, Molly was a sprinter. Columns were her format, not narrative. In time, Random House would publish other successful collections of columns by her, and she also collaborated on two books with Louis Dubose, another great Texan writer, about George W. Bush, whom she always called "Shrub."

I worked well with Molly, but accepted the fact that as a New York publisher, I was a valuable ally to be sure, but not really qualified to be a friend. At my invitation, Molly came to big-time Random House sales events and was a featured speaker at the annual meeting of the Association of American Publishers in Florida. On that occasion, she chose to give a stern lecture on the importance of courage in defending the First Amendment. The audience was polite. I think they would have preferred funny Molly.

I lost contact with her when I left Random House, though I did keep up reading about her seven-year battle with cancer that eventually took her life in 2007. Through most of that time Molly kept up her schedule of speeches, columns, accepting deserved awards, and always honing her reputation as a shit-kicking, badass, hard-drinking Texan who could hold her own with the roughest-toughest denizens around her.

In 2019 a feature documentary about her was released, called *Raise Hell: The Life and Times of Molly Ivins*. The film makes clear what I had always suspected about who she really was, and confirms the vivid and poignant portrait of her in *Molly Ivins: A Rebel Life*, a biography by Bill Minutaglio and W. Michael Smith published by PublicAffairs ten years earlier.

She never married, and the documentary points out that the love of her life died in a motorcycle accident when they were very young. She was a very heavy drinker, probably an alcoholic. She seemed gregarious but except for a very few close friendships, she was essentially a loner to the point of loneliness. She put up a barrier to most people.

Her fellow Texan, the journalist Mimi Swartz, has written that "as her fame grew, [Molly] was sometimes better experienced at a distance than close up."

The documentary shows—unequivocally and perhaps unintentionally—that Molly's outrageous persona was acquired. She was not born that way. She was raised in a gated community in Houston. Her father was a top-level oil executive. She went to a private girls school and landed at Smith College. She loved Paris and spoke fluent French. There are photographs of young Molly in various stages of adolescence and young adulthood when she looked more a debutante than a cowgirl.

Late in life, her father, dying of cancer, committed suicide. He was, from all accounts, a domineering presence. While she clearly differed from her father in politics and style, I think she understood, where family was concerned, "you got to dance with them that brung you," the title of one of her books.

Watching the movie, I understood that Mary Tyler Ivins (her legal name) invented a character called Molly and inhabited her completely and very successfully. The distance that I and others felt was a signal that she didn't really want us to press too deeply behind her bravado. Molly was brilliant as were her insights about people and politics. Still, I now believe that being the Molly she devised was harder than it looked.

~

ANDY ROONEY WAS BEST KNOWN for his weekly commentary at the end of each episode of CBS's *60 Minutes*. He was also a hugely popular book author, releasing number one bestsellers that mainly consisted of the columns he wrote for his newspaper syndicate. For some reason, long forgotten, Andy was miffed at his publisher, Putnam (for an ethical lapse, not about money). In his continuing quest to bring more commercial authors to Random House, Bob Bernstein called Andy, and a $1 million advance was agreed for the next collection. I was to be the editor. We called the book *Not That You Asked*.

Andy said that he did not do promotion for his books. "I write them," he said. "You sell them." Even so, I did once spot a copy of the book over his shoulder on *60 Minutes*. Over time, as Andy became more comfortable at Random House, he agreed to do a few in-store signings and seemed to enjoy them because old friends would often show up. Andy and I did appearances at places like the 92nd Street Y and the Union Club in Chicago in which I would ask questions designed to elicit the sort of observations about life that his audiences so liked.

Not That You Asked did only okay by the standards of Andy's previous books, selling about 100,000 copies, not nearly enough to earn back the advance. As per the terms of the contract, Random House had paid half, with the balance of the advance still to be paid in installments down the line. I hadn't acquired the book, but the way these things tend to be measured, the write-off would be attributed to me.

I approached Andy (I think by phone) and said something like, "Well, we published columns for which you had already been paid once and you've gotten $500,000 from us. We're about to lose the other $500,000 we owe you on the deal. That makes no sense." So Andy instructed his agent not to accept the additional money. The contract was revised accordingly. The agent was baffled. Bob Bernstein said he had never heard of anything like that happening. That was Andy.

Next Andy decided to write a memoir of his experiences as a *Stars and Stripes* reporter in World War II. This was the only autobiography Andy would ever publish. He called it *My War*, and in it he described his romance with the incomparable Marge when he was an undergraduate at Colgate and she was at Smith, along with his wartime experiences, which were worth retelling. He flew with the Eighth Air Force, joined American forces entering Buchenwald, and drank with Hemingway in Paris. He thought Ernest was a puffed-up bore. The advance was $250,000. The book did well, selling about 60,000 copies. That was it for Andy and me until I ran into him on the street in 1999 after PublicAffairs had been launched. His CBS office was nearby.

"Know any good publishers?" he asked. Let me think about it, I said.

A year earlier, Andy had been one of the featured characters in Tom Brokaw's hugely successful book about World War II veterans, *The Greatest Generation.* I got the idea of reclaiming the rights to *My War* and reissuing it to look like Brokaw's book and with a cover blurb from him. I priced the book at $19, cheap for a hardcover, and lo and behold, *My War* sold 120,000 copies in its new hardcover edition and many more in paperback.

Andy now saw some virtue in our dealings. We struck an agreement, more or less on a napkin. He'd supply the material—columns, letters, the *60 Minutes* pieces in transcripts. PublicAffairs would compile them and then split the net proceeds with him 50/50, after deducting expenses and overhead. There would be no advance paid and Andy would have to trust that the accounting was fair. This was clearly an unusual relationship. But because I was the CEO of a startup and the largest personal investor, I could make up rules that otherwise would not be possible.

Andy liked the PublicAffairs people, and they enjoyed working with him. His assistant at CBS, Susie Bieber, was invaluable. The books did well. Every six months, I would walk down the street to Andy's office (eventually accompanied by Susan Weinberg when she became publisher) and deliver Andy a check. He'd take out a magnifying glass to see if it was real. Over time, Andy's proceeds exceeded $1 million, which meant that so did PublicAffairs' share.

Andy continued working into his nineties. After the great producer Don Hewitt (another PublicAffairs author who had worked with Andy at *Stars and Stripes*) was eased out from *60 Minutes*, Andy retired also. Two weeks later, watching television, he had a heart attack and died.

Andy was a man of remarkable talents, skill, perspective, and integrity. One of the lines of his I most admired was this: "Personally, I don't much like the idea of abortion, but I like the people who are for it better than I like the people who are against it." Rooney could summarize profound thoughts with indelible humor.

～

THERE WERE VERY FEW marquee figures on the losing side of the Cold War. Perhaps the most celebrated was Markus Wolf, who was the head of East Germany's foreign intelligence service in the Stasi, the state's equivalent of the KGB. He was known as "the man without a face" because for decades he was never photographed, which only added to his mystique. It was widely said by the experts that Wolf was very good at his nefarious job. And yet he was never portrayed in the West as a torturer or thug. I wondered how a spy could succeed in managing his image.

When I met Wolf in 1995 at a restaurant in what had been East Berlin, I was impressed with his good looks in a trench coat and jaunty beret. He could have been a Hollywood star in a movie about the East-West espionage game. He spoke good English.

The agent Andrew Nurnberg, who was remarkably skilled in unusual clients—he and I had worked with Boris Yeltsin, among others—offered Random House world rights for the book. Germany was likely to be the major market for the book, but none of the German publishers would touch the project. After the Berlin meeting, Random House secured the rights for $750,000. To justify that amount, the lawyers drafted a very explicit paragraph in the contract saying, in so many words, *This better have a lot of cool stuff in it, or we won't publish it.*

I retained a British writer named Anne McElvoy, who had written a lively book about East Germany, as the coauthor. In a relatively short time I began to worry about the book's revelatory contents, as I read the material that was emerging from McElvoy's sessions with Wolf.

Things soon reached a critical point, and I decided to try another approach. I recruited Larry Malkin, who had done so well working on the Anatoly Dobrynin book and several others, to assist. (McElvoy would still receive cover credit and would go on to a major career in British journalism.) Larry's energy and his willingness to endure my prodding made him a good choice. Geoff Shandler of Times Books, Larry, and I went to Berlin to reboot the inquisition.

I summarily reduced Wolf's advance and said that I had the right to reduce it further unless we got the narrative we had been promised. Ever genial (he would serve us delicious dumplings in his apartment), Wolf started talking about how the Mossad had tried to recruit him and the efforts by the CIA to turn him. I still felt we were getting a fraction of what he knew, but it was getting to be usable.

There was still no German publisher willing to take the book on. My old friend Craig Whitney of the *Times* was now in Europe, spoke fluent German, and was knowledgeable enough about the subject to have written a good book about Cold War spy trades. His job was to get enough of the nitty gritty to make the book sufficiently interesting to a German audience. Wolf came up with a good closing line for his introduction: "Any history worthy of the name can not only be written by the winners."

Ullstein Verlag, a very respected German publisher, signed on to publish the book with Whitney's additions, and it sold 120,000 copies there, three times as many as we sold in the English-language markets. Promotion in the United States was undermined by the State Department's refusal to grant Wolf a visa. I complained in a *Times* op-ed, to no avail. *The New Yorker* called *Man Without a Face* "a curious biography, defiant, apologetic, bitter, funny, sordid, boastful, and it is also unexpectedly well written and mostly entertaining."

Years later, PublicAffairs reissued the book in paperback. Wolf never made it to America and died in 2006 at age eighty-three.

~

WORKING WITH THE world's most illustrious figures was exceptionally tricky. During my time at Random House, I was brought in to work with three of them: Gianni Agnelli, Pamela Harriman, and Rupert Murdoch. All three of these personages were alarmed to learn that books were being written about them by journalists and decided to do their own. But none of these projects made it to publication.

Gianni Agnelli, the most glamorous man in Italy, whose family owned Fiat, came to Random House because of Alberto Vitale's Italian background. Agnelli hired Roger Cohen, a *Wall Street Journal* reporter who later became a columnist for *The New York Times*, to write the book. I can only recall one meeting with Agnelli, in Vitale's office. He had signature style choices, wore his watch over his shirt cuff, and never used the buttons on his button-down shirt collar. I'm sure I was dazzled. We agreed to $300,000 as the advance. And Mondadori, the leading Italian publisher not owned by Agnelli's conglomerate, paid us $1 million, all on signing with an 18 percent royalty, a spectacularly lucrative deal. We had a celebratory dinner at a fancy restaurant and issued a press release announcing the acquisition.

A year or so later, the manuscript arrived. It was fine, but when Agnelli read it, he decided he didn't want to publish it after all. In his view every sentence would be scrutinized in the Italian press and omissions would be highlighted. He canceled the contract and returned the advance with interest. We paid back Mondadori. I kept a copy of the manuscript and when Agnelli died in 2003 asked Roger whether it was worth approaching the family about releasing what was Agnelli's only autobiography. Cohen said the moment had passed. I have lost track of where that unpublished book landed among my files.

Pamela Harriman led one of the starriest lives of the twentieth century. At nineteen she married Randolph Churchill, Winston's son, and lived at 10 Downing Street during the war. She had numerous lovers of note then and thereafter, including Edward R. Murrow, the great CBS correspondent, and also Gianni Agnelli. When she married Averell Harriman, a very wealthy Democratic Party stalwart and former governor of New York, she became a major Washington hostess, at whose table Clark Clifford had so memorably called Ronald Reagan "an amiable dunce."

In the 1970s, she and Harriman visited Moscow, and Suze and I had entertained them in our apartment with caviar, chilled vodka, and brown bread. That merited for me, at least (Pamela showed more interest in men than their spouses), recognition when she decided to publish a memoir.

At the time, the writer Sally Bedell Smith was embarked on a biography. Mort Janklow brought Pamela's proposed book to Random House for a substantially larger advance. She arranged with Christopher Ogden, a *Time* magazine correspondent, to be the coauthor, and they soon had more than forty hours of taped interviews. The Random House publicity department prepared a press release highlighting what we all assumed would be the book's tales of Pamela's experiences. Exactly what happened next is not clear, but word came back that Pamela couldn't do that kind of book and was calling off the project. She had not, however, concluded her contract with Ogden, who took the position that the interview transcripts were his to use. Why her lawyers permitted that is beyond my imagining. Ogden wrote his book. Sally Bedell Smith wrote her book. I last saw Pamela when she was ambassador to France during the Clinton administration. She greeted me warmly, so no hard feelings. Pamela died in Paris in 1997, taking her stories with her.

The last of this troika was Rupert Murdoch, the global media mogul and bastion of the right-wing establishment, who was persuaded to write a book by Lord George Weidenfeld, the great British publisher and friend to the mighty. Weidenfeld then brought the US rights to Random House. The focus was to be a year in Murdoch's life, which turned out to be an especially difficult one, filled with business challenges. There was a coauthor, Peter Brimelow, deemed acceptable politically. The biography Murdoch wanted to offset was being written by my friend William Shawcross, whom it was assumed would be critical. I met with Murdoch in his office on Sixth Avenue to discuss strategy. But less than fifty pages in, Murdoch pulled out. When I next saw Willie and told him that Rupert had canceled his book, my friend dropped to one knee and kissed my hand. As it happens, Willie's book was perhaps the most favorable book ever done about Murdoch's power and influence the world over.

What a dinner party it would have been: Peggy, Molly, Andy, Agnelli, Pamela, Murdoch, and Markus Wolf.

Chapter 23

The Talmud

ONE MORNING IN 1988, I got a call from Pam Bernstein, a literary agent at the William Morris Agency. At a publishing dinner years before we had discussed my fascination with the culture of Hasidic Jews in Brooklyn, about which I knew very little. She told me now that she was representing one of the most important and exciting projects in decades, a complete retranslation of the Talmud into English by Rabbi Adin Steinsaltz, a revered scholar in Jerusalem, with his contemporary commentary. Privately I thought that if I had thirty seconds to define the Talmud or else, I would be in desperate trouble. I looked it up and found this definition: "From the Hebrew word 'to learn,' . . . a large collection of writings containing a full account of civil and religious laws of the Jews." That sounded right to me.

Pam and her boss, Owen Laster, came to Random House and met with Bob Bernstein and me. Their description of the project was impressive—volumes and volumes of what would become a classic version of the Talmud to be read for centuries. Bob was smitten and said we would do the project. He offered a very substantial advance of hundreds of thousands of dollars per volume that would cover the costs of development and production, specialized designers, and printers.

Bob then went to lunch with his close friend and adviser Bernie Fishman, a lawyer. Bob returned to my office looking pale and troubled. He sat down and said that Bernie had told him it would be nuts to take on the Talmud. As a youth, Bernie said, he had done everything possible to avoid studying the sacred texts and was sure that sales of our series would be tepid. We made a mistake, Bob said, and directed me—sheepishly—to fix the problem. I called Pam and said Bob had decided to rescind the offer. Not surprisingly, she was beyond furious. What an insult, she declared. She had already told the rabbi about the deal.

It was a miserable moment for all concerned. Somehow, we recovered and agreed to do the project for, as I recall, $50,000 a book, about 10 percent of our original offer. There would also be considerable additional expense in mounting a promotion that would cater to a specific audience prepared to spend significantly for a library of books for very observant Jews.

Rabbi Steinsaltz's headquarters were in Jerusalem, on a street almost certainly centuries old and in space that probably had never been updated, aside for electricity. His staff took translations and comments and designed elegant large-sized volumes of the type known as coffee-table books. It was agreed that we would publish the first two volumes for the Hanukkah season of 1989. Bob had left Random House by then, so the behemoth became all mine. There would be a reference guide and a book about issues like the purpose of marriage. It was never clear how many volumes Random House would publish, although Bob and I anticipated twenty. Ultimately, Random House published twenty-two.

Page layouts and a very handsome jacket treatment were created. Steinsaltz's Aleph Foundation was well connected in New York's elite Jewish community and a specialized marketing/publicity firm joined the effort. But over the summer of 1989, the production of pages seemed to be slowing. Somewhat alarmed, I called Jerusalem and harangued Baruch Goldberg, the foreman of the production group, telling him we had to drastically step up progress, and that his team needed to work around the clock to meet our encroaching deadline. You will have to work nonstop, I demanded, including on Rosh Hashanah in early September. Baruch had heard enough. "Peter," he said, "our people have died for less. We will not work on Rosh Hashanah."

I then went to the Random House design director and ordered him to go to Israel to oversee the process. He said he needed a passport. The next day he showed up in my office, closed the door, and said, "I'm afraid to fly." Foiled. My next plan was to have Baruch's people go every day to Ben Gurion Airport and find a young Yeshiva student returning to the United States who would agree to carry the pages. Then I would dispatch someone to Kennedy Airport to retrieve the material. Somehow the gambit worked, and we put the first two volumes into production.

Now we had to find a way to make the Steinsaltz Talmud an event worthy of its ambition. One idea was to convene a series of master classes where the rabbi would meet with prominent people who might spread the word. We hosted several sessions at Random House that attracted an array of notables, including the great theatrical producer Joseph Papp and the real estate mogul Mort Zuckerman.

The *New York Times* publishing reporter Edwin McDowell was persuaded to write a piece about the undertaking. In the course of the story he identified me as "the editor" of the Talmud. I was told that this caused a disturbance in Orthodox circles. "What does he know?" was the appropriate question. And some observed: "He's Greek!"— not being able to figure out what kind of name "Osnos" was. I pitched the project to editors at the *New York Times* and *Washington Post* book sections, highlighting the prestige of Steinsaltz as a sage. Neither of these editors was Jewish, and they probably had less of an idea about the Talmud than I did. But reviews by major writers were commissioned to be finished in time for the book launch in December.

The publicity department booked the rabbi on major television shows to explain his work. The one I remember best was *Good Morning America*, where the host was Joan Lunden, a Jewish convert. After the appearance, the producer called Carol Schneider, the publicity director, and said that if Steinsaltz was going to do any more television, he should trim the hair from his beard around his mouth so he could be better understood. The great violinist Itzhak Perlman hosted an event at his home. Si Newhouse's wife, Victoria, asked for a private lunch with the rabbi, which Joni Evans hosted at her apartment in the Olympia Towers on Fifth Avenue.

Steinsaltz took it all with aplomb, but he was not by nature or appearance a showman. We urged him to speak slowly enough for people to understand his message through his deeply accented English. We did not pass along any grooming advice.

The books made their mark. In my parents' building on Central Park West, neighbors would stop me to say what a great thing we were doing at Random House. My response was to recommend that they commit to acquiring the whole series as it came out. Our marketing partner designed sales material. We bought lists of Jews to solicit. My favorite was labeled "South Florida Wealthy."

For some reason, the rabbi was not satisfied. He came to my office to complain. Listening for a while, I finally blurted, "Rabbi, I am not your wife, calm down." The young publicist in the room, Malka Margolies, an observant Jew, gasped at my insolence. The moment passed.

Those first two volumes did well, selling about 50,000 copies each over time. Each successive volume sold less. After I left Random House, I lost track of the project. I was amused to learn that the editor assigned to oversee the venture was Joy de Menil, from a very wealthy family of art collectors and philanthropists in Houston.

I have the first two volumes on my shelf in leather binding. They look beautiful. I will confess, however, that I never did more than skim a few pages. I hope I will be forgiven. At least I made the series happen, against considerable odds. When I checked in 2020 on the financial results of the series, I was told it had been "successful."

Rabbi Steinsaltz died in Jerusalem on August 7, 2020, at the age of eighty-three. The extensive *New York Times* obituary called him a "towering scholar of the bedrock Jewish texts who spent four and a half decades writing a 45-volume translation of the Babylonian Talmud and made it accessible to hundreds of thousands of readers." The closing quote from Steinsaltz reflected the enormity of the project he had undertaken, more challenging than he had anticipated: "Sometimes when a person knows too much, it causes him to do nothing. . . . It seems it's better sometimes for a man, as for humanity, not to know much about the difficulties and believe more in the possibilities."

I exchanged emails about Steinsaltz with David Remnick, the editor of *The New Yorker*, who had interviewed him at length and read from among his sixty books on philosophy, mysticism, theology, and zoology. "He managed to be both a great scholar and popularizer, a tough trick," David said.

Reading Steinsaltz's obituary, I was surprised to realize that he was in his early fifties when I first met him. Great sages are never supposed to be what now seems to me to be young.

In recent years, my own advancing age and my growing understanding of what it had meant to my parents, my brother, and my Polish family to be Jewish has ignited my own sense of being a Jew. I had always known I was, of course, and my early experiences at Cheshire Academy had highlighted that, as had my essentially accidental enrollment at Brandeis among a great many Jews who were observant, which I was not. As I've mentioned, I was embarrassed to have been bar mitzvahed, for which I really was unprepared.

When my grandson Peter Sanford, age thirteen and one-quarter Jewish, decided—entirely for reasons of his own—that he wanted to be bar mitzvahed, Katherine tasked me to be his spiritual adviser while he was taught to read Hebrew by a pro. I observed that the entirety of his Jewish education to that point consisted of seeing *Fiddler on the Roof* on Broadway and being cast as Tevye in a summer take-off for the children at Lakeside, renamed Lakesidetovka. Katherine's family regularly joined in Seders with friends that I suspect were very multicultural. I bought a book called *Torah for Dummies*, and each week Peter and I would explore by phone another of the five books that make up the sacred text. My resources were limited. I told him to watch Charlton Heston in the film *The Ten Commandments* as a portrayal of the Exodus he was reading about. Together we understood that the Torah was a guide to life that recognized that ultimate goals of sanctity were unreachable on this earth. Being a young man of his generation, he also thought that the Torah was inexcusably sexist.

I've also grappled with what it means to be a Jew in contemporary America. In 2018 PublicAffairs published an illuminating personal book by Robert Mnookin of Harvard Law School called *The Jewish American Paradox*. The thesis is that it has never been easier to be Jewish in the United States—discrimination is no longer a real issue, and Jews are among the most prominent people in a great many fields. And yet an overwhelming majority of Jews—perhaps as high as 70 percent—are marrying outside the faith. And Israel, once a symbol of post-Holocaust pride, has become a source of division, not just among Jews but also among those who believe that the Palestinians were and continue to be brutally repressed.

In recent years, anti-Semitism has again become visible enough to be taken seriously. Under its former leader Jeremy Corbyn, the British Labour Party came a cropper in large measure because of its anti-Semitic tendencies. There have been incidents of hate crimes in Europe and around the United States. Great Jewish papers like *The Forward* in New York and *The Chronicle* in the UK struggle to stay extant. The campus BDS movement (boycott, divestment, sanctions)—to essentially treat Israel as an apartheid-type regime—was acknowledged by many university leaders to be more than a simmering problem.

So how do I feel, ersatz publisher of the Talmud and Torah amateur that I am?

Jews are by any definition a minority, wherever they are—except in Israel. So are a great many other Americans: Native Americans, African Americans, Latinx, and Asians, who have largely joined Jews in the category of being resented for their achievement.

Bias, harassment, oppression, even annihilation are the realities of human history, including in this country. The Pilgrims were refugees from religious persecution; Africans were enslaved for centuries and still struggle for genuine equality; Italians and the Irish "need not apply." The Chinese were excluded, the Japanese were interned, and the tribes we called Indians were driven from territory that had been theirs since time immemorial.

One consequence of the way a majority of Jews came to America, through Ellis Island, is that descendants tend to know little about their family's past. The standard line is something like "my great-grandparents came from somewhere in the Pale or in the Ukraine." Some people visit the "old country" in an effort to connect with their heritage, but that is not typical. Part of the phenomenon of being Jewish in the United States (and doubtless in Western Europe) is the re-invention of lives so very different from the ones that gave people in shtetls their identity and challenges. And finally, the spectrum of Jewishness is very wide, Haredi to secular, blue-eyed to dark-skinned, rich to poor. Jews come in very many shades, but when it comes to anti-Semitism, they tend to look alike.

Being a Jew is and should be a source of pride when it is associated with our survival against history. But it is also a considerable responsibility, to cherish what is right and oppose what is wrong, wherever it is found.

Chapter 24

Puzzles and the Endgame

AFTER LIVING IN BROOKLYN HEIGHTS for three years, Suze and I decided that in the summer of 1987 we would move into her family's home in Greenwich, Connecticut. It was a farmhouse built in the 1750s on three and a third acres on Round Hill Road, then and thereafter one of the fanciest addresses in that fancy community. Our house was not one of the estates or McMansions that were taking over the neighborhood. Being so old, it had the charms and challenges of its age. Suze's grandparents lived in it for about forty years, and then her parents took it over for about ten years when Ambassador Sherer was appointed to a diplomatic post at the United Nations.

As I wrote earlier, there was a small outbuilding where we used to go with the children while the main house was rented in the 1980s. Why, we reasonably asked, were we not living in the house ourselves? So we rented out and eventually sold the Brooklyn apartment and made the change. We gave up central air-conditioning and private schools for an extended heat wave (and emergency window units) and Greenwich public schools. We stayed for twenty-seven years. After Katherine married, she and her husband, Colin, and their (eventually) three children lived in what had been the garage turned into a cozy updated house that suited them well. Suze's mother, Carroll, now a widow, joined us in the early 2000s. So for several years we were a four-generation establishment—with nary a day, I can proudly declare, of any tension of consequence.

289

Carroll (MaMere) died in 2012, at home. And as the house was jointly owned by all of us in the family, it was sold to a high-end Fairfield country architect and developer. He bought it the first day it was for sale, told us how much he admired it, and then scheduled its demolition. The grand house he built instead and priced at almost $13 million has never sold.

I was named publisher of Times Books in 1989. The book inventory was very small. My predecessor, Jon Segal, had moved to Knopf as a senior editor and most of the contracts had, appropriately, moved with him. What I found in the cupboard was *The American Heart Association Cookbook*; a never-fulfilled contract for a memoir by Abe Rosenthal, the former executive editor of *The New York Times*; a personal finance guide to the 1990s by a *Times* columnist, Gary Klott, who had quit before it was published; and the backlist of *New York Times* crossword puzzles—as I soon discovered, a very valuable asset. Some staff turnover followed, and our new team consisted of a small, but as I think about it now, excellent group. Steve Wasserman, the editorial director, was a book person to his core, serious to the point occasionally of self-parody, but willing to wear a sandwich board outside a Mafia trial to promote a book of mob transcripts. Steve's editorial commitment—I will always remember his migraine over the missing Clinton manuscript—was boundless. Everyone liked him even better after human resources told him to stop smoking cigars in his office. Four talented editors—Ruth Fecych, Henry Ferris, Paul Golob, and Betsy Rapoport—rounded out the editorial team. They would later be joined by Geoff Shandler. Karl Weber and John Mahaney became our business books editors. Each had specialties of interest and talent. They were younger than the venerables at the Random House trade imprint, and we were not a stuffy bunch.

Annik LaFarge and then Carie Freimuth were our associate publishers, young women of charisma and talent guiding us through Random House's protocols and politics. Mary Beth Murphy (later Roche) handled our publicity with charm and judgment. She later became a senior executive at Macmillan. The art director was Robbin

Schiff, who designed the iconic Obama cover and had a brilliant long run at Random House. The books' interiors were designed by Naomi Osnos, who in addition to being a fine book designer was also my sister-in-law. (She was already working at Random House when I took over Times Books, so no nepotism was involved.) Darrell Jonas was my assistant. When she finally retired in 2016, I said it was the longest relationship I had with a woman, other than my mother and my wife.

Together, we pulled off a steady stream of unlikely triumphs—instant books on big issues that became huge bestsellers like *Saddam Hussein and the Crisis in the Gulf* by Judy Miller and Laurie Mylroie, written and released in six weeks following Saddam's invasion of Kuwait in 1990, and selling about 400,000 paperback copies; *The Clinton Health Care Plan*, which became the standard text first for and later against the legislation that eventually failed; Newt Gingrich's *Contract with America* for the Republicans. We paid no advances for government documents and relatively small ones for our instant narratives. After Knopf paid $9 million for a book by Pope John Paul II, we sent a young editor to Rome to pick up his lengthy encyclical on life and death, and it became a bestseller for the price of airfare and a hotel.

Having sold Times Books to Random House in 1984, *The New York Times* no longer seemed interested in what we were doing. I changed the colophon to Times Books/Random House. Still, *New York Times* staff writers couldn't shake the belief that publishing anywhere but us was more prestigious. That was the case even though in the Segal era, writers like David Shipler and Joe Lelyveld won Pulitzer Prizes for books about their overseas assignments. We had to scramble to be shown the most desirable books coming out of the paper's work.

Except, however, for the crosswords. They were ours by contract and they made money. My association with the crosswords would have been more meaningful to me if I had been a fan, which I was not—no offense, I just didn't do them. Gradually we leveraged the *Times* brand, adding *The Washington Post* and most of the other major newspaper puzzles. Then my friend Eli Segal (he of so many other joint adventures) bought *Games* magazine. *Games'* editor was Will Shortz, who later became a puzzle superstar as the *Times* puzzle editor and through his weekly appearances on NPR. I hired Stanley Newman, a puzzle entrepreneur, to run the list. Stan held a record for finishing the hardest puzzles in the shortest times. From his home basement, Stan was also the impresario of leading crossword puzzle organizations and competitions.

At some point, it was decreed that Random House would divide the imprint into two parts: Times Trade and Times Puzzles and Games, the same company with separate profit and loss spreadsheets. Accepting that arrangement was a mistake because from then on, every quarterly financial review showed robust earnings for puzzles and the usual mix of successes and failures on the trade side.

For one year I negotiated unsuccessfully with the *Times* to acquire the CD-ROM rights to crosswords. Had I made the deal, the money would have been lost because CD-ROM never took off as a viable format for publishing. Sometimes failure is actually preferable to success.

Over time, Times Books published Jimmy Carter, Bill Clinton, Barack Obama, Paul Volcker, Boris Yeltsin, and Robert McNamara. Even so, the imprint remained one of Random House's lesser entities, or so it seemed to me.

The bigger company was growing, and internal competition was intense. The Random House Trade imprint was under stress because the Vintage imprint of trade paperbacks had been moved to Knopf, adding a major asset to an imprint that was already strong and hobbling "Little Random," which now had to put Vintage revenue "below the line," an artifice that accountants insisted meant that the money didn't count. The Crown Publishing Group was acquired from its family ownership by Si Newhouse without much due diligence, and it was soon discovered that a significant part of its earnings came from pornographic videos in the mail order division. That did not last. When Alberto Vitale replaced Bob Bernstein, the focus on finances in the company was increased, with regular business reviews intended, at least it seemed to me, to emphasize our shortcomings rather than acknowledge our strengths.

I had the fantasy of announcing to Alberto (who, I should say, seemed to like me when he was not looking at my profit-and-loss statement) that he reminded me of my session with the prime minister of Iceland when I was reporting there. After forty-five minutes or so, she stood up and I stood up and then we sat down again, because my next interview was with the country's culture minister and she was that, too. The two parts of Times Books were really the same people in the same space, but that was not how the accountants wanted us to be considered.

At Times Books, we operated essentially on our own. In a remodeling, we were moved from the eleventh floor to the remote twenty-sixth floor, where I had a great corner view but had to take two elevators to get to the Random House floor and the executive offices, which gave us a somewhat out-of-sight-out-of-mind character. We were joined in that space by the contracts and permissions staff. This was a stripped-down floor, no frills and older furniture.

In early 1996, I had lunch with Harry Evans, who as publisher of Random House Trade was my nominal boss. Harry was a brilliant editor and an even more lustrous showman. He had given the imprint added cachet, shared with his wife, Tina Brown, the editor of *Vanity Fair* and later, *The New Yorker*. Harry was on a roll with huge bestsellers like Colin Powell's memoir, a big (and hollow) buy of Marlon Brando's autobiography, and *Primary Colors*, the political *roman à clef* that caused a sensation because the author was "Anonymous," eventually revealed to be the *Newsweek* columnist Joe Klein. The imprint published a glossy promotional magazine and spared, as far as I could tell, no expense.

Times Books, on the other hand, was projecting a significant revenue deficit on the trade side and the booming puzzle sales were deemed another business. In the tangled way costs are allocated, Times Trade was paying a share of the lavish style elsewhere in the building, which we couldn't really afford. My business managers explained to me that our books were on the whole doing fine, but our numbers were badly impacted by the high cost of the added allocations. Senior editors at Random House had a regular use of "town cars." At the Four Seasons restaurant, Random executives had a permanent rolling tab. Renovations were expensive and never did make it to the twenty-sixth floor.

My big idea for dealing with the deficit was the secret Clinton book, *Between Hope and History*. And I had proposed to Vitale starting a business books imprint and got authority to do so and to hire two outstanding senior editors—Karl Weber and John Mahaney. The hitch was that we were told to budget a profit for this venture in the first year, which on reflection was ridiculous.

This was the peak of what was known as the superstore era, when Barnes & Noble and Borders were expanding, adding stores with expansive shelves and coffee bars. They would buy books for all the stores, centrally, and then return them after a few weeks or months. Very few of the books we published had that kind of national potential. I realized that our books were a form of wallpaper for them. Our rate of returns, unsold inventory, grew to about 40 percent. The blame was deemed to be our faulty judgment in acquisition and overprinting. In the effort to bring in more commercial titles, the size of our advances was going up as well. In one of my very last acquisitions, Times Books paid nearly $1 million for a book by a specialist in anorexia, an eating disorder then considered a crisis among teenage girls. The author had been featured twice in admiring pieces on ABC's major magazine show, *20/20*. She turned out to be more a phony than a savior and was trashed in places like *People* magazine. Her clinic in Canada was shut down. Fortunately, I was gone when the book was published and flopped.

I began to sense that my standing as a publisher was being questioned by others elsewhere in the company who had Vitale's ear. This was nothing specific. I could sense the condescending aroma beneath the glamour of Random House under Harry, in which we were something of a junior varsity. I began to imagine my exit options. I had been recruited and was a finalist for the position of president of National Public Radio years earlier, but I withdrew when I recognized that I wasn't qualified for some of the aspects of the job, such as working with hundreds of local stations, and that it would have meant a major pay cut and a move to Washington. I was approached by the outgoing president of the Association of American Publishers to apply for his job but sensed that I wasn't right for a position that eventually went to a former member of Congress.

And yet I had been given a lucrative new Random House contract the year before because there was a widely believed rumor that I would be offered the job of publisher of Simon & Schuster. It turned out—I never told anyone—that when the recruiter reached me, the job was to be the publisher of American Automobile Association books.

By the summer, with the Clinton book hanging in the balance, I was told to redo budgets, including deep cuts in staff. I remember one evening going to the theater with Suze to see the great comic musical *A Funny Thing Happened on the Way to the Forum*. I was not in the mood for light entertainment, and we left at intermission. *The New York Times* ran a feature on puzzle publishing in which I was quoted, saying, "Many people do crossword puzzles the way other people exercise," I said. "It's the original inactive game." The writer added that I was the publisher of Times Books, the "premier publisher of crossword books."

"We sold five or six million copies a year," I said. "I wasn't particularly a crossword visionary. It was simply a way to make money."

Is this where twelve years in book publishing had led me?

Then, on August 29, 1996, Józef Lionel Osnos, age ninety-two, died of natural causes at Roosevelt Hospital, very peacefully. My mother, Marta Bychowski Osnos, had died in 1993 at age eighty-three.

"I am now an orphan," Robert said.

"Well, yes," I replied, "but you are sixty-five."

We had a small burial. Józef had outlived most of his peers.

The Clinton book had finally shipped. I was asked to lunch by Alberto Vitale and Harry Evans a week or two later at the Four Seasons, where we were seated at a featured banquette. I did not tell them about my father. Instead, they told me I could have thirty days to redo the Times Books budgets to reflect a shift to news-you-can-use "soft reference" and away from risky trade books. I could have countered with our publishing of Carter, Clinton, McNamara, Volcker, and all those rabbits. But I wasn't in the mood.

At the end of lunch, when Harry went to the men's room, I said, "Alberto, you've been through this kind of discussion any number of times. I have not. What are you really trying to tell me?" I knew I was effectively being told to leave Times Books.

Alberto replied that he and Harry wanted me to go back to focusing on high-profile books at the Random House imprint and that Times Books would be about puzzles and reference. Ironically, this would involve, as I recall, a transfer of the Times Books imprint and staff to the division of the company known as RIP, Random Information Publishing.

Oddly, I don't remember being upset. I was clearly tired of the tension. On Sunday, Harry with his inimitable good cheer called to say how glad he was I would be returning full time to his fold. And my first book, he said, would be Donald Trump's third book. I was alone in the house. It was raining. I put down the phone and said, "Wow." I walked to the end of the lane, and when Suze came home, I told her I was going to quit on Monday, which I did. She was completely supportive, despite the obvious unknowns.

When my resignation was announced, it merited full stories in *The New York Times*, *The Wall Street Journal*, and the publishing trade media. While the articles were flattering, the suggestion was that I was a part of the increasing concentration on commercial successes, rather than the serious to earnest books I had been doing. That was true in its way, but I didn't like the idea of being cast as a martyr.

When *The New York Observer* published a whole column about me, I summoned the discipline not to read it. And never did.

Well, almost never. A cache of material was found in my brother's closets after he died in 2020 and included was the *Observer* column. Among other things it said, "Mr. Osnos let down his guard against the tide washing him right out of the publisher's office." The article also described me as "the prickly son of European refugees whose intellectual gravitas won him membership in the left-wing, do-good media elite currently overshadowed by Mr. Evans' mode of working-class-bloke-made-good showmanship." And finally, it said that there had been "tensions" with Harry. Maybe someone saw that, but Harry and I remained on excellent terms until his death in September 2020, and no one I know reads *The New York Observer* anymore.

It isn't really possible to retrace what happened in the last year or so at Random House. I have concluded that in every office there are competitions and resentments. Rather than make it sound as though Times Books was a business disappointment, I might have been told that asking me to return to the full-time editing of big books was a compliment, perhaps with a raise and a new title. That did not happen, of course. This was as close as I ever got to the feeling of being fired. I didn't like it, but I wasn't all that troubled, either. When I met privately with Vitale to say that I had decided to start my own publishing company, he said that if he were ten years younger, he would do the same thing.

Steve Wasserman also knew the imprint's role was going to change and, fortuitously, landed a new gig as the books editor of the *Los Angeles Times*, for him a dream job. There was no purge at Times Books. Karl Weber left and made a very successful career out of being a freelance editor, writer, and publisher. John Mahaney stayed on until he joined PublicAffairs years later. Should we have done things differently at Times Books in my seven years there? There's no answer to that question. As an entity, Times Books no longer exists. *New York Times* reporters are much sought after to write books. And the *Times* has a whole department that reframes *Times* content for books by publishers of all kinds, who then get reams of free advertising in the print paper, where actual paid advertising is on what appears to be an inexorable decline.

On October 1, 1996, I left the building at 201 East 50th Street for the last time.

A month later, Random House gave me a going away party, hosted by Vitale and Harry at the Century Association, one of New York's private clubs. The company commissioned a sturdy glass book ornament inscribed:

> For Peter Osnos
> editor and publisher
> with the affection
> and esteem
> of his colleagues at
> Random House
> November 1996.

Someone liked the object enough to have two made.

PART FOUR

~

Shopkeeper

Chapter 25

One Word, Cap A

OVER THE SUMMER OF 1996, sensing that my time at Random House might be running short, I sketched out a plan for a new publishing enterprise. It would focus on books about public affairs, topical but hopefully enduring. I envisioned the audience as the people who listen to NPR and read *The New Yorker*, *The Economist*, nonfiction books, and top-tier newspapers. I recognized that this was a small slice of the total US population, but it was an identifiable constituency. My business model had to fit the potential.

I compared the fate of most books to what I remembered of the experience in school. Students who received a B or better tended to say, "I got." Students who received a B- or less would say, "The teacher gave me." For too many authors, the publishing experience was of the latter kind.

On the day that an agent secures what is known as a "six-figure deal"—the iconic number—everyone is pleased. Then the author pays the agent 15 percent, pays taxes of something like 25 to 30 percent and keeps the rest, which for a year's work is barely the minimum wage. Meanwhile, the publisher has paid the full six figures and unless the book is more than a minor success, takes a write-down on that investment. I didn't think that this would be the right equation for the sort of books I favored.

The mid-1990s was also one of those periods when publishers appeared to be losing confidence in what were known as midlist books, those that were not ticketed to be bestsellers and not the type that became backlist staples. I hated the term *midlist*, which reminded me of *mediocre*. Times Books was pivoting to reference as I described. Basic Books, one of the most established serious imprints with fifty years of history, was being shut down at HarperCollins, and the Free Press had lost its venerable publisher, Erwin Glikes, who had died a few years earlier, and seemed to be drifting.

The internet was in a very early stage, and the concept of digital books hadn't yet been taken seriously. While booksellers and publishers always see a future of some peril and are right to be careful, the result is what I thought of as stasis rather than innovation in our time-honored field. As I like to say, the first book in print was Gutenberg's Bible. And the second book was called, effectively, *Publishing Is Dead*.

I had developed a friendship with Richard Leone, the president of the Twentieth Century Fund, and we had partnered on books and lunch. Leone had a background in politics and public service and wanted to encourage the foundation's publications program. On the day I decided to leave Random House, we spoke, and he said, come to the fund as a fellow with an office, a stipend, and an assistant. That enabled me to say publicly that I had a plan for my next objective: to start my own publishing house. Privately, I was relieved not to have to make an announcement about seeking new challenges or comparable palaver.

On the evening that the stories of my resignation appeared, Ben Bradlee and Sally Quinn called to find out what had happened, in itself a compliment that they cared enough to ask. After all, I had been gone from the *Post* for more than a decade. When I described my idea, Bradlee said, "Ha, captain of your own ship!" In a phrase he said it all. My ship would turn out to be a rowboat, but it was mine to captain.

Józef's estate included my parents' apartment in the Beresford, with the proceeds to be shared between Robert and me. The sale went through quickly and with my share in hand I knew that I could go to investors and match what I would ask others to put in. Having your own resources as a start is essential, if not indispensable, to establishing a new company.

The next month was, in every way, amazing enough to make a person believe in destiny. Eli Segal, he who keeps showing up and will again, had been retained by a Washington investor named Frank Pearl to join Perseus Capital LLC. His position was amorphous, as was, I recognized, the mission of Perseus. Frank had made a fortune working as a lawyer for the original leveraged buyout experts, who had flipped Hallmark Cards, for example, and made a vast return. Pearl and his wife, Geryl, sailed around the world and when he returned to Washington, he joined the boards of the Brookings Institution and the Kennedy Center, and he also founded a publishing house called Counterpoint Press.

Counterpoint was led by Jack Shoemaker, who had worked at Pantheon Books and had good taste in literary fiction. Pearl set up Shoemaker and his small staff in the same building as Perseus's offices. Counterpoint had designer furniture and an exotic fish tank, and its beautifully produced books started making an impact. I had read a *Washington Post* feature after the author Gina Berriault won a major prize. Eli told me that Frank wanted to expand his publishing interests and had hired as an adviser Charlie Heyward, who had been a senior figure at Simon & Schuster and Little, Brown.

Frank was a dapper fellow of the type that had a personal chef; homes in Palm Beach, Rappahannock (Virginia), and Martha's Vineyard; a private plane; and a Washington residence full of elegant trappings. In our first meeting, he said he wanted to work with me and would underwrite the whole startup costs of my venture. I responded that I wanted a partnership, using my inheritance (I didn't call it that) and outside investors. He agreed.

Brian Lamb, another good friend—the founder of C-SPAN and whose books I had published at Times Books—told me that he knew of a possible investor who lived "up there in Connecticut." Bob Rosencrans was a much-admired leader in the cable television industry and had been the founder of many channels that were making tons of money. More to the point, in the late 1970s, when Brian came up with the concept of a cable public affairs television network to cover Congress and provide extensive programming on issues in the public interest, Rosencrans had been his first backer. Brian considered Bob his cofounder.

Rosencrans had a small office in Greenwich where he and a partner managed their media holdings. When I called him and asked where he lived, the answer was Round Hill Road. Really, I said, so do we. What number? 331. We were at 272, a quarter mile away.

Charlie Heyward and I drew up a simple business plan—about ten people investing equal amounts getting to as much as $4 million; Pearl's support in developing sales and distribution infrastructure; and a concept for the books and possibly a nonprofit affiliate to host events and design educational activity. To my astonishment, Bob said yes and added that I could use his name, which I soon learned was persuasive to others I approached.

I was scheduled to visit Evan in Beijing, where he was studying that semester (I had never been to China), and then go to Vietnam with our cousins, Scott and Laura Malkin. I can't be sure of the exact sequence now. I did, however, apparently go on that trip with a major head start on the resources for my imprint, which, most startup entrepreneurs will agree, is not usually the case.

From a little office on the top floor of the Twentieth Century Fund's townhouse at 41 East 70th Street, I spread the word and had meetings with potential supporters. My friend Peter Jennings, the superstar anchor of ABC News, joined at $50,000, warning me that his only other private investment was a failed salsa company. His name added glamour. My brother joined, as did Eli and some notable business figures. One of my favorite encounters was with a Wall Street mogul who had a position in the Clinton administration. He and his wife listened, and the man's response was "You clearly did not go to Harvard Business School." True, I replied, "but if I had and you hadn't, we'd be on the other sides of the table." He did not participate.

Years later, when I ran into the wife at an event, she told me she now owned a bookstore and had divorced the husband. We shook hands warmly.

Frank Pearl carried himself as something of a grandee, but when Suze and I met his parents, it turned out that they were from an unprepossessing neighborhood in Chicago and had a legal practice that supported a cottage rental in Union Pier, a town near Lakeside on the eastern shore of Lake Michigan. Lakeside was the summer home of prominent WASP families and the University of Chicago professors they patronized. Union Pier was a destination for Jewish and some Black families. Suze and I found it reassuring to discover that Pearl was a self-made aesthete and multimillionaire.

I began working with Perseus on the partnership contract. I had a young lawyer at Williams & Connolly as my adviser and the exceptionally good will of Charlie Heyward. I grappled with concepts like preferred and common shares and apportioning the majority. With money in hand, my commitment to fine points was, I guess, a little casual. In the end, I allocated 53 percent of the business to Perseus, in recognition of the fact that it would do all the distribution and financial work. It took me years to understand that in a crisis 47 percent might as well be 1 percent.

My nonprofit idea faded because it would be just too hard to manage. But Richard Leone was a great host at the Twentieth Century Fund. I joined in its activities, got assistance from its staff, and enjoyed my time on the Upper East Side of Manhattan. Richard would again give me credibility on other ventures in the future and was literally—and, alas, he is no longer alive to hear this—one of the most important people in my life. From 1996 until 2011, when he retired, I was associated with the fund. Starting in 2006, I wrote a weekly column called "Platform" that was circulated by the fund and appeared on *The Daily Beast* and then on *The Atlantic*'s website.

Frank Pearl's publishing vision was real. He wanted to establish a consortium of publishers—I called them startups and castoffs—that would share services but have their own editorial identities. Henry Louis Gates, the peripatetic Harvard professor, was funded for $2 million to create an African American encyclopedia called *Africana*. When HarperCollins announced it was closing Basic Books, Pearl offered to buy it. The deal had nearly closed when Rupert Murdoch's News Corporation, the owner of HarperCollins, said that as a piece of the bigger company the sale price would undervalue the whole enterprise. Soon, News Corp took a huge write-down on the business, and at this lower valuation, the Basic sale went through. Addison-Wesley decided to sell its trade division to focus solely on educational publishing; two months later the division, redubbed Perseus Books, joined the group. The academic publisher Westview Press came next, followed by the eclectic independent Da Capo Press.

The Perseus Books Group was taking shape. Jack McKeown, with whom I had worked at Random House, was named CEO. Matty Goldberg, who became a close friend as "supermensch," was sales director, and his young assistant Sabrina Bracco had the makings of a star, which she became.

As I began to shape the concept, I decided that the company should have a clear set of principles that could be grasped without a great deal of explanation. The notion of "mentor" appealed to me. I devised a form of tribute to the three people who had been most instrumental in my career: Izzy Stone, Ben Bradlee, and Bob Bernstein. I approached Jeremy Stone, Izzy's eldest son, and asked for his sanction, which I got. I went to Bradlee expecting that he would consider my pitch, at the least, odd. Instead he seemed to be flattered and agreed. So did Bob Bernstein. My plan was to have a colophon made up of the letters BBS. A colophon is the emblem of a publishing imprint, the Random house and the Knopf borzoi, for instance.

I even thought of naming the company BBS, like CBS or IBM. I was dissuaded by those who said, "You'll know what it means, but no one else will." Next, I thought of naming the company Mentor, until a friend pointed out that there already was an imprint called that.

I was stymied until one day, Peter Malkin, one of my investors (he was an admirer of Bob Rosencrans), said Why not call it Public Affairs? I did my research and discovered that there had been a publishing house in Washington called Public Affairs Press, run by Morris B. Schnapper. An article in *The Washington Post* many years earlier had called him "a redoubtable gadfly." I found him living in Silver Spring, no longer publishing but engaged with the greater world.

I put in a call, explained who I was, and said that I would like to meet him about using the Public Affairs name in some way. He invited me to his small home, where the first floor was completely covered in books. He was a widower. Neighbors and relatives looked in on him. His mind and spirit were lively, and when I made my pitch, he said he would think about it. The next day he called and said I could adopt the name and he would not "expect compensation or any other consideration." I promised that we would recognize his legacy in some way, and we did in our tribute page included in every book.

As I pondered being called Public Affairs Press, it occurred to me that we would be called, shorthand, as PAP, not the message I wanted to send. So, I modified the brand to PublicAffairs—one word, cap A. We were still in a relatively early stage of the internet, but I wanted a way to distinguish us from public affairs offices that were prevalent in searches. That was the right move, although it led to decades of chasing people who wanted to call it Public (space) Affairs or Public Affairs Press.

The New York Times took the position that we could not amalgamate the two words and would not do so. William Safire, the paper's language columnist, dealt with the issue in one of his columns. I appealed to Allan Siegal, the guardian of *Times* style, who said no. Okay, I said, from now on your name to me is Irving and not Allan, because I say so. He eventually relented and on November 1, 1999, our name was spelled correctly in the paper of record.

On the street one day I ran into Edwin Schlossberg, a highly regarded designer. We had both been Principals for a Day at our alma mater, PS 166. And when I was president of the student council in sixth grade, Ed had been second vice president. He had married Caroline Kennedy, President Kennedy's daughter, so I liked to say that Ed and I had met in politics. Ed offered to help with PublicAffairs' branding, and the meetings he convened with his staff were invaluable. He helped me focus the company's message, which led to the tribute to the "values, standards, and flair" of Ben, Bob, and Izzy and the elegant design for our books, stationery, and ads. Ed's assistance was worth a great deal more than he asked to be paid.

May 29, 1997, was a day to be remembered. It was Suze's fiftieth birthday, and her cousin Carroll Bogert and I organized a surprise birthday party at Carroll's spacious Upper East Side apartment. There was a great turnout of friends, family, and Suze's high school and college roommates. We decorated the front hall with blown-up photographs of the honoree at various stages of her life.

Also, that morning *The New York Times* ran a news story about a new publishing company being launched and called Public Affairs (sigh). It said all the right things about who we were and our aspirations. News of a small startup in the paper of record was a boost to our visibility. It helped that our friend John Darnton was the *Times*'s culture editor.

Now the job became to create an actual company—staff, offices, and books to be published. Robert Kimzey was the person at Human Rights Watch who managed the organization's publications. For seven years he had reported to Suze. She told me that he would be a very good person to help pull things together. She also said that if I hired him, she would kill us both. I did and she didn't. As managing editor, Kimzey was nothing short of genius on all the important parts of establishing a publishing enterprise. He handled everything from tables and chairs to the design of our office and then overseeing the output of books as well as editing several. He later described the experience as "Mr. Toad's Wild Ride."

One of Robert's great strengths was his ability to manage temperaments—an essential quality in dealing with a startup entrepreneur who was determined but ignorant in many ways; authors whose vulnerabilities need to be accommodated; and a small staff signing on for what they couldn't exactly know.

Lisa Kaufman, who had been so talented as my assistant at Random House twelve years earlier, was working in marketing at Viking Penguin. She joined PublicAffairs as a senior editor and marketing director. Very few people are equally good at both skills and Lisa was. Lisa was also calm, another great asset.

Hiring for our top editing position led to an interesting moment. I had been given the name of a former assistant to the legendary Robert Silvers at *The New York Review of Books*. He had excellent credentials, and we got along when we met. I offered him the job. He started to haggle with me over the terms he wanted in a contract. After thinking it over, I decided we were not a good match and withdrew the offer.

Geoff Shandler, who was still at Random House as an aspiring editor, had worked well with me on several projects. He accepted my offer—no fuss. Geoff had grown up in Santa Fe and had a relaxed vibe, especially in his attire. On Fridays in the warmer months, he wore orange shorts and clogs. One of Geoff's first acquisitions, for $25,000, was a book called *Blind Man's Bluff* about US-Soviet submarine competition in the Cold War by two young reporters, Christopher Drew of *The New York Times* and Sherry Sontag, a freelancer. It had been under contract to Simon & Schuster but was canceled for being late. The formidable agent Esther Newberg at ICM essentially tossed the book to us. It became a huge bestseller with more than 400,000 hardcover copies sold. HarperCollins bought the paperback rights for $1 million. When we recovered the rights ten years later, the book became a backlist bestseller for us.

After twenty-three years, it remains the best-selling book PublicAffairs has ever published.

Gene Taft was a publicist at Viking, referred to us by Lisa. He was hired as publicity director. Gene was superb at his job. He was the only person of the original staff who I didn't know, and I watched with amazement and amusement Gene's commitment to his work and the Boston Red Sox. When I finally directed him to take a few days off, he went to Red Sox spring training. Gene was a true Bostonian and the case of Whitey Bulger, a local mobster, caught his eye. Two *Boston Globe* reporters, Dick Lehr and Gerry O'Neill, dominated the story, and Gene suggested getting them to write a book. Geoff acquired the project and with Gene organized a rollout that featured ads on the Boston T and other attention getters. Published in 2000, *Black Mass* was another big bestseller. We sold the paperback rights again for hundreds of thousands of dollars to HarperCollins.

In 2015 *Black Mass* was released as a major feature film starring Johnny Depp as Bulger, who remained a celebrity in the years he managed to avoid arrest and then was murdered in prison. This is now another PublicAffairs backlist perennial.

When Gene came in one morning and said he was moving to Washington, was planning to get married, and would go out on his own, I couldn't have been more surprised if he switched allegiance to the Yankees. Gene and I were the two more volatile personalities in the group, and we clashed occasionally. We are now and forever fast friends.

And finally, Kate Darnton joined as an all-around assistant. She came from the distinguished Darnton family of journalists and scholars. She was at Oxford University Press, and as soon as I met her, I knew she would be a great asset and she was. She eventually became a senior editor and could handle even the grumpiest of authors with calm and resolve. I was sad to see her go, with her husband and eventually three children, to India and later the Netherlands. She wrote and published a children's book and got a master's degree in art history.

Reading these descriptions now, they have the flavor of book acknowledgments that are so effusive they make my teeth ache from the sweetness. But the accolades are deserved—and PublicAffairs' astonishing success in our early years was a result of their talents and, for better or worse, my vision.

∼

WE NEEDED AN OFFICE. Our first meetings were at the Twentieth Century Fund's offices. Robert shared space with a busted treadmill. Somewhere I had read that *The New York Review of Books* was vacating its space on the thirteenth floor at 250 West 57th Street, between Broadway and Eighth Avenue, which it had occupied since its founding in 1963. The version I heard was that the publication had produced an advertising solicitation that described the building as "shabby and Raymond Chandleresque." Building management countered that the *Review*'s offices were a mess and that it should not bother to renew its lease. The idea of taking over such hallowed space appealed to me and, in a stroke of coincidence, the owner of the building was the Malkin family, with whom I had become connected through marriage into the Russell clan and because they were investors in PublicAffairs.

Robert handled our negotiations and with the assistance of his brother, an architect, designed the offices. The biggest issue of dispute was air-conditioning. Bob Silvers tended to work around the clock, and in the summer when the building shut off air-conditioners at 5 P.M., he complained, finally installing his own window unit (probably in violation of some city code). The building insisted that we supply our own air system, at our expense, and they would provide the overhead ducts.

My father's old firm, Airvel, came to our support (though my father had died), and we got an excellent central system. When we saw the ducts, they looked way too large, better suited to the Lincoln Tunnel than an office. More discussion, but the lease was finally signed, and we were to move in during September 1997.

Renovation was not complete, and we were given temporary space on the eighteenth floor, recently vacated by some sort of small stock brokerage, which showed signs of a sudden departure. Next door was Candid Productions, a documentary filmmaking company owned by the well-known ice skating commentator Dick Button. Down the hall was a dental practice that we all started to use.

The building tenants were an eclectic assortment of small offices: an acupuncturist, a disbarred lawyer doing tax returns, *American Cheerleading* magazine, the great historian Robert Caro, and the notorious literary agent Andrew Wylie. A Vietnamese woman would circulate in the afternoon with snacks and drinks for sale. There was a newsstand in the lobby. Across the street was Coliseum Books, one of the city's best independent booksellers, a no-frills establishment with clerks who sat on an elevated platform and looked down at customers, especially when they were asking for a book that was not in stock.

By Christmas we had decorated Suite 1825 with decorative lights, which we never took down as work on our permanent space continued. There is now a gauzy glow to those early days, nostalgia we all feel.

I had brought with me my good assistant from the Twentieth Century Fund, Erica Brown. She was a mellow Californian. I heard her one day saying in exasperation to the phone company, "I have the patience of a saint, but this is ridiculous." And Robert hired as his assistant a woman whom he met because she helped produce the fund's reports. I had forgotten to alert Leone to this and he was, understandably, irritated, sensing (probably correctly) that I thought that PublicAffairs would be more fun than the fund. I am still sorry.

Perseus Capital was looking for New York offices and we brought Frank Pearl over to take a look at the building. Pearl doubtless thought the premises well below his standards and took space someplace swankier. I never saw them. I think Frank only came to our offices once more in the next decade.

At long last, we moved into Suite 1321. I located a photograph of Bob Silvers and Barbara Epstein as young editors in the office and framed it on a wall near our conference room with a plaque that read: "*The New York Review of Books* was edited in these offices from 1963–1997." We unveiled the plaque in Silvers's presence at our opening cocktail party, which got a fine turnout.

One day in the fall of 1997, when we were still in Suite 1825, George Stephanopoulos, Bill Clinton's former communications director, called at the suggestion of Bill Novak, who had been hired as George's coauthor for a book about his time working on the campaign and in the White House. George asked whether based on my Washington experience I could advise him on the book. I agreed, but I told him that my fee was that he pay for the advance on one of our books. He chose Muhammad Yunus's book about the development of microlending, a brilliant initiative to enable mostly small groups of women working together in Bangladesh to establish a business—a shared sewing machine, for example. The advance was $30,000. Our first check as a company was $15,000 from George for the first half. Framed, it became an indelible part of our company lore. *Banker to the Poor* was published in June 1999, with a note inside thanking George for his generosity. Yunus would later win the Nobel Peace Prize, and the book was a bestseller.

George did most of his own writing, with Bill's help, and he and I would consult regularly on Fridays. In January 1998 he showed me the first chapter, which extolled Clinton and said that unlike Richard Nixon, Clinton had overcome his demons—namely, his womanizing.

That weekend came the first word of the Lewinsky story in the Drudge Report. As the story moved into the mainstream media and more details emerged, George was so astonished and appalled that he became the first person to mention the possibility of impeachment on air. At our final session, I told George that he had to have an answer to the question of whether he had seen any sign of the Lewinsky affair while he was at the White House. He could see Clinton flirting with staff, he said, but really he had no idea of what was happening. In his acknowledgments, George thanked me for "shrewd" counsel.

PublicAffairs' first list was scheduled for the fall of 1998. My sense was that we needed to make a marketing splash. Our catalog was magazine-size and every one of the nine books—six hardcovers and three paperback reprints—received two pages. Other publishers' catalogs were digest-sized and allotted only one page to most books. In addition, we created an audio catalog (what today would be called a podcast) in which Faith Middleton, who hosted an award-winning program on Connecticut's NPR network, interviewed our authors. We would continue that tradition for several years, making the audio catalogs available on cassettes and later as CDs.

Here is how we described ourselves: "Our books are for a particular community of intelligent, non-doctrinaire, politically and socially engaged people; people interested in the world around them and the world of ideas. If you are part of that community, we hope you'll find something to interest you in the pages that follow. We hope that, over time, you'll come to recognize us a symbol that means: Here's my kind of book."

For the cover we found a book jacket for a 1944 book called *Runyon a la Carte* by Damon Runyon, a writer who captured New York's gritty edge of the time. The image, celebrating PublicAffairs, was a couple running to get out of view from me waving flashlights in their general direction. Little did we know when we chose the image that as the catalog circulated, the country would be mesmerized by Bill Clinton's now public affair with Monica Lewinsky and we would find our first bestseller as a result.

The first books were:

Lawyer: A Life of Counsel and Controversy by Arthur Liman, who had just died. He was one of the brightest graduates of Yale Law School and we joined Yale in sponsoring events on Liman's career in New York, Washington, Los Angeles, and New Haven.

The Sword and the Olive: A Critical History of the Israeli Defense Force by Martin van Creveld, a respected writer on military affairs. I don't believe I ever met him.

Legends of the Plumed Serpent: Biography of a Mexican God by Neil Baldwin, who was the executive director of the National Book Foundation, a very visible position in the book world. At a dinner for him at the annual spring booksellers convention, we invited the owners of a dozen of the most important independent bookstores in the country. They all came.

Others Unknown: The Oklahoma City Bombing Case and Conspiracy by Stephen Jones, the chief defense counsel for Timothy McVeigh, who was executed as the perpetrator of the 1995 bombing at a federal building that killed 168 people. Jones contended that there were others involved in the conspiracy and that McVeigh exaggerated his role. Doubleday had acquired the book but dropped it, letting Jones keep the advance. The argument Jones made was strong, but no one believed it.

Blind Man's Bluff: The Untold Story of American Submarine Espionage by Christopher Drew and Sherry Sontag. I realized this was going to be a hit when I saw a C-SPAN piece on one of our book signings with a long line of submariners buying multiple copies. This book really did have stories that were not previously known.

Fortress America: The American Military and the Consequences of Peace by William Greider. This book started as a three-part series in *Rolling Stone*, where my much-admired former boss at *The Washington Post* was now working. Greider was a bestselling author and superb writer and we got the book because for some reason Simon & Schuster didn't want it.

There were three paperbacks:

When the War Was Over: Cambodia and the Khmer Rouge Revolution by Elizabeth Becker. The definitive account of the Khmer Rouge genocide after a war that Americans kickstarted and then ignored.

Last Wish by Betty Rollin, a bestseller in hardcover about the profound issue of assisted suicide.

Fear No Evil by Natan Sharansky. I reissued this book that had meant so much to me at Random House. More than twenty years later, it is still in print.

The Liman book was our first release and it was reviewed in *The New York Times*. Our small staff was in our makeshift conference room on our rented chairs when David Kirkpatrick, the publishing reporter of *The Wall Street Journal*, called to tell me that Kenneth Starr's report on the Clinton-Lewinsky case would be released on Friday, September 11, and to ask if PublicAffairs would publish Starr's report in book form. He remembered that at Times Books I had published "instant books" from public documents. Of course, I said, perhaps a touch ahead of myself.

Immediately I called my old pal Bob Kaiser, now the managing editor of *The Washington Post*, and asked if the paper would give us a disc of the report and its first-day coverage of the story. Neither of us can remember whether we had discussed this before. Now it was real. I said that I would pay the *Post* a royalty on sales. Bob and I quickly agreed, and I called Kirkpatrick back to tell him that PublicAffairs had a partnership with the *Post*. He called around to other publishers, who were not interested, so PublicAffairs got the lede of the next morning's story.

By the end of Wednesday, September 9, at least one other publisher had decided to release the report, but we were the early mover and Amazon, only three years old at that point but already a factor in bookselling, asked us if we had a cover that it could post on the site. Our freelance art director, Evan Gaffney, produced an elegant design, approved by the *Post*. We sent it off to Seattle.

On Friday evening, Robert, Geoff, and I went to Washington and waited for the *Post* to give us a government-issued disc of the report and access to the paper's full first-day coverage. By then we knew that the *Post* and the *Times* would be publishing the full report as print supplements the next morning. And the Government Printing Office had a version that could be downloaded, although that was still a very tedious process. At 8 P.M. I got a call in the *Post* newsroom from Bill Curry, a former *Post* reporter who was Amazon's spokesman. He told me that our book was number one on Amazon's list of bestsellers.

We had a national bestseller before we had even touched the disc. Clearly this was a new world. Robert and Geoff rushed off to a printer we had designated in Virginia, and by early the next morning the presses were rolling. Our sales director, Matty Goldberg, had alerted our distributor, HarperCollins, of the plans and somewhere short of 100,000 books started shipping on Saturday, September 12. What I didn't know until later was that Jack McKeown, Perseus's CEO, had ordered the book to be air-shipped to major accounts at $1 a copy for a $12.95 book.

Had the book tanked, the future of PublicAffairs might well have been in doubt. Fortunately, that did not happen. *The Starr Report* sold nearly 200,000 copies—much more than the competing versions. We did a follow-up on the supporting material called *The Starr Evidence*, which included the text of Clinton's grand jury testimony. It was also a bestseller, though on a smaller scale. The *Times* ran a feature story headlined, "Steamy Report Aids a Publisher's Debut." I was quoted as saying, "I didn't know when we chose PublicAffairs for this company's name that we literally meant public affairs, but that's the way it worked out." All in all, this was a combination of publishing skill and daring along with almost incredible luck.

Next up was our acquisition of George Soros's global capitalism book, followed by the success of *Blind Man's Bluff*. By year's end we had four bestsellers out of twelve books. We received positive stories in national media—I particularly remember a full-page feature in *Newsweek*—and had revenues well beyond our forecast of a first-year loss. With the benefit of hindsight, I should have taken half of that money and banked it against less flush times. That did not occur to me, and Perseus was able to say how profitable their new business was. Frank Pearl hosted a lavish Christmas party at the French embassy in Washington to celebrate. I didn't make it because I was at a Soros event in New York that night.

The *New York Post* ran a piece over the Christmas holidays under the headline "PublicAffairs' Hit Debut." The reporter, Karen Angel, wrote: "For an independent publisher of serious non-fiction, Peter Osnos is behaving very strangely. In his first season of publishing, he has launched four books onto national bestseller lists."

"It's a phenomenal strike rate," said Harry Evans to the *Post*.

We were now in a publishing rhythm with a mix of hardcovers and paperbacks, including some reprints I wanted to add from other publishers: there were five novels by Jim Lehrer, the host of *NewsHour*, whom I had published at Random House. I wasn't planning to publish fiction but made an exception for Jim because of his public standing and the accessibility of his novels, which arose from his experience and background. We reissued Ward Just's *To What End*, one of the earliest reporter's books on the Vietnam War. Ward was the *Post*'s correspondent in 1966 and 1967 and one of the very best for any news organization. He was a great favorite of Ben Bradlee's for his skill and style. He left to write fiction for the balance of his long career. Ward pounded away on an old Smith-Corona typewriter and smoked unfiltered cigarettes. He had the best of macho charm, and I thought of him as the Humphrey Bogart of books.

Phyllis Grann was the legendary CEO and editor extraordinaire of Penguin Putnam, invariably described as the first woman to reach that position in publishing. When she left Putnam, Random House retained her as its vice-chair. A year or so later, I visited her there, and when I asked how it was going, she replied, with astonishing candor, that she had a big title and little influence. I replied that she could have influence with me and that since I knew money was not her issue, I asked her to become a consultant to us for an annual fee of $10,000. She agreed.

Phyllis would come to the office from time to time and to our sales presentations. Her mere presence at a meeting elevated its standing, and her advice was bracingly direct. Phyllis also helped me understand balance sheet bookkeeping, which would later become more important than I had realized. I don't believe I ever thanked Phyllis properly, so I am doing that now.

Perseus was giving us the essential services. Our small sales team was augmented by HarperCollins's considerable staff, to whom we paid a distribution fee. I didn't pay close attention to the financial conditions at Perseus because we were paying our bills—sometimes at the last possible moment, a policy known as "cash management." Only later did I come to realize that the financial management at Perseus was just short of chaotic.

Our office on 57th Street was separate from the company's main office. And because I was the CEO, a significant investor, and a member of the Perseus Books Group board of directors (which almost never met), I was able to establish many of our own policies. For instance, I set up a corporate American Express account, and every employee had a card. There was a single monthly bill, which meant employees didn't have to float the company waiting to be reimbursed. In the eighteen years we held that account, no one ever abused it. Amex gave us points for our spending, which we used for things like airfare and hotels.

Because of the nature of our books, we concluded that they might sometimes be harder to find in many bookstores. So we devised an advertisement for *The New York Review of Books* built around the headline: "How to Buy a PublicAffairs Book." The message was: If you don't see it, ask for it. It can be ordered. Once we had a fully operational website, we started selling books from it. This is a practice which not surprisingly booksellers hate because it interferes with their sales. We were too small for anyone to notice, and over time our effort added to our numbers, where every dollar counted.

Geoff Shandler was so successful as an acquirer and editor that he was willing to entertain an offer from Little, Brown, one of the most established imprints in the business, to become a senior editor there. He was the first of the team to leave and I said that it proved we were not bulletproof. Paul Golob, who had been a wonderful colleague at Times Books and was now working as an editor at the *New York Times* editorial page, took the job.

Meanwhile, the Times Books imprint at Random House had been shuttered, and the name was resold by the paper to Henry Holt. Because the last home for the imprint at Random had been in the Information Publishing division, we gathered all our staff from over the years for an RIP party. It had been a good run.

Chapter 26

No Longer a Startup,
Not Yet an Antitrust Case

ON PUBLICAFFAIRS' FIFTH ANNIVERSARY we took
out a two-page ad in *Publishers Weekly* listing every book we had published with the headline as above. I still use the quip and it always
gets a chuckle. Suze and I hosted a fifth-anniversary picnic in Greenwich for the whole staff, authors, and several investors. It was a beautiful spring day and the mood was excellent. There was also a dinner
at the Century Association for all the investors and our senior staff.
Tables were carefully arranged so everyone could feel important.
With Bradlee and Jennings on hand, there was considerable star
power. On the morning of the dinner, Frank Pearl called me to say he
wasn't going to make it. Not possible, I said, you need to be there. I
had come to realize that Frank was only truly comfortable on his
various home turfs, with his personal chef. Otherwise he was not in-
clined to show up. But he did come. His wife, Geryl, did not.

Frank's personal ambitions were considerable. He wanted to join
the Century Association and the Council on Foreign Relations, and
I became a sponsor at both places. Once accepted, he rarely came to
either venue. After the 2000 election, with George W. Bush in the
White House, Frank added two celebrity vice-chairs to Perseus Capital: Jim Johnson had been CEO of Fannie Mae and was a major
figure in Democratic politics; and Richard Holbrooke, who I had, of
course, worked with at Random House (the Clifford book and his
memoir) and was a friend, had become famous by negotiating an end
to the Balkan wars. In a Democratic administration Johnson would

have been a good bet to be secretary of the treasury and Holbrooke, to be secretary of state. That never came to pass—not in 2000, and not when John Kerry lost to Bush in 2004. Holbrooke once remarked to me that now that he was vice-chair of Perseus, I worked for him. No, I said, you work for Pearl. He is my partner.

Perseus Capital had $2 billion under management and added a fund with George Soros's firm for pharmaceutical investments. The book company was growing also. Running Press, a Philadelphia-based publisher that specialized in novelty and illustrated books, was acquired. From the outset, I could tell that Running Press was of little interest to Frank. Some smaller specialized companies were added in fields like health and parenting.

The actual business practices of Perseus Capital remained opaque to me. Frank Pearl was a mystery wrapped in an enigma, and I never figured him out. He would stay in the fanciest suite at the St. Regis in New York, fly on his private plane while his senior bankers (except for Holbrooke and Johnson) flew commercial on the same routes. He dieted until he was svelte, mastered tennis with a coach, joined prestigious boards, and lined his offices with bookshelves and art. He clearly enjoyed being a publisher at the loftiest level. I almost never heard from him.

I decided to raise another million dollars of capital for PublicAffairs and added impressive investors, including Martin Whitman, one of the country's leading value investors, and Ben Heineman, a close friend who was the general counsel of General Electric. But though my investors and I had put in more money than Perseus Capital, Perseus still held a majority of the equity. The total investment in PublicAffairs was still under $4 million, a fact that would become relevant years later. I've often wondered what would have happened if I had used one of the financial experts among our investors as an adviser rather than handle these issues myself. On one hand, we would have gotten a better deal. On the other hand, we might not have gotten any deal at all. I'll never know.

Mort Janklow, one of the most formidable of New York literary agents, had found working with me compatible, although his private opinion of publishing (he once told me) was that it was a "jerk" business. He brought PublicAffairs a major biography of Franklin D. Roosevelt by Conrad Black, the owner of major newspapers in the United States and Canada, and later a convicted felon for his business shenanigans. I brought in William Whitworth, a highly respected former editor of *The Atlantic Monthly*, to edit the book, which weighed in at 1,134 pages, not counting endnotes, bibliography, and index. Whitworth spent eleven months on the project. The book was destined to be a great success until Black's indictment. While awaiting trial he wrote an equally high-quality book for us about Richard Nixon. Most of Black's convictions were overturned, although he did spend three years or so in prison. He returned to Canada and wrote an approving biography of Donald Trump, who then gave him a full pardon. Black was a paradoxical figure, eloquent and even learned on the page and vexed when it came to some of his personal life choices.

Janklow also represented Wesley Clark, the four-star general who had commanded US forces in the short war in Kosovo in 1999. His book, *Waging Modern War*, was so successful that Clark became a viable candidate for the Democratic presidential nomination in advance of the 2004 election. My old friend Eli Segal was running the campaign, and at one point Clark was the front-runner. PublicAffairs published a second book with him and years later a third. It turned out that Clark was a better general than a politician.

In 2004, Pearl decided to replace Jack McKeown as CEO with David Steinberger and Joe Mangan. They had been colleagues at Booz Allen Hamilton, a major management consultant. David had held senior positions on the business side at HarperCollins, and Joe was an operational specialist with a background in all matters technical. He had also completed the Ironman triathlon and was a skydiver, two achievements I especially respected.

The new leadership started to shake up the company, knowing much more about its financial frailties than I did. PublicAffairs was left intact. Chief financial officers came and went, including one who at the first sales meeting he attended fell asleep. On one fateful spring day, Evan was in Falluja for the *Chicago Tribune*, then the center of violence in the Iraq war, and Katherine was briefly hospitalized with a minor pregnancy scare. I should have stayed home, not realizing how tense I was. Instead, I went to a meeting at the Perseus offices where multiple layoffs were announced. And then Steinberger left for lunch. I was furious and made no effort to hide my feelings. Finally, Joe Mangan had to calm me down.

I called Frank Pearl on the issue and was told he would call me back. He did not. Months later, I decided to test my instincts about the financial situation and hired my own accountant and lawyer. I added Sabrina Bracco, who was working at Perseus in sales while attending business school at night, to support our "strategic review." For months we did our best to extract numbers from the latest chief financial officer, Tom Allen. Frustrated, I began to line up the means to buy out Perseus Capital and arrange for separate distribution through HarperCollins, on better terms than I was getting through Perseus. This would reduce our costs by hundreds of thousands of dollars. Perseus Capital's directors (but not Pearl) became increasingly fierce, writing letters to my home warning me that PublicAffairs would not be allowed to leave under any circumstances. And giving me a deadline to drop my buyout efforts. It was, I can say in hindsight, creepy.

And then Justine Tenney, my personal accountant—not the expensive one I had hired—looked at the balance sheet and discovered that every dollar we paid as advances to authors, an asset on the balance sheet, was being doubled by someone, rendering the numbers meaningless, if not worse. I realized that I could not ask investors to add money if the company's performance record was so unreliable. My buyout plans were not viable.

As I had so often done before, I turned to Eli, in part because I had such confidence in him and also because he had been the one who had introduced me to Pearl. Rather than resign and lose the company, I decided to step down as CEO and get off the Perseus

Books so-called board while still retaining a role in publishing books. Why did I give up the job? I had waged a battle and lost because the other side was playing unfairly. I did not want to abandon PublicAffairs, and yet I knew that I couldn't overcome the money issues I had uncovered. I believed Perseus would continue to support PublicAffairs financially, which they did thereafter.

Susan Weinberg, who had recently been let go as the head of the HarperCollins trade department, was hired (with my approval) to replace me as publisher. She knew our list well, having been the buyer of the paperback rights to *Blind Man's Bluff* and *Black Mass* for a total of $1.5 million. She apparently was not told the reasons why I was giving up my publisher role, merely that she could have the job.

I arranged with my friends at *Newsweek*, who had offices across the street, to rent an office there at $200 a month to give Susan the space to assume management of the imprint, while I would continue to acquire and shape our books. Susan was the right partner for me because her background was different from mine. She had an MBA and experience in marketing. When it came to the editorial side of the business, she didn't feel she had to compete with me and my connections. At Perseus, a new CFO was named, the first to really know what he was doing. I did not ask nor ever could get an explanation, to this day, of how the balance sheet became so screwed up. I suspect that the bookkeepers themselves may not have known. In Moscow we used to say that it was sometimes difficult to discern whether some matter of concern was sinister or incompetent. That was my view about this financial mismanagement.

On July 14, 2005, Keith Kelly, the media business reporter for the *New York Post*, wrote a story under the headline "Osnos Turns a Page—Stepping Down from Imprint He Started." I told Kelly, "The second most important thing to do when you start something is to step back from the management at some point." I would now be known as "founder and editor-at-large." The story noted that in our first eight years PublicAffairs had published three hundred books, including fifty bestsellers.

Kelly also wrote, "While Osnos may have been the visionary, some sources say that it was not always a smooth ride with investors who were looking for a return on their money. 'I don't think he made a heck of a lot of money for himself or his investors,' said one."

Well, maybe, but for those eight years the company paid the salaries of all the employees, the advances to authors, and all expenses. My parents, whose money from the apartment sale was so essential, would have been satisfied with that. David Steinberger and I got past the financial friction of the prior year and worked well for the remaining years of our collaboration. I found it harder to justify the way Perseus Capital had handled this dispute.

Chapter 27

The Caravan Moves On

FROM MY SMALL OFFICE in the *Newsweek* building and with Susan Weinberg now in charge at PublicAffairs, I embarked on two self-invented projects that would prove to be a personal plus and, in retrospect, publicly successful.

When *Shelf Awareness*, a publishing newsletter, interviewed me about my plans going forward, I talked generally about my concern that books like those published by PublicAffairs needed a better distribution model. I was convinced that serious nonfiction books were losing sales because retailers were out of stock or the title was unavailable in the format a customer wanted. This was before e-books started to take hold, but printing books on demand and models for audio delivery were already gaining a role in the industry. From a concept I wrote in the summer of 2005, what became the Caravan Project came into focus. One of my favorite pieces of personal philosophy had come from John Scanlon, once described in *The New York Times* as "a public relations man who brought cunning, bare-knuckle tenacity and the nimbleness of a leprechaun to promoting the interests of his high-profile clients." Confronting a crisis, Scanlon would say, "The camel shits and the caravan moves on." People with sensitivity about language would say, "the dog barks," etc.

Emerging from my battle with Perseus over accounting, I decided to call my project Caravan, which also described the objective of creating multi-platform publishing: traditional print, on-demand printing, e-books, audio, digital audio, and large print. With the objective of serving university and nonprofit presses, I was able to recruit Kate

Torrey, the director of the University of North Carolina Press (a close friend of Suze's from boarding school days) to be cofounder. I hired Della Mancuso, whom I had admired at Random House, to handle production. Ingram, the country's largest book wholesaler, joined us with its divisions that handled on-demand printing, and it was developing ways to deliver e-books to bookstores. An audio specialist devised a plan for using downtime in public radio studios to record what were then still books on CDs.

We received a starter grant of $225,000 from the John D. and Catherine T. MacArthur Foundation. It is worth noting that I came to know the foundation president, Jonathan Fanton, when he was president of the New School and a member of the board of Human Rights Watch. He and I had been tasked as members of a three-person search committee to recommend a successor to Bob Bernstein as chair. We solicited interest from several New York luminaries, all of whom declined. One day, Maureen White and I, a majority of the search committee, decided that Jonathan should be our choice. He agreed and went on to be a superb chair, moving the organization from Bob's founding spirit to the more formal structure of what was becoming a global organization. The point here is that when I approached Jonathan years later and he recommended me to the program officer Elspeth Revere, I was not a stranger. Over time I understood that raising money almost always requires more than having a good idea. The donor needs to trust the asker. And to Jonathan and Elspeth, my thanks for that.

Over the course of the project, which ran for four years, thirteen university and nonprofit presses participated, representing a cross-section of sizes and experiences in digital initiatives: they were Beacon Press, the University of California Press, the University of Chicago Press, Columbia University Press, the Council on Foreign Relations Press, Harvard University Press, Island Press, Kent State University Press, the University of Michigan Press, the University of Wisconsin Press, and Yale University Press. Here is an excerpt from our final report on what we achieved:

The publishers contributed 139 books that were distributed in some or all of these formats: e-books,
print on demand, large print on demand, and down-
loadable audio. Caravan's sales vendors included Ingram, Overdrive, Sony Reader, Lightning Source,
E-Music, and Audible. Libraries and independent
and chain booksellers were offered the books for re-
tail distribution. In every case, the Caravan formats
supplemented the books' original print publication
and all revenues from sales flowed to the publishers.

I became an advocate for Caravan's work. We had panels at Book
Expo America, the new name for what once was the American Booksellers Association convention, and the yearly meeting of the Association of American University Presses and other conferences. Caravan
was profiled in *BusinessWeek* and *The Washington Post*, and the project
received coverage in *The New York Times*, *The Wall Street Journal*, *Publishers Weekly*, and elsewhere.

As Caravan gained momentum, MacArthur gave us another $1
million grant. The Carnegie Corporation of New York added
$200,000, and the National Association of College Bookstores do-
nated $25,000—one of the largest grants in its history. Ingram pro-
vided invaluable in-kind support, including helping Caravan shape
its online presentation on Caravan.org and helping with marketing
and technical innovation. The American Booksellers Association endorsed Caravan. The Century Foundation (the new twenty-first-
century name for the Twentieth Century Fund) named me a senior
fellow for media—a reunion of sorts, since that is where I first moved
to devise PublicAffairs. And again, an indispensable show of support
from Richard Leone. After the first year, Kate Torrey needed to focus
on her duties at UNC Press, so I became executive director of the
project.

Kent Freeman, an Ingram executive, joined Della Mancuso and
me in visits to leading independent booksellers and to Borders, then

the second-largest national chain. We made our pitches, prepared marketing material, and worked with the stores on establishing a way to collect sales revenue. That aspect of the project never really took hold. Booksellers seemed skeptical at best that e-books would be meaningful for them. Borders had been enthusiastic at the start but never could put into place our demonstration. The weaknesses we saw meant that when Borders went bankrupt a few years later, I was not altogether surprised. In 2007, Amazon launched the Kindle. Overnight, e-books were available on demand. I bought my first Kindle as soon as it was released and had it working in under a minute.

The brick-and-mortar booksellers, already wary of Amazon's competition, did not ramp up their e-book offerings. Barnes & Noble eventually did release the Nook and invested heavily in it. But Kindle dominated the market. In fact, "Kindle" became almost a generic term, the way "Xerox" and "Scotch tape" had in the past. Even today, the brick-and-mortar stores still regard digital delivery as marginal to their businesses. In 2020, when the coronavirus pandemic meant that stores had to close and customers could no longer visit or peruse, knowing how to ship print books efficiently was critical.

The conclusion to our final Caravan report was this:

> Information and entertainment are indispensable commodities in the organization of civilization. We are clearly at a major junction in the way books are made available. Whatever the outcome in the short term, books in various forms will endure—in your hand, on the screen, in your ear. As The Caravan Project has demonstrated, the choice will increasingly be made by readers about where, when and how to take advantage of the best of scholarship and creativity.

Our motto, which remains a guiding principle for publishing today, is: Good Books. Any Way You Want Them Now.

∼

IN MID-JANUARY 2006, what was then commonly referred to as a blog, but which I called a column, appeared on the Century Foundation's website and was distributed to a mailing list. I called it *Platform*. That was the beginning of a weekly writing routine through 2014, revived in 2017. The first column was called "Media and Journalism: Yesterday, Today and Tomorrow." Reading it now, the column remains topical. The details are different, but the basic themes are the same. "Will great newspapers survive? Hard to say. But there will always be a place, indeed a need for great journalism," was how *Mother Jones*, whose website picked up the column, summarized my argument.

In a way this was an early foray into personal digital distribution. The column never appeared anywhere in print. The Century Foundation mailing list showed 561 names. How many people actually read it, I'll never know. An early column suggesting that Katie Couric invest half her $15 million salary into her nightly news broadcast, where the budget was being cut, was picked up by *Romenesko*, at the time a closely read media aggregator. I felt something akin to having a front-page story in my *Washington Post* days.

About two years later when Tina Brown launched *The Daily Beast*, I offered her the column gratis, and after another year or so, *The Atlantic* began to feature it on its website and gave me the status of "correspondent." An appearance on the site's homepage made the column very visible to what was a growing audience of online readers. When I revived the column under the name *Peter Osnos' Platform*, I put it on Medium.com, which has millions of users and tens of thousands of contributors. The appeal to me is that publication of my ideas does not involve a submission to a busy editor somewhere who may or may not want the effort. I think of the columns as "brain exercise," a way to summarize my ideas and reread them later.

I now realize that editors at leading publications have a great deal of good material to choose from and no one will take my work as a favor. I recently submitted a piece to the *Columbia Journalism Review*, where I was vice-chair for six years. It was accepted, but when it was finally used—two months later—it was sliced in half. So, I put the full thing on Medium.com, adding that a portion of it had appeared on CJR.com. It went up immediately. It then became my goal to learn the patterns of social media, and I put the columns on Facebook and Twitter to see how those sites worked. I had the editorial help of a young former colleague, Athena Bryan, who added a related graphic for each piece. Last I checked I had over a thousand page views a month on Medium, an infinitesimally small number but better than zero. As I write, there have been about five hundred columns, dating back to that first one in January 2006.

The prevalence of digital social media is a form of twenty-first-century literacy, I concluded, and I decided to learn how it worked. I eventually acquired 1,150 "friends" on Facebook and almost 400 on Twitter, mainly by posting pieces I had written. As a test, I put up the sticky "Crazy Uncle Donald" anecdote from Mary Trump when her book about the Trump family came out to see how many people would respond to an exclusive insight to a story at the top of the news. About sixty did on Facebook and none on Twitter, evidence that you may think you are reaching a bigger audience than you are because a robot algorithm selects who really cares what you have to say. Robots are not editors.

In 2019, I decided to ask David Remnick, the editor of *The New Yorker*, whether he would be interested in an article about my experiences editing and publishing Donald Trump's *The Art of the Deal*. It appeared on NewYorker.com and got a very satisfying reaction. I told people it was a fragment from the book you are reading. What surprised me most, however, was the number of people, mostly my generational cohort, who asked, "Is it only online?" which was the case. Clearly being in print has not lost its cachet.

A recent *Platform* column was called "The Resilience of Analog." My favorite example of this is the astounding popularity of podcasts in recent years. What is a podcast? Radio on demand, a new way of listening to a one-hundred-year-old delivery system.

∽

IN THE WAKE OF my stepping back in 2005, Susan Weinberg's leadership of PublicAffairs was undisputed. I no longer did the hiring or setting of sales and budget goals. I did join in various ways in the acquisition and publishing of books. The most exciting book came in the spring of 2008. It was called *What Happened: Inside the Bush White House and Washington's Culture of Deception* by Scott McClellan, who had served as George W. Bush's press secretary from 2003 to 2006, after many years in the Bush orbit. Lisa Kaufman was asked by a literary agent whether she might be interested in a book by him. I joined her on the call with Scott and asked him if he knew who, as a publisher, we were. He said he did and was ready to write a book that we would be proud to publish. Here is how the Associated Press later described the book:

> McClellan has burned the talking points and his bridges in writing this book, and the results are a more sophisticated assessment than most anything his former colleagues turned out. "What Happened" provides a telling and unflattering glimpse of Bush and his White House, and also makes an important commentary on Washington's poisonous political climate—one that Bush promised to change but did not, McClellan writes.

What Scott described as "one of the most painful experiences in my life" came in 2005, when he realized that what he had told reporters at a daily briefing two years earlier was not true. It concerned the leaking of classified information about CIA officer Valerie Plame in retaliation for her diplomat husband's revelation about the administration's hyping of evidence that Saddam Hussein was developing a nuclear weapon to justify the invasion of Iraq. "I had unknowingly passed along false information," he wrote, "and five of the highest-ranking officials in the administration were involved in my doing so . . . [including] the president himself."

A snippet of the story had been included in our catalog months before the book was published and caused a flurry of anticipation.

Susan Weinberg, Whitney Peeling, who was then our publicity director (and a forever fan favorite), Lisa, and our sales team scripted a rollout befitting an unusually hot title, complete with an embargo and an agreement with *The New York Times* to break the story. The release was scheduled for a Tuesday, but on the Thursday before, Mike Allen, one of the most intrepid of Washington newshounds, bought a copy at a Washington store and at 7 P.M. posted on *Politico* that it was "scathing." By 9 P.M. the story was leading the news on CNN. While we had shipped 30,000 books or so, in the next forty-eight hours we had orders for 80,000 more. That also happened to be the weekend of BookExpo America in Los Angeles, which added to the excitement.

The news coverage was vast and among conservatives, splenetic. Rush Limbaugh on his daily radio broadcast with an audience of millions unleashed a harangue about Scott and "a guy named Peter Osnos" who was his publisher. He called me a "huge, far-left liberal" who was bankrolled by George Soros. The best line, however, was mine. Limbaugh said with apparent resentment that I had once called him in a column "bombastic, aggressive, and mean." And he concluded by saying I was "probably the guy who wrote McClellan's book." Actually, Scott with Lisa's editorial guidance had done an excellent job telling the story, the whole story. As we had done so often, we recruited Karl Weber (late of Times Books) as a book doctor on the manuscript. His assistance, Lisa reminds me, was essential.

We knew we had a hit and a problem. The book would sell out immediately, especially in the country's independent bookstores, which had only taken a very few copies per store. We calculated that a regular reprint would take too long to arrive, and we very much wanted to land at number one on the *New York Times* bestseller list in the one-week window before a new book by the enormously popular humorist David Sedaris was scheduled to be published.

We tracked down John Ingram, the CEO of Ingram, who was at his Princeton reunion. Joe Mangan, the Perseus operations executive, and I asked John if he would be willing to produce 7,500 hardcover copies in Ingram's print-on-demand machinery and ship them by air to the accounts that needed them most. I think the cost was $5 per copy. But it was worth it. We made it to number one, for one week.

But the fuss went on. There was a congressional hearing in which Scott was vilified by the Republicans and I was publicly identified as the originator of this outrage. It was flattering, to be honest—and less disconcerting than being called a CIA agent by the KGB in Moscow. We eventually sold 300,000 copies. To his lasting credit, Scott never flinched under the pressure and moved his family to the Northwest, where he works as a college administrator. The scandal was huge at the time, but by the standards of the Trump era, it was comparatively short-lived. No one went to prison. From this distance, however, I have come to believe that the Bush administration—from the president and his entire top tier—took the country to war on false pretenses, and as I write those conflicts are continuing.

The corruption that Scott uncovered in his White House days was a symptom of a much greater problem in which trust, confidence, and privacy have steadily eroded under the pressure of political money, self-interest, and the media's essential but damaging need to share anything provocative.

Chapter 28

Pearl Dive

IN LATE 2011, Frank Pearl was diagnosed with lung cancer. He died the following May. His obituary in *The New York Times* described him as "a lawyer and investor in Washington who entered the book business on a quest to publish the serious, quality literature that he felt large corporate publishing houses had neglected." (The *Times* also noted that the news of Frank's passing "was announced by the lawyer, Vernon E. Jordan, Jr., a close friend.")

This was a true portrayal of Frank's vision and the *Times* called the Perseus Books Group "a major player in the publishing industry, an authority in titles on politics, foreign affairs, history and current events, the largest independent book distributor in the country." The obit even caught the distinction between the imprints the company owned and those, like PublicAffairs, that were partnerships.

The Century Association asked me to write an appreciation for the "Memorial" section of the leather-bound annual yearbook. I no longer have the volume, but my guess is that it was filled with the respect I felt and left out my frustrations with Perseus Capital and the book group's financial management.

Then on July 19, 2013, a major story appeared in *The Washington Post* under the byline of Thomas Heath with the headline: "Legendary Financier Frank Pearl Left Behind a Huge Legacy—of Mystery." After describing Frank's lavish lifestyle and high-level connections, Heath dropped the bomb:

Sustaining this life was Pearl's work in private equity and Perseus, the Pennsylvania Avenue firm he created. Pearl, its founder and sole owner, was in the business of buying and selling companies with borrowed money. Perseus has directed hundreds of millions of dollars to investments such as Converse sneakers, Ritz-Carlton Hotels and book publishers such as PublicAffairs.

Now lawsuits filed by major banks that had extended him loans and his own firm alleged fraud by the man once known for his Midas touch. Bank of America, TD Bank, Eagle Bank and Perseus have filed claims against Pearl's estate in D.C. and Federal courts.

In all they are seeking $50 million.

For Perseus Capital the downward spiral was fast. In time, the firm relocated from those elegant offices on Pennsylvania Avenue to East-West Highway in Bethesda, a busy commercial street hardly in keeping with Frank's self-image. I wondered what had happened to all the books he had displayed in his office, a source of pride that he had never shared with the hundreds of people who had made them possible. Perseus Capital was eventually liquidated. All its monies, including those that had provided capital to the books group, had to be unloaded to an acquirer of "distressed" funds. The outcome of those lawsuits never became public. I did find records that cases were dismissed. There were certainly private settlements of some kind.

The buyer of Perseus's funds was Centre Lane Partners in New York, which described itself as "an experienced, cohesive team that brings to bear a combination of relevant skills and experiences, including . . . distressed investing, corporate finance, mergers and acquisitions, restructuring and operations." I was, to put it mildly, not privy to the complexities of what was happening despite knowing that I had a fiduciary responsibility to the PublicAffairs staff, the authors, and the investors—or to put it another way, to protect the company.

I did know that the process of selling the funds was fraught. At least one major pension fund rejected the Perseus fire-sale plan, and it had to be redrawn. Finally, the deal was made. To be as clear as possible, it was not the book companies that were in financial trouble, it was the value of the funds that provided working capital for the publishers. David Steinberger, the CEO, and his CFO, Charles Gallagher, were the only book executives to engage with Centre Lane. I once shared an elevator with one of their junior analysts. That was it.

I have since thought deeply about whether I was right by instinct to be, by my standards, passive. Had I demanded to know everything that was happening to the books group and how it affected PublicAffairs, there would have been an added layer of contention and probably legal expenses that I believed were not in our interest. So I let events go on around me. I could do that because I knew that Steinberger and Gallagher were under very great pressure themselves. Their priority was holding the company together and they were doing their best. I did not object to cuts in my already much lower salary. Only one of the PublicAffairs staff was "let go," in the corporate euphemism. There was some discussion about restructuring our business model, but that never went anywhere. In all, therefore, our rowboat stayed afloat in what were very stormy seas, much more turbulent than anyone seemed to realize, except for me.

By this time, Susan Weinberg had been elevated to oversee all the Perseus imprints. Clive Priddle, our senior-most editor, was now the publisher of PublicAffairs, with my support. The staff underwent routine changes, the most significant of which was the return of Jaime Leifer, who had started as Gene Taft's assistant and learned the ropes from him before moving to *The New Yorker*'s publicity department for two years. She was now ready to come home as the new director of publicity, replacing Whitney Peeling, who was so impressed working on the book by Muhammad Yunus that she quit and went to work for him in Bangladesh.

Centre Lane had no interest in publishing books, and so the whole company was put up for sale, which entailed the framing of the financial history to be examined by any potential acquirer. Here again I had only the vaguest notion of what that process was like. In late May 2014,

Steinberger told me that a buyer had been identified for the publishing imprints: Hachette Book Group, the very large American division of the French conglomerate Lagardère, the leading publisher in France. A few years earlier, Hachette had bought the Time Warner book division, one of the "big five" American publishers—the others being Penguin Random House (owned by Bertelsmann in Germany), Macmillan (also German-owned), HarperCollins (part of the sprawling Murdoch empire), and Simon & Schuster, which had landed in what is now called ViacomCBS.

After seventeen years, PublicAffairs would go from being a small independent to becoming a small, wholly owned piece of a behemoth.

The Perseus Books Group had developed a significant share of the book distribution market, which meant handling sales and fulfillment for publishers who did not maintain their own warehouses or sales teams. This was a major achievement by Steinberger and his executives. In 2007, after rescuing Publishers Group West from bankruptcy, David and Joe Mangan had been named Publishers of the Year by *Publishers Weekly*, a genuine distinction. Distribution is a less risky proposition than being a publisher. Clients pay a fee for every book sold. As long as clients pay their bills and operating expenses are kept under control, distribution can be very profitable. The prospective buyer of this side of the company was the Ingram Book Group. I had worked so well with Ingram on Caravan and in other ways that I especially liked that possibility.

The partnership agreement I had signed with Perseus Capital included provisions for what would happen to PublicAffairs in a sale. We would be "dragged" along. There were contractual minutiae that contemplated a buyout by us, but I had abandoned that concept in 2005 when I realized that our financial records were too questionable to take to bankers or investors. In our meeting Steinberger presented the deal to me with a shocking kicker. He said that Perseus's accounting showed that over the years PublicAffairs had amassed an intra-company debt of around $17 million, which was much more than its value would ever be in a sale. That was the first time I had ever heard of a debt to Perseus, which would mean they had advanced us a great deal of money over the years without ever discussing it with me. I did recall that Pearl had assured me that we would always have the cash we needed without being charged interest. I notified the investors about the developments—telling them they would not be getting any return on their investment—and prepared for the sale to go through. It did not, for reasons that were never explained. I was told—informally—that Ingram had found issues in the way shipping costs were charged that had to be dealt with.

In time, the deal was revived. On December 9, 2015, a letter was sent to the PublicAffairs investors signed by Steinberger and by me. The key section read: "The purchase price for the assets of PublicAffairs [will] be substantially less than its debts and there would be no return for the members." The letter went on to say "it is likely to be beneficial to you to sell your investment in PublicAffairs to Perseus for a nominal sum," which was $100. The investors were asked to agree and return a signed paper by the end of the year, which they all did.

What that meant was that once in 2014 and again in 2015, I had to explain to each of the investors—family, friends, and those whose understanding of these issues was much greater than mine—that PublicAffairs had been a success, except for the fact that their ownership share was now worth just a hundred dollars—as was mine—and there was a supposed intracompany debt that in a single year had increased to about $19 million.

Several of the savviest investors—including Marty Whitman at Third Avenue Value—urged, but mercifully did not demand, that I challenge these numbers. I recognized, again, that a real audit of the numbers was impossible. (I was told by one of our most astute financial staff that no number at Perseus before 2009 could be trusted.) I chose to believe that my intracompany debt was actually a calculation of my share of the company's overall debt that had been accrued by Perseus Capital's policy of financing much of its investments with debt. One of the lessons I had learned as an entrepreneur—I called myself a shopkeeper—is that accounting can be fungible to meet the needs of the person doing the counting. As long as there is enough cash on hand to manage operations, the bottom line can be adjusted to meet the needs of the people filing the tax returns, especially in a privately held company.

Most of the investors assured me that they were proud of their association with PublicAffairs and that they had not expected a greater return on their money than the books we sent them and their satisfaction with the company's reputation for quality. I did get one email sent to me inadvertently that made the point I had heard before—Osnos is a fine editor but, well, only a middling businessman. I am reluctant to plead guilty because whatever my strategy was—accident or design—it enabled PublicAffairs to be acquired by Hachette, which to my relief and regard did not in any meaningful way change our business model. That did not mean that nothing changed. In *The Wall Street Journal* I found an ad that declared boldly: "The average company lasts 20 years. So, what does it take to last to 100?" I framed it.

Over the past year or two, I have spoken to as many former colleagues as possible about how the business at Perseus was managed but have gotten little insight. No one can remember being asked to do anything unethical. Nonetheless, a great amount of financial juggling must have gone on. Business expertise, I've concluded, is as much an art as a science and I was better at the former than the latter, which turned out to be enough to sustain the company through its financial travails, thank goodness.

After the sale of Perseus Books went through, Steinberger, Mangan, and Gallagher had to sue Centre Lane to get their piece of the sale price. That case was also privately settled. When David and I discussed the sale process recently, it became clear that his main recollection was relief that I had not contested the debt figure. I had recognized that a challenge would have been expensive and fruitless and probably would have ended up destroying the company. Sometimes it is best to sublimate the urge to retaliate.

The version of events I have described above are almost entirely mine. The details of what happened are mired in the mists of time, dubious (at best) records, and the fact that all of this was ultimately more important to me than to anyone else involved.

PART FIVE

Reflections

Chapter 29

Wrinkles

FOR REASONS I CANNOT EXPLAIN, I have always avoided wrinkles. In junior high school, I made sure my pants had a crease. In Vietnam other reporters would say I could spend days on the road and still come back looking somewhat starched. There are pictures of me in the office in Moscow wearing a three-piece suit. I've always been known as a snappy dresser. A greeting from a former colleague seeing me after a long while was "Mr. Haberdasher." Sally Quinn, arbiter of Washington standards, had after all deemed me the best-dressed man at *The Washington Post*.

But this avoidance of wrinkles extended to much more significant issues in life. I had discovered what I describe as "emotional deflection," parking my reaction to life challenges rather than immediately reacting to them. Physical danger in Vietnam and KGB harassment in the Soviet Union, for example, were largely deflected. I do not remember real fear in either situation when it would have been understandable to be scared. This isn't courage, I believe. It is a form of denial. This was a characteristic shared by my father and brother as well. Józef lost most of his family in the Holocaust and almost never talked about them or that fact, though he did put a stone in Warsaw's Jewish cemetery with all their names. Robert's insistence that he had not been a "victim" of the Nazis as a child was true, but somewhere in his soul that fear had to have made a mark. It is well past time that I can discuss these matters with either Robert or Józef, so we will have to take my word for it.

You may recall that I had a short first marriage that ended without fuss, and that I paid the legal fees in stamps from Laos. At *The*

Washington Post, Random House, and for the most part at PublicAffairs, I navigated around the inevitable pressures of coping with other humans without being easily undone. As a result, I was never so addled by setbacks or exultant in successes to lose perspective on what was really at stake. I did not weep, although I did grieve, when my parents and then my brother died. In retrospect, I find that surprising. It was not callousness. I am not sure what it was.

In my family, for a very, very long time, I underestimated how some of my closest relatives felt about the way I had dealt with them years before. Children, for instance, have a way of absorbing experiences, slights, and support that shape responses decades later. Frustrated parental rebukes are never forgotten. I remember that once I was so furious about something that my mother poured cold water on my head to calm me down. That was at least sixty-five years ago.

Most memorably, I have had temper outbursts when my frustration level reached a high pitch. This is more than just a vent. And when that happened—it did not happen often—those on the receiving end have been startled to see me in such disarray. Usually, I deal with obstacles and provocations in three steps, starting with good-humored irony, then stentorian clarity, and only finally by going ballistic in what is probably rage, an explosion from within. I cannot answer the question of why all this has been the case. I now understand how Robert's traumatic childhood in wartime led to his insistence that he was never a "victim," allowing him to bury anger that rarely surfaced. Yet when it did, it was especially striking. If our parents were permanently bruised by their loss of family and livelihood because they were Jews, I never saw evidence of it. On the eve of my departure for Moscow in 1974, Robert expressed fury with me. It came out of nowhere. It went nowhere. I am told that there are letters Robert wrote about me to our parents when they were concerned about my teenage antics. I am certain that I never wrote to anyone about my feelings about Robert—at least I think that is the case. I was recently shown one letter to my parents, written from Cheshire, apologizing for something that is not described therein.

Late into my eighth decade I am increasingly aware of the fact that every life has its wrinkles, of the kind that can't be addressed by having them pressed. The ability to manage these is central to how things eventually work out.

Here in brief, with a minimum of name-calling, are my reflections on what is broadly defined as mental health. I describe this because I believe the subject casts the darkest shadow—the wrinkles—on my otherwise fortunate life.

The language of psychology was around me my entire growing-up years. My grandfather was a contemporary of Sigmund Freud and one of the earliest physicians in Poland to practice in the emerging field known as psychiatry. My uncle Gustav was a student of Freud and became one of the world's most prominent psychoanalysts. My brother had a fifty-year career in psychiatry. I majored in psychology in college, and one of my most memorable courses involved a year-long engagement with a committed patient at Met State, a massive institution in Massachusetts.

I had a conventional susceptibility to teenage and collegiate ups and downs. In college, there was the time I did lose my temper after a girl broke up with me and I smashed my hand through a glass door. Did I intend to hurt myself? I doubt it. My first visit to a psychiatrist, as described earlier, was in Washington when I was working for Izzy Stone. The doctor prescribed an introduction to his daughter, a way of telling me I should stop working so hard.

My self-described attitude has always been "aggressive optimism," feeling that the way to confront a problem was to believe you could solve it. And yet, in half a dozen instances, I was by the medical definition clinically depressed. In the worst bout, in 2011, I had myself hospitalized on a closed ward at McLean Hospital, an affiliate of Harvard Medical School. I thought it would be cool—after all, James Taylor had been a patient. The book and movie *Girl, Interrupted* was a hit. I had even published Alex Beam's portrait of McLean Hospital, *Gracefully Insane*, a few years earlier.

Not only was McLean associated with Harvard; it had a campus I had seen when I would drive my Brandeis professor Hortense

Calisher to visit her son there when he was a patient. Now, I received a rude awakening. After being admitted and a cursory check-in process, I was, being over sixty, placed on a locked ward with geriatric patients, deemed eligible for electroconvulsive therapy (ECT), and left after a miserable month (Suze says it was only two weeks) in no better shape than when I arrived. Even the exercise bike on the ward was busted. Restorative it most certainly was not. I suppose its only merit was that I now know what it is like to be incarcerated.

An indelible impression is what it felt like to be thought of and treated as a patient. All anyone there knew about me was that I was hospitalized. The daily visit from the shrink, except when he was away on weekends, was humiliating, as was standing in line for meds in the morning. The ECT doctor and his nurse were thoughtful and kind as they zapped my head. In that respect, they were different from most of the rest of the staff. Trust me, you do not want to be a patient in a mental hospital, even one associated with the Ivy League. The bill was large and fortunately covered by insurance.

Self-analysis by and large is worth what you paid for it. I think that being sent to an eight-week sleepaway camp when I was three years old was not a plus. My parents didn't always arrange a babysitter when they went out, and I would put a knife under my pillow to protect myself and for a while would throw up regularly. They were not cruel or insensitive. They had to rearrange their lives completely and didn't really know the rules of American parenting. As I said, childhood has a way of embedding into one's adulthood.

Dealing with these depressive episodes in detail would not make them any clearer to anyone. But I have drawn conclusions about the differences between aggravated stress and mental illness, the difference between personality disorders and personality. A famous *New Yorker* cartoon shows a patient telling his doctor that he has an inferiority complex. After listening a while, the doctor declares, "Actually, you are inferior."

I have an especially strong view on the role of psychiatric medication, which is now at least as prevalent in medical treatment as analysis once was. Psychologists and counselors focus on talk therapy because, among other things, they do not prescribe drugs. But the use of "meds" by MDs is virtually universal. My first exposure to the perils of pills came in the year when I was traveling to Israel to work with Natan Sharansky. I had started taking Halcion, a sleeping pill, on flights and for days after. The wild success of Donald Trump's *The Art of the Deal* compared to the disappointment of Natan's *Fear No Evil* led me to try Xanax to deal with my upset. The mix was poisonous.

In time, I had to stop going to the office to gather myself and was in trouble. On the eve of my planned return to Random House, I was so addled that Suze and I went to the emergency room at Greenwich Hospital. A young psychiatrist on duty there asked what I was taking and told me to stop immediately, that night. I did. And the next morning I was well enough to make the trip to New York and on the way to recovery. Only later was it disclosed that the Halcion-Xanax combination could lead to psychotic symptoms. The novelist Philip Roth and the director Mike Nichols wrote about sieges that were very much like mine. A biography of Nichols reported that a Halcion addiction almost cost him his career—and because he contemplated suicide, his life.

Was I upset about the situation of the two books? Yes. I felt enormous pressure to succeed at Random House on my terms. Was I mentally ill? All I know is that the drugs apparently turned stress into sickness.

In 1996, when the pressure at Random House felt intense and I didn't see a way to solve the financial issues, even by acquiring and releasing a secret book by the president of the United States and being hailed as the world's leading publisher of crosswords, a psychiatrist in Greenwich prescribed Prozac, which I took daily for the next twelve years. In that period, I devised, started, and led PublicAffairs. I recently reread a memo I wrote in 2005, when I was at loggerheads with Perseus, explaining my side of the financial dispute; I was surprised to see that it was lucid, even learned. My only contact with the psychiatrist, other than renewing the prescription, was when he asked me to evaluate short stories he was writing. I didn't want anyone to know about the Prozac so would leave it off my list of medications when I went to see any other doctors.

In 2008 or so, the shrink and I agreed to taper the drug because neither of us now thought it was necessary and didn't know what the effect of long-term use might be.

In the summer of 2009, our whole family flew to Beijing to pick up a two-year-old girl. Katherine and her husband, Colin, were adopting from an orphanage. She was to be called Mae. They had waited for four years. An airline clerk upgraded us to business class when she heard why we were traveling. She said we were doing God's work.

Katherine had agreed to take a child with special needs. The medical records in a seven-page memorandum that was translated and shared with a doctor at home claimed that the little girl had had a single fever seizure with no apparent consequences. An adorable toddler awaited, who took exceptional pleasure from the little flashing lights on her sneakers. Within a day or two, we noticed that something was not right. After all, she had been in an orphanage with nine hundred children where milk was delivered from a mechanical device.

The story of what happened over the next year is Katherine and Colin's to tell, if they choose. But one night, sitting on our screened porch in Lakeside, Katherine left no doubt that she recognized that Mae was autistic and nonverbal. As far as anyone knows, this is not a condition that can be reversed. More than a decade later, Mae is beloved. Her brothers are amazing with her. Katherine and Colin have adapted to all the changes that were inevitable in their life. Katherine found a sign in an antique store and put it over the door to Mae's room. It says, "Warrior Mouse."

At home, my mother-in-law, MaMere, was weakening but maintaining her customary style and élan. When she had moved back to the family home in Greenwich, Suze became the CEO of our four-generation household, with Katherine and family living next door. There was a succession of caregivers of varying quality. For a while,

Suze's younger brother, Tony, lived with us while he was regrouping after changes in his life. MaMere died at home in the fall of 2012, at the age of eighty-eight. She had made careful arrangements for what would happen afterward, the most significant of which was the sale of the Greenwich property, which was owned in shares by everyone in the immediate family down to the babies.

That meant a prolonged period of deaccessioning the contents of a house that had been in the family for about ninety years. And the house was put up for sale. Local agents said that the house was a teardown at a time when new mansions in Greenwich were in demand. As I wrote, on the first day, a prominent Fairfield County architect offered the asking price. The real estate agent said to take it. The buyer was acquiring the John Knapp House, with a plaque from the Greenwich Historical Society dating the house to 1760, beams in the living room and beveled glass in the dining room with the name of a past owner, Peck, scratched into one panel. Almost as soon as the deal closed—a tangled story that is Suze's to describe—the buyer had declared he was tearing it down. The local paper put that story on the front page, fortunately without our names. The house he put up was vast and soulless. I like to say it had North Korean style and Saudi Arabian charm. It remains for sale after more than three years and several cuts in price. He even changed the address from 5 Brynwood Lane (a nonentity) back to 272 Round Hill Road because that sounded more desirable. We were on a corner, so both were technically true.

I watched Suze wrestle with the sale and complexities, which were many. Experts were consulted. Suze was the family's lead. And I was on the sidelines.

And then came my growing recognition of the mess at Perseus Capital. I had known for years that the numbers I was being shown were fraught at best. I focused on assuring myself that PublicAffairs was as safe as possible. Susan Weinberg was doing a terrific job and when she was promoted in the company, Clive Priddle, a highly skilled editor, took her position and learned to be a publisher. (They really are different jobs.)

Somewhere in that time frame I began to fret. I remember being alarmed one night when I was alone at home and couldn't find my keys. I went back to the Greenwich doctor and that began a sustained period in which my mood and demeanor gradually went from aggressive optimism to agitated despair.

Over the next few years, I saw four psychiatrists plus two referrals to eminent senior consulting doctors. I saw four psychologists for what was called cognitive therapy, meditation, and breathing exercise. I tried a noninvasive new treatment called Transcranial Magnetic Stimulation, which involved a device on my head. The doctor said it was covered by insurance. We never saw a dime. I spent that self-imposed period at McLean, at one point sitting in a circle with other patients banging on a tambourine. Suze kept a list of the drugs that were being prescribed in the unending effort to change my state of mind. There were antipsychotics and an increasing dose of Ativan, which was intended to reduce anxiety. I went to the office and pretended to be working. I wrote my weekly *Platform* columns, and although the process was slower, they weren't bad. I exercised daily and twice a week before dawn with a trainer. I would kayak on Long Island Sound listening to music or singing at the top of my lungs. Suze and I kept up as much as possible of our busy lives. In time, anyone who knew us understood that, for all my facade, I was not myself. If I talked to friends or family about the condition, I have no recollection of it.

The most graphic literary portrayal of clinical depression is William Styron's account of his debilitating and essentially chronic illness, *Darkness Visible*. I can confirm that at its worst, thoughts of suicide are not unusual. Those who have never been stricken cannot imagine what pain it can cause you and those around you. I'm sure I did my best to mask my situation. I do know that the darkness was quite visible even if it was not discussed.

Finally, in 2015, a friend of Suze's recommended a doctor whose name I will use: Carolyn Douglas. It took a year, but in weekly sessions she guided me through what started as relief and became recovery. With agreement, we started tapering all the drugs. My head began to clear and I started to react in welcome ways. I went on a weeklong PEN America mission to meet with civil society activists in Hong Kong, at the urging of the new owners of PublicAffairs at Hachette. While there I visited my distinguished tailor at A-Man Hing Cheong in the Mandarin Hotel and had a jacket made, a sure sign I was getting better.

Dr. Douglas parried my gratitude and said that a conversation or two she had with Suze had helped her greatly in understanding me and our relationship. There was more to the treatment than that. She was calm, thoughtful, and genuinely interested. I take a daily pill now. Whether it has any effect, I'll never know because it would be folly (also the name of our dog) to take a chance and stop.

What are my lessons from those experiences with mental illness? Yes, chemical changes happen in the brain under stress, especially when medications are hurled at the patient, under the principle of throwing it against the wall to see what sticks. I go back to that *New Yorker* cartoon about the fellow with the inferiority complex. I was definitely upset by three matters—my granddaughter's condition, the sale of our home, and the dangers to the business I had created, not to mention the fact that, for the most part, solutions to these problems defied my instinct for action.

I will never know, of course, whether this siege could have been avoided by early understanding that these problems were at the core of what I thought was important. In my view, "What's wrong now?" is as good a question for therapists as how you were treated as a child. Mental illness is still stigmatized in our culture. I was reluctant to ask our insurance companies to pay for it and when I did (except for the hospitalization), I received only a portion of what I was paying. In dealing with doctors and therapists whose specialty is psychology, patients tend to be regarded as the nail and doctors as the hammer. Lawyers like to do law. Painters paint. Dentists take care of teeth. Therapists may—just may—see problems to be resolved in the ways they were taught rather than with the default of common sense. As the cliché goes, just saying.

There will be wrinkles in the best of lives. All of us have vulnerabilities we may not recognize and cannot ascribe to anything in particular. I remember my brother's early insight in his practice to what he called a genetic predisposition to addictive behavior with drugs or alcohol. In Vietnam, for example, where I saw that GIs had easy access to heroin, mostly in cigarettes, a notably smaller number of users stayed on drugs when they returned from their wartime tours. They tended to be the soldiers from the most difficult backgrounds and surroundings. Decades later, the nationwide opioid epidemic showed that addictive drugs are not geographically defined. Some addiction is genetic, and some is acquired. Alcoholism does appear to run in families, which suggests a genetic link. Addiction is physical. It is mental. It has many causes and consequences.

Stress starts at birth and ends with your last breath. It fluctuates. It is inevitable and to the extent possible should be accepted as such. It is more than normal.

Chapter 30

Families, Communities, and Work

FAMILIES, FOR WORSE and mainly better, are the basic organizing principle of the human race. In the past fifty years or so, the definition of family has been extended from the traditional models of the past. And yet the basic meaning is the same: these are the people we consider closest to us, either by heritage or assumption. All of us surely can attest that these relationships are not always smooth, for any number of reasons. My grandfather Zygmunt Bychowski had always introduced himself to my father, the man courting his daughter, as if he didn't remember meeting him previously: a way of signaling that he thought Józef's family was less distinguished than his own, or so it was widely believed. As soon as Marta and Józef married they moved to Paris, perhaps to get out of the way. There are countless examples of this sort of friction. And yet, no matter how frayed, family bonds are usually immutable.

Until they were very old, my parents convened the family for Thanksgiving and Passover, the closest thing to religious and/or secular holidays that were observed. The standing assumption was that the reading of the Haggadah would be trimmed so that everyone could get to their favorite part, the song "Dayenu," or, in English, "It Would Have Been Enough"— in our family's interpretation, it would have been enough that the food was good, but so is the company. The Osnos and Bychowski families have histories that can be traced hundreds of years—now that I have done the research—and if not for the Holocaust, it would surely be a bigger family. The sacred part of the Seder was the annual reading of a prayer that had been added to recognize the murder of the 6 million in the Holocaust.

The Russell family of Lakeside, which I joined nearly fifty years ago, now numbers about eighty people who are directly tied to Paul and Carroll Russell, Suze's grandparents, and their land on Lake Michigan, a wedding gift from "Uncle Harold" Swift, scion of the meatpacking family, a "confirmed bachelor," as they were then called. The original Big House is now fourteen houses, four on the compound and the rest nearby. I cannot speak for everyone, but my sense is that the Lakeside connection is a central touchstone for all who can claim to be a Russell.

On the day Suze and I got married in 1973, I became what the extended Russell family calls an "outlaw," their word for those of us who have married in. For many years now, every new member has endured the outlaw song rendered by others in that category wearing a bandanna with words adapted from "Rawhide" by Frankie Laine (the theme song from a movie about outlaws): "Rollin', rollin', rollin', keep them doggies rollin'." Lest you be misled, "outlaw" is a term of honor.

I was the first person in the extended Russell family who was Jewish. The reach of families can be wide, and it is fun to uncover through research anyone who is part of the clan. In Suze's family and mine one can find associations with Elizabeth Browning and Emily Dickinson, the great architect Stanford White (who in turn was related to John Jacob Astor), a Red Army colonel exiled to Siberia and another Polish officer executed at Katyn, the mother of André Citroën, the chess coach to a world champion in Russia, an all-American football player at the University of Chicago, and the man who, it is said, introduced rice to Japan. Quite a group.

And then there are the communities that exist alongside family: churches, synagogues, and mosques; the Scouts; Alcoholics Anonymous; the Authors Guild; fraternities and sororities; neighbors. Most people are joiners, members of one community or another. Aside from family, I realize now that by instinct I never became a devoted member of any universe other than the very loose one of journalists. For Suze and me, our close friendships came from a cross-section of our experiences at home and abroad. And as I have grown older, I have become more aware of what it means to be a Jew, not as a member of a synagogue or fraternal group, but rather through an awareness of our history of travail and triumph. Family is my community.

Among the gentry in places like New York, Washington, Boston, or San Francisco, there is the tendency, which I do not like, to see the achievements of your offspring as a reflection of your own success. *Did the kid go to (or get into) the right schools? Are they heading to the right career for people of our cohort?* Children have become symbols of status, along with the tribal identification of where your weekend house is located. Okay, that does seem a bit cynical. But it is my view. I don't want to brag. That is why there is so little in this book about Katherine and Evan and their spouses, Colin Sanford and Sarabeth Berman. (Scour the earth and you will not find a better son-in-law or daughter-in-law.) I don't describe (but adore) Ben, Peter, Mae, Ollie, and Rose either, all works in progress.

Words cannot express my love for these folks. Katherine is daring, which is why she has performed so many feats of physical prowess and mastered so many careers as a student, parent, mother, and all-around professional. She has a degree from New York University in art history, a stellar list of devoted luminaries to her yoga instruction in Greenwich, and state certification as a social studies teacher in California. When a short film was made about Katherine's leadership of a trip by her eighth grade class from Lagunitas Middle School to the iconic civil rights sites in Georgia and Alabama, the credits acknowledged my daughter as "a force of nature." In high school Evan became editor of the school paper and president of the senior class, and he wrote his first stories as an intern at the *Greenwich Time*. At Harvard he became president of his "finals" club—a dented chalice since he had to take responsibility for the behavior of other members. He has won the National Book Award for Nonfiction and a raft of prizes in journalism. When I told the legendary broadcaster Tom Brokaw that I was writing a memoir, he said it could be called *I Am Evan Osnos's Father*.

I'll settle for those characterizations and, after checking, so will Suze.

In today's world the broader meaning of family and community is flexible. It is as important a definition of civilization as it has always been, however you choose to define it.

~

THIS BOOK HAS BEEN a recitation of my career, the activities that provided income, recognition, and, at times, disappointment. The generation to which I belong has been mislabeled "silent" and came after the "greatest"—those who fought in World War II. "Silent" is the wrong term. My generation included Martin Luther King Jr. at the beginning and Mick Jagger at the end. In my time, men (and the women like my mother who chose to work in their field) still believed in careers. You joined an enterprise and expected to rise in it until retirement with a pension. It was possible to think of your work colleagues as an alternate family. Because so many of us were the children of Depression-era parents or, as in my case, refugees, we tended toward the "professions"—law, medicine, academia with tenure—or industry and manufacturing, large companies which made things everyone needed.

Few of us in the class of '64 at Brandeis opted for the news business or even less conventional pursuits, but those that did seem to have done all right. As time went on, security became less of a factor in work life. It was desirable to be in riskier parts of finance or rock and roll. The next phase was tech and entrepreneurship at the top and the gig economy for the masses, including even college graduates. It was unusual to land at a company expecting to stay for the duration, which made employees pretty much transient, both to themselves and their bosses.

What was called journalism when I joined the field in the mid-1960s has become media, and it encompasses *The New York Times* and websites like BuzzFeed and Breitbart. On screens and over the air, these venues too often look eerily similar in design if not in content. In the internet age, media has been upended, with that story still unfolding. It will continue to do so. One of the basic truths is that evolution and innovation are eternal, until they are destroyed by nature or human blunder.

I can, however, attest to the lingering prestige and benefits of working or studying at one place or another. At Harvard the freshman class were always told that at the end of the year, half of them would have an experience that was unique: they would be in the bottom half of the class. When hired by the *Times*, journalism's Harvard, arriving staff soon discover that they could well be in the bottom of the class, in an obscure corner of the institution or underappreciated. With the benefit of distance, I attribute the neurotic competitiveness I've always seen at the *Times* to the dismay of not being as high-echelon as you thought you were, combined with the burdens of talent and ambition. The *Post* had its status ranks also but we were buoyed by the charisma of Ben Bradlee and, over time, the courage of Katharine Graham. And being number two is often easier than being number one. (It must be said here that those of us in the newsroom used to joke that we could retire if we got a nickel for every sentence that began, "The trouble with *The Washington Post* is ...")

When I left the *Post* in 1984 to start another career, it was still somewhat unusual to do so. It was not thought to be necessary to leave journalism, except that older "ink-stained wretches" were forgiven for going into better-paying positions in public relations. Over the years the definition of success has largely changed. It is no longer just the standing of where you work; it is whether you can get properly rewarded for it—at all the unicorns in Silicon Valley, for instance, or those lucrative appearance contracts with CNN or MSNBC, or a book with a large advance. Reporters in national media can tell you how many followers they have on Twitter and Instagram, in the way that syndicated columnists a half century ago knew how many papers took their stuff.

Another major change has to do with age. If you make it to sixty-five, the actuarial prediction is that you will last until eighty-five, which means that one-third of your adult life comes after what was long thought of as the time to retire. How to make the most of that extended period of life is not yet properly understood. My personal suggestion is to replace the notion of retirement with what I consider repositioning. After thirty years or so in one's chosen career, you can opt for the rocking chair—which becomes a wheelchair—or set out in some other direction.

Try something else, and recognize that whatever it is, it won't be at the same level of rank or income as the job you are leaving behind. Reinvent the work arc that still usually ends with a cliff and make it a downward slope instead.

There is no doubt that ageism is a modern fact, when people are living so much longer than they used to. The desired target of advertising, after all, is still someone twenty-five to fifty-four. Beyond that people are considered old at sixty and elderly at seventy. Ads for the older folks on the evening news are almost all related to medical matters: Viagra (they've stopped, the market must be saturated), diabetes, memory loss, back pain, heart disease.

I would argue that the final third of life is as diverse as the first two-thirds in terms of health, happiness, and style. There are people doing just fine and those who decline, just as there are people who are tall and those who are short and teenagers with or without acne.

I became especially aware of the perils of aging in the workplace when PublicAffairs was acquired by Hachette Book Group in 2016. I was no longer an owner and did not want to fill out timecards as an employee. I was over seventy and had outside interests and opted for CONSULTANT (all caps) attached to my email address, which I always said was better than PEDOPHILE. Over time it became clear that as a result of this choice I became something of an outsider at the company I had founded. As a consultant, it was decreed that I should not have a permanent workstation in the open-plan offices. I resented this, of course, and probably could have challenged it, but decided it wasn't worth the embarrassment of having to ask. What I considered support for my younger colleagues, it became apparent over a year or two, they thought of as interference. They had jobs they had earned and wanted to perform well in them. It takes unusual self-confidence to invite a former boss—who no longer sets your pay or does your annual review—to partner on a project. That is not always what happens, but I recognized that it was the norm. Successors in leadership need space to show their professional prowess to their current bosses, not the past ones. Approbation from your supervisors is a tangible form of compensation these days for employees when money in publishing, as it always has been, is tight.

The epiphany moment came when a really valued staff member blurted, "You don't trust me!" I most certainly did. I just wanted to use my experience to augment hers. That was when I made the command decision, without any announcement, to speed up my withdrawal from the imprint's work and said that the books I was working on would be my finale. I soon knew that I felt better having made that decision and so, I'm sure, although they did not realize it, did the very fine PublicAffairs team. When I told publishing people, including at PublicAffairs, that I was doing the reporting for this book, the response was oddly muted. Other people's recollections of the past were much less vivid than mine, and no one ever told me what they really thought of me. When I said I was trying to figure out the financial picture at Perseus, one senior colleague remarked, "You are like a dog with a bone about that stuff." Yes, but the meat on that bone was the source of our two decades of good work.

If there is a roadmap to the process of stepping back, I have never seen it. If I had, I would have known that once PublicAffairs was sold and I was the oldest person in the Hachette offices, it was time to move on. But now that I have done it, *emeritus* and *founder* don't sound so bad. As often was the case, Ben Bradlee summed it up well, when he observed after he was no longer executive editor of the *Post*, "On the day after you stop being the boss, you'll start to find out who cares enough to return your calls." It is important to remember that this is natural—even if it can be infuriating—and not to take it too personally.

What made the disengagement process essentially painless was the fact that PublicAffairs at Hachette was doing well. Its 2019 results hit all the right targets that measure a publisher's performance—backlist, returns of unsold inventory, and reported profit. The pandemic in 2020 upended everything. Yet, even so, sales from a single book from BoldType (formerly Nation Books), Ibram X. Kendi's 2015 National Book Award–winning *Stamped from the Beginning*, made the imprint's numbers look good by the standards of the year. BoldType is overseen by PublicAffairs, which gets credit for its revenue.

Clive Priddle's editorial team scored solid successes, especially with economics and business books. Abhijit V. Banerjee and Esther Duflo, the authors of *Poor Economics: A Radical Rethinking of the Way to Fight Global Poverty*, were awarded the Nobel Prize in Economics in 2019.

My last adventure at PublicAffairs started in 2018 when, after reading Jeff Bezos's thoughtful shareholder letters, I contacted Jay Carney, Amazon's executive in Washington (Carney was a former press secretary to President Obama and a *Time* magazine bureau chief), with the idea of collecting everything Bezos had said or written into a book. It took two years but Bezos, personally, signed the contract, with all his revenues going to philanthropy. There was a glitch about Hachette's sales term with Amazon, by far its largest retailer, so we partnered with Harvard Business Review Press to release the book.

Susan Weinberg used to choose what she called "a PublicAffairs moment" at sales conferences, meaning something that was not a routine move for a publisher. This was certainly the case with Bezos. By far the world's richest man, the nemesis of independent booksellers and one of the major entrepreneurs of all time, was publishing a book with us. And his money would go to charity. I never met Bezos as I had all those presidents and luminaries. He is a busy fellow. He did inscribe a book to me praising the "perfect execution" of the product.

I am fine with that. Just as we eventually downsize our living arrangements, we should downsize our ambitions. The success you have had cannot be taken away from you, unless you stay so long that they tell you to, please, leave.

Work and family are the pillars of our world, and as with the sturdiest of pillars they need to be refurbished, reconstructed, or reexamined occasionally.

Chapter 31

Time Present and Time Past

ON JUNE 16, 2015, the day Donald J. Trump descended the escalator at Trump Tower and declared that Mexicans were "rapists" and he should be president of the United States, we entered the Trump era. Not just the man himself, but all he represents about our social fabric and politics in the broadest sense.

I'm guessing that the Trump era will find a place among the most momentous and contentious periods in our history, not bloody or existential as the Civil War was, but nearly as divisive. With the global coronavirus pandemic unfolding in the spring of 2020, Lawrence Summers, a former secretary of the treasury and president of Harvard, called this the greatest challenge to Americans since Pearl Harbor and the war that followed. Within weeks, the resulting economic collapse was being compared to the Great Depression. Because the rhetoric of politics has been overheated for so many years, when a genuine crisis—the pandemic and its consequences—arrived, there weren't really superlatives left to portray the seriousness of the situation.

Trump's chaotic, untethered, uniquely selfish approach to leadership was bound, one way or another, to culminate in catastrophe. All of his life's turmoil—defying every benchmark for failure in business or personal relationships—and his escapes as president from his two impeachment convictions finally careened into an uncontrollable natural disaster. It almost seems enough to make a nonbeliever think there really is something to destiny—which I have come to believe there is, not preordained by a cosmic force yet determined by factors both tangible and indefinable.

The Trump years, especially when compared to the dignified, misleading calm of Barack Obama's two terms, have highlighted every fault line in our culture: inequality, grievance, bias, paranoia, racism, and corruption. Our country's collective history is a record of never-ending efforts to foster the ideals of our Constitution. These goals have been fractured, and the test going forward will be how and when we recover them.

A national tendency, exaggerated by the pervasiveness of the internet and social media and by their bias in favor of the provocative over the reassuring, sends a message of decline that is stronger than the concurrent improvements in diversity and gender awareness. In my early days with Izzy Stone, I wrote what I thought of as my "Not one Negro" stories as I uncovered government agencies without any Black employees. There is a great deal yet to be done, but who can deny that we have a far better approach to ritualized discrimination than was true in the past? Nonetheless, those who say that racial injustice is America's original sin are right. Poverty everywhere in the world is still too prevalent, but that is less the case than it was even fifty years ago. Climate change is a demonstrated and acute danger. And yet the means to deal with it are available in advances in science and energy. The issue is whether this generation or the next will mobilize to use them for the benefit of survival.

We have been whipsawed by the pace and frenzy of events. By the time this book will be read, the coronavirus and Trump sagas will have entered another stage. Trump's fate and his record of sidestepping obstacles in business, politics, and his private life will undergo a variety of tests in the coming years. We should not forget, however, that in the space of just two months or so in 2020, the nation endured the ultimate political drama of presidential impeachment at a time of record high stock markets and low unemployment, and spiraled in what felt like an instant into an economy in collapse and dread of what could happen to loved ones in a war against an invisible enemy.

There is a saying that a week is a long time in politics. That is ever more the case when events cascade rather than evolve, as they now so often do.

~

AS THIS BOOK TOOK SHAPE, I encountered, quite literally, bits and pieces—some in the trunk, some in a closet, some in a drawer, some online. They are to a large extent the texture in this narrative. Will the memoirist of a hundred years from now have these things to work from? Unlikely. So as a publisher I find myself telling friends and acquaintances to write down their thoughts and recollections— one page a day, and in 365 days you have a manuscript. Do it with a pen and a notebook. Or write it directly on the computer. Or dictate it to yourself. Just get it down. Don't think of publishing what you do, necessarily, to an audience outside your circle. Most strangers will not be interested. I always wondered why several of my authors who had led amazing lives and wrote well about them were in despair because *The New York Times* did not review their book.

I started to write this narrative for my family. It turned out to be for me, at least, ultimately much more meaningful than just a hand-off to future generations. I had the chance to completely review my life up to this moment. To be honest, I liked what I found more than I thought I would. If you want to preserve the past, and trunks in the attic are not an option, write it down, copy it, put it in a safe place, and share it with those who want to see it. I tell authors that books or journals are better than a building because they cannot be torn down and they will have your name on it. To accompany this book, I have created a virtual attic—anespeciallygoodview.com—where the material I have relied on will be posted. I believe in taking advantage of the best of technology, as we always have, or we would still be living in caves.

It is also important to acknowledge that the "old" way of doing things is not always bad, and sometimes better than inscrutable tech improvements designed by engineers. Why do we hit Start to close

Microsoft Outlook? After all, a car with roll-up windows and a simple dashboard has fewer things that can go wrong.

Two additional observations as I draw to a close: When you are asked to buy an expensive service contract to be sure all that new-fangled stuff is kept working, the seller knows that the margin of profit is usually greater on the contract than the original sale price. So, buyer beware. And when you are presented with the accounting for any business or financial transaction, it is wise to assume that the people who have counted the numbers want to make it look as good or bad as possible depending on which perspective serves their interests best. This is my business degree in LL—Life Learning.

As I mentioned at the start, in the process of writing this book, it has only been read by people who, for one reason or another might be interested in what it says. Now the book will be available to readers of other generations, including millennials. So let's revisit my calculations: my first memories and stories are from the 1940s, about 80 years ago. Eighty years before that was 1860. So if reading about these events and personalities seems remote to you, it is. This is, in a way, a book of history, not always historically significant but certainly some of it was.

I'd like to end this story where it began: with the outbreak of World War II and a young couple, who happened to be my parents, losing everything except their wits as around them violence took the lives of tens of millions. They made their way to India and then safety in the United States. I was along for that journey, in a basket to begin with. Believing in the power of resilience has become something of a cliché to offset our embedded gloom and strife at events and crises. If the human race, for all it has been through over the millennia, were not resilient, we certainly would not have gotten this far.

That is so often said, because it is right.

A VIRTUAL ATTIC

Victoria Roberts

*"Whatever you do in there all day is fine with me,
so long as it's not writing a memoir."*

A VIRTUAL ATTIC

In 2014, as Suze and I prepared to move to an apartment from our home in Connecticut, the challenge of what to do with the contents of all those trunks, boxes, and files in the attic and garage loomed large. The collection of letters, photos, articles, tapes, notebooks, and memorabilia of one kind or another went as far back as early in the twentieth century from her side of the family, my side, and our decades together.

Eventually, a plan was developed. Some of the material went to archives at alma maters, some were converted to CDs and digital files, some are still crammed in boxes in closets. Books and vinyl records went to interested libraries.

A good many of these items in a variety of formats will be available on a website we have developed called anespeciallygoodview.com in what is a virtual attic. A sample of that material follows in this appendix featuring things related to the book.

What is not there are thousands of emails we've sent because these were mostly deleted and what remains is too fleeting in thought and cursory in topic as to be of any real use.

And that is the point of the virtual attic. In the future will we have as much to preserve as we have in the past? Will we have handwritten letters, photos on shiny stock of childhood, family, holidays, pets, and travel? Certainly, there will be much less to save. The shared history that was in those trunks, boxes, and files will have to be assembled in other ways, which will not be an easy task.

Technology and the urge to remember will certainly devise ways to take account of our lives. After all, humans have come a long way from cave paintings. But for now, let's preserve what we have in the best way possible, which is by scanning, copying, and linking, and to the extent we can, put them on computers, in safe places at home, or long-term storage.

The site, anespeciallygoodview.com, will have links to a variety of places where pictures and words can be found, including YouTube, Flickr, and Medium.com by searching under the Osnos name.

SECOND LOOKS

In recent years and especially while working on this book, I have visited and written about many of the places that were meaningful in my life. These were Bombay (now Mumbai), Poland, Britain, Vietnam, Cambodia, Russia, and Israel. None of those trips fundamentally changed my understanding of those places. But the passage of time and twists of history enhanced my judgments about them. I wrote pieces about all these trips for what I called *Peter Osnos's Platform* on the Medium site and then posted them on social media. I called the writing "brain exercise" because they were a way to use my thoughts beyond simply holding forth to family and friends. I also wanted to explore how social media worked. There are many more pieces there than in this collection, all of which can be read in full. What are they? Essays? Articles? Blogs? Does it matter what they are called?

I was born in Bombay but had never been back until 2019, when Suze and I took our teenage grandsons, Ben and Peter, on a weeklong visit with the objective of re-creating as nearly as we could the experiences of my parents and brother from the summer of 1940 until the end of 1943, when they left on the USS *Hermitage*. We saw the hospital where I was born, the apartment houses where my family lived (even meeting a ninety-nine-year-old neighbor named "Auntie Nora"), the sites where they worked, and the school in Panchgani that Robert attended. India had welcomed Józef, Marta, and Robert—and eventually me as well. It is a country so vast that the point of our tiny measure of gratitude to the Indians and colonial-era British is that if you desperately need to acclimate— and if your hosts permit you to—the odds are that you'll be okay even very far from home.

I wrote an article about a 2018 visit to Warsaw and Krakow titled "There's Something About Poland." What that meant was that my attraction to my parents' homeland surpassed the reality that they had to flee to avoid anti-Semitism and certain execution by the Nazis. Warsaw today rivals other European cities for sass and class, but that urbanity coexists with religious and social conservatism that has been present throughout the country's history. There are many books about the "Polish Problem" of living between Russia and Germany, the neighboring nations that have overwhelmed Poland in the past. Perhaps that is why the Polish language is replete with ironic imagery that reflects its people's wariness about the future of their state.

My years of living in London, as I've written, made me an Anglophile, a friendly critic. With Winston as one of my middle names, that was probably pre-ordained.

Vietnam and Cambodia, two countries that suffered the brutal consequences of American intervention in their internal political order, have rebounded in impressive ways, even if neither country comes close to the standards of liberal democracy. I can attest that more than forty years after the wars that annihilated much of their populations, their recovery has restored time-honored strengths of character and beauty.

I was last in Russia just after the millennium to meet with Boris Yeltsin about his book. Russia today has a personality compatible with its history. It is again an autocracy, with enormous inequality and a largely controlled public across the vastness of a land spanning twelve time zones. There is a youth culture connected to Western styles that in the future may turn out to be important. For now, I say you can take communism out of Russia, but you can't take the Russians out of Russia.

I've made a number of visits to Israel, most recently a decade ago for the wedding of Natan and Avital's daughter. The Sharanskys now have six grandchildren. The land of Israel has never been a placid place and is not now. I've written about my concerns over how the politics of the country have developed. Yet after visiting Auschwitz in 2018 and seeing the remnants of the hundreds of thousands of Jews executed there, I have a better sense of why so many Israelis take the position of "Never Again."

Suze and I went to China and Egypt when Evan was working there and visited Nepal while Katherine was a student in Kathmandu. We had a family trek through the Himalayas to celebrate our twenty-fifth anniversary. All these destinations qualify as enlightening. The only way to appreciate the complexity of human beings is to see how they live and cope.

The full text of all these pieces and more as far back as 2008 can be found at Medium.com under Peter Osnos, TheAtlantic.com, or TheDailyBeast.com.

～

The telegram received in spring 1943 with notice that a US visa
was available. I have no idea how Marta and Józef reacted.
In late December, they left India.

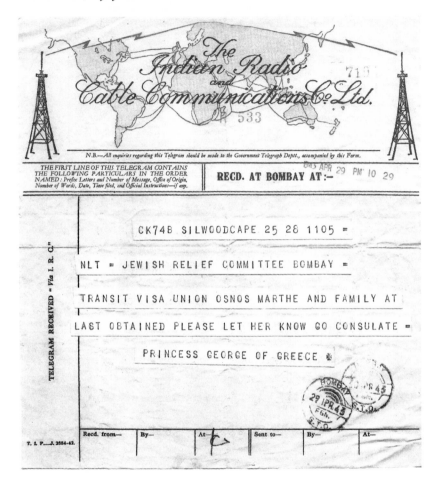

The birth certificate that makes me and anyone else who sees it smile.
"Caste: Polish" is an unusual designation.

Certificate of Birth Registry.   2040 VII / 277

PUBLIC HEALTH DEPARTMENT.
REGISTRATION OF BIRTHS AND DEATHS,

Bombay, 11th November 1943.

No. 1204 OF 1943.

Date of Registry___ 30th October 1943
Date of Birth___ 13th October 1943
Names of Parents___ Joseph Osnos — Marta Osnos
Address of Parents___ Maskati Court, Queens Road, Esplanade
Caste___ Polish
Occupation___ Manager
Sex___ Male
Name of Child___ Peter Lionel Winston

L.M. & S., D.P.H.
Executive Health Officer.

These pictures were on the cover of a short book that Marta and Robert
wrote about their travels from Poland to the United States.
The full book can be found at www.anespeciallygoodview.com.

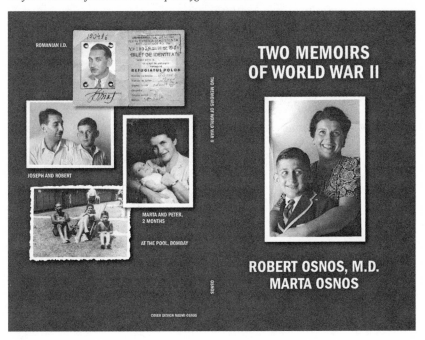

ROMANIAN I.D.

TWO MEMOIRS
OF WORLD WAR II

JOSEPH AND ROBERT

MARTA AND PETER,
2 MONTHS

AT THE POOL, BOMBAY

ROBERT OSNOS, M.D.
MARTA OSNOS

COVER DESIGN NAOMI OSNOS

Suze and I in Vietnam, 1971.

*The CIA makes it clear, contrary to Soviet allegations, that I did not
have any connection to American intelligence.*

MEMORANDUM FOR: Director of Central Intelligence

FROM :

SUBJECT : Allegations Linking U. S. Correspondents
in Moscow with the CIA

1. As you know, a story appeared in this morning's
edition of the New York Times reporting that the Soviet
Weekly "Literaturnaya Gazeta" for 26 May 1976 contains an
article alleging that three American correspondents in
Moscow are associated with the Central Intelligence Agency.
In addition, a copy of a State Department cable dated 25 May
1976 has been obtained which contains information along
parallel lines. The State Department received the information
from the Chicago Tribune correspondent in Moscow. (Copies
of the Times article and State Cable are attached.)

2. Complete Agency traces have been conducted in the
names of the six American correspondents mentioned in the
Times article and/or State Department cable.

3. As a result of our traces the following information
was developed: There is no record in Agency files of

There is a file in the
Office of Security regarding Peter Osnos (Washington Post)
but it contains only references to several stories written
by Mr. Osnos about the Agency. There is no file on

A piece on moving from the Foreign to the National Desk at The Washington Post,
written with a touch of humor, which infuriated my successor as foreign editor.

No More Champagne

The Washington Post
By Peter Osnos[1]
December 4, 1979

Some thoughts on moving from the foreign desk to the national desk of this newspaper:

1) It is, on the whole, easier to pose as an expert on foreign matters than domestic ones.

Last summer, after the fall of the shah of Iran, Somoza of Nicaragua and Idi Amin of Uganda, but before the downfall of Emperor Bokassa of the Central African Empire and the demise of Park Chung Hee of South Korea (not a good year for dictators) came the end of Franciso Macias Nguema, president of Equatorial Guinea, overthrown by his nephew, Lt. Col. Teodoro Obiang Nguema.

A tyrant if ever there was one, Macias presided for 11 ghastly years over an island sand spit off the coast of West Africa with a separate smidge on the mainland inhabited by two tribes: Fangs and Bubis. American relations with the country were suspended in 1976 when our visiting ambassador extraordinary and minister plenipotentiary was denounced by the local deputy chief of protocol, who delivered what was described as a "rambling, polemical, at times almost incomprehensible" diatribe against the United States.

All that is fact, solemnly recorded on page one of *The Post*. But suppose it were all made up. How many readers would be in a position to seriously quibble?

Fangs, Bubis, Shiites, mullahs and Pol Pot—for all the miracles of modern technology and communication, the globe is still replete with exotic crannies and (to us) mysterious passions. A foreign editor and his colleagues can, with some diligence, successfully pretend to be wiser and more knowledgeable about the obscure than ordinary folks.

Not so on national.

Anyone who takes the trouble to pick up a newspaper has background, experience and, therefore, strong views on inflation, taxes and presidential politics. Try for example, posing as an oracle on Chappaquiddick. Or gas lines. Or rising prices. Where national affairs gets technical—on the finer points, say, of nuclear power—there are so many bona-fide know-it-alls, committees, studies and panels that journalists end up, more often than not, as conduits for someone else's views in the current debate.

All this affects the way stories get written. It seems acceptable (although it shouldn't be) for trench-coated correspondents in distant lands to employ such sturdy terms of self-certainty as "Most modern day Europeans believe. . ." or "Indeed. . ." or "Hence. . ." or

---

[1]The writer, formerly foreign editor of *The Post,* recently was named national editor.

"Moreover. . ." But it is clear to me already that similar stuff from Dubuque or Sioux City sounds ridiculous.

2) It is definitely easier from the vantage point of national editor to develop sympathy for the problems of the president.

Hard as it may be to organize the world, the fact is that Russians, Chinese and Iranians, never mind Fangs and Bubis, don't vote. People here do—or at least are entitled to. Jimmy Carter is therefore besieged by more special interests angered over action, inaction or reaction than any one individual should reasonably be expected to bear. Whites, blacks, rich, poor, young, old, North, South—each must have its say.

The Post national staff is also responsible for national security matters: the State Department, the Pentagon, the CIA. These concerns seem relatively antiseptic and manageable compared with the multitude of pressing domestic issues. Mistakes at home probably won't kill you the way war would. But the harassment could drive you nuts.

Big business complains bitterly about administration economic policies—like U.S. Steel did the other day when it closed down some outmoded plants—and so does big labor, which, after all, lost the 13,000 jobs. Getting something through Congress, a seemingly sensible measure to control soaring hospital costs, for instance, is a major frustration, arousing, as it did in this case, the formidable forces of free-enterprise medicine.

Or consider energy legislation. Everyone knows it is essential to do something, but deciding exactly what is a nightmare. Proposals get so weighted down with the preference of groups—from travel agents to the people who design rationing stamps—that the effect is enervating.

Add to that a special prosecutor investigating President Carter's chief of staff on a potential felony charge; 11 Republican candidates for president and a Democratic hopeful who is heir to one of the few magical names in American politics and no wonder Jimmy Carter looks older, wiser, sadder and skinnier than he did on the stump in 1976.

3) Word of a change in job gets around fast in Washington, especially to the people who do mailing lists.

Within a week after moving into the new job, my mail began to change. There were more press releases from trade associations and government agencies and fewer invitations to embassy national days and similar entertainments. Since most of those embassy shindigs come at *Post* deadline time and from a news standpoint are usually unproductive, I rarely went. Still, it was pleasant to have that small stack of creamy, thick cards summoning me to champagne and smiles.

Invitations to cocktails with tire manufacturers just don't have the same impact. The difference is that when embassies do the wooing we prefer to call it diplomacy. But when it's folks from home, that's lobbying.

Copyright © 1979 *The Washington Post*

Reagan's ancestral village was my last dateline as a correspondent for the Post.

Reagan's Homecoming Excites Irish Village

The Washington Post
By Peter Osnos
April 6, 1984

What can this Tipperary village of about 300 persons expect to get from being the homeland of Ronald Reagan's ancestors? "A sense of standing," said Con Donavan, the amiable shopkeeper who has represented Ballyporeen on the county council for 24 years.

For a few hours on the first weekend in June, Reagan, en route to the western economic summit in London, will be paying homage to his roots and, incidentally, reminding millions of Irish Americans that he is one of them. But for a humble farming community whose name in Irish means "town of the small potatoes," the presidential visit is a very big deal.

Over coffee in the back of his store ("everything sold from a needle to an anchor"), Donavan said that he is hoping for a special allocation from the government to spruce up the derelict sites and older facades on the main street. The old crank-up telephones are being replaced by an automatic system. And plans are under way to accommodate the needs of what he called "the Reagan juggernaut" to Ballyporeen's simple sanitary, eating and sleeping facilities.

Preserving decorum in the unaccustomed glare of international attention seems to be a central theme.

"I hope south Tipperary will be prepared to avail of the onslaught," Donovan told his fellow councilors at a meeting earlier this month.

The price of mistakes, others at the session agreed, will be to make Ballyporeen look foolish. "We have had a small bit already and they should be given no more chances to make dirt out of us," said Councilor P.J. Maher, referring to jocular local news accounts such as an *Irish Times* story headlined "Ballyporeen Honors Its Big Spud."

Shortly after the 1980 election, Debrett's Peerage Ltd., the London-based genealogical specialists, traced Reagan back to his great-grandfather Thomas Regan, who was a dirt farmer in Doolis, a patch of rolling land adjoining Ballyporeen. Thomas' son Michael emigrated to England in the 1840s, married a Tipperary lass and crossed the Atlantic, settling in Illinois. For unexplained reasons, he added an "a" to his surname. Ronald Reagan came two generations later.

To mark their good fortune, the people of Ballyporeen staged an inaugural parade in pouring rain on the day Reagan took office in Washington. John O'Farrell, a leading local pub keeper—the town has six pubs—changed the name of an adjoining club where musical acts appear on weekends to the "Ronald Reagan Lounge."

O'Farrells have been pub keepers on this corner since at least 1810 and the entrepreneurial spirit flourishes. He started to sell, along with T-shirts and other items, small packets of the old sod retrieved by hand from Doolis by his wife Mary. Upstairs under lock and key is a gift shop with Irish souvenirs that the couple hope to sell to tourists this summer and for as long as the appeal lasts of seeing where America's 40th chief executive came from.

"There is a tremendous sense of pride in knowing that someone could leave from here penniless and have a descendant become president," said O'Farrell as rough-hewn customers headed up to the bar for pints of dark Guinness stout at a hefty $1.25 per glass. "Most of the price goes to taxes," he noted.

From the beginning of his administration, Ballyporeen longed for a visit by Reagan. Several times there were false alarms, particularly last fall when Secret Service men were reported to be checking out the area. On that occasion it was Reagan's son Ron who was coming to do research for a magazine article.

By the time the rumors proved to be true and while most townspeople were thrilled at the prospect, a certain amount of cynicism was expressed over Reagan's choice of an election year to make a pilgrimage. A columnist for the local weekly *Avondhu* wrote that for most people outside of Ballyporeen the announcement of the visit is "merely a source of sarcastic humor."

To counter that stance, Patrick Cooney, Ireland's defense minister, told a dinner audience that the president of the United States should always be welcome here. "We as a people owe a debt to that country," he said. "It offered a haven for our forefathers in times of great national distress and, indeed, for over a century it provided opportunity for young Irish people who did not have the like at home."

Part of the clucking over the visit is that invidious comparisons are invariably drawn between Reagan's Irish ancestry and John F. Kennedy's. Reagan is no longer Roman Catholic. His mother raised him as Protestant. Moreover, Kennedy had living relatives in County Wexford with whom he could commune when he came in 1963. There are no identifiable Reagan kin in Ballyporeen.

There isn't even a grave in the Templetenny cemetery with the family name. It is assumed that the stone sunk into the rich earth with the passage of time.

A plaque has been erected saying that this must be the place where Reagan's ancestors were laid to rest.

But the proof of Reagan's Irish blood is unassailable. It resided in the graceful hand of the scribe for the registers of Ballyporeen parish for baptisms and marriages. Translated from the Latin, its entry for Sept. 3, 1829, reads: "I baptized, Michael, son of Thomas Regan and Margaret Murphy of Doolis; godparents: William Regan and Catherine Walsh. Signed Fr. Martinus Redmond."

The announcement of my job at Random House.

RANDOM HOUSE, INC.

201 EAST 50TH STREET, NEW YORK, N.Y. 10022
TELEPHONE 212 751-2600

TO EVERYONE AT RANDOM HOUSE

     We are delighted to announce that Peter Osnos, London Bureau
Chief of The Washington Post, will join Random House on April 1st
as Senior Editor in the Adult Trade department.

     Peter has been with The Washington Post for 18 years in a
variety of major domestic and foreign positions. Before taking
the London assignment he was National Editor, Foreign Editor,
Moscow correspondent and Saigon bureau chief. For the past three
years, he has also been a commentator for National Public Radio,
and has contributed articles and book reviews to such magazines
as Foreign Affairs, The Atlantic and The New Republic.

     We expect that Peter will quickly become an integral part
of the Random House trade operation, originating projects of his
own, handling major books already under contract, and participating
in the overall editorial decision-making process and future
development of the department.

                              Jason Epstein

                              Tony Schulte

January 11, 1984

An article in The New York Times *that provided insights into my parents' lives that I only realized during the writing process. Photo © The Beresford by David Shankbone*

Splendor, at Last

The New York Times
By Peter Osnos[1]

In September 1929, a few weeks before the stock market crash, a three-towered apartment building in late Italian Renaissance style opened on the corner of Central Park West and 81st Street. It was named the Beresford, after the hotel it replaced, and was a masterwork of the architect Emery Roth, a Jewish emigrant from the Austro-Hungarian Empire whose background limited his chances for commissions to build on the posh east side of the park.

"And what a creation!" exclaims Andres Alpern in his book "Luxury Apartment Houses of Manhattan: An Illustrated History" (1992, Dover Publications). Two hundred feet square and 22 stories high, the building had three elegant entrances and only one or two apartments—simplexes and duplexes—to a floor. It looked like a European fortress, Mr. Alpern wrote, and was every bit as lavish as the era that was about to end. Today, in another gilded age for Central Park West, the Beresford is once again a New York symbol of grandeur.

For nearly half of its 75 years, the Beresford was home to my parents, Joseph and Marta, and I came to understand over time that it was more than a residence to them. Although their apartment was relatively modest by Beresford standards, the splendor made them

---

[1]Peter Osnos is the publisher and chief executive officer of PublicAffairs, the New York publishers.

feel prosperous. Living there provided a sense of connection to the comfortable, secure life they were forced to leave behind, when they fled the Nazi onslaught of Europe.

The named Central Park West apartment buildings of the early 20th century, like the Majestic, the San Remo and the Eldorado, were different from the numbered residences along Fifth and Park Avenues in that they were not "restricted," which meant that many of the residents were Jews. In the 1930's and 40's, these people were what was loosely known as "All Rightniks," second- or third-generation Jewish merchants and professionals who were associated with solid West Side temples like Rodeph Sholom and B'nai Jeshurun. There were a cut below the wealthy "Our Crowd" set of German Jews at Temple Emanu-El, but they still sent their children to private schools and expensive summer camps.

As the situation worsened in Europe in the late 1930's, a flow of wealthier Jews got out, and they too found their way to Central Park West. My parents were not part of that lucky group. They grew up on Warsaw and spent much of the 30's in Paris. But they were back in Poland when the war started in 1939, and only by acts of great daring and good luck did they manage to escape. They made their way across Romania, Turkey and Iraq, and found refuge in Bombay, where they lived until securing visas to the United States.

A troop ship transported them across the Pacific, and in the spring of 1944, they arrived by train in New York. My parents were in their late 30's, my brother, Robert, was almost 13. I was still in a basket, barely 6 months old, with an Indian birth certificate that declared "Caste: Polish."

Joseph and Marta found an apartment in the Belnord on 86th Street and Broadway, another fabulous neo-Classical stone pile that had started to get a little shabby. The rent was about $125 a month for seven rooms, split among three families, and some of the furniture came from the Salvation Army. But it was a great place to be a child. There was a large courtyard where bike riding and ball playing were permitted. Over time, the other people in our apartment moved out, and my parents, with what in retrospect seems like amazing equanimity, re-established careers and even bought a summer home on a lake in New Jersey. It is hard to believe that they were barely a decade from their harrowing escape.

The Beresford also had its ups and downs. According to "Luxury Apartment Houses of Manhattan," the building had a hard time dealing with the effects of the Great Depression. In 1940, it was sold in tandem with the San Remo Apartments for a total of $25,000 over the mortgages for the two buildings. Much of the West Side was also in decline and many "All Rightniks" made the move to the suburbs and the East Side. Nonetheless, Central Park West still had those fabulous buildings of the 20's, and in 1962, the Beresford became a co-op.

My parents bought their first apartments for $18,000. A few years later they upgraded to the more expensive 8B—the cost was $40,000, if I recall—with a better view, one that looked south across the Museum of Natural History over the park to Central Park South.

By then I was in college, so the Beresford didn't have the gauzy glow for me that the Belnord did. But for my parents, I now realize, it had enormous significance. With its ornate trimmings and moldings, the door and elevator men, the view of the park, the Beresford represented the lifestyle they had expected for themselves before the war. It had taken them 20 years to do it, but when Joseph and Marta moved into the Beresford, they had completed their journey back to where they felt they belonged. I don't remember them ever speaking about this, yet I know how important it was for them to reclaim the graciousness in their lives to match the courage and energy they had expended in rescuing themselves and their sons.

My favorite Beresford moment came in the mid-1960's when I was preparing to move to New York for graduate school at Columbia. My mother was eager for me to live at home. But after years of living in dorms and student housing, I was skeptical. "Mother," I said with a clear sense of priorities, "what if I want to entertain a girl?"

The next day, a Saturday, it was raining heavily, and a young woman friend came for a visit. My mother disappeared and returned soaking wet moments after the girl had left. "Where have you been?" I demanded. She replied, "I didn't want you to think I was interfering with your privacy."

Eventually, I chose to live with two other guys on West 99th Street, where my share was about $100 a month. But for another three decades, I was a regular visitor to the Beresford. We celebrated my mother's 80th birthday and my father's 90th in the spacious living room, dining room and entry hall. Both of them slept their last nights there before they died. In so many ways, the Beresford and Apartment 8B was the finish line for them, the terminus of their remarkable life journeys.

Today, the Beresford is home to moguls and superstars. As an address, it is more splendid than ever, beautifully maintained and worth every penny, I suspect, of the millions it costs to buy into it. Every time I pass the place, I pay my respects to the enduring beauty of the building and the tradition of urban good living it represents. Mostly, however, I honor it on behalf of my parents, whose strength and style it served so well.

Copyright © *The New York Times*

"*Tracy, this is Gene. He also read the Nancy Reagan
book in unbound galleys.*"

John F. Kennedy Jr. on Robert McNamara. I thought these comments were especially striking because no one else of his public visibility ever said anything remotely comparable.

Time Magazine's 75th Anniversary Celebration Toast
by John F. Kennedy to Robert S. McNamara 3/3/98

PERHAPS NO TWO PRESIDENTS LINKED BY HISTORY HAD LESS IN COMMON THAN LYNDON JOHNSON AND JOHN KENNEDY. BUT ONE THING THEY DID SHARE WAS AN ENDURING RESPECT AND AFFECTION FOR ROBERT MCNAMARA.

MR. MCNAMARA SERVED AS SECRETARY OF DEFENSE IN THOSE ADMINISTRATIONS FOR SEVEN YEARS. YEARS THAT WERE AMONG THE MOST TUMULTUOUS IN MODERN AMERICAN HISTORY. DURING THAT TIME, HE SERVED HIS COUNTRY WITH EXCEPTIONAL LOYALTY, INTEGRITY, DEDICATION.

AFTER LEAVING PUBLIC LIFE, HE KEPT HIS OWN COUNSEL, THOUGH IT WAS BY FAR, THE HARDER CHOICE.

YEARS LATER, ROBERT MCNAMARA DID WHAT FEW HAVE DONE. HE TOOK FULL RESPONSIBILITY FOR HIS DECISIONS AND ADMITTED THAT HE WAS WRONG. JUDGING FROM THE RECEPTION HE GOT, I DOUBT MANY PUBLIC SERVANTS WILL BE BRAVE ENOUGH TO FOLLOW HIS EXAMPLE.

SO TONIGHT, I WOULD LIKE TO TOAST SOMEONE I'VE KNOWN MY WHOLE LIFE, NOT AS A SYMBOL OF PAIN WE CAN'T FORGET, BUT AS A MAN. AND I WOULD LIKE TO THANK HIM FOR TEACHING ME SOMETHING ABOUT BEARING GREAT ADVERSITY WITH GREAT DIGNITY. AN ADVERSITY ENDURED ONLY BY THOSE WHO DARE ACCEPT GREAT RESPONSIBILITY.

The Washington Post's *coverage of the launch of PublicAffairs in 1997.*

Big-Picture Books

The Washington Post
By David Streitfeld
May 29, 1997

Washington investor Frank Pearl must have been having a good time with Counterpoint, his literary press here, because yesterday he announced the creation of a second publishing house.

More imprints—"either formed from scratch or acquired"—will be announced in the coming months. "We are encouraged that our idea that you can do high-quality publishing profitably is correct," said Pearl, who made his fortune doing leveraged buyouts in the 1980s with former treasury secretary William Simon and other partners.

The new house is called PublicAffairs, and will naturally specialize in books by public figures and journalists. It is the brainchild of Peter Osnos, who was head of Times Books until last fall. His authors included Jimmy Carter, Bill Clinton, Robert McNamara, Paul Volcker and Boris Yeltsin, as well as many journalists.

These are, as ever, rocky times in the publishing world, and serious books that specialize in Washington-oriented issues are finding the going especially bleak. Earlier this month, HarperCollins folded Basic Books, one of the leading nonfiction imprints, into the parent company. Addison-Wesley, another former fount of serious nonfiction, has also announced severe cutbacks. Other houses are cutting back more quietly.

When Osnos left Times, he said it was increasingly difficult to publish the kinds of books he wanted within the confines of its parent company, the Random House conglomerate. More and more crossword puzzle books and brain-twister compilations had to be acquired to pay for books on, say, tax reform.

PublicAffairs is an attempt to control costs and manage distribution in ways that are difficult for the large publishers, which have huge overhead. Deals are being worked out with PBS's "Frontline" documentary show and the Twentieth Century Fund to develop properties jointly, while marketing, accounting and other support staff will be shared with Counterpoint and the future imprints.

"We want to provide authors with the means to be able to write these books, and we want to be able at the same time to meet all the costs and demands of running a business. That's the equation we have to bring together," Osnos, 53, said yesterday from New York, where PublicAffairs will be based.

While the 54-year-old Pearl is the majority owner of PublicAffairs through the Perseus Capital investment firm he runs, there are a half-dozen minority investors, including ABC News anchor Peter Jennings, former C-SPAN chairman Robert Rosencrans and Osnos himself. The press will issue 25 to 30 books a year, starting in the fall of 1998.

PublicAffairs, Osnos said, is "a tribute to the standards, values and flair of three persons who have served as mentors to countless reporters, writers, editors and book people of all kinds, including me": the late muckraker I.F. Stone, former Washington Post executive editor Benjamin C. Bradlee and former Random House chairman and Human Rights Watch founder Robert L. Bernstein.

Indeed, for a while Osnos toyed with the idea of naming the publisher BSB, after the trio's initials. While that notion was ultimately rejected, each book from the press will have an emblem with the initials BSB, and a note at the back explaining its significance.

"Well, God love him" Bradlee commented yesterday. "It's original. Because it means something to him, it means a lot to me, too." Stone and Bernstein were, he added, "good company."

The press is a tribute to a fourth pioneer as well: Morris B. Schnapper, who for decades ran a now-defunct outfit called Public Affairs Press. Schnapper, now in his eighties and living in Silver Spring, gave his blessing to the enterprise.

Schnapper published Harry Truman, Gandhi, Arnold Toynbee and over 1,000 others, but things have changed since his heyday. The problem, Osnos said, is that costs are out of control. "If I give you $100,000 to write a book, you'll give 10 percent to your agent and $30,000 to Uncle Sam. If it takes 18 months to write the book, you'll be working essentially for minimum wage," he said.

Say the book sells 12,000 copies, which is often considered a good sale. This doesn't earn the publisher enough money to cover the expenses as well as the author's advance. For everyone, it's a losing game.

Said Osnos, "The author isn't getting what the author needs, and the publisher isn't getting what the publisher needs. The only way it can work is if there are books that significantly exceed the royalty advance, and pick up the slack for all the others"—a high-risk style of operating that can yield big losses more easily than it brings bonanzas.

Adam Bellow, editorial director of the Free Press—owned by Simon and Schuster, it is the most prominent public affairs imprint—said he wished Osnos luck and hoped the venture would succeed. He added, however, that "there's a reason why the big publishers are turning away from this type of books, and it's not just the celebrity author system or the high cost of doing business in a conglomerate. There's still a limit to how many copies of a serious book you can sell on a policy issue."

These days, political books are in a trough. "I just don't think there's an audience for them," Bellow said. "People are not paying attention to politics, because there doesn't seem to be anything at stake. There's a mood of distemper."

Lynn Chu, literary agent for House Speaker Newt Gingrich and other Washington figures, concurred. "I just got really sick of reading the same repetitive tripe," she said. "Conservatives are so boring. They keep repeating themselves. Who cares? And the

Democrats are even worse, as usual. The left is dead. I supposed that's good. But somehow, it's no fun anymore. What you like to see is a good hand-to-hand fight."

Osnos, who spent the early part of his career as a reporter and editor for The Washington Post, firmly believes there is a market for Washington-oriented books. "The audience I'm interested in are the millions of people who listen to NPR, C-SPAN, 'Frontline' and Jim Lehrer." He's convinced he can make the economics work. So is Frank Pearl. His attempt to form a new style of publishing conglomerate ranks among the most ambitious in the field in the past decade, which has tended to see more shutdowns than start-ups. It will probably push the deeply private Pearl further into the spotlight. "I hope not," he said uneasily.

Copyright © *The Washington Post*

Our first big hit, The Starr Report.

A Steamy Report Aids a Publisher's Debut

The New York Times
By Doreen Carvajal
September 21, 1998

By rather brief tradition, the literature of choice at the year-old PublicAffairs publishing house started by the Random House refugee Peter Osnos is intelligent and reflective—serious nonfiction scorned by conglomerates seeking best-seller profits.

So how is it that Mr. Osnos's leading title on his debut list this fall is a breast-heaving 421-page tale of unrequited love, of a tormented affair of a young woman scorned and a married man scarred, of an impossible relationship characterized by bodice-ripper sentiments and romance-book regrets? A book brimming with sentiment like: I "cannot ignore what we have shared together. I don't care what you say, but if you were 100 percent fulfilled in your marriage I never would have seen that raw, intense sexuality."

Expect no grainy photographs for your $10 purchase, but there's not much else left to the imagination in "The Starr Report"—That Book—which PublicAffairs started shipping before dawn last Monday with a dignified crimson-and-gray cover and the complete text of the report of the Whitewater independent counsel Kenneth W. Starr, chronicling President Clinton's relationship with the White House intern Monica S. Lewinsky. Also included are the White House rebuttal and early news articles from The Washington Post about the steamy Government document, which makes "The Valley of the Dolls" read like a phone book.

"I didn't know that when we chose PublicAffairs for this company's name that we literally mean public affairs, but that's the way it worked out," Mr. Osnos, 54, said dryly from the company's headquarters—spare, dorm-like offices that share the 18th floor of the Fisk Building in midtown Manhattan with the nonliterati, like Arista Dental and Dentogenic Studios.

———

The company's maiden catalogue does indeed boast serious books, like Arthur L. Liman's posthumous memoir of his legal career and the Iran-Contra investigation, and Neil Baldwin's exploration of Mexico and the myth of Quetzalcoatl, the principal god of the Aztecs. But the company has printed far more copies of "The Starr Report" than of any of the nine other titles, with 300,000 books shipped on the first day, and Mr. Osnos is poised to gamble by printing still more. "We could print hundreds of thousands right now," Mr. Osnos said. "We are still going to print as conservatively as we can because we don't know how long this is going to last."

But for now, copies of "The Starr Report" are moving as if they were Stephen King paperbacks—and are a far better bargain for Mr. Osnos than a blockbuster novel would be because his company can publish the Government document without paying advances to its authors, subsidizing expensive book tours or sparring with agents. By some estimates, PublicAffairs could easily make more than a half a million dollars in profits if the books continue to sell briskly.

"We're sold out in Cincinnati, Denver, Paramus, Dallas and Las Vegas," an exuberant Mr. Osnos marveled before bolting from his office to meet another company employee to debate how many more copies to print. (To be sure, PublicAffairs has at least two competitors, which also report brisk sales of Mr. Starr's report—a $5.99 mass-market paperback by Pocket Books, part of Viacom's Simon & Schuster unit, and a $9.99 trade paperback from a small California publisher, Prima.)

It is a rather odd state of public affairs for Mr. Osnos, a former reporter and editor at The Washington Post who left Random House two years ago as the publisher of its Times Books imprint. One of the last books he published there was a slim political work by President Clinton, which certainly failed to match the sales power or Oval Office sizzle of "The Starr Report."

As the publisher of Times Books—once owned by The New York Times Company—Mr. Osnos came to believe that the system for publishing serious books was flawed and the audience for them too limited to support standard author advances and corporate overhead. It bothered him that "Times Books was doing more and more consumer reference books and crossword puzzles, and I wanted to do public-affairs books," he said.

So he resigned to start his own company, and set about looking for partners to share the costs of author contracts. "PBS Frontline" signed on in return for exclusive rights to produce documentaries tied to the books it helped underwrite. His plan also attracted minority investors like the ABD News anchor Peter Jennings and the former C-Span chairman Robert Rosencrans. It also prompted Frank H. Pearl, a lawyer and chairman of the venture capital firm Perseus Capital, to buy a majority interest and make PublicAffairs a part of his expanding publishing group, which also includes Basic Books, a bastion of scholarly works, and Counterpoint, a literary press.

For his part, Mr. Osnos has no qualms about making a publishing debut with a Government page-turner of Oval Office romance and footnotes that helpfully provide the definition of telephone sex and Ms. Lewinsky's dry-cleaning habits—or lack thereof.

"I do not have a moment's doubt that a report by this special counsel, recommending the impeachment of the President of the United States, is a historic document," Mr. Osnos said.

"I cannot think of anything more substantive," he added. "Do you think I should curl my lip at the President of the United States? I'm not in the business of judging whether history is elegant or not. History in this case is degrading."

"The Starr Report"—as The Book—could have a significant impact on the fledging Pub-licAffairs, letting it subsidize more projects and "change our sense of what is possible," Mr. Osnos said.

Is there a sequel? Mr. Osnos is waiting for 2,800 more pages of evidence.

Copyright © *The New York Times*

PublicAffairs is a publishing house founded in 1997. It is a tribute to the standards, values, and flair of three persons who have served as mentors to countless reporters, writers, editors, and book people of all kinds, including me.

I. F. Stone, proprietor of *I. F. Stone's Weekly,* combined a commitment to the First Amendment with entrepreneurial zeal and reporting skill and became one of the great independent journalists in American history. At the age of eighty, Izzy published *The Trial of Socrates,* which was a national bestseller. He wrote the book after he taught himself ancient Greek.

Benjamin C. Bradlee was for nearly thirty years the charismatic editorial leader of *The Washington Post.* It was Ben who gave the *Post* the range and courage to pursue such historic issues as Watergate. He supported his reporters with a tenacity that made them fearless, and it is no accident that so many became authors of influential, best-selling books.

Robert L. Bernstein, the chief executive of Random House for more than a quarter century, guided one of the nation's premier publishing houses. Bob was personally responsible for many books of political dissent and argument that challenged tyranny around the globe. He is also the founder and was the longtime chair of Human Rights Watch, one of the most respected human rights organizations in the world.

. . .

For fifty years, the banner of Public Affairs Press was carried by its owner Morris B. Schnapper, who published Gandhi, Nasser, Toynbee, Truman, and about 1,500 other authors. In 1983 Schnapper was described by *The Washington Post* as "a redoubtable gadfly." His legacy will endure in the books to come.

Peter Osnos, *Founder and Editor-at-Large*

ACKNOWLEDGMENTS

A LONG LIST OF PEOPLE enabled the stories in this memoir to be told. A great many of them are in the narrative either by name or in spirit.

A smaller group was responsible for the preparation of the book.

Lisa Kaufman and Paul Golob, esteemed long-time colleagues, were the editors. Each brought an expert's eye to the project; I asked for and got rigorous editing. Athena Bryan, who is much earlier in her editing career, made interpretive comments to minimize generational misunderstandings. Bill Warhop did a careful copy edit.

Christine Marra is the managing editor for the book and its fledgling publisher, Platform Books LLC. Maryellen Tseng created the design and, with the counsel of Pete Garceau, the art director for PublicAffairs, the jacket.

The media outreach was overseen by Whitney Peeling. She chooses very carefully which books to represent. I was honored to be one of them.

Literary agent Kathy Robbins helped me decide the right way to have it published.

Then there are Matty Goldberg, Sabrina McCarthy, and the sales team at Two Rivers/Ingram. We worked closely together at the Perseus Books Group for two decades. I couldn't imagine asking anyone else to sell it.

Finally, there is Susan Sherer Osnos, wife, mother, grandmother, lover, friend, adviser, editor, who after fifty years I can still make laugh.